# Politicians & Diapers Should Be Changed Frequently

.... and for the same reason

## VOLUME 1

Dr. Fredric L. Frye

Copyright © 2013 Dr. Fredric L. Frye
All rights reserved.
ISBN: 1492872741
ISBN 13: 9781492872740

# TABLE OF CONTENTS

| | |
|---|---|
| Title page | i |
| Table of Contents | v |
| Dedication | vii |
| Acknowlegments | ix |
| Preface | xiii |
| Political Humor and Wisdom | 1 |
| Other Nations, Ethnicities, and Regions as Subjects of Humor | 69 |
| Golf and Golfers | 197 |
| Body Parts | 233 |
| Bodily Functions | 277 |
| On Blondes | 301 |
| Bars and Drunks | 333 |
| Child-Related Humor | 361 |
| English for Foreigners | 373 |
| The Results of Our Current Educational System | 383 |
| Bumper Stickers | 409 |
| Darwin Award Nominees | 413 |
| Why Chickens Cross Roads | 425 |
| Haiku and Zen for the Masses | 441 |
| Growing Old Gracefully | 451 |
| Glossary an Other Useful Explanations | 539 |
| About the Author | 549 |

# DEDICATION

To my wife, Brucye, of almost 60 years, and our two children. Lorraine, and Erik, to our two grandsons, Noah, and Ian. Also to Professor Emeritus, Milton Hildebrand, a polymath of a man who has served as a model for me to emulate in my scientific endeavors, dealing with others, and in recognizing and writing humor in its many forms. If it had not been for his decision to publish his book, *Laugh and Love,* under his own name, rather than under a pseudonym, I might very well have used a pseudonym when authoring this title. His academic reputation survived after *his* book was published; I suspect that *mine* will do likewise.

# ACKNOWLEGMENTS

This literary effort is, to a substantial degree, a work compiled from e-mailed material from a wide variety of "correspondents." Beginning in 1980, family members, friends, colleagues in my own profession, as well as others in the related health and natural science fields of endeavor, began exchanging bits of humor. At first, I merely printed out those bits that I found humorously appealing and saved them in a file. Soon that file and the amount of time, paper, and printer ink far exceeded what I could ever have imagined.

Once home computing became more widespread and recording media became more efficient, I switched to saving these materials on floppy disks, and then, eventually, on USB flash drives.

Obviously, proper attribution to those from whose fevered brains many of the jokes and/or bits of wit and wisdom originated can not be properly given because the majority of these gems arrived as anonymous contributions, passed from one person to another. As an author of numerous scientifically rigid papers and textbooks, and co-author or contributing author of multi-authored texts, I am acutely aware of plagiarism; after all, I have been the victim of my own writing being plagiarized. That said, it is virtually and actually impossible to give proper attribution to the vast majority of the pieces contained in this book. Where attribution was possible, it was cited appropriately..

# ACKNOWLEGMENTS

The major contributing "correspondents to whom I am indebted for providing the morsels that completed this meal are (in alphabetical order): Gary Averbach, Jason Albertson, Dr. Robert Baker, Dr. Stephen Barten, Helen Benton, my brother-in-law, Dan Burshtine, my former student and now colleague, Cinzia Cordella, my late father, Ben Frye, Jim Foster, my sister and brother-in-law, Susan and Howard Goldstein (Howard also designed the cover and its illustrations), my daughter Lorraine Frye-Wilson, my former student and now esteemed colleague, Dr. Candalaria Gonzalez, Dr. Steve Grimes, Dr. Robert Klein, Dr. Angelo Lambiris, Dr. Derek Lyon, my step-brother, Brad Lefton, my colleague, Dr. Chris Knott, my former luminous star student and "second son," Dr. Douglas R. Mader, my London publisher and dear friend, Michael Manson, my former student and now colleague, Dr. Jöerg Mayer, Dr. Rick Shapiro, Dr. Howard Schwartz, who, over the many years of our friendship, undoubtedly has provided the most contributions to this effort. Terry Shultz provided numerous goodies, as did Willow Trent, RN, who has never been at all shy in her selection of what to send to me, Dr. Mike and Ella Tyler whose wit is always smile-worthy, Clifford Warrick, a very special individual who has consistently shown his predilection for precious nuggets of wry humor, my eldest grandson, Noah Wilson, with his ability to see humor where others might not. Frances "Chirp" Winter provided numerous nuggets and, especially witty puns; my childhood buddy, Irwin Zane, and our dear friend of nearly fifty years, Margery Zelles, sent many others worthy of inclusion. If I have omitted anyone else, please forgive my oversight.

Special appreciation is due to Brucye, my loving wife and very best friend for nearly 60 years. Over the decades that we have lived together, she has selflessly taken time away from her many other chores to serve as the primary editor of my books and papers – long before the advent of the word processor. While our tastes for humor might vary somewhat, she has a keen sense of what to leave "on the cutting room floor."

Lastly, this is the second book that I have written or edited that strays from my usual scientific output. The first was an excursion into humor was *"Phyllis, Phallus, Genghis Cohen – and other creatures that I have known."* I hope that the readers of this latest effort enjoy perusing this book as much as they apparently did with "Phyllis–" which is still selling copies after almost thirty years in press. With the publication of this book, I shall now return to more academic literary pursuits.

Be well – it certainly beats the alternative!!

# PREFACE

In 1980, when I began working on this book, I decided to *compile*, rather than *write*, much new material. Some required a bit of editing in order to correct the English or punctuation. I set out to be faithful to those who have been sending humor of all kinds to me via the Internet or via conventional mail. In doing so, I set aside "Political Correctness" and let the chips fall where they may.

Being in my seventh decade of life, I have witnessed the changes brought about in our culture during the nineteen thirties through the early years of the new millennium. Those, who were brought up and entered their 'teens and early twenties during the 1960s and early 1970s appear, when compared to their parents' generation, to have lost much of their collective sense of humor. Whether it was because of the anti-war movement(s), the ready availability of the birth control pill, the rise of the "Woman's Movement," the zeal with which so many young adults embraced the social and economic trends and opportunities, or other changes in our society, can only be surmised. Where once ethnic humor was commonplace, it is now considered to be socially and politically insensitive – unless the humor is aimed at, and/or delivered by, a member of that particular ethnic or national group. Be that as it may be, there is still a rich wellspring of humor out in America that is tapped and distributed via e-mail. At the same time, we have witnessed the rise and fall of cults and various political

## Preface

movements that have been characterized by members who willingly quaff cyanide-laced KoolAid®, had themselves electively castrated as part of readying themselves for embarkation on space ships following in the wake of the Hale-Bopp comet, indulged and placed great store in such pseudo-scientific beliefs in reflexology, iridology, coffee enemas, laetrile treatment for cancer, engaging in mind-altering drugs and any and all means of instant gratification. The Era of Permissiveness is upon us but, strangely, that very permissive attitude often lacks the toleration to benignly laugh at ourselves – or others – as once we did.

In editing these pieces, I tried to excise only those parts that I considered mean-spirited or disgustingly gross. But then again, *my* tastes might not necessarily be shared by some of my readers. If you will look, you will find just about equal numbers of humorous bits that skewer the Democrats, as well as Republicans. Admittedly, the advent of the self-proclaimed Tea Party Republicans in their zeal to upset the national applecart, are very easy targets for humorists. After all, many of these objects of derisive humor come from the southern states (and Alaska) and, when carefully parsing their raving pronouncements, one is left questioning how they *could* have been elected by an *intelligent* electorate. Perhaps, in even considering the response to that question, the answer becomes glaringly obvious! It was that thought that occasioned the title of this book! Damn it, we deserve better representation in Washington, D.C.

Many, if not most, politicians suffer from a mental malady termed *Illusion of Confidence,* a common state in which people overestimate their abilities (Mario Livio, *Brilliant Blunders: from Darwin to Einstein*). It was Charles Darwin who observed that: "Ignorance more frequently begets confidence than does knowledge." That stipulated, before taking the time and effort to e-mail or snail-mail me a note of righteous indignation, read a bit further and save yourself the exertions.

As I have noted in the chapters dealing with both religion and other nationalities and ethnicities, there is a preponderance of both Jewish and Catholic humor. In the first category, the people of the "Hebrew persuasion" have a particularly rich tradition of self-derisive humor. In the second, it may be that the very nature of the Roman

Catholic Church, with its studied concentration upon sexuality (or lack of it – except for procreation – and priestly and sisterly abstinence), are sufficient reason for humor. Never-the-less, both religions appear to be greatly over-represented when compared with other faiths.

I once had the suspicion that there are only so many original jokes in existence, with many having multiple versions. Indeed, what may appear to be novel ones are, in reality, newly minted permutations of age-old tales, canards, limericks, puns, and stories with the subjects of those tales only changed slightly or rearranged to suit a specific social, political, or economic milieu. That stated, I am *now* convinced that there actually *are* truly novel jokes. The advent of new technology has given rise to new jokes, humorous tales, and inspired wit have changed the ledger substantially.

As much as I would like to cite the provenance of each and every piece to avoid the charge of plagiarism, it is impossible to do so because the vast majority of the material arrived anonymously – or at least with no discernable authorship. Almost all were received as e-mailed missives and, therefore, had entered the public domain electronically.

As the compiler of these objects of humor, I can claim little or no credit for their originality. I have edited many, if not most, so that they are more easily read and their tense and singularity or plurality are consistent. Wherever the provenance of a story or joke is known, I have given proper attribution. Some, in particular, were from my late father's fertile and eclectic mind. I have purposely left them undocumented; however, my sister and I know which ones they are! My brother-in-law as well as several of my esteemed professional colleagues contributed many of what I consider to be the very best. Others are from former students with whom I have maintained close ties. I have credited the many people who have contributed pieces in the Acknowledgments. A few were my own creation. They too, shall remain anonymous. Many of items contained herein are decidedly raunchy and/or scatological. The "S" word, "F" word, if appropriate to the subject, were left in as received. I made little effort to Bowdlerize them because to do so would be intellectually dishonest. As our Elizabethan forebears knew – and practiced so well – colorful

# Preface

language is often the spicy condiment with which we flavor, enliven and entertain one another in our varied discourses.

Many pieces were left on the "cutting room floor" during editing this mass of individual examples of humor, wit, and wisdom. However, their excision from the body of material was *not* done for political reasons nor was it done for concern for those who might cringe at expletives.

I created categories into which most tales, stories, and jokes fit best. That said, I identified many which would fit naturally into more than one category; some in as many as three categories. Whenever that was perceived, I tried to chose the one into which the fit was most appropriately comfortable. However, in some instances, I included particularly germane pieces in more than a single category. For instance, some that featured the elderly (of both genders), animals, religion, ethnicity or national origin, or wit and wisdom, were placed in two or more of these respective chapters.

As this project was nearing completion, its manuscript length amounted to over 400,000 words and it was readily apparent that it would be impossible to publish it as a single-volume book. Accordingly, I selected those topic chapters that most readily matched the political and social milieu in late 2013. One or more volumes are planned in the near future. To be completely candid, the behavior of the U.S. Congress under its present leadership was a major factor in deciding to publish this first volume now!

Early in the conception of this compendium, I chose *not* to use my real name. I am a professional who did not wish to forfeit my professional image as a scholar. Now that over thirty years have passed since I first started collecting this material, and my scholarly credentials have been established, I suspect that my image can withstand any attack based upon the prudery of others

You don't stop laughing because you grow old; you grow old because you stopped laughing. Let that be lesson well learned.

Enjoy the examples of humor that I hope are new to *your* memory.

Fredric L. Frye
30 September, 2013

# POLITICAL HUMOR AND WISDOM

If nothing else can convince you that our current political system is dysfunctional, remember that Founding Fathers *never, ever* conceived of public service in the office of the U.S. Presidency and Vice Presidency, Senate, or Congressional representatives as life-long tenures once elected. Consider the recent effects of our aging cadre of septuagenarian, octogenarian, and even older officials' recurring run every two or six years. We have had such luminaries as Senators Strom Thurmond and Robert Bird – and many others – who have grown fossil-like whilst serving in their elected – and re-elected offices, often from gerrymandered, so-called "safe" seats. Presently, our *dys*functional and *mal*functional system was partially engendered and, certainly exacerbated, by the advent of the so-called "Tea Party". Many of its adherents were born well after the end of the Second World War and are unaware – or merely ignoring the history of our national political system that led us both *into* and *out* of the Great Depression and economic resurgence since 1945.

I am not an advocate of forced term-limits; however, I am, *firmly* convinced that both our U.S. Senate, and especially, our House of Representatives, foster an unhealthy tendency to keep electing too many candidates of dubious quality and cerebral competency. The gerrymandering of political districts by both parties, is in my opinion, disgraceful and selfish. When congressional and senatorial seats can be won by voters who constitute a minority of the voters in these gerrymandered districts, something is very, very wrong and should be addressed and corrected by people whose first allegiance is to our nation's health, rather than their specific rationale to hold and remain in office. It is for that reason, as if there were not abundant *other* reasons for declaring:

**"POLITICIANS AND DIAPERS SHOULD BE CHANGED FREQUENTLY — AND FOR THE SAME REASON."**

As I was preparing this manuscript for publication, the House of Representatives was about to shut down the government to which they had sworn an oath to defend and protect. Aha! Although the above dictum is not original with me, it fairly *screamed* to be employed as the title of this book! I heard that shriek loud and clear. If only the likes of Senator Ted Cruz, Representatives Michelle Bachmann, Louie Gohmert, Mike Lee, ex-governor Sarah Palin, Speaker of the House John Boehner, and their fellow obstructionists, would listen, they too might very well hear that shriek and think more of their statutory obligations than of their political careers. That hope is equally directed to the members of the Democratic Party. Harry Reid and Nancy Pelosi, are you listening too?

• • •

WASHINGTON, D.C. (AP) - A major research institution has recently announced the discovery of the heaviest chemical element known to science. The new element has been tentatively named "Governmentium." Governmentium has 1 neutron, 12 assistant neutrons, 75 deputy neutrons, and 11 assistant deputy neutrons, giving it an atomic mass of 312. These 312 particles are held together by forces called morons, which are surrounded by vast quantities of lepton-like particles called peons. Since Governmentium has no electrons, it is inert. However, it can be easily detected as it impedes virtually every reaction with which it comes into contact.

A minute amount of governmentium causes one reaction to take over 4 Days to complete when it would normally take less than a second.

Governmentium has a normal half-life of 3 years; it does not decay, but instead undergoes a reorganization in which a portion of the assistant neutrons and deputy neutrons exchange places. In fact, Governmentium's mass will actually increase over time, since each reorganization will cause some morons to become neutrons, forming isodopes. This characteristic of moron-promotion has led some scientists to speculate that Governmentium is formed whenever morons reach a certain quantity in concentration. This hypothetical quantity is referred to as "Critical Morass". You will know it when you see it.

• • •

A late-middle-aged chap came home one night accompanied by a chimpanzee wearing a three-piece pin-striped suit, gleaming white-on-white French-cuff dress shirt, a Homburg hat, two-toned wing-tipped shoes, spats, and a fine Italian cravat, knotted squarely under his chin. In his left hand, he carried a splendid walking stick. In the chimp's left lapel was a "Romney" campaign. The fellow's wife of many years shrieked, "Where the hell did you get that filthy monkey?!"

"Honey, he's *NOT* a monkey; he is a chimpanzee; and, furthermore, he is not filthy; please do not hurt his feelings; he is *very* sensitive!"

"I don't care what you call him or how clean he is, what the blazes is doing in our home? Also, look at that Romney pin in his suit's lapel. How could you bring into our home, a conservative Republican?"

"Oh that; well, I too was a bit concerned when I first saw it; however, it turns out that, after I discussed his political views with him, he realized that he was part of the forty-seven percent that Mitt Romney knew would *never* vote for him. He only wears that pin because he could not find one from the Obama campaign that didn't clash with his suit. I suspect that he is, at heart, more of an Independent thinker. Look, let's not be nit picking about his political leanings. You've always regretted that we were never able to have children. Well, he'll be our son! Look, it was you who always mourned the fact that we didn't have the sound of tiny feet in our home."

"You're wacked-out crazy, that's what you are! Democrat, Republican, Independent — where is he going to eat?" demanded the now nearly hysterical wife.

"Honey, this little chap dines with impeccable manners; he shall take his meals with us; just you wait and see how he knows which salad, dinner, or dessert fork – or teaspoon, tablespoon or even demitasse spoon, or butter, or steak knife to use and which wine to drink with each course. As I said, he is VERY cultured. Just calm yourself and think of the possibilities."

"Well, just where will he take care of his toilet needs?"

"Right where you and I do, my dear; I am confident that you will find that he not only takes care of himself, but he'll also put the seat down when he is finished and replenish the toilet paper when a roll needs to be replaced. As a matter of fact, he is quite accustomed to using a bidet after using the toilet for number two. Since we do not have one, perhaps we should consider having one installed. You will find him to be a perfect gentleman," replied the husband in good humor.

"Al right; you say that he'll eat with us and use our bathroom; but, where the hell is he going to sleep? We have a one bedroom apartment"

"After he has had his after dinner brandy and a cigar, and watched a little late evening television, he'll shower, put on his silken pajamas, and then curl up in bed with us."

"With US In OUR bed! But, what about the smell? screamed the wife, at the very thought of sharing her bed with the chimp.

"Look, I got used to it, I'm certain that he'll get used to it!" replied the husband calmly.

• • •

## A Primer on Political Science

I bought a new Lexus 350 and returned to the dealer the next day complaining that I couldn't figure out how the radio worked.

The salesman explained that the radio was voice activated. "Watch this!" he said, "Nelson" The Radio replied, "Ricky or Willie?"

"Willie!" he continued and *"On The Road Again"* came from the speakers. Then he said, "Ray Charles!", and in an instant *"Georgia On My Mind"* replaced Willie Nelson.

I drove away happy, and for the next few days, every time I'd say, Beethoven," I'd get beautiful classical music, and if I said, "Beatles," I'd get one of their songs.

Yesterday, a couple ran a red light and nearly creamed my new car, but I swerved in time to avoid them. I yelled, "Ass Holes!"

Immediately the French National Anthem began to play, sung by a chorus of Jane Fonda and Barbara Streisand, Glenn Beck, Michael Savage, Sean Hannity, and Rush Limbaugh, backed up by Michael Moore and The Dixie Chicks, with John Kerry on guitar, Al Gore on drums, Louie Gohmert on harmonica, Sara Palin on Souzaphone, Governor Rick Perry on fiddle, Mich McConnell on washboard, Nancy Pelosi on tambourine, Michelle Bachmann on kazoo, Harry Reid on spoons, Steve Ducie on swinette, Bill Clinton on sax, Christine O'Donnal on a broom stick, Bill O'Reilly on scotch, Senator Ted Cruz obstructing, and Dick Cheney guarding them all with his trusty shotgun.

Oh, I *LOVE* this car!

• • •

## The Best Lay-off Letter Ever

No wonder this guy is the boss, he is *sharp*! You can't be any fairer than this guy. This is an actual letter from an industrialist trying to operate his firm in today's South Africa. I received this copy on 3 September, 2013 from a colleague living there.

Dear Employees:

As the CEO of this organization, I have resigned myself to the fact that Jacob Zuma is our President and that our taxes and government fees will increase in a BIG way.

To compensate for these increases, our prices would have to increase by about 10%. But, since we cannot increase our prices right now due to the dismal state of the economy, we will have to lay off sixty of our employees instead. This has really been bothering me since I believe we are family here and I didn't know how to choose who would have to go. So, this is what I did:. I walked through our employee parking lot and looked for cars with ANC bumper stickers and then decided that these folks will be the ones to let go. I can't think of a more fair way to approach this problem. They voted for change... I gave it to them. See the rest of you at the annual company picnic. Regards, Pieter

• • •

After dying a grisly death in Abbotabad, Pakistan, and burial at sea, Osama bin Laden made his way to the Pearly Gates. There, he was greeted by George Washington.

"How dare you attack the nation I helped conceive!" yelled Washington, slapping Osama in the face.

Patrick Henry came up next. "You wanted to end the American's liberty, so they gave you death!" Henry punched Osama in the nose.

James Madison came next and said, "This is why I allowed the government to provide for the common defense!" He seized a sledge hammer and whacked Osama's knee.

Osama was subjected to similar beatings from John Randolph, James Monroe and 67 other people who had the same love for liberty and America.

As he writhed on the ground, Thomas Jefferson hurled him back toward the gate where he was to be judged.

As Osama awaited his journey to his final very hot destination, he whined, "This is not what I was promised!"

An angel replied, "I told you there would be 72 Virginians waiting for you. "What did you think I said?"

• • •

### Democrat

Your neighbor has no cows..
You feel guilty for being successful.
You push for higher taxes so the government can provide cows for everyone.

### Republican

You have two cows.
Your neighbor has none.
So?

### Socialist

You have two cows.
The government takes one and gives it to your neighbor.
You form a cooperative to tell him how to manage his cow.

### Communist

You have two cows.
The government seizes both and provides you with milk.
You wait in line for hours to get it.
It is expensive and sour.

### Capitalism American Style

You have two cows.
You sell one, buy a bull, and build a herd of cows.

### Bureaucracy American Style

You have two cows.
Under the new farm program the government pays you to shoot one, milk the other, and then pours the milk down the drain.

### American Corporation

You have two cows.
You sell one, lease it back to yourself and do an IPO on the 2nd one.
You force the two cows to produce the milk of four cows.
You are surprised when one cow drops dead.
You spin an announcement to the analysts stating you have downsized and are reducing expenses.
Your stock goes up.

*Or*
### American Capitalism

You have two cows. You sell one, and force the other to produce the milk of four cows. You are surprised when the cow drops dead.

### Traditional Capitalism

You have two cows. You sell one and buy a bull. Your herd multiplies, and the economy grows. You sell them and retire on the income.

### Nazism

You have 2 cows. The Government takes both and shoots you.

### Bureaucratism

You have 2 cows; the Government takes both, shoots one, milks the other and throws the milk away...

### Enron Venture Corporation

You have two cows. You sell three of them to your publicly listed company, using letters of credit opened by your brother-in-law at the bank, then execute a debt/equity swap with an associated general offer so that you get four cows back, with a tax exemption for five cows. The milk rights of the six cows are transferred via an intermediary to a Cayman Island company secretly owned by the majority shareholder who sells the rights to all seven cows back to your listed company. The annual report says the company owns eight cows, with an option on one more. Sell one cow to buy a new president of the United States, leaving you with nine cows! No balance sheet provided with the release. The public buys your bull.

### Arthur Anderson LLC, Corporation

You have no cows. You shred all documents that Enron has any cows, take two cows from Enron for payment and attest that Enron has nine cows.

### English Corporation

You have two cows. They both go mad and have to be "put down."

### French Corporation

You have two cows.
You go on strike because you want three cows.
You go to lunch and drink wine.
Life is good.

### Swiss Corporation

You have 5000 cows, none of which belong to you. You charge others for storing them.

### Indian Corporation

You have two cows.
You worship them.

### Chinese Corporation

You have two cows.
You have 300 people milking them.
You claim full employment, high bovine productivity, and arrest the newsman who reported the numbers.

### Japanese Corporation

You have two cows.
You redesign them so they are one-tenth the size of an ordinary cow and produce twenty times the milk.
They learn to travel on unbelievably crowded trains.
Most are at the top of their class at cow school.

Or

You have no cows. You then create clever cow cartoon images called Cowkimon and market them worldwide.

### German Corporation

You have two cows.
You engineer them so they are all blonde, drink lots of beer, give excellent quality milk, and run a hundred miles an hour.
Unfortunately they also demand 13 weeks of vacation per year.

Or

You have two cows. You re-engineer them so they live for 100 years, eat once a month, and milk themselves.

### Italian Corporation

You have two cows but you don't know where they are.
You break for lunch.
Life is good.

### Russian Corporation

You have two cows.
You have some vodka.
You count them and learn you have five cows.
You have some more vodka.
You count them again and learn you have 42 cows.
The Mafia shows up and takes over regardless of how many cows you really have.

### Taliban Corporation

You have all the cows in Afghanistan, which are two.
You don't milk them because you cannot touch any creature's private parts.
You get a $40 million grant from the US government to find alternatives to milk production but use the money to buy weapons.

### Iraqi Corporation

You have two cows.
They go into hiding.
They send radio tapes of their mooing.

### Polish Corporation

You have two bulls.
Employees are regularly maimed and killed attempting to milk them.

### Belgian Corporation

You have one cow.
The cow is schizophrenic.
Sometimes the cow thinks he's French, other times he's Flemish.
The Flemish cow won't share with the French cow.
The French cow wants control of the Flemish cow's milk.
The cow asks permission to be cut in half.
The cow dies happy.

### Florida Corporation

You have a black cow and a brown cow.
Everyone votes for the best looking one.
Some of the people who actually like the brown one best accidentally vote for the black one.
Some people vote for both. Some people vote for neither. Some people can't figure out how to vote at all. Finally, a bunch of guys from out-of-state tell you which one you think is the best-looking cow.

### California Corporation

You have millions of cows.
They make real California cheese.
Only five speak English.
Most are illegal.
Arnold likes the ones with the big udders.

• • •

### Presidential Humor

"Political Correctness is a doctrine, fostered by a delusional, illogical minority, and rabidly promoted by an unscrupulous mainstream media, which holds forth the proposition that it is entirely possible to pick up a turd by the clean end."

• • •

Our good buddy Bill Clinton was assigned a new intern named Sally. Being the polite gentleman he is, Bill went to visit Sally and ask her if she needed any questions answered. She said no, so President Bill asked, "Have you seen the presidential clock yet?" Sally replied, "I haven't even heard of the presidential clock."

Bill then replied, "Well let's go to my office, so I can show it to you."

Sally was a little taken aback, and she stated, "With all the problems you've had lately, I don't think we should."

Then Bill said, "Ahh, it's just a clock and I promise I won't try anything."

Sally then agrees to go with him.

Bill leads her to the Oval Office, shuts and locks the door behind them and then drops his pants to the floor.

Sally is flabbergasted and says, "Mr. President, that is the presidential cock, not the presidential clock."

Bill looks at her and says, "Sally, by my definition, if you put two hands and a face on it, it's a clock.

• • •

I met a fairy today that said she would grant me one wish.

"I want to live forever," I said.

"Sorry," said the fairy, "I'm not allowed to grant wishes like that!"

"Fine," I said, "then I want to die after Republicans in Congress gets their heads out of their asses!"

"You crafty bastard," said the fairy.

• • •

If you run naked around a tree, at a speed of 185,999 miles per second, there is a distinct possibility of fucking yourself. Or, you can vote for the more radical Tea Party candidates and achieve the same result. –Alphonse Einstein

• • •

During a recent staff meeting in Heaven, God, Moses, and Saint Peter concluded that the behavior of Bill Clinton, Gary Condit, and Anthony Weiner had brought about the need for an eleventh commandment.

They worked long and hard in a brain storming session to try to settle on the wording of the new commandment, because they realized that it should have the same style, majesty and dignity as the original ten. After many revisions, they finally agreed that the eleventh commandment should be: "Thou shall not comfort thy rod with thy staff."

• • •

Russian President Vladimir Putin called President George W. Bush with an emergency, "Our largest condom factory has exploded," the Russian President cried.

"My people's favorite form of birth control. This is a truly a disaster!"

"Mr. Putin, the American people would be happy to do anything within their power to help you," replied the U.S. President.

"I do need your help," said Putin. "Could you possibly send 1,000,000 condoms, ASAP, to tide us over?"

"Why certainly! I'll get right on it," said Bush.

"Oh, and one more small favor, please?" said Putin.

"Yes?"

"Could the condoms be red in color and at least 10 inches long and 4 inches in diameter?" asked Putin.

"No problem," replied the President.

With that, George W. hung up the phone and then called the President of the Amalgamated Latex Condom Company.

"I need a favor. You've got to send 1,000,000 condoms over to Russia right away."

"Consider it done," said the CEO of ALCC.

"Great! Now listen. They have to be red in color, 10 inches long, and 4 inches in diameter."

"Easily done. Anything else?"

"Yeah," said Bush. "On each one print the words 'MADE IN TEXAS, SIZE SMALL.'"

• • •

### Are you a Democrat, a Republican, or a Redneck?

Here is a little test that will help you decide.

You are walking down a deserted street with your wife and two small children. Suddenly, an Islamic terrorist with a huge knife comes around the corner, locks eyes with you, screams obscenities, praises Allah, raises the knife, and charges at you. You are carrying a Kimber 1911 cal. 45 ACP, and you are an expert shot. You have mere seconds before he reaches you and your family. What do you do?

**Democrat's Answer:**

Well, that's not enough information to answer the question! Does the man look poor or oppressed? Have I ever done anything to him that would inspire him to attack? Could we run away? What does my wife think? What about the kids? Could I possibly swing the gun like a club and knock the knife out of his hand? What does the law say about this situation? Does the pistol have appropriate safety built into it? Why am I carrying a loaded gun anyway, and what kind of message does this send to society and to my children? Is it possible he'd be happy with just killing me? Does he definitely want to kill me, or would he be content just to wound me?

If I were to grab his knees and hold on, could my family get away while he was stabbing me? Should I call 9-1-1? Why is this street so deserted? We need to raise taxes, have "Paint & Weed Day" Can we make this a happier, healthier street that would discourage such behavior. I need to debate this with some friends for a few days and try to come to a consensus. This is all so confusing!

**Republican's Answer:**
BANG!

**Redneck's Answer:**
BANG! BANG! BANG! BANG! BANG! BANG! BANG! BANG! BANG! BANG! BANG! BANG! Click..... (Sounds of reloading) BANG! BANG! BANG! BANG! BANG! BANG! BANG! BANG! BANG! Click Daughter: "Nice grouping, Daddy! Were those the Winchester Silver Tips or Hollow Points?! "Can I shoot the next one?!"
Wife: 'You ain't taking that to the Taxidermist!

• • •

A cowboy named Bud was overseeing his herd in a remote mountainous pasture in California when suddenly a brand-new BMW advanced out of a dust cloud towards him. The driver, a young man in a Brioni suit, Gucci shoes, YSL tie, and RayBan sunglasses, leaned out the window and asked the cowboy, "If I tell you exactly how many cows and calves you have in your herd, will you give me a calf?"

Bud looked at the man, obviously a yuppie, then looked at his peacefully grazing herd and calmly answered, "Sure, Why not?"

The yuppie parked his car, whipped out his Dell notebook, connected it to his Cingular RAZR V3 cell phone, and surfed to a NASA page on the Internet, where he calls up a GPS satellite to get an exact fix on his location which he then feeds to another NASA satellite that scans the area in an ultra-high-resolution photo. The young man then opened the digital photo in Adobe Photoshop and exported it to an image processing facility in Hamburg, Germany. Within seconds, he received an email on his Blackberry that the image has been processed and the data stored. He then accessed an MS-SQL database through an ODBC connected Excel spreadsheet with email on his Blackberry and, after a few minutes, received a response. Finally, he printed out a full-color, 150-page report on his hi-tech, miniaturized HP LaserJet printer and finally turned to the cowboy and proudly exclaimed, "You have exactly 1,586 cows and calves."

"That's right. Well, I guess you can take one of my calves," said Bud.

He watched the young man select one of the animals and looked on amused as the young man stuffed it into the trunk of his car.

Then Bud said to the young man, "Hey, if I can tell you exactly what your business is, will you give me back my calf?"

The young man thinks about it for a second and then said, "Okay, why not?"

"You're a Democratic U.S. Congressman," said Bud.

"Wow! That's correct," said the yuppie, "But how did you guess that?"

"No guessing required, Sonny" answered the cowboy. "You showed up here even though nobody called you; you want to get paid for an answer I already knew, to a question I never asked. You tried to show me how much smarter than me you are; and you don't know a thing about cows... this is a herd of sheep. Now give me back my dog!"

• • •

Being able to laugh at yourself is a rare quality in a leader. It's one thing George W. Bush can do that Bill Clinton couldn't. Unfortunately, as we bid farewell to Bushisms, we must conclude that the joke was mainly on us.

1. "Our enemies are innovative and resourceful, and so are we. They never stop thinking about new ways to harm our country and our people, and neither do we."— Washington, D. C., Aug. 5, 2004

2. "I know how hard it is for you to put food on your family."–Greater Nashua, N. H., Chamber of Commerce, Jan. 27, 2000
3. "Rarely is the question asked: Is our children learning?"–Florence, S. C., Jan. 11, 2000.
4. "Too many good docs are getting out of the business. Too many OB/GYNs aren't able to practice their love with women all across the country." – Poplar Bluff, Mo., Sept. 6, 2004
5. "Neither in French nor in English nor in Mexican."–declining to answer reporters' – questions at the Summit of the Americas, Quebec City, Canada, April 21, 2001
6. "You teach a child to read, and he or her will be able to pass a literacy test."— Townsend, Tenn., Feb. 21, 2001.
7. "I'm the decider, and I decide what is best. And what's best is for Don Rumsfeld to remain as the secretary of defense." – Washington, D. C., April 18, 2006.
8. "See, in my line of work you got to keep repeating things over and over and over again for the truth to sink in, to kind of catapult the propaganda." – Greece, N. Y., May 24, 2005.
9. "I've heard he's been called Bush's poodle. He's bigger than that."–discussing former British prime minister Tony Blair, as quoted by the Sun newspaper, June 27, 2007.
10. "And so, General, I want to thank you for your service. And I appreciate the fact that you really snatched defeat out of the jaws of those who are trying to defeat us in Iraq."— meeting with Army Gen. Ray Odierno, Washington, D. C., March 3, 2008.
11. "We ought to make the pie higher."– South Carolina Republican debate, Feb. 15, 2000.
12. "There's an old saying in Tennessee–I know it's in Texas, probably in Tennessee— that says, fool me once, shame on– shame on you. Fool me–you can't get fooled again." –Nashville, Tenn., Sept. 17, 2002.
13. "And there is distrust in Washington. I am surprised, frankly, at the amount of distrust that exists in this town. And I'm sorry it's

the case, and I'll work hard to try to elevate it." –speaking on National Public Radio, Jan. 29, 2007.
14. "We'll let our friends be the peacekeepers and the great country called America will be the pacemakers" – Houston, Sept. 6, 2000.
15. "It's important for us to explain to our nation that life is important. It's not only life of babies, but it's life of children living in, you know, the dark dungeons of the Internet." — Arlington Heights, Ill., Oct. 24, 2000.
16. "One of the great things about books is sometimes there are some fantastic pictures." – U. S. News & World Report, Jan. 3, 2000.
17. "People say, 'How can I help on this war against terror? How can I fight evil?' You can do so by mentoring a child; by going into a shut-in's house and say I love you." — Washington, D. C., Sept. 19, 2002.
18. "Well, I think if you say you're going to do something and don't do it, that's trustworthiness." – CNN online chat, Aug. 30, 2000.
19. "I'm looking forward to a good night's sleep on the soil of a friend." –on the prospect of visiting Denmark, Washington, D. C., June 29, 2005.
20. "I think it's really important for this great state of baseball to reach out to people of all walks of life to make sure that the sport is inclusive. The best way to do it is to convince little kids how to – the beauty of playing baseball." –Washington, D. C., Feb. 13, 2006

• • •

## The Demographics of American Newspapers

1. The Wall Street Journal is read by the people who run the country.
2. The Washington Post is read by people who think they run the country.
3. The New York Times is read by people who think they should run the country and who are very good at crossword puzzles.

4. USA Today is read by people who think they ought to run the country, but don't really understand The New York Times. They do, however, like their statistics shown in pie charts.
5. The Los Angeles Times is read by people who wouldn't mind running the country - if they could find the time-and if they didn't have to leave Southern California to do it.
6. The Boston Globe is read by people whose parents used to run the country and did a poor job of it, thank you very much.
7. The New York Daily News is read by people who aren't too sure who's running the country and don't really care as long as they can get a seat on the train.
8. The New York Post is read by people who don't care who is running the country as long as they do something really scandalous, preferably while intoxicated, and who like their news as pictures and/or cartoons.
9. The Miami Herald is read by people who are running another country, but need the baseball scores.
10. The San Francisco Chronicle is read by people who aren't sure if there is a country or that anyone is running it; but if so, they oppose all that they stand for. There are occasional exceptions if the leaders are handicapped minority feminist atheist dwarves who also happen to be illegal aliens from any other country or galaxy, provided, of course, that they are not Republicans.
11. The National Enquirer is read by people trapped in line at the grocery store.
12. The Seattle Times is read by people who have recently caught a fish and need something in which to wrap it.
13. The Berkeley Gazette is read by people with a new puppy whose house training is just beginning.

• • •

The following is from a contest on Long Island, NY. The requirements were to use the two words Lewinsky (as in Monica) and Kaczynski (Unabomber) in a limerick. Here are the three winners:

### Third place:

There once was a gal named Lewinsky,
Who played on a flute like Stravinsky
'Twas "Hail to the Chief"
On this flute roast of beef
That stole the front page from Kaczynski.

### Second place:

Said Clinton to young Ms. Lewinsky
We don't want to leave clues like Kaczynski.
Since you look such a mess.
Use the hem of your dress
And wipe that stuff off of your chinsky.

### And the winning entry:

Lewinsky and Clinton have shown
What Kaczynski must surely have known
That an intern is better
Than a bomb in a letter
When deciding how best to be blown

• • •

50,000 people went to a baseball game, but the game was rained out and a refund was due. The team was about to send out refunds when the Democrats stopped them and suggested that they send out refund amounts based on their interpretation of fairness. After all, if the refunds were made based on the price each person paid for the tickets, most of the money would go to the richest people. This plan pays: People in the $10 seats will get back $15, because they have less money to spend. People in the $15 seats will get back $15, because that's fair. People in the $25 dollar seats make a lot of money and don't need a refund. People in the $50 luxury seats will have to pay another $50, because they have way too much to spend. The people driving by the stadium who couldn't afford to watch the game, will get $10 each (even though they didn't pay anything to get in) because they need the most help. Now *What* about the Democrats do you *not* understand?

• • •

It was getting a little crowded in Heaven, so God decided to change the admittance policy. The new law was that, in order to get into Heaven, you had to have a really bad day on the day that you died. The policy would go into effect at noon the next day. So, the next day at 12:01 the first person came to the gates of Heaven. The Angel at the gate, remembering the new policy, promptly asked the man, "Before I let you in, I need you to tell me how your day was going when you died."

"No problem," the man said. "For some time now I have been suspicious of my wife having an affair. So today I decided to come home for lunch early to surprise her. When I opened the door to my 25th floor apartment I knew that something was up. My wife was standing in the kitchen half naked, but her lover was nowhere in sight; immediately I began searching for him. My wife was crying and yelling at me as I searched the entire apartment. Just as I was about to give up, I happened to glance out onto the balcony and noticed that there was a man hanging off the edge by his fingertips! The nerve of that guy! Well, I ran out on to the balcony and stomped on his fingers until he fell to the ground. But wouldn't you know it, he landed in some trees and bushes that broke his fall and he didn't die. This ticked me off even more. In a rage, I went back inside to get the first thing I could get my hands on to throw at him. Oddly enough, the first thing I thought of was the refrigerator. I unplugged it, pushed it out onto the balcony, and tipped it over the side. It plummeted 25 stories and crushed him! The excitement of the moment was so great that I had a heart attack and died almost instantly."

The Angel sat back and thought a moment. Technically, the guy did had a bad day–it was a crime of passion. So, the Angel announces, "OK sir. Welcome to the Kingdom of Heaven," and let him in.

A few seconds later the next guy came up. "Greetings, friend: before I can let you in, I need to hear about what your day was like when you died." The man said, "No problem. But you are not going to believe this; I was on the balcony of my 26th floor apartment doing my daily exercises. I had been under a lot of pressure so I was really pushing hard to relieve my stress. I guess I got a little carried away, slipped, and accidentally fell over the side! Luckily, I was able to catch myself by my fingertips on the balcony below mine. But all of a sudden this crazy man comes out of his apartment, starts cussing, and stomps on my fingers. Well of course I fell. I hit some trees and bushes at the bottom, which broke my fall so I didn't die right away. As I'm laying there face up on the ground, unable to move and in excruciating pain, I see this guy push his refrigerator of all things off the balcony. It falls the 25 floors and lands on top of me killing me instantly."

The Angel was quietly laughing to himself as the man finishes his story. "I could get used to this new policy," he thought to himself. "Very well sir," the Angel announced. "Welcome to the Kingdom of Heaven," and he permitted the man to enter. A few seconds later, President Clinton arrived at to the gate. The Angel was almost too shocked to speak. Thoughts of assassination and war pour through the angel's head. Finally he said "Mr. President, please tell me what it was like the day you died."

Clinton replied, "OK, picture this. I'm naked inside a refrigerator..."

• • •

## Bill and Al

Bill and Hillary had Al and Tipper Gore over for dinner at the White House. In the middle of dinner, Al excused himself to use the bathroom. After a couple minutes, he came back. They finished dinner and Al and Tipper left for home.

On the way home, Al turned to Tipper and said, "Did you know that Bill has got a solid gold urinal in his bathroom? How can we tell the American people we are serious about cutting the budget when the President has a solid gold urinal?"

Tipper said, "There must be some mistake, I'll call Hillary when we get home and find out."

When they get home, she called Hillary and said, "is it true that Bill has a solid gold urinal in his bathroom?"

Hillary put her hand over the telephone receiver and said, "Bill, I just found out who peed in your saxophone!"

• • •

## "Bubba Vita "

(A classic piece of email humor, that made the rounds.)

NEW YORK. Opening night at the The Metropolitan Opera this coming season will be the world premiere of a new opera on Bill Clinton:"*Il Bubba Vita*," Composed by Giuliani Veritas. It will be performed in Italian. The following is a summary of what is expected to be regarded as a modem masterpiece of political satire and verissimo drama:

### Act I

Bill Clinton has been elected President of the United States by an overwhelming margin. The Republicans are devastated and angry and are trying to find their way back to power. As the curtain rises on the opera, the House Republicans are meeting with Ken Starr with the object of trying to find a way to remove Bill

Clinton from the Presidency. The opening chorale, "We must find a way" ("*Creato grandissimo floozi scandala*") is sung as a sextet. In an impressive recitative, Tom Delay sings, "Where will we find a helper?" ("*Dredgi uppulia una Granda Bimba*"). The House Republicans exit.

Paula Jones enters stage right with a mirror, singing her plaintive "Why can't I find a man?" ("*Mia schnozola es humongo*"). Tom Delay and Newt Gingrich enter from the other wing. They Spot Paula and sing the duet, "Why not her?" ("*la flooza perfecta*"). They meet and take Paula to a small cafe where they hatch their plot in hushed tones. Paula tells them of her meeting in a hotel with Clinton years earlier and how her fortunes have collapsed since then. Delay and Gingrich offer to help. They sing the aria, "Your luck has changed" ("*Nozjobbo e' rewardo*").

## Act II

The House Republicans reconvene with the news of Paula's relelations. They sing in jubilation, "We must tell the world" ("*Fono tabloido*"). The rear curtain rises to reveal the Chorus of Media, who sing the chorale, "Tell us more, but only the truth" ("*Sexio scandala hypo sweepi*"). Gingrich enters with Pat Robertson. They sing the duet, "He must go" ("*Hypocriti pious crappola*"). Robertson offers to make time on his television program to expose the charges.

At the House Republicans' suggestion, Paula initiates a lawsuit. The Paula Jones scandal becomes the topic of conversation throughout the country. The Chorus of Lawyers enters from the right to sing the jubilant grand chorale, "We must do our duty" ("*Molto, molto grande moola*"). Ken Starr meets with the House Republicans to plan the next steps. They sing the aria, "We will save the country" ("*Sleezi connivo, la media soccituppo*"). Starr promises to convene a grand jury that will send charges to the Congress. He sings, "The truth will be known" ("*Whitewater non starto, il probo la flooza epidemio*"). The Chorus of Lawyers sings a reprise of "We must do our duty" as the act ends.

## Act III

Linda Tripp enters the stage arm in arm with Ken Starr. She is wearing a headset. She is singing, "Monica is my dearest Friend" ("*Lo sono la oichida witchi occidenta*"). She tells Starr about the secret tapes that she has made of conversations with Monica Lewinsky. Starr takes them from her and sings, "We've got him now" ("*Presidente droppo pantaloni*"). Starr hurries off to the Grand Jury to call Monica as a witness.

In Scene 2, Monica enters the grand jury room where the Chorus of Lawyers asks her questions. They sing the recitative, "How did it happen?" ("*C'Panti hong, la flashi*"). Monica sings the long passionate aria, "We were meant for each other" "('*Nonsmoko el producto, phalli symboglio*").

In the third scene, Hillary and Bill are sitting in the Lincoln Bedroom discussing the revelations about Monica. Hillary sings, "I will stand by you" ("*Tu jercho estupido, io removo tu equippamento*"). Bill replies with, "She was the only one" ("*Non counto Gennifer, Paula, piu molto bimba forgetta*"). They embrace.

## Act IV

Sam Donaldson is interviewing Henry Hyde in the Capitol Building. The Chorus of Lawyers hums in the background. Hyde sings the aria, "We believe in something" ('*Impeaccho hippi bastardo*"). Donaldson sings a recitative in answer, "We only want the truth" ("*Mio toupee eslippo*").

The great trial begins in the Senate. Trent Lott reacts to public opinion polls showing that the President has a 76% approval rating with the public with the poignant aria, "What is right is not popular" ("*Partia repubblico commitini suicido*"). The Chorus of lawyers sings the chorale, "Principles come first" ("*Mio adultero non counto*") with great flourish. Henry Hyde, Bill McCullum, and Tom Delay stand before the Senate to present their case. They sing the somber trio, "How can you not convict?" ("*Evidensi multo flimsioso*").

Finally, in a moving chorale, the Chorus of Lawyers sings "For the good of the nation, we must acquit" ("*Senatorios non stupido*"). After the vote is announced, Henry Hyde, Tom Delay, Trent Lott, and Bill McCollum leave the Senate Chamber singing the grand quartet, "We still know the truth" ("*Wasto multo millioni*") as the Act ends.

## Epilogue

The President sings the contrite aria, "I am 'very sorry" ("*Revengo Futuro furioso*") as the Chorus of Media circles him shouting their questions. They sing, "Who will believe us?" ("*Publicca degustanta es in media*"). Monica Lewinsky crosses the stage with her new literary agent, Ken Starr. They sing, "It is still not over" ("*Publishi grande bucchi, Dolare millioni*") as the final curtain falls on this epic drama.

• • •

Father O'Malley rose from his bed. It was a fine spring day in his new Washington DC parish. He walked to the window of his bedroom to get a deep breath of the beautiful day outside. He then noticed there was a jackass lying dead in the middle on his front lawn. He promptly called the US Senate for assistance. The conversation went like this:

"Good morning. This is Representative Mitch McConnell. How might I help you?"

"And the best of the day te yerself. This is Father O'Malley at St. Brigit's. There's a jackass lying dead in me front lawn.

Would ye be so kind as to send a couple o' yer lads to take care of the matter?"

McConnell, considering himself to be quite a wit, replied with a smirk, "Well now father, it was always my impression that you people took care of last rites!"

There was dead silence on the line for a long moment.

Father O'Malley then replied: "Aye, that's certainly true, but we are also obliged to notify the next of kin.

• • •

**Politics Explained**

A little boy went to his dad and asked, "What is Politics?"

Dad replied, "Well son, let me try to explain it this way:

I'm the head of the family, so call me The President. Your mother is the Administrator of the money, so we call her the Government. We're here to take care of your needs, so we'll call you the People. The nanny, we'll consider her the Working lass. And your baby brother, we'll call him the Future. Now think about that and see ifit makes sense."

So the little boy went off to bed thinking about what Dad has said. Later that night, he heard his baby brother crying, so he got up to check on him. He found that the baby had severely soiled his diaper. So the little boy went to his parent's room and found his mother sound asleep. Not wanting to wake her, he went to the nanny's room. Finding the door locked, he peeked in the keyhole and saw his father in bed with the nanny. He gave up and went back to bed.

The next morning, the little boy say's to his father, "Dad, I think I understand the concept of politics now."

The father said, "Good, son. Tell me in your own words what you think politics is all about.

The little boy replied, "The President is screwing the Working Class while the Government is sound asleep. The People are being ignored and the Future is in deep shit."

• • •

## The Oil is Low

There are a lot of folks who can't understand how we came to have an oil shortage here in the USA. Well, there's a very simple answer. Nobody bothered to check the oil. We just didn't know we were getting low. The reason for this is purely geographical. All the oil is in Alaska, Oklahoma, Texas, Louisiana, Wyoming, etc.

All the dipsticks are in Washington, DC.

• • •

The Pope was visiting Washington, DC and President Bush took him out for an afternoon on the Potomac... sailing on the presidential yacht. They were admiring the sights when, all of a sudden, the Pope's hat (zucchetto) blew off his head and out into the water. Secret service guys started to launch a boat, but Bush waved them off, saying "Wait, wait. I'll take care of this. Don't worry."

Bush then stepped off the yacht onto the surface of the water and walked out to the Holy Father's little hat, bent over and picked it up, then walked back to the yacht and climbed aboard. He handed the hat to the Pope amid stunned silence.

The next morning, the Washington Post carried a story, with front page photos, of the event. The banner headline read: "Bush Can't Swim."

• • •

One day a florist went to his usual barber for a haircut. After the cut he asked the barber about his bill. "I am sorry, I cannot accept money from you. I am doing community service this week." The florist was pleased and departed the shop. The next morning when the barber went to open his shop, there was a "thank you" card and a dozen roses waiting at his door.

Later a cop came in for a haircut and he also tried to pay the barber. The barber replied, "I am sorry I cannot accept money from you.

I am doing community service this week." The cop was happy and left the shop. The next morning the barber went to open his shop, there is a "thank you" card and a dozen donuts waiting at his door.

A life-long Democrat came for a hair cut and when he asked the barber what he owed, the barber replied, "I am sorry I cannot accept money from you. I am doing community service this week." The Democrat was very happy and left. The next morning when the barber opened his shop, a dozen Democrats were lined up waiting for free haircuts.

• • •

George W. Bush was walking through an airport last week, when he saw an old man with white hair, a long white beard, wearing a long white robe and holding a staff. He walked up to the man, who was staring at the ceiling, and said "Excuse me sir, aren't you Moses?"

The man stood perfectly still and continued to stare at the ceiling, saying nothing.

Again George W. asked, a little louder this time, "Excuse me sir, aren't you Moses?"

Again the old man stared at the ceiling motionless without saying a word.

George W. tried a third time, louder yet. "Excuse me sir, aren't you Moses?"

Again, there was no movement or words from the old man. He continued to stare at the ceiling.

One of George W's aides asked him if there was a problem, and George W said, "Either this man is deaf or extremely rude. I have asked him three times if he was Moses, and he has not answered me yet."

The man, still staring at the ceiling finally replied, "I *can* hear you and yes, I am Moses, but the last time I spoke to a bush, I spent 40 years wandering in the wilderness.

• • •

I just received my tax return for 2012 back from the IRS. It puzzles me!!! They are questioning how many dependents I claimed. I guess it was because of my response to the question: "List all dependents?"
I replied:
12 million illegal immigrants;
3 million crack heads;
42 million unemployed people on food stamps,
2 million people in over 243 prisons; Half of Mexico; and –
535 persons in the U.S. House and Senate."

Evidently, this was NOT an acceptable answer. I keep asking myself, who the Hell did I miss?

• • •

British Intelligence reported yesterday that Saddam Hussein had issued a general order that all woman in Iraq must shave off all their pubic hair.

Tony Blair thinks Saddam is taking the Anti-Bush campaign a bit too far.

• • •

After numerous rounds of "We don't even know if Saddam is still alive", Saddam Hussein decided to send George W. a letter in his own writing to let him know that he is still in the game. Bush opened the letter and it appeared to contain a coded message:

**370HSSV-0773H.**

George W. couldn't figure it out so he typed it out and emailed it to Colin Powell. Colin and his aides had no clue either so they sent it to Condoleza Rice, and she, also couldn't understand the cryptic note. Then she sent the message to the CIA. No one could solve it so it went to the NSA and then to MIT and NASA and the Secret Service... the list got longer and longer.

Eventually they asked Mossad in Israel for help. Cpt. Moishe Pippick took one look at it and replied: "Tell the President he is looking at the message upside down and backwards."

• • •

Hillary Clinton visited a primary school to talk about the world. After her talk she offered question time. One little boy puts up his hand, and the former Secretary of State asked him what his name was.

"Billy" "And what is your question, Billy?"

I have three questions. First - whatever happened to your medical health care plan; second – why would you run for President after your husband shamed the office; and third – whatever happened to all those things you took when you left the White House?"

Just then the bell rings for recess. Hillary Clinton informed the kiddies that they will continue after recess.

When they resume Hillary said, "Okay where were we? Oh, that's right, question time. Who has a question?"

A different little boy puts his hand up; Hillary points him out and asks him what his name is.

"Steve" "And what is your question, Steve?"

"I have five questions. First - whatever happened to your medical care plan; second – why would you run for President after your husband shamed the office; third – whatever happened to all those things you took when you left the White House; fourth – why did the bell ring 20 minutes early; and fifth – what happened to Billy?"

• • •

Late one night, a mugger wearing a ski mask jumped into the path of a well-dressed man and stuck a gun in his ribs.

"Give me your money", he demanded.

Indignant, the affluent man replied, "Hey, watch it - I'm a United States Congressman!"

"In that case," replied the mugger, "give me MY money."

• • •

Hillary Clinton was out jogging one morning along the parkway when she tripped, fell over the bridge railing and landed in the creek below.

Before the Secret Service guys could get to her, 3 kids who were fishing pulled her out of the water. She was so grateful she offered the kids whatever they wanted.

The first kid says, "I want to go to Disneyland."

Hillary says, "No problem, I'll take you there on my special Senator's airplane."

The second kid says, "I want a new pair of Nike Air Jordan's."

Hillary said, "I'll get them for you and even have Michael sign them!!"

The third kid says, "I want a motorized wheelchair with a built in TV and stereo headset!"

Hillary is a little perplexed by this and says, "But you don't look like you're handicapped."

The kid says, "I will be after my dad finds out I saved your ass from drowning.

• • •

**The Politically - Correct Little Red Riding Hood**

There once was a young person named Little Red Riding Hood who lived on the edge of a large forest full of endangered owls and rare plants that would probably provide a cure for cancer if only someone took the time to study them.

Red Riding Hood lived with a nurture giver whom she sometimes referred to as "mother", although she didn't mean to imply by this term that she would have thought less of the person if a close biological link did not in fact exist. Nor did she intend to denigrate the equal value of nontraditional households, although she was sorry if this was the impression conveyed.

One day her mother asked her to take a basket of organically grown fruit and mineral water to her grandmother's house.

"But mother, won't this be stealing work from the unionized people who have struggled for years to earn the right to carry all packages between various people in the woods?"

Red Riding Hood's mother assured her that she had called the union boss and gotten a special compassionate mission exemption form.

"But mother, aren't you oppressing me by ordering me to do this?"

Red Riding Hood's mother pointed out that it was impossible for women to repress each other, since all women were equally oppressed until all women were free.

"But mother, then shouldn't you have my brother carry the basket, since he's an oppressor, and should learn what it's like to be oppressed?"

And Red Riding Hood's mother explained that her brother was attending a special rally for animal rights, and besides, this wasn't stereotypical women's' work, but an empowering deed that would help engender a feeling of community.

"But won't I be oppressing Grandma, by implying that she's sick and hence unable to independently further her own selfhood?"

But Red Riding Hood's mother explained that her grandmother wasn't actually sick or incapacitated or mentally handicapped in any way, although that was not to imply that any of these conditions were inferior to what some people called "health."

Thus Red Riding Hood felt that she could get behind the idea of delivering the basket to her grandmother, and so she set off.

Many people believed that the forest was a foreboding and dangerous place, but Red Riding Hood knew that this was an irrational fear based on cultural paradigms instilled by a patriarchal society that regarded the natural world as an exploitable resource, and hence believed that natural predators were in fact intolerable competitors.

Other people avoided the woods for fear of thieves and deviants, but Red Riding Hood felt that in a truly classless society all marginalized peoples would be able to "come out" of the woods and be accepted as valid lifestyle role models.

On her way to Grandma's house, Red Riding Hood passed a woodchopper, and wandered off the path, in order to examine some flowers. She was startled to find herself standing before a Wolf, who asked her what was in her basket. Red Riding Hood's teacher had warned her never to talk to strangers, but she was confident in taking control of her own budding sexuality, and chose to dialogue with the Wolf.

She replied, "I am taking my Grandmother some healthful snacks in a gesture of solidarity."

The Wolf said, "You know, my dear, it isn't safe for a little girl to walk through these woods alone."

Red Riding Hood said, "I find your sexist remark offensive in the extreme, but I will ignore it because of your traditional status as an outcast from society, the stress of which has caused you to develop an alternative and yet entirely valid world view.

Now, if you'll excuse me, I would prefer to be on my way."

Red Riding Hood returned to the main path, and proceeded towards her grandmother's house. But because his status outside society had freed him from slavish adherence to linear, Western-style thought, the Wolf knew of a quicker route to Grandma's house. He burst into the house and ate Grandma, a course of action affirmative of his nature as a predator. Then, unhampered by rigid, traditionalist gender role notions, he put on Grandma's nightclothes, crawled under the bedclothes, and awaited developments.

Red Riding Hood entered the cottage and said, "Grandma, I have brought you some cruelty free snacks to salute you in your role of wise and nurturing matriarch."

The Wolf said softly "Come closer, child, so that I might see you."

Red Riding Hood said, "Goodness! Grandma, what big eyes you have!"

"You forget that I am optically challenged," replied the wolf.

"And Grandma, what an enormous, long nose you have."

"Naturally, I could have had it fixed to help my acting career, but I didn't give in to such societal pressures, my child."

"And Grandma, what very big, sharp teeth you have!"

The Wolf could not take any more of these speciest slurs, and, in a reaction appropriate for his accustomed milieu, he leaped out of bed, grabbed Little Red Riding Hood, and opened his jaws so wide that she could see her poor Grandmother cowering in his belly.

"Aren't you forgetting something?" Red Riding Hood bravely shouted. "You must request my permission before proceeding to a new level of intimacy!"

The Wolf was so startled by this statement that he loosened his grasp on her.

At the same time, the woodchopper burst into the cottage, brandishing an ax.

"Hands off!" cried the woodchopper.

"And what do you think you're doing?" cried Little Red Riding Hood. "If I let you help me now, I would be expressing a lack of confidence in my own abilities, which would lead to poor self esteem and lower achievement scores on college entrance exams."

"Last chance, sister! Get your hands off that endangered species! This is an FBI sting!" screamed the woodchopper, and when Little Red Riding Hood nonetheless made a sudden motion, he sliced off her head.

"Thank goodness you got here in time," said the Wolf. "The brat and her grand-mother lured me in here. I thought I was a goner."

"No, I think I'm the real "victim, here," said the wood chopper. "I've been dealing with my anger ever since I saw her picking those protected flowers earlier. And now I'm going to have such a trauma. Do you have any aspirin?"

'Sure," said the Wolf.

"Thanks."

"I feel your pain," said the Wolf, and he patted the woodchopper on his firm, well padded back, gave a little belch, and said "Do you have any Maalox?"

• • •

President Clinton was being entertained by an African leader. They spent the day discussing what the country had received from the Russians before the new government kicked them out.

"The Russians built us a power plant, a highway, and an we learned to drink vodka and play Russian roulette."

President Clinton frowned. "Russian roulette's not a friendly, nice game."

The African leader smiled. "That's why we developed African roulette. If you want to have good relations with our country, you'll have to play. I'll show you how."

He pushed a buzzer, and a moment later six magnificently built, nude women were ushered in. "You can choose anyone of those women to give you oral sex." He told Clinton.

This gained Clinton's immediate attention, and he was ready to make his choice, when a thought occurred to him. "How on earth is this related to Russian roulette?"

The African leader smiled and replied, "One of them is a cannibal."

• • •

The government announced today that it is changing its emblem to a condom because it more clearly reflects the government's political stance.

A condom stands up to inflation, halts production, destroys the next generation, protects a bunch of pricks, and gives you a sense of security while you're actually being screwed.

Damn, it just doesn't get more accurate than that.

• • •

A little old lady called 911. When the operator answered she yelled, "Help, send the police to my house right away! There's a damn Republican on my front porch and he's playing with himself."

"What?" the operator exclaimed!

"I said there is a damn Republican on my front porch playing with himself and he's weird; I don't know him and I'm afraid! Please send the police!" the little old lady repeated.

"Well, now, how do you know he's a Republican?"

"Because, you damn fool, if he were a Democrat, he'd be screwing somebody!"

• • •

"It doesn't get any better (worse?) than this.

Jessie Jackson has added former Chicago democratic congressman Mel Reynolds to Rainbow/PUSH Coalition's payroll. Reynolds was among the 176 criminals excused in President Clinton's last-minute forgiveness spree.

Reynolds received a commutation of his six-and-a-half-year federal sentence for 15 convictions of wire fraud, bank fraud and lies to the Federal Election Commission. He is more notorious, however, for concurrently serving five years for sleeping with an underage campaign volunteer. This is a first in American politics: an ex-congressman who had sex with a subordinate... won clemency from a president who had sex with a subordinate... then was hired by a clergyman who had sex with a subordinate.

His new job?

Youth counselor!

*IS THIS A GREAT COUNTRY OR WHAT?*

• • •

## Classic Version:

The ant worked hard in the withering heat all summer long, building his house and laying up supplies for the winter. The grasshopper thought he was a fool and laughed and danced and played the summer away. Come winter, the ant was warm and well fed.

The grasshopper had no food or shelter so he died out in the cold.
*MORAL OF THE STORY:* Be responsible for yourself!

## Modern Version:

The ant worked hard in the withering heat all summer long, building his house and laying up supplies for the winter.

The grasshopper thought he was a fool and laughed and danced and played the summer away. Come winter, the shivering grasshopper called a press conference and demanded to know why the ant should be allowed to be warm and well fed while others are cold and starving. CBS, NBC, ABC, and CNN showed up to provide pictures of the shivering grasshopper next to a video of the ant in his comfort able home with a table filled with food.

America was stunned by the sharp contrast. How can this be, that in a country of such wealth, this poor grasshopper was allowed to suffer so?

Kermit the Frog appeared on Oprah with the grasshopper, and everybody cried when they sing "It's Not Easy Being Green." Jesse Jackson staged a demonstration in front of the ant's house where the news stations film the group singing "We shall overcome". Jesse then has the group kneel down to pray to God for the grasshopper's sake.

Nancy Pelosi and Chuck Shumer exclaimed in an interview with Wolf Blitzer that the ant had gotten rich off the back of the grasshopper, and both call for an immediate tax hike on the ant to make him pay his "fair share."

Finally, the EEOC drafts the "Economic Equity and Ant i- Grasshopper Act", retroactive to the beginning of the summer.

The ant was fined for failing to hire a proportionate number of green bugs and, having nothing left to pay his retroactive taxes, his home was confiscated by the government.

Hillary got her old law firm to represent the grasshopper in a defamation suit against the ant, and the case was tried before a panel of federal judges that Bill appointed from a list of single-parent welfare recipients.

The ant lost the case.

The story ends as we see the grasshopper finishing up the last bits of the ant's food while the government house he is in, which just happens to be the ant's old house, crumbles around him because he doesn't maintain it.

The ant has disappeared in the snow.

The grass hopper is found dead in a drug-related incident and the house, now abandoned, is taken over by a gang of spiders who terrorize the once peaceful neighborhood.

*MORAL OF THE STORY*: Vote Independent (currently; the Tea Party activists have destroyed the Republican Party as we once knew it – and the Democrats are becoming increasingly moribund.

• • •

### Noah

If Noah had lived in the United States in the year 2003, the story may have gone something like this. And the Lord spoke to Noah and said, "In one year, I am going to make it rain and cover the whole earth with water until all flesh is destroyed. But I want you to save the righteous people and two of every kind of living thing on earth. Therefore, I am commanding you to build an Ark."

In a flash of lightning, God delivered the specifications for an Ark. In fear and trembling, Noah took the plans and agreed to build the ark. Remember, said the Lord, "you must complete the Ark and bring everything aboard in one year."

Exactly one year later, fierce storm clouds covered the earth and all the seas of the earth went into a tumult. The Lord saw that Noah was sitting in his front yard weeping.

"Noah!" He shouted. "Where is the Ark?"

"Lord, please forgive me," cried Noah. "I did my best, but there were big problems. First, I had to get a permit for construction, and your plans did not meet the building codes. I had to hire an engineering firm and redraw the plans. Then I got into a fight with OSHA over whether or not the Ark needed a sprinkler system and approved floatation devices. Then, my neighbor objected, claiming I was violating zoning ordinances by building the Ark in my front yard, so I had to get a variance from the city planning commission. Then, I had problems getting enough wood for the Ark, because there was a ban on cutting trees to protect the Spotted Owl. I finally convinced the U.S. Forest Service that I really needed the wood to save the owls. However, the Fish and Wildlife Service won't let me take the 2 owls. The carpenters formed a union and went on strike. I had to negotiate a settlement with the National Labor Relations Board before anyone would pick up a saw or hammer. Now, I have 16 carpenters on the Ark, but still no owls. When I started rounding up the other animals, an animal rights group sued me. They objected to me taking only two of each kind aboard. This suit is pending."

"Meanwhile, the EPA notified me that I could not complete the Ark without filing an environmental impact statement on your proposed flood. They didn't take very kindly to the idea that they had no jurisdiction over the conduct of the Creator of the Universe. Then, the Army Corps of Engineers demanded a map of the proposed flood plain. I sent them a globe."

"Right now, I am trying to resolve a complaint filed with the Equal Employment Opportunity Commission that I am practicing discrimination by not taking atheists aboard. The IRS has seized my assets, claiming that I'm building the Ark in preparation to flee the country to avoid paying taxes. I just got a notice from the state that I owe them some kind of user tax and failed to register the Ark as a 'recreational water craft'. And finally, the ACLU got the courts to issue an injunction against further construction of the Ark, saying that since God is flooding the earth, it's a religious event, and, therefore unconstitutional. I really don't think I can finish the Ark for another five or six years." Noah waited. The sky began to clear, the sun began to shine, and the seas began to calm. A rainbow arched across the sky. Noah looked up hopefully. "You mean you're not going to destroy the earth, Lord?"

"No," He said sadly. "I don't have to. The government already has."

• • •

TO: Honorable Secretary of Agriculture
Washington, D.C.

Dear Sir;

My friend, Ed Peterson, over at Wells Iowa, received a check for $1,000 from the government for not raising hogs. So, I want to go into the "not raising hogs" business next year. What I want to know is, in your opinion, what is the best kind of farm not to raise hogs on, and what is the best breed of hogs not to raise? I want to be sure that I approach this endeavor in keeping with all governmental policies. I would prefer not to raise razorbacks, but if that is not a good breed not to raise, then I will just as gladly not raise Yorkshires or Duroc Jerseys.

As I see it, the hardest part of this program will be in keeping an accurate inventory of how many hogs I haven't raised. My friend, Peterson, is very joyful about the future of the business. He has been raising hogs for twenty years or so, and the best he ever made on them was $422 in 1968, until this year when he got your check for $1000 for not raising hogs.

If I get $1000 for not raising 50 hogs, will I get $2000 for not raising 100 hogs? I plan to operate on a small scale at first, holding myself down to about 4000 hogs not raised, which will mean about $80,000 the first year. Then I can afford an airplane.

Now another thing, these hogs I will not raise will not eat 100,000 bushels of corn. I understand that you also pay farmers for not raising corn and wheat. Will I qualify for payments for not raising wheat and corn not to feed the 4000 hogs I am not going to raise?

Also, I am considering the "not milking cows" business, so send me any information you have on that too.

In view of these circumstances, you understand that I will be totally unemployed and plan to file for unemployment and food stamps.

Be assured you will have my vote in the coming election.

Patriotically Yours,

Jack Smith

P.S. Would you please notify me when you plan to distribute more free cheese?

• • •

You gotta love the Government! This is an actual letter sent to a man named Ryan DeVries by the Michigan Department of Environmental Quality, State of Michigan. This guy's response is hilarious, but read the State's letter before you get to the response letter.

SUBJECT: DEQ File No.97-59-0023; T11N; R10W, Sec. 20; Montcalm County Dear Mr. DeVries: It has come to the attention of the Department of Environmental Quality that there has been recent unauthorized activity on the above referenced parcel of property.

You have been certified as the legal landowner and/or contractor who did the following unauthorized activity:

Construction and maintenance of two wood debris dams across the outlet stream of Spring Pond. A permit must be issued prior to the start of this type of activity. A review of the Department's files shows that no permits have been issued. Therefore, the Department has determined that this activity is in violation of Part 301, Inland Lakes and Streams, of the Natural Resource and Environmental Protection Act, Act 451 of the Public Acts of 1994, being sections 324.30101 to 324.30113 of the Michigan Compiled Laws, annotated.

The Department has been informed that one or both of the dams partially failed during a recent rain event, causing debris and flooding at downstream locations. We find that dams of this nature are inherently hazardous and cannot be permitted. The Department therefore orders you to cease and desist all activities at this location, and to restore the stream to a free-flow condition by removing all wood and brush forming the dams from the stream channel. All restoration work shall be completed no later than January 31, 2003.

Please notify this office when the restoration has been completed so that a follow-up site inspection may be scheduled by our staff. Failure to comply with this request or any further unauthorized activity on the site may result in this case being referred for elevated enforcement action.

We anticipate and would appreciate your full cooperation in this matter. Please feel free to contact me at this office if you have any questions.

Sincerely,
David L. Price, District Representative, Land and Water Management Division Re: DEQ File No. 97-59-0023; T11N; R10W, Sec. 20; Montcalm County.

Dear Mr. Price,

Your certified letter dated 12/17/02 has been handed to me to respond. I am the legal landowner but not the Contractor at 2088 Dagget, Pierson, Michigan. A couple of beavers are in the process of constructing and maintaining two wood "debris" dams across the outlet stream of my Spring Pond. While I did not pay for, authorize, nor supervise their dam project, I think they would be highly offended that you call their skillful use of natures building materials "debris." I would like to challenge your Depart-ment to attempt to emulate their dam project any time and/or any place you choose. I believe I can safely state there is no way you could ever match their dam construction skills, their dam resourcefulness, their dam ingenuity, their dam persistence, their dam determination and/or their dam work ethic.

As to your request, I do not think the beavers are aware that they must first fill out a dam permit prior to the start of this type of dam activity.

My first dam question to you is: (1) Are you trying to discriminate against my spring Pond Beavers, or (2) do you require all beavers throughout this State to conform to said dam request? If you are not discriminating against these particular beavers, through the Freedom of Information Act, I request completed copies of all those other applicable beaver dam permits that have been issued. Perhaps we will see if there really is a dam violation of Part 301, Inland Lakes and Streams, of the Natural Resource and Environmental Protection Act, Act 451 of the Public Acts of 1994, being sections 324.30101to 324.30113 of the Michigan Compiled Laws, annotated.

I have several concerns. My first concern is; aren't the beavers entitled to legal representation? The Spring Pond Beavers are financially destitute and are unable to pay for said representation – so the State will have to provide them with a dam lawyer. The Department's dam concern that either one or both of the dams failed during a recent rain event, causing flooding, is proof that this is a natural occurrence, which the Department is required to protect. In other words, we should leave the Spring Pond beavers alone rather than harassing them and calling their dam names.

If you want the stream "restored" to a dam free-flow condition please contact the beavers – but if you are going to arrest them, they obviously did not pay any attention to your dam letter, they being unable to read English.

In my humble opinion, the Spring Pond Beavers have a right to build their unauthorized dams as long as the sky is blue, the grass is green and water flows downstream. They have more dam rights than I do to live and enjoy Spring Pond. If the Department of Natural Resources and Environmental Protection lives up to its name, it should protect the natural resources (Beavers) and the environment (Beavers' Dams).

So, as far as the beavers and I are concerned, this dam case can be referred for more elevated enforcement action right now. Why wait until 1/31/2003? The Spring Pond Beavers may be under the dam ice then and there will be no way for you or your dam staff to contact/harass them then.

In conclusion, would like to bring to your attention to a real environmental quality (health) problem in the area. It is the bears! Bears are actually defecating in our woods. I definitely believe you should be persecuting the defecating bears and leave the beavers alone. If you are going to investigate the beaver dam, watch your step! (The bears are not careful where they dump!)

Being unable to comply with your dam request, and being unable to contact you on your dam answering machine, I am sending this response to your dam office.

• • •

Bill Clinton, Al Gore and George W. Bush died and found themselves standing on the other side of the Jordan River looking across at the Promised Land. The Archangel Michael was standing on the other side and shouted over to the three surprised Americans, "Contrary to what you have been taught, each of you will have to wade across the Jordan River."

As Michael saw their perplexed looks, he assured them by saying, "Don't worry, you will sink only proportionally, according to your sins on earth. The more you have sinned, the more you will sink into the water."

The three American sages of political lore looked at one another, trying to determine who would be the first brave soul to cross the Jordan River.

George W. Bush volunteered to go first. Slowly he began to wade out into the river, and slowly the water began to get higher and higher, filling his cowboy boots, reaching to his waist. George began to sweat, thinking of all his sins that were coming back to haunt him. He was beginning to wonder if he would ever see the other side.

Finally, after what seemed like an eternity, he began to emerge on the river's bank. As he ascended to the other side, he looked behind him to see which one of the other brave souls was going next. A shock of surprise registered on his face, as he saw Al Gore almost in the middle of the river, and the water was only up to his ankles. He turned to Michael and exclaimed, "I know Al Gore. Al Gore is a friend of mine, and he has sinned much, much more than that!"

Before the Archangel Michael could reply, Al Gore shouted back, "I'm standing on Clinton's shoulders!"

• • •

An eighteen-year-old girl told her Mom that she thinks that she is pregnant. Very worried, the mother went to the drugstore and bought a pregnancy test kit. The test result showed that the girl was, indeed, pregnant. Shouting, cursing, and crying, the mother demanded, "Who did this to you? I want to know!"

The girl picked up the phone and made a call. Half an hour later a Ferrari stopped in front of their house. A distinguished man with gray hair and dressed in a very expensive suit stepped out and entered the house. He sat down in the living room with the girl's father and mother and told them, "I want to introduce myself. I am senator O'Reilly an chairman of the Senatorial Committee on Foreign Affairs. Your daughter has informed me of the situation. However, I can't marry her because of my wife and family but, I'll take care of my responsibility and will tell you this: that if a girl child is born, I will bequeath her 2 retail stores, a townhouse, a beach-front villa and a 1,000,000 bank account. If a boy is born, my legacy will be a couple of factories and a $2,000,000 bank account. If it is twins, a factory each and $1,000,000 each. However, if there is a miscarriage, what do you think I should do?"

At this point, the father, who had remained silent, places a hand firmly on the man's shoulder and tells him, "You'll have to screw her again!"

• • •

Bill and Hillary were at the Yankee's home opener, sitting in the first row, with the Secret Service people directly behind them. One of the Secret Service guys leaned forward and said something to Bill.

Clinton stared at the guy, looked at Hillary, looked back at the agent, and shrugged his shoulders. Then Bill picked up Hillary by the coat collar and the seat of her pants, and dropped her right over the wall into the field.

She was kicking and swearing and screaming, and the crowd went wild. They were cheering, applauding, and high-fiving.

Bill was bowing and smiling, when the agent leaned forward and said, "I said, they want you to throw out the first *PITCH*!"

• • •

Ted Cruz called Eric Kantor into his home office one day and said, 'Eric, I have a great idea! I know how we can win back middle America and secure my presidential victory in 2016; I'll choose you as my running mate'.

'Great, but how do you propose we go about that, asked Eric?

"Well," Ted responded, "We'll go down to a local Wal-Mart, get some cheezy clothes and shoes, like most middle Americans wear and then we'll stop at the pound and pick up a Labrador. When we look the part we'll go to a nice old country bar in middle America, and we'll show them that we really enjoy the countryside and show admiration and respect for the hard working people living there."

A few days later, all decked out and with the requisite Labrador at heel, they set off from New York in a westerly direction. Eventually they arrived at just the place they were looking for. With dog in tow they walk into the bar. They step up to the bar and the bartender takes a step back and say's, "Aren't you Ted Cruz and Eric Kantor?"

Eric answered, "yes we are, and what a lovely town you have here. We were just passing through and Ted suggested that we stop and take in some local color."

They then ordered a couple of cocktails from the bartender and proceeded to drink them down, all the while chatting up a storm with anyone who would listen.

All of a sudden, the bar room door opened and a grizzled old farmer came in. He walked up to the Labrador, lifted its tail and looked underneath, shrugged his shoulders and walked out the door.

A few moments later, in came another old farmer. He walked up to the dog, lifted its tail, looked underneath, scratched his head and then left the bar. Over the course of the next hour or so, another four or five farmers came in, lifted the dog's tail, and went away looking puzzled.

Eventually Ted and Eric could stand it no longer and called the bartender over. 'Tell me' said Ted, 'why did all those old farmers come in and look under the dog's tail like that? Is it some sort of old custom?

"'Good Lord no," said the bartender. "It's just that someone has told them that there was a Labrador in this bar with two assholes!".

• • •

## Israeli Politics Made Simple

What happens when a fly falls into a coffee cup?

The Italian - throws the cup, breaks it, and walks away in a fit of rage.

The German - carefully washes the cup, sterilizes it and makes a new cup of coffee.

The Frenchman - takes out the fly, and drinks the coffee.

The Chinese - eats the fly and throws away the coffee.

The Russian - Drinks the coffee with the fly, since it was extra with no charge.

The Israeli - sells the coffee to the Frenchman, the fly to the Chinese, drinks tea and uses the extra money to invent a device that prevents flies from falling into coffee.

The Palestinian - blames the Israeli for the fly falling in his coffee, protests the act of aggression to the UN, takes a loan from the European Union to buy a new cup of coffee but uses the money to purchase explosives and then blows up the coffee house where the Italian, the Frenchman, the Chinese, the German and the Russian are all trying to explain to the Israeli that he should give his cup of tea to the Palestinian.

• • •

**Something to Annoy Everyone or any Ethnicity**

I've just come out of the shop with a meat and potato pie, large chips, mushy peas & a jumbo sausage. A poor homeless man sat there and said "I've not eaten for two days!' told him "I wish I had your fucking will power!"

• • •

A fat girl served me food in McDonald's at lunch time. She said "Sorry About the wait." I said "Don't worry fatty, you're bound to lose it eventually."

• • •

I have a new pick up line that works every time. It doesn't matter how gorgeous or out of my league a woman might be, this line is a winner and I always end up in bed with them. Here's how it goes

"Excuse me love, could I ask your opinion? Does this damp cloth smell like chloroform to you?"

• • •

Years ago it was suggested that an apple a day kept the doctor away. But since many the doctors in the United Kingdom are now Muslim, I've found that a bacon sandwich works best!

• • •

I hate all this terrorist business. I used to love the days when you could look at an unattended bag on a train or bus and think to yourself "I'm having that."

• • •

I took my Biology exam last Friday, and failed. I was asked to name two things commonly found in cells. Apparently "Blacks" and "Mexicans" were not the correct answers.

• • •

Man in a hot air balloon is lost over Ireland. He looks down and sees a farmer in the fields and shouts to him "Where am I?"

The Irish farmer looks back up and shouts back 'Ya canna kid me ya flash bastard. You're in that fookin' basket."

• • •

I had a trivia competition shot to pieces until the last question which I got wrong. The question was "Where do women have the curliest hair?"

The answer I should have given was "Fiji."

• • •

## Political Humor And Wisdom

### Council Complaints Letters

The following are genuine clips from: Durban (South Africa) Council complaint letters:

1. My bush is really overgrown round the front and my back passage has fungus growing in it.
2. He has this huge tool that vibrates the whole house and I just can't take it anymore.
3. It's the dogs mess that I find hard to swallow.
4. I want some repairs done to my cooker as it has backfired and burnt my knob off.
5. I wish to complain that my father hurt his ankle very badly when he put his foot in the hole in his back passage.
6. And their 18 year old son is continually banging his balls against my fence.
7. I wish to report that tiles are missing from the outside toilet roof. I think it was a bad wind the other night that blew them off.
8. My lavatory seat is cracked, where do I stand?
9. I am writing on behalf of my sink, which is coming away from the wall.
10. Will you please send someone to mend the garden path. My wife tripped and fell on it yesterday and now she's pregnant.
11. I request permission to remove my drawers in the kitchen.
12. 50% of the walls are damp, 50% have crumbling plaster and 50% are plain filthy.
13. I am still having problems with smoke in my new drawers.
14. The toilet is blocked and we cannot bath the children until it is cleared.
15. Will you please send a man to look at my water it is a funny color and not fit to drink.
16. Our lavatory has broken in half and is now in three pieces.
17. I want to complain about the farmer across the road, every morning at 6 am his cock wakes me up and it's now getting to much for me.

18. The man next door has a large erection in the back garden, which is unsightly and dangerous.
19. Our kitchen floor is damp. We have two children and would like a third so please send someone round to do something about it.
20. I am a single woman living in a downstairs flat and would you please do something about the noise made by the man on top of me every night.
21. Please send a man with the right tool to finish the job and satisfy my wife.
22. I have had a clerk of works down on the floor six times but I still have no satisfaction.

• • •

## An Example of the United Kingdom's Political Sense of Humor

Dear Brits,

Due to the current financial situation caused by the slowdown of economy, your Government has decided to implement a scheme to put workers of 40 years of age and above on early retirement. This scheme will be known as RAPE (Retire Aged People Early). Persons selected for RAPE can apply for the SHAFT scheme (Special Help After Forced Termination).

Persons who have been RAPED and SHAFTED will be reviewed under the SCREW programme (Scheme Covering Retired Early Workers).

A person may be RAPED once, SHAFTED twice and SCREWED as many times as the Government deems appropriate.

Persons who have been RAPED can only get AIDS (Additional Income for Dependants and Spouse) or HERPES (Half Earnings for Retired Personnel Early Severance).

Obviously persons who have AIDS or HERPES will not be SHAFTED or SCREWED any further by the Government.

Persons who are not RAPED and are staying on will receive as much SHIT (Special High Intensity Training) as possible.

My government has always prided itself on the amount of SHIT it gives Brits.

Should you feel that you do not receive enough SHIT, please bring to the attention of your local Member of Parliament. They have been trained to give you all the SHIT you can handle.

Enjoy the future.

Yours sincerely,

Gordon Brown.

• • •

The Sierra Club and the U.S. Forest Service were presenting an alternative to the Wyoming ranchers for controlling the coyote population. It seems that after years of the ranchers using the tried and true method of shooting or trapping the predators, the Sierra Club had a "more humane" solution to this issue. What they were proposing was for the animals to be captured alive. The males would then be castrated and let loose again. This was ACTUALLY proposed by the Sierra Club and by the U.S. Forest Service. All of the ranchers thought about this amazing idea for a couple of minutes. Finally an old fellow wearing a big cowboy hat in the back of the conference room stood up, tipped his hat back and said; "Son, I don't think you understand our problem here... these coyotes ain't fuckin' our sheep... they're eatin' 'em!"

• • •

Two alligators were sitting at the side of the swamp near Washington, DC. The smaller one turned to the bigger one and said, "I can't understand how you kin be so much bigger 'n me. We're the same age, we was the same size as kids. I just don't git it."

Well," said the big 'gator, "What you been eatin' boy?"

"Republican Congressional Politicians, same as you," replied the small 'gator.

"Hmm. Well, where do y'all catch 'em?"

"Down to the side of the swamp near the parkin' lot by the Capitol."

"Same here Hmm. How do you catch 'em?"

"Well, I crawls up under one of them Lexus and wait fer one to unlock the car door. Then I jump out, grab 'em on the leg, shake the shit out of 'em, and eat 'em!"

"Ah!" says the big alligator, "I think I see your problem. You ain't gettin' any real nourishment. See, by the time you get done shakin' the shit out of a Republican Congressman, there ain't nothin' left but an asshole and a briefcase."

• • •

A farmer was selling his peaches door to door. He knocked on a door and a shapely 30-something woman dressed in a very sheer negligee answered the door. He raised his basket to show her the peaches and asked, "Would you like to buy some peaches?"

She pulled the top of the negligee to one side and asked, "Are they as firm as this?"

He nodded his head and said, "Yes ma'am," and a little tear ran from his eye.

Then she pulled the other side of her negligee off asking, "Are they nice and pink like this?"

The farmer said, "Yes," and a tear came from the other eye.

Then she unbuttoned the bottom of her negligee and asked, "Are they as fuzzy as this?"

He again replied, "Yes," and broke down crying.

She asked, "Why on earth are you crying?"

Drying his eyes on his shirt sleeve, he replied, "The drought got my corn, the flood got my soy beans, the weevils got my cotton, a tornado leveled my barn, I voted for George Bush and then, Obama and now I think I'm gonna get fucked out of my peaches!"

• • •

### Yiddish Curses for Republican Jews:

May you sell everything and retire to Florida just as global warming makes it uninhabitable.

May you live to a hundred and twenty without Social Security or Medicare.

May you make a fortune, and lose it all in one of Sheldon Adelson's casinos.

May you live to a ripe old age, and may the only people who come visit you be Mormon missionaries.

May your son be elected President, and may you have no idea what you did with his goddamn birth certificate.

May your grandchildren baptize you after you're dead.

May your insurance company decide constipation is a pre-existing condition.

May you find yourself insisting to a roomful of skeptics that your great-grandmother was "legitimately" raped by rampaging Cossacks.

May you feast every day on chopped liver with onions, chicken soup with dumplings, baked carp with horseradish, braised meat with vegetable stew, latkes, and may every bite of it be contaminated with *E. Coli*, because the government gutted the E.P.A and the F.D.A.

May you have a rare disease and need an operation that only one surgeon in the world, the winner of the Nobel Prize for Medicine, is able to perform. And may he be unable to perform it because he doesn't take your insurance. And may that Nobel Laureate be your son.

May the state of Arizona expand their definition of "suspected illegal immigrants" to "anyone who doesn't hunt."

May you be reunited in the afterworld to come, with your ancestors, who were all socialist garment workers.

• • •

## Great Political Truths

1. In my many years I have come to a conclusion that one useless man is a shame, two is a law firm, and three or more is a congress. – John Adams
2. If you don't read the newspaper you are uninformed, if you do read the newspaper you are misinformed. – Mark Twain
3. Suppose you were an idiot. And suppose you were a member of Congress. But then I repeat myself. – Mark Twain
4. I contend that for a nation to try to tax itself into prosperity is like a man standing in a bucket and trying to lift himself up by the handle. –Winston Churchill
5. A government which robs Peter to pay Paul can always depend on the support of Paul. – George Bernard Shaw
6. A liberal is someone who feels a great debt to his fellow man, which debt he proposes to pay off with your money. – G. Gordon Liddy
7. Democracy must be something more than two wolves and a sheep voting on what to have for dinner. –James Bovard, Civil Libertarian (1994)
8. Foreign aid might be defined as a transfer of money from poor people in rich countries to rich people in poor countries. – Douglas Case, Classmate of Bill Clinton at Georgetown University.
9. Giving money and power to government is like giving whiskey and car keys to teenage boys. – P.J. O'Rourke, Civil Libertarian
10. Government is the great fiction, through which everybody endeavors to live at the expense of everybody else. – Frederic Bastiat, French economist (1801-1850)

11. Government's view of the economy could be summed up in a few short phrases: If it moves, tax it. If it keeps moving, regulate it. And if it stops moving, subsidize it. –Ronald Reagan (1986)
12. I don't make jokes. I just watch the government and report the facts. – Will Rogers
13. If you think health care is expensive now, wait until you see what it costs when it's free! – P. J. O'Rourke
14. In general, the art of government consists of taking as much money as possible from one party of the citizens to give to the other. –Voltaire (1764)
15. Just because you do not take an interest in politics doesn't mean politics won't take an interest in you! – Pericles (430 B.C.)
16. No man's life, liberty, or property is safe while the legislature is in session.– Mark Twain (1866)
17. Talk is cheap, except when Congress does it. – Anonymous
18. The government is like a baby's alimentary canal, with a happy appetite at one end and no responsibility at the other. – Ronald Reagan
19. The inherent vice of capitalism is the unequal sharing of the blessings. The inherent blessing of socialism is the equal sharing of misery. – Winston Churchill
20. The only difference between a tax man and a taxidermist is that the taxidermist leaves the skin. – Mark Twain
21. The ultimate result of shielding men from the effects of folly is to fill the world with fools. – Herbert Spencer, English Philosopher (1820-1903)
22. There is no distinctly Native American criminal class, save Congress. – Mark Twain
23. What this country needs are more unemployed politicians. – Edward Langley, Artist (1928-1995)
24. A government big enough to give you everything you want, is strong enough to take everything you have. – Thomas Jefferson
25. We hang the petty thieves and appoint the great ones to public office. – Aesop

• • •

## Five Best Sentences

1. You cannot legislate the poor into prosperity, by legislating the wealthy out of prosperity.
2. What one person receives without working for, another person must work for without receiving.
3. The government cannot give to anybody anything that the government does not first take from somebody else.
4. You cannot multiply wealth by dividing it.
5. When half of the people get the Idea that they do not have to work, because the other half is going to take care of them, and when the other half gets the idea that it does no good to work because somebody else is going to get what they work for, that is the beginning of the end of any nation!

• • •

Nelson: "Order the signal, Hardy."

Hardy: "Aye, aye sir."

Nelson: "Hold on, that's not what I dictated to Flags. What's the meaning of this?"

Hardy: "Sorry sir?"

Nelson (reading aloud): "England expects every person to do his or her duty, regardless of race, gender, sexual orientation, religious persuasion or disability.– What gobbledygook is this?"

Hardy: "Admiralty policy, I'm afraid, sir. We're an equal opportunities employer now. We had the devil's own job getting 'England' past the censors, lest it be considered racist."

Nelson: "Gadzooks, Hardy. Hand me my pipe and tobacco."

Hardy: "Sorry sir. All naval vessels have now been designated smoke-free working environments."

Nelson: "In that case, break open the rum ration. Let us splice the main brace to steel the men before battle."

Hardy: "The rum ration has been abolished, Admiral. Its part of the Government's policy on binge drinking."

Nelson: "Good heavens, Hardy. I suppose we'd better get on with it; Full Speed ahead."

Hardy: "I think you'll find that there's a 4 knot speed limit in this stretch of water."

Nelson: "Damn it man! We are on the eve of the greatest sea battle in history. We must advance with all dispatch. Report from the crow's nest please."

Hardy: "That won't be possible, sir."

Nelson: "What?"

Hardy: "Health and Safety have closed the crow's nest, sir. No harness; and they said that rope ladders don't meet regulations. They won't let anyone up there until a proper scaffolding can be erected."

Nelson: "Then get me the ship's carpenter without delay, Hardy."

Hardy: "He's busy knocking up a wheelchair access to the foredeck Admiral."

Nelson: "Wheelchair access? I've never heard anything so absurd."

Hardy: "Health and safety again, sir. We have to provide a barrier-free environment for the differently abled."

Nelson: "Differently abled? I've only one arm and one eye and I refuse even to hear mention of the word. I didn't rise to the rank of admiral by playing the disability card."

Hardy: "Actually, sir, you did. The Royal Navy is under represented in the areas of visual impairment and limb deficiency."

Nelson: "Whatever next? Give me full sail. The salt spray beckons."

Hardy: "A couple of problems there too, sir. Health and safety won't let the crew up the rigging without hard hats. And they don't want anyone breathing in too much salt - haven't you seen the adverts?"

Nelson: "I've never heard such infamy. Break out the cannon and tell the men to stand by to engage the enemy."

Hardy: "The men are a bit worried about shooting at anyone, Admiral."

Nelson: "What? This is mutiny!"

Hardy: "It's not that, sir. It's just that they're afraid of being charged with murder if they actually kill anyone. There's a couple of legal-aid lawyers on board, watching everyone like hawks."

Nelson: "Then how are we to sink the Frenchies and the Spanish?"

Hardy: "Actually, sir, we're not."

Nelson: "We're not?"

Hardy: "No, sir. The French and the Spanish are our European partners now. according to the Common Fisheries Policy, we shouldn't even be in this stretch of water. We could get hit with a claim for compensation."

Nelson: "But you must hate a Frenchman as you hate the devil."

Hardy: "I wouldn't let the ship's diversity coordinator hear you saying that sir. You'll be up on disciplinary report."

Nelson: "You must consider every man an enemy, who speaks ill of your King."

Hardy: "Not any more, sir. We must be inclusive in this multicultural age. Now put on your Kevlar vest; it's the rules. It could save your life"

Nelson: "Don't tell me - health and safety. Whatever happened to rum, sodomy and the lash?"

Hardy: As I explained, sir, rum is off the menu! And there's a ban on corporal punishment."

Nelson: "What about sodomy?"

Hardy: "I believe that is now legal, sir."

Nelson: "In that case...... kiss me, Hardy."

• • •

The teacher said, "Let's begin by reviewing some History. Who said 'Give me Liberty, or give me Death'?"

She saw a sea of blank faces, except for Little Akio, a bright foreign exchange student from Japan, who had his hand up: "Patrick Henry, 1775," he said.

"Very good!

Who said, 'Government of the People, by the People, for the People, shall not perish from the Earth'?"

Again, no response except from Little Akio: "Abraham Lincoln, 1863."

"Excellent!" said the teacher continuing, "Let's try one a bit more difficult –

Who said, 'Ask not what your country can do for you, but what you can do for your country'?"

Once again, Akio's was the only hand in the air and he said: "John F. Kennedy, 1961."

The teacher snapped at the class, "Class, you should be ashamed of yourselves, little Akio isn't from this country and he knows more about our history than you do."

She heard a loud whisper: "Fuck the Japs."

"Who said that? – I want to know right now!? She angrily demanded.

Little Akio put his hand up, "General Douglas MacArthur, 1945."

At that point, a student in the back said, "I'm gonna puke.'

The teacher glared around and asked, 'All right! – Now who said that?"

Again, Little Akio said, "George Bush to the Japanese Prime Minister, 1991."

Now furious, another student yelled, "Oh yeah? – Suck this!"

Little Akio jumped out of his chair waving his hand and shouted to the teacher, "Bill Clinton, to Monica Lewinsky, 1997!"

Now, with almost mob hysteria, someone said, "You little shit! – If you say anything else – I'll kill you!"

Little Akio frantically yelled at the top of his voice, "Michael Jackson to the children called to testify against him, 2004."

The teacher fainted. As the class gathered around the teacher on the floor, someone said, "Oh shit, we're screwed!"

Little Akio said quietly, "The South African people, when Jacob Zuma was elected President, May 2009."

• • •

An Irishman in a wheel chair entered a restaurant one afternoon and asked the waitress for a cup of coffee. The Irishman looked across the restaurant and asked in a lilting brogue, "Sure and is that Jesus sitting over there?"

The waitress nodded "yes."

So the Irishman told her to give Jesus a cup of coffee on him.

The next patron to come in was an Englishman with a markedly hunched back. He shuffled over to a booth, painfully sat down, and asked the waitress for a cup of hot tea. Like the first chap, he also glanced across the restaurant and asked, "My word; is that Jesus over there?"

The waitress nodded, so the Englishman instructed the waitress to give Jesus a cup of hot tea, my treat.

The third patron to come into the restaurant was a Redneck on crutches. He hobbled over to a booth, sat down and hollered, "Hey there, sweet thang, How's about gettin' me a cold glass of Coke!"

He, too, looked across the restaurant and asked, "Whoa now, is that God's boy over there?"

The waitress nodded in the affirmative, so the Redneck said to give Jesus a cold glass of coke, on his bill.

As Jesus got up to leave, he passed by the Irishman, touched him and said, "For your kindness, you are healed."

The Irishman felt the strength come back into his legs, got up, and danced a jig out the door.

Jesus also passed by the Englishman, touched him and said, "For your kindness, you are healed."

The Englishman felt his back straightening up, and he rose up his hands, praised the Lord and did a series of back flips out the door.

Then Jesus walked towards the Redneck. The Redneck jumped up and yelled, "Don't touch me! I'm drawin' disability!"

• • •

## An Interesting Observation:

1. The sport of choice for the urban poor is BASKETBALL.
2. The sport of choice for maintenance level employees is BOWLING.
3. The sport of choice for front-line workers is FOOTBALL.
4. The sport of choice for supervisors is BASEBALL.
5. The sport of choice for middle management is TENNIS.

And 6.. The sport of choice for corporate executives and officers is GOLF. The amazing conclusion: The higher you go in the corporate structure, the smaller your balls become—there must be a boat load of people in Washington playing marbles!!!

• • •

As this book was being prepared for submission to the publisher. the following lengthy piece was aired on Home Box Office's *Real Time with Bill Maher* on September 27th, 2013. Certainly, there are certainly many who do not share Maher's politics, nor his use of colorful expletive-laced language. However, what he had to say resonates with probably an equal number of people, if not a substantially greater majority, especially younger people and minorities. Because I found it germane to the tone of this chapter and the title of this book, I have reproduced it here in its entirety: Also, because it was aired on the very cusp of when this title was being readied for submission. It had to be added at the end of this chapter.

*New Rule: Conservatives who love to brag about American exceptionalism must come here to California, and see it in person. And then they should be afraid – very afraid. Because while the rest of the country is beset by stories of right-wing takeovers in places like North Carolina, Texas and Wisconsin, California is going in the opposite direction and creating the kind of modern, liberal nation the country as a whole can only dream about. And* not only can't the rest of the country stop us – we're going to drag you along with us.

It wasn't that long ago that pundits were calling California a failed state and saying it was ungovernable. But in 2010, when other states were busy electing whatever Tea Partier claimed to hate government the most, we elected a guy who actually liked it, Jerry Brown.

Since then, everything Republicans say can't or won't work – gun control, immigration reform, high-speed rail – California is making work. And everything conservatives claim will unravel the fabric of our society – universal healthcare, higher taxes on the rich, gay marriage, medical marijuana – has only made California stronger. And all we had to do to accomplish that was vote out every single Republican. Without a Republican governor and without a legislature being cock-blocked by Republicans, a $27 billion deficit was turned into a surplus, continuing the proud American tradition of Republicans blowing a huge hole in the budget and then Democrats coming in and cleaning it up.

How was Governor Moonbeam able to do this? It's amazing, really. We did something economists call cutting spending AND raising taxes. I know, it sounds like some crazy science fiction story, but you see, here in California, we're not just gluten-free and soy-free and peanut-free, we're Tea Party free! Virginia could do it, too, but they're too busy forcing ultrasounds on women who want abortions. Texas could, but they don't because they're too busy putting Jesus in the science textbooks. Meanwhile their state is so broke they want to replace paved roads with gravel. I thought we had this road-paving thing licked in the 1930s, but not in Texas. But hey, in Dallas you can carry a rifle into a Chuck E. Cheese, 'cause that's freedom. Which is great, but it wasn't so great when that unregulated fertilizer plant in Waco blew up. In California, when things blow up, it's because we're making a Jason Statham movie.

California isn't perfect, but it is in our nature from being on the new coast to be up for trying new things – and maybe that's why the right wingers are always hoping we fail. On the campaign trail last year, Mitt Romney warned that if we didn't follow his conservative path, "America is going to become like Greece, or... Spain, or Italy, or... California." And that was a big laugh line with Mormons, because Greece, Spain and Italy have some art and poetry and theatre, but nothing like Salt Lake City. Yes, Mitt sure hates California, which is why he moved to San Diego. To the house with the car elevator.

What conservatives fear about California being a Petri dish for the liberal agenda is well-founded. For example, as The Affordable Health Care Act a.k.a. "Obamacare" gets implemented here much more successfully than predicted, the movement to just go all the way to a single payer system is gathering steam. It actually passed the legislature twice, but was vetoed by Schwarzenegger, who argued it didn't go far enough to cover the children of that natural, beautiful love between a man and a cleaning lady.

In lots of areas, California seems to have decided not to wait around for the knuckle-draggers and the selfish libertarian states to get on board. They can mock "European style democracies" all they want, we are building one here, and people like it – the same way when Americans come back from a vacation in Europe they all say the same thing: "Wow, you can see titties on the beach!" But they also remark on the clean air, the modern, first world infrastructure, the functioning social safety net, and bread that doesn't taste like powdered glue. And they wonder, "Why can't we get that here?" Unless they're Republicans, in which case they wonder, "How can people live like that?"

Well, swallow hard, guys, because California is eventually going to make all Americans live like that. Why? Because we're huge. The 12th largest economy in the world, the fifth largest agricultural exporter in the world, and of course number one in laser vaginal rejuvenation. There's 40 million of us – so, for example, when California set a high mileage standard for any car sold in this state, Detroit had to make more fuel-efficient cars; we're just too big a slice of the market, and it would be too expensive to make one car for us, and another for shit-kickers who want something that runs on coal. It's so ironic – the two things conservatives love the most, the free market and states rights – are the two things that are going to bend this country into California's image as a socialist fagtopia. Maybe our constipated Congress can't pass gun control laws, but we just did. Lots of 'em. Because we don't give a shit about the NRA. Out here that stands for "Nuts, Racists, and Assholes." So while the rest of America is debating whether it's a good idea to allow guns in bars or a great idea to allow guns in bars, California is about to ban lead bullets. Which is a no-brainer, because bullets don't need lead, and lead kills birds and gets into the food supply of people who hunt their own food. Which explains why Ted Nugent is such a raving lunatic.

While other state governments are working with Jesus to make abortion more miserable – because otherwise women would use it for weight loss – California is making it easier. We actually have a guy dancing on the street corner dressed as the Statue of Liberty spinning a big arrow that says, "Abortions!" And a new law will even let nurse practitioners perform abortions. And dog groomers can aid assisted suicides by Skype.

California was the first state to legalize medical marijuana, our minimum wage is almost three dollars higher than the national rate, and in 10 years a third of our electricity will come from renewable energy and 15 percent of our cars will be electric.

And while Republicans in the rest of the country are threatening to deport every immigrant not named Ted Cruz, California just OK'd driver's licenses for undocumented aliens. That's right, we're letting them drive cars – just like white people! You Red Staters may ask, "How come they're lettin' Meskins drive?" Well, it's because they have to get to their jobs. You see, here in California we're embracing the modern world – we can't be worrying about all the nonsense that keeps Fox News viewers up at night when they should be in bed adjusting their sleep apnea mask. Our state motto is, "We're Too Busy for Your Bullshit."

*The bottom line is that we are moving the country's largest economy into a place where we can all be health-insured, clean air-breathin', gay-married, immigrant-friendly citizens who don't get shot all the time. And my message to the rest of America is: do not resist. Kneel before Zod! California has been setting the trends in America for decades, from Silicon Valley to silicone tits, and it's not going to stop now. We say jump – you say, "Please sell me new exercise clothes for jumping." We said put cilantro in food, and dammit, you did, you put cilantro in food, even though neither one of us knows what it is. Almond milk? We just had some extra almonds and thought we'd fuck with you. The enormous earlobe hole? You're welcome. We also invented the genius bar, where the kid with the enormous earlobe hole takes your MacBook in the back and fills it with animal pornography.*

- Bill Maher, host of HBO's Real Time with Bill Maher

# OTHER NATIONS, ETHNICITIES, AND REGIONS AS SUBJECTS OF HUMOR

Why does a Canadian cross the road?
To get to the middle.

• • •

I was at my bank today; there was a short line. There was just one lady in front of me, an Asian lady who was trying to exchange Japanese yen for dollars. It was obvious that she was more than slightly irritated.

She asked the teller, "Why it change? Yesterday, I get two hunat dolla fo yen. Today I only get hunat eighty? Why it change?" The teller shrugged his shoulders and said, "Fluctuations."

The Asian lady says, "Fluc you white people too"

• • •

After living in the remote countryside of Ireland all his life, an old Irishman decided it was time to visit Dublin. In one of the stores he picked up a mirror and looked in it. Not ever having seen one before, he remarked at the image staring back at him. 'How 'bout that!' he exclaimed, "Here's a picture of me Fadder."

He bought the mirror thinking it was a picture of his dad, but on the way home he remembered his wife didn't like his father, so he hung it in the shed, and every morning before leaving to go fishing, he would go there and look at it.

His wife began to get suspicious of these many trips to the shed. So, one day after her husband left, she went to the shed and found the mirror. As she looked into the glass, she fumed, 'So that's the ugly bitch he's runnin' around with.'

• • •

A hooded robber burst into a North Dakota bank and forced the tellers to load a sack full of cash.

On his way out the door, a brave North Dakota customer grabbed the hood and pulled it off, revealing the robbers face. The robber shot the customer without a moment's hesitation. He then looked around the bank and noticed one of the tellers looking straight at him. The robber instantly shot him also.

Everyone in the bank, by now very scared, looked intently down at the floor in silence.

The robber yelled, "Well, did anyone else see my face?"

There are a few moments of utter silence in which everyone was plainly to afraid to speak. Then, one old Norwegian named Ole tentatively raised his hand without looking up said, "My wife got a pretty good look at ya."

• • •

### Subject: Alerts around the world

The British are feeling the pinch in relation to recent terrorist threats in Islamabad and have raised their security level from "Miffed" to "Peeved." Soon, though, security levels may be raised yet again to "Irritated" or even "A Bit Cross." Brits have not been "A Bit Cross" since the blitz in 1940 when tea supplies all but ran out. Terrorists have been re-categorized from "Tiresome" to a "Bloody Nuisance." The last time the British issued a "Bloody Nuisance" warning level was during the great fire of 1666.

The French government announced yesterday that it has raised its terror alert level from "Run" to "Hide". The only two higher levels in France are "Collaborate" and "Surrender." The rise was precipitated by a recent fire that destroyed France's white flag factory, effectively paralyzing the country's military capability.

It's not only the French who are on a heightened level of alert. Italy has increased the alert level from "Shout loudly and excitedly" to "Elaborate Military Posturing." Two more levels remain: "Ineffective Combat Operations" and "Change Sides."

The Germans also increased their alert state from "Disdainful Arrogance" to "Dress in Uniform and Sing Marching Songs." They also have two higher levels: "Invade a Neighbor" and "Lose."

Belgians, on the other hand, are all on holiday as usual, and the only threat they are worried about is NATO pulling out of Brussels.

The Spanish are all excited to see their new submarines ready to deploy. These beautifully designed subs have glass bottoms so the new Spanish navy can get a really good look at the old Spanish navy.

Americans meanwhile are carrying out pre-emptive strikes on all of their allies, just in case.

New Zealand has also raised its security levels - from "baaa" to "BAAAA!" Due to continuing defense cutbacks (the Air Force being a squadron of spotty teenagers flying paper aeroplanes and the navy some toy boats in the Prime Minister's bath), New Zealand only has one more level of escalation, which is "Shit, I hope Australia will come and rescue us". In the event of invasion, New Zealanders will be asked to gather together in a strategic defensive position called "Bondi."

Australia, meanwhile, has raised its security level from "No worries" to "She'll be right, mate." Three more escalation levels remain: "Crikey! I think we'll need to cancel the Barbie this weekend" and

"The Barbie is cancelled." There has not been a situation yet that has warranted the use of the final escalation level.

• • •

### Excellent Question from a Son to a Father

A young Arab asked his father, "What is that weird hat you are wearing?"

The father said, "Why, it's a 'chechia' because in the desert it protects our heads from the sun."

"And what is this type of clothing that you are wearing?" asked the young man.

"It's a 'djbellah' because in the desert it is very hot and it protects the body." said the father.

The son asked, "And what about those ugly shoes on your feet?

His father replied, "These are 'babouches", which keep us from burning our feet in the desert."

"So tell me then," added the boy. "Yes, my son?"

"Why are you living in Bradford, England, and still wearing all this shit?"

### Ed Zachary Disease

A woman was very distraught at the fact that she had not had a date or any sex in quite some time. She was afraid she might have something wrong with her, so she decided to seek the medical expertise of a sex therapist. Her doctor recommended that she see the well known Chinese sex therapist in Shanghai, Dr. Chang.

So she went to see him. Upon entering the examination room Dr. Chang said "OK take off all your crose."

The woman did as she was told.

"Now get down and craw reery, reery fass to odderside of room."
Again the woman did as she was instructed.

Dr. Chang then said, "OK, now craw reery, reery fass back to me." So she did.

Dr..Chang shook his head slowly and said, "Your probrem vewy bad. You haf Ed Zachary disease. "Worse case I ever see. Dat why you not haf sex or dates."

Worried the woman asked anxiously, "Oh my God Dr. Chang what is Ed Zachary Disease?"

Dr. Chang sighed deeply and replied, "Ed Zachary Disease is when your face look Ed Zachary like your ass."

• • •

Ole and Sven were playing golf when Sven pulled out a cigar but he didn't have a lighter. So he asked Ole for a light.

"Ya, shure, I tink I haff a lighter," he replied, reached into his golf bag, and pulled out a 12-inch BIC lighter.

"Yimiiny Cricket!" exclaimed Sven, "Vhere did yew get dat monster?"

"Vell," replied Ole, "I got it from my Genie."

"You haff a genie?" Sven asked, in astonishment.

"Ya, shure, he's right here in my golf bag," said Ole.

"Could I see him?"

Ole opened his golf bag and out popped the genie.

Sven said, "Hey der! I'm a good friend of your master. Vill you grant me vun vish?"

"Yes I will", the genie said.

So Sven asked him for a million bucks and the genie hops back Into the golf bag and left him standing there waiting for his million bucks. Suddenly the sky begins to darken and the sound of a million waterfowl was heard.

Sven yelled to Ole, "1 asked for a million bucks, not *ducks*!"

Ole answers, "Ya, I forgot to tell yew, da genie is hard of hearing. Do yew really tink dat I asked him for a 12-inch BIC?"

• • •

The Mexican maid asked for a pay increase.

The wife was very upset about this and decided to talk to her about the raise.

She asked, "Now Maria, why do you want a pay increase?"

Maria: "Well, Señora, there are tree reasons why I wanna increaze. The first is that I iron better than you."

Wife: "Who said you iron better than me?"

Maria: "Jor huzban he say so."

Wife: "Oh yeah?"

Maria: "The second reason eez that I am a better cook than you."

Wife: "Nonsense, who said you were a better cook than me?"

Maria: "Jor hozban did."

Wife increasingly agitated: "Oh he did, did he?"

Maria: "The third reason is that I am better at sex than you in the bed."

Wife, really boiling now and through gritted teeth asks, "And did my husband say that as well?"

Maria: "No Señora... The gardener did."

Wife: "So how much do you want?

• • •

## Holistic Medicine

Abdul the came to America from the Middle East and he was only here a few months when he became very ill. He went to doctor after doctor, but none of them could help him.

Finally, he went to an Arabic doctor who said: "Take dees bucket, go into de odder room, poop in de bucket, pee on de poop, and den put your head down over de bucket and breathe in de fumes for ten minutes."

Abdul took the bucket, went into the other room, pooped in the bucket, peed on the poop, bent over and breathed in the fumes for ten minutes. Coming back to the doctor he said, 'It worked. I feel terrific! What was wrong with me?'

The doctor said.... "You were homesick."

• • •

A Greek and Italian were sitting in a Starbuck's one day discussing who had the superior culture. Over triple lattes the Greek guy proudly announced, "Well, we have the Parthenon."

Arching his eyebrows, the Italian replies, "We have the Coliseum."

The Greek retorted, "We Greeks gave birth to advanced mathematics."

The Italian, nodding agreement, said, "But we built the Roman Empire."

And so on and so forth, until the Greek came up with what he thought would end the discussion. With a flourish of finality he exclaimed, "We invented sex!"

The Italian replies, "Ah, that is entirely true, but it was we Italians who introduced it to women"

• • •

A class of five-year old school children returned to the classroom after playing in the playground during their recess time. The teacher said to the first child "Hello Becky, what have you been doing this playtime?"

Becky replied "I have been playing in the sand box."

"Very good," responded the teacher "If you can spell 'sand' on the blackboard, I will give you a cookie"

Becky duly goes and writes 'S A N D' on the blackboard.

"Very good" says the teacher and gives Becky a cookie.

The teacher then sees a boy and asked, "Freddie, what have you been doing in *your* playtime?"

Freddie replied "Playing with Becky in the sand box."

"Very good' said the teacher; "If you can spell 'box' on the blackboard, I will also give you a cookie."

Freddie duly goes and wrote 'B O X' on the blackboard.

"Very good" said the teacher and gave Freddie a cookie.

The teacher encountered her next student: "Hello Mohammed, have you been playing in the sand box with Becky and Freddie?"

"No," replied Mohammed, "'I wanted to, but they would not let me. Every time I went near them they started throwing sand at me, calling me nasty names and asking to see under my jacket in case I had explosives"

"Oh dear," exclaimed the teacher; "That sounds like blatant racial discrimination to me. "I'll tell you what, if you can spell 'blatant racial discrimination' I will give *you* a cookie too."

• • •

## Chicken Surprise

A couple went for a meal at a Chinese restaurant and ordered the 'Chicken Surprise.' Soon the waiter brought the meal, served in a lidded cast iron pot.

Just as the wife was about to serve herself, the lid of the pot rose slightly and she briefly saw two beady little eyes looking around before the lid slammed back down.

"Good grief, did you see that?" she exclaimed to her husband. He hadn't, so she asked him to look in the pot. He reached for it and again the lid rose all by itself, and he saw two little eyes looking around before it slammed down with a crashing sound.

Rather perturbed, he called the waiter over, explained what was happening every time the lid was approached, and he demanded an explanation.

"Please sir," said the waiter, "what you order?"

The husband replied, "Chicken Surprise"

"Ah! So sorry," replied the waiter, "I bring you Peeking Duck."

• • •

An Ontarian wished to become a Newfoundlander. He went to a neurosurgeon and asked, "Is there anything that you can do to me that would make me into a Newfie?"

"Sure, it's easy" replied the neurosurgeon. "All I have to do is to remove one-third of your brain, and you'll be a Newfie. The Ontarian was pleased and immediately underwent the operation. However, the surgeon's scalpel slipped and instead of excising one-third of the patient's brain, he accidentally removed *TWO-THIRDS* of his patient's brain. He was terribly remorseful, and waited impatiently beside his patient's bed as the poor chap recovered from the anesthetic.

As soon as the fellow was conscious, the neurosurgeon said to him, "I'm terribly sorry, but there was a ghastly accident. Instead of removing one-third of your brain, I excised two-thirds of your brain."

The patient replied, "Qu'est-ce que vous avez dit, monsieur doctor?"

• • •

A professor at the Auburn University was giving a lecture on Paranormal Studies. To get a feel for his audience, he asks, "How many people here believe in ghosts?"

About 90 students raised their hands.

"Well, that's a good start. Out of those who believe in ghosts, do any of you think you have seen a ghost?"

This time, about 40 students raised their hands.

"That's really good. I'm really glad you take this seriously. Has anyone here ever talked to a ghost?"

About 15 students raised their hand.

"Has anyone here ever touched a ghost?"

Three students raised their hands.

"That's fantastic. Now let me ask you one question further. Have any of you ever made love to a ghost?"

Way in the back, Mustafa raised his hand.

The professor took off his glasses and said, "Son, all the years I've been giving this lecture, no one has ever claimed to have made love to a ghost. You've got to come up here and tell us about your experience."

The Middle Eastern student replied with a nod and a grin, and began to make his way up to the podium. When he reached the front of the room, the professor asked, "So, Mustafa, tell us what it's like to have sex with a ghost?"

"Oh shit, Professor, from back there, I thought you asked, "Has anyone here ever made love to a goat?"

• • •

An Irish boy stood crying at the side of the road. A man asked "What is wrong?"

The boy replied "Me ma is dead."

"Oh bejaysus" the man exclaimed. "Do you want me to call Father Duffy for you?"

The boy replied "No tanks mister, sex is the last ting on my moind at the moment."

• • •

An American, a Scot, and a Canadian were in a terrible car accident. They were all brought to the same emergency room, but all three of them died before they arrived. Just as they were about to put the toe tag on the American, he stirred and opened his eyes. Astonished, the doctors and nurses present asked him what had happened.

Said the American, "I remember the crash, and then there was a beautiful, light; and then the Canadian, the Scot, and I were standing at the Gates of Heaven. St. Peter approached us and said that we were all too young to die, and that for a donation of $50.00, we could return to Earth. So of course, I pulled out my wallet and gave him the $50.00; the next thing I knew, I was back here."

"That's amazing!" exclaimed one of the doctors, "But what happened to the other two?"

"Last I saw them," replied the American, "The Scot was haggling over the price, and the Canadian was waiting for the government to pay for his."

• • •

In a skirmish between Newfoundland and Nova Scotia, the Newfies were lobbing grenades; the Nova Scotians were pulling the pins and throwing them back.

• • •

The train was quite crowded, so a U. S. Marine walked the entire length looking for a seat, but the only seat left was taken by a well dressed, middle-aged French woman's poodle.

The war weary Marine asked, "Ma'am, may I have that seat?"

The French woman just sniffed and said to no one in particular, "Americans are so rude. My little Fifi is using that seat."

The Marine walked the entire train again, but the only seat left was under that dog.

"Please, ma'am. May I sit down? I'm very tired."

She snorted, "Not only are you Americans rude, you are also arrogant!"

This time the Marine didn't say a word; he just picked up the little dog, tossed it out the train window, and sat down.

The woman shrieked, "Someone must defend my honor! This American should be put in his place!"

An English gentleman sitting nearby spoke up, "Sir, you Americans often seem to have a penchant for doing the wrong thing. You hold the fork in the wrong hand. You drive your autos on the wrong side of the road. And now sir, you seem to have thrown the wrong bitch out the window!

• • •

## CONFUCIUS DIDN'T SAY

Man who wants pretty nurse must be patient.

• • •

Passionate kiss, like spider web, leads to undoing of fly.

• • •

Better to be pissed off than pissed on.

• • •

Lady who goes camping must beware of evil intent.

• • •

Squirrel who runs up woman's leg will not find nuts.

• • •

Man who leaps off cliff jumps to conclusion.

• • •

Man who runs in front of car gets tired; man who runs behind car gets exhausted.

• • •

Man who eats many prunes get good run for money.

• • •

War does not determine who is right, it determines who is left.

• • •

Man who fight with wife all day get no piece at night.

• • •

It takes many nails to build a crib, but one screw to fill it.

• • •

Man who drives like hell is bound to get there.
Man who stands on toilet is high on pot.

• • •

Man who live in glass house should change clothes in basement.

• • •

Man who fish in other man's well often catch crabs.

• • •

But CONFUCIUS **DID** SAY

"A lion will not cheat on his wife, but a Tiger Wood."

"Self praise is no recommendation"

• • •

# Other Nations, Ethnicities, And Regions As Subjects Of Humor

A French Canadian guest, staying in a hotel in Edmonton, phoned Room Service for some pepper.

"Black pepper or white pepper?" inquired the concierge.

Toilet pepper!" responded the guest.

• • •

An Aussie who had lived all of his life in the Outback came into civilization to visit a friend and was asked immediately what he would like to see or do on this, his first visit to modern life.

"I have heard about trains; could you arrange for me to see one mate?"

So his friend drove him down to the nearest railroad track and they waited. Soon, a train came into view and it approached and blew its whistle, the unsophisticated Aussie just stood there at trackside and was hit by a glancing blow by the locomotive as it passed by. Many broken bones, contusions, and scrapes later, he was recuperating at his friend's station (ranch). His friend was about to make him a cup of tea and had put the kettle on the stove. Soon the kettle began to steam and squeal, whereupon the rustic Aussie took a cricket bat form the corner and beat the kettle to a unrecognizable pile of metallic rubble.

"Mate, why the hell did you do that!?" asked his astonished host.

The Aussie replied, "You've got to kill them fuckers before they grow up!"

• • •

Pierre, a very brave and famous French fighter pilot, took his girlfriend Marie, out for a pleasant little picnic by the River Seine. It was a beautiful day, and love was in the air. Marie leaned over to Pierre and said, "Pierre, kiss me!"

Our hero grabbed a bottle of Merlot and splashed it on Marie's lips.

"Pierre, what are you doing?!"

"I am Pierre, the very brave and famous pilot! When I have red meat, I like to have red wine!"

"Marie smiled and they started kissing. Then things began to heat up and Marie turned to Pieere and said, "Pierre, mon cher, kiss me lower!"

Pierre immediately tore open Marie's silken blouse, grabbed a bottle of Chardonnay, and poured it over Marie's heaving breasts.

Bewildered by this, Marie cried, "Pierre, what **are** you doing?!

"Marie, I am Pierre, the very brave and famous fighter pilot! When I have white meat, I like to have white wine!" They resumed their passionate interlude and then things really began to steam up. Marie then whispered softly into Pierre's ear, "Oh Pierre, kiss me lower."

"Our hero then ripped off Marie's panties, grabbed a bottle of cognac, and poured it over her lap and struck a match, setting the cognac alight.

Marie shrieked and dove into the Seine. Standing waist-deep in the river, Marie threw up her arms and screamed furiously. *"PIERRE, WHAT IN THE HELL DO YOU THINK YOU ARE DOING?!"*

Our hero stood up defiantly and exclaimed, "I am Pierre, the very brave and famous fighter pilot! When I go down, I go down in flames!"

• • •

Two Irishmen were sitting in a small town pub, when Aidan bragged to Sean, "You know, I had me every woman in this town, except, of course me mother and me sister."

"Well," Sean replied, "Between you and me we got 'em all."

• • •

Flynn and Mike landed themselves jobs in a local sawmill just outside Dublin. Just before the morning break, Flynn yelled out, "Mike, I've just lost me finger!"

## Other Nations, Ethnicities, And Regions As Subjects Of Humor

"Have ye now?" inquired Mike. "And how did you do it?"

"I just touched this big, shiny spinning thing here like this. DAMN! There goes another one!"

• • •

Two Canadians were sitting in a bar, getting bored, playing "20 questions." The first Canadian tried to think of a word and, after a pondering, came up with the word: *moosecock.*

The second Canadian tries his first question, "Is it to eat?"

The first guy thinks a moment, then laughed and replied you *could* eat it."

The second Canadian said, "Is it a *moosecock*?"

• • •

Paddy said to Mick, "Christmas is on Friday this year". Mick said, "Let's hope it's not the 13th then."

• • •

On the first day of Grade Three, Johnnie's teacher asked the students to count to 50. Many of them did very well, some counting as high as 37. But Johnnie did extremely well; he made it to 100 with only 3 mistakes. At home, he told his Dad how well he had done.

Dad told him, "That's because you are from Newfoundland, son."

The next day, in language class, the teacher asked the students to recite the alphabet. Some made it to the letter "K;" again, Johnnie went all the way through, missing only the letter "M." That evening, Johnnie once again brought his dad up to date.

Dad explained to him, "That's because you are from Newfoundland, son." The next day, after Physical Education, the boys were taking showers. Johnnie noted that, compared with the other boys in his grade, he seemed to be overly "well-endowed." This confused him.

That night, he asked his father, "Dad, they all have little tiny ones, but mine is at least 10 times bigger than theirs. Is that because I'm from Newfoundland?"

"No son," explained his dad, "That's because you are 18."

• • •

The Shapiros, a Jewish couple living in England, won twenty million pounds in the National Lottery. They immediately set out to begin a life of luxury. They bought a magnificent mansion in Knightsbridge and surrounded themselves with all the material wealth imaginable. Then they decided to hire a butler. They found the perfect butler through an agency, very proper and very British, and brought him back to their home.

The day after his arrival, they instructed him to set up the dining room table for four, as they were inviting the Cohens to lunch. The couple then left the house to do some shopping.

When they returned, they found the table set for eight. They asked the butler why eight, when they had specifically instructed him to set the table for four.

The butler replied, "The Cohens telephoned and said they were bringing the Blintzes and the Knishes"

• • •

## Japanese Hotel Service

A Canadian salesman checked into a futuristic hotel in Tokyo. Realizing he needed a haircut before the next day's meeting, he called down to the desk clerk to ask if there was a barber on the premises.

"I'm afraid not, sir," the clerk told him apologetically, "but down the hall from your room is a vending machine that should serve your purposes."

# Other Nations, Ethnicities, and Regions As Subjects Of Humor

Skeptical but intrigued, the salesman located the machine. There was a placard sating that the haircut would cost 250 yen. He inserted his credit card, and OK's the transaction, then stuck his head into the opening, at which time the machine started to buzz and whirl. Fifteen seconds later the salesman pulled out his head and surveyed his reflection, which reflected the best haircut of his life.

Two feet away was another machine with a sign that read, 'Manicures, 500 Yen.

"Why not?" thought the salesman. Again, he paid the fee by credit card, inserted his hands into the slot, and the machine started to buzz and whirl. Fifteen seconds later he pulled out his hands and they were perfectly manicured.

The next machine had a sign that read, "This Machine Provides a Service Men Need When Away from Their Wives, 100 Yen."

The salesman looked both ways, paid by credit card, unzipped his fly, and with some anticipation, stuck his member into the opening. When the machine started buzzing, the guy let out a shriek of agony and almost passed out. Fifteen seconds later it shut off. With trembling hands, the salesman was able to withdraw his tender unit ....which now had a button sewn neatly on the end.

• • •

A Frenchman and an Italian were seated next to an Englishman on an overseas flight. After a few cocktails, the men began discussing their home lives.

"Last night, I made love to my wife four times." The Frenchman bragged, "And this morning, she made me delicious crepes and she told me how much she adored me."

"Ah, last night, I made love to my wife six times!" the Italian responded. "And this morning she made me a wonderful omelet and told me that she could never love another man."

When the Englishman remained silent, the Frenchman smugly asked, "And how many times did you make love to your wife, monsieur?"

The Englishman replied, "Once."

"Only once, Senore?" the Italian snorted. "And what did she say to you this morning?"

"Don't stop!"

• • •

### An Interesting piece of history!

In 1272, the Arabs invented the condom, using a goat's lower intestine. In 1873, the British somewhat refined the idea by taking the intestine out of the goat first.

• • •

An Englishman, a Scotsman, and an Irishman were all to give speeches to the Deaf Society. All were determined to make a lasting impression on their audience.

The Englishman went first and to the surprise of his colleagues, started by rubbing first his chest and then his groin. When he finished, the Scotsman and the Irishman asked him what the bloody hell he was doing up there at the podium.

"Well," he replied, "by rubbing my chest, I indicated breasts and thus, 'Ladies' and rubbing my groin, I indicated balls and, thus, 'Gentlemen.' So, my speech commenced started 'Ladies and Gentlemen."

On *his* way up to the podium, the Scotsman thought to himself "I'll go that English bastard one better" and began his speech by making an antler symbol with his fingers above his head, before also rubbing his chest and his groin. When he finished, his colleagues asked what he was doing.

"Well," he explained, "By imitating antlers and then rubbing my chest and groin, I was signing "Dear Ladies and Gentlemen."

On his way up to the podium, the Irishman thought to himself "I'll go those mainland buggers one further" and started his speech by making an antler symbol with both of his raised hands, rubbing his chest, then his groin, and then masturbating furiously.

When he finished, his colleagues asked him what he was doing up there.

"Well, me buckos, by imitating antlers, rubbing my chest, then my groin, and then masturbating, I was starting my speech by saying "Dear Ladies and Gentlemen, it gives me great pleasure —."

• • •

What does a Canadian say when you step on his foot?
"Sorry"

• • •

Mahoney said to his friend, Duffy, "I haven't been feelin' myself lately."

"Tis a good thing, too – that was a nasty habit you had," responded, Duffy.

• • •

Ahmed found himself stranded in the vast wastes of the desert and was nearly dead from thirst when his sandaled foot kicked up an old Manichewitz wine bottle. He bent over, picked it up, and peered inside. To his delight, he found a few drops of liquid and quickly removed the top. Lo' and behold, out popped a Jewish genie – complete with long black caftan, fur hat, and long sideburns.

"*So vhat kann I do for you? You've got three vishes,*" queried the genie.

Ahmed thought for a moment and responded first, I would like to be in a beautiful spot where water and trees are plentiful.

Immediately, he found that he and the genie had been transported to a lush oasis with running brooks and many splendid date palms.

"Second, Ahmed told the genie that he wanted great wealth.

The genie, said, *"Is zat all; oy, daht's an easy one to grant."*

Again, Ahmed was astonished to find that his filthy robes had been transformed into a glistening set of immaculate coverings that a sultan would envy.

The genie reminded him that he had one more wish to fulfill.

Ahmed relied, "Well, I would like to be white and surrounded by lovely women."

*Shazzaam*! He found that he had been transformed into a tampon.

The moral of this tale: when dealing with a Jewish genie, there is always a string attached.

• • •

A Saskatchewan farmer and his wife, on their way back home in January, were at the airport in New York awaiting their flight. They are dressed in heavy boots, parka, scarf, mittens, etc. An older couple standing nearby was intrigued by their manner of dress.

The wife said to her husband: "Look at that couple. I wonder where they're from?"

He replied: "How would I know?"

She countered: "You could go and ask them."

He said: "I don't really care. You want to know, you go and ask them."

She decided to do just that and walked over to the couple and inquired, "Excuse me. Looking at your dress, I wondered where you were from."

The farmer replied: "Saskatoon, Saskatchewan ".

The woman returns to her husband who asked: "So, where are they from?"

She responded, "I don't know. They don't speak English"

• • •

## Other Nations, Ethnicities, And Regions As Subjects Of Humor

Two Irishmen, Flanagan and Ryan, were adrift in a lifeboat following a dramatic escape from a burning freighter. While rummaging through the lifeboat's emergency provisions, Flanagan stumbled across an old lamp. Secretly hoping that a genie would appear, he rubbed t he lamp vigorously. To his amazement, a genie *did* came forth. This particular genie, however, stated that he could only deliver one wish, not the standard three.

Without giving much thought to the matter, Ryan blurted out, "Make the entire ocean into Guinness!"

The genie clapped his hands with a deafening crash, and immediately the entire sea turned into the finest brew ever sampled by mortals. However, simultaneously, the genie vanished. Only the gentle lapping of Guinness on the hull broke the stillness as the two men considered their circumstances.

Flanagan looked disgustedly at Ryan, whose wish had been granted. After a long, tension-filled moment, he spoke, "Nice going matey; now we're going to have to piss in the boat!"

• • •

Saddam Hussein was sitting in his office wondering whom to invade next when his telephone rang. "Hallo, Mr. Hussein!," a heavily accented voice said:

"This is Paddy down at the Harp Pub in County Sligo, Ireland. I am ringing to inform you that we are officially declaring war on you!"

"Well, Paddy," Saddam replied, "This is indeed important news! How big is your army?"

"Right now," said Paddy, after a moment's calculation, "there is myself, my cousin Sean, my next door neighbor Seamus, and the entire dart team from the pub. That makes eight of us!"

Saddam paused. "I must tell you, Paddy, that I have one million men in my army waiting to move on my command."

"Begorra!" said Paddy. "I'll have to ring you back!"

Sure enough, the next day, Paddy called again. "Mr. Hussein, the war is still on! We have managed to acquire some infantry equipment!"

"And what equipment would that be, Paddy?" Saddam asked.

"Well, we have two combines, a bulldozer, and Murphy's farm tractor."

Saddam sighed. "I must tell you, Paddy, that I have 16,000 tanks and 14,000 armored personnel carriers. Also, I've increased my army to 1-1/2 million since we last spoke."

"Saints preserve us!" said Paddy. "I'll have to get back to you."

Sure enough, Paddy rang again the next day. "Mr. Hussein, the war is still on! We have managed to get ourselves airborne! We've modified Harrigan's ultra-light with a couple of shotguns in the cockpit, and four boys from the Shamrock Pub have joined us as well!"

Saddam was silent for a minute and then cleared his throat. "I must tell you, Paddy, that I have 10,000 bombers and 20,000 fighter planes. My military complex is surrounded by laser-guided, surface-to-air missile sites. And since we last spoke, I've increased my army to TWO MILLION!"

"Jesus, Mary, and Joseph!" said Paddy, "I'll have to ring you back."

Sure enough, Paddy called again the next day. "Top o' the mornin', Mr. Hussein! I am sorry to tell you that we have had to call off the war."

"I'm sorry to hear that," said Saddam. "Why the sudden change of heart?"

"Well," said Paddy, "we've all had a long chat over a bunch of pints, and decided there's no way we can feed two million prisoners."

• • •

Once upon a time lived a king who had a Jewish advisor. The king relied so much on the wisdom of his Jewish advisor, that one day he decided to elevate him to the post of Head Advisor. After it was announced, the other advisors objected. After all, "It was bad enough," the other advisors complained, just to sit in counsel with a Jew. But to allow one to 'Lord it over them,' was just too much to bear." Being a compassionate ruler, the King agreed with them, and ordered the Jew to convert.

What could the Jew do? One had to obey the King, and so he did. As soon as the act was done, the Jew felt great remorse for this terrible decision. As days became weeks, his remorse turned to despondency, and as months passed, his mental depression took it toll on his physical health. He became weaker and weaker. Finally he could stand it no longer. His mind was made up. He burst in on the king and cried, "I was born a Jew and a Jew I must be. Do what you want with me, but I can no longer deny my faith."

The King was very surprised. He had no idea that the Jew felt so strongly about it. "Well, if that is how you feel," he said, "then the other advisors will just have to learn to live with it. Your wise counsel is much too important to me to do without. "Go and be a Jew again," he said.

The Jew felt elated. He hurried back home to tell the good news to his family. He felt the strength surge back into his body as he ran. Finally, he burst into the house and called out to his wife. "Rifka, Rifka, we can be Jews again, we can be Jews again."

His wife glared back at him angrily and said, "You couldn't wait until after Passover?"

• • •

An Irishman who had a wee bit too much to drink was driving home from the pub one night and, of course, his car was weaving violently all over the road. A constable pulled him over.

"So," said the constable to the driver, "Where have you been?"

"Why, I've been to the pub of course," slurred the drunk with a smile.

"Well," relied the officer, "It looks like you've had quite a few to drink this evening."

"I did indeed," the drunk replied with a smile.

"Did you know," said the constable standing straight and with his arms folded across his chest, "that a few intersections back, your wife fell out of the car?"

"Oh, thank heavens," sighed the drunk, "For a minute there I thought I'd gone deaf!"

• • •

As you probably know, there is a certain group, caste, or religion, in India where the women apply a red spot on their foreheads. You have probably wondered what this is for. The answer is actually very simple. When they are married, their husband gets to scratch it off to see if he won a convenience store, or a motel.

• • •

Brenda O'Toole, was home making dinner, as usual when Tim Finnegan arrived at her door.

"Brenda, may I come in?" he asked. "I've something to tell ya."

"Of course you can come in, Tim. But, where's me husband?"

"That's what I'm here to tell ya, Brenda. There was an accident down at the Guiness brewery —."

"Oh God no!" cried Brenda. "please don't tell me—"

"I must, Brenda. Your husband, Seamus is dead and gone. I'm sorry."

Finally she looked up at him, "How did it happen?"

"It was terrible, Brenda. He fell into a vat of Guiness stout and drowned."

"Oh my dear Jesus; but you must tell me true now, Tim. Did he at least die quickly?"

"Well, no Brenda ___."

"No?"

"Fact is, he got out to pee three times to pee."

• • •

Mary Clancy went up to father O'Grady in tears after his saying Sunday mass.

Father O'Grady inquired, "So what's bothering you, dear?"

Oh, Father, I've got terrible news. My husband passed away last night."

Oh, Mary, that's is truly terrible news; tell me, did he have any last requests?"

Mary replied, "Aye and that he did Father."

The priest inquired, "What did he ask, Mary?"

She replied, "Please Mary, put that damned gun down!"

• • •

A young Muslim kid can't find his mother in the supermarket. The store attendant asks "What does your mother look like?"

The kid says "How the fuck should I know?"

• • •

Two aliens landed in the Arizona desert near an abandoned gas station. They approached the gas pumps and one of them said to it "Greetings, Earthling. We come in peace. Take us to your leader."

The gas pump, of course, did not respond. The alien repeated the greeting and there was still no response. Annoyed by what he perceived as the gas pump's haughty attitude the alien drew his ray gun and said impatiently, "Greetings earthling, we come in peace. How dare you ignore us this way? Take us to your leader or I will fire."

The other alien shouted to his comrade, "No, you must not anger him..." but before he could finish his warning the first alien fired. There was a huge explosion that blew both of them 200 meters into the desert where they landed in a heap.

When they finally regained consciousness the one who fired turned to the other one and said, "What a ferocious creature. It nearly killed us. How did you know it was so dangerous?"

The other alien answered, "If there is one thing I have learned in my travels through the galaxy, it's if a guy has a penis he can wrap around himself twice and then stick in his own ear, don't screw with him."

• • •

A man is traveling a route and sees a sign "Apples–£5 each."

"Five pounds?" exclaims the man, "I'll have to stop just to protest about that."

"I see you're charging five pounds for apples, is that right?"

"Oh, yes", says the countryman, "They, be real good apples, them."

"No apples are worth a fiver," complains the man.

"These are Sir. You see this side of the apple is like the best apple you ever tasted, see. But this corner of it is blueberry. What's more, this other corner is peach. And over here, well, that's nectarine–all for five pounds."

The man doesn't believe it.

"Go on Sir, 'ave a bite, you'll buy some, I promise ya."

The man takes a bite. Sure enough, it's everything the countryman promised and more.

"I'll have some." Says the man, and he left. A little way down the road, the man saw another sign: "Apples–£10 each". He can't believe it. "Ten quid—for an apple—outrageous! I'll have to stop just to tell him there only a fiver down the road. And so, he does. The countryman is unperturbed.

"No Sir, these apples be different, like. 'way different any others you ever had." "But ten pounds an apple, that can't be right."

"Well, Sir ", says the countryman, "You see this here apple, is like a complete roast dinner all in one. This side...well that's your roast beef, see, and over here well that potatoes and greens; see, on the corner here there's the equivalent of a nice bottle of red wine, and on the other side – well, that's your dessert. Try it Sir; buy some."

The man tries the apple – the countryman is exactly right–so he buys a few.

Further down the road, the man sees another sign which *really* takes him aback:

"Apples- -£100 each."

"Ridiculous", he says, "I'm going to show him what I got for ten pounds"

At the farm, the man protested strongly, "No one can charge a hundred pounds for an apple and get away with it."

"Ahh", says the grocer, "These apples are like none what you 'ave; these are real special, sir. Why these apples are quite simply the best bit of pussy what you've ever 'ad. You won't get none better!"

"You've got to be kidding me." Says the man.

"Oh no Sir. Go on, you just take a bite of that there apple Sir, and you will agree with me that it's the best bit of pussy you've ever had."

The man was unsure. But, then, goes for it, and takes a big bite.

"Er, my god man, that's revolting, disgusting, absolutely horrible, I'm not paying for that, it tastes like shit."

"Oh, no, Sir..." added the grocer hurriedly,"...I think you should turn that one round!!"

• • •

King Arthur was in Merlin's laboratory where the great wizard was showing him his latest creation. It was a chastity belt, except it had a rather large hole in the most obvious place which made it basically useless.

"This is no good, Merlin!" the King exclaimed, "Look at this opening. How is this supposed to protect my lady, the Queen, when I'm on a long quest?"

"Ah, sire, just observe," said Merlin. He then selected his most worn out wand, one that he was going to discard anyway. He inserted it in the gaping aperture of the chastity belt whereupon a small guillotine blade came down and cut it neatly in two.

"Merlin, you are a! genius!" said the grateful monarch. "Now I can leave, know-ing that my Queen is fully protected." After putting Guinevere in the device, King Arthur then set out upon a lengthy Quest.

Several years passed until he returned to Camelot. Immediately he assembled all of his knights in the courtyard and had them drop their trousers for an informal 'short arm' inspection. Sure enough, each and every one of them was either amputated or damaged in some way. All of them, that is, except Sir Galahad.

"Sir Galahad," exclaimed King Arthur. "You are my one and only true knight! Only you among all the nobles have been true to me. What is it in my power to grant you? Name it and it is yours."

But, alas, Sir Galahad was speechless.

• • •

There was a cruise ship going through some rough waters that ended up sinking just off the coast of a small deserted island off the coast of County Cork, Ireland.

There where only 3 survivors' 2 guys and a girl. They lived there for a couple of years doing what was natural for men and women. After several years of casual sex all the time, the girl felt really bad about what she had been doing. She felt having sex with both guys was so bad that she killed herself.

It was very tragic but the two guys managed to get through it and after a while nature once more took it's inevitable course.

Well, a couple more years went by and the guys began to feel absolutely horrible about what they were doing. So they buried her.

• • •

Back in the time of the Samurai there was a powerful emperor who needed a new head Samurai, so he sent out a declaration throughout the country he was searching for one. A year passed, and only 3 people showed up: a Japanese Samurai, a Chinese Samurai and a Jewish Samurai.

The emperor asked the Japanese warrior to come in and demonstrate why he should be head Samurai. The Japanese Samurai opened a match box, and out popped a bumblebee. Whoosh! went his sword, and the bumblebee dropped dead on the ground in 2 pieces. The emperor exclaimed: "That is impressive!"

The emperor then asked the Chinese warrior to come in and demonstrate his skills. The Chinese Samurai also opened match box, and out buzzed a fly. Whoosh, Whoosh! went his sword, and the fly dropped dead on the ground in 4 small pieces. The emperor exclaimed: "That is really VERY impressive!"

The emperor then had the Jewish Samurai demonstrate why he should be the selected as the head Samurai. The Jewish chap also opened a match box and out flew a gnat. His flashing sword went Whooooosh! Whooooosh! But the gnat was still alive and flying around.

The emperor, obviously disappointed, asked: "After all of that, why is the gnat not dead?" The Jewish Samurai smiled. "Well," he replied, "circumcision is not meant to kill."

• • •

This young swimmer from the Australian Olympic team managed to sneak his new girlfriend, a gorgeous Danish gymnast, into his room at the Olympic Village. Once she was inside, he quickly switched out all the lights and they rapidly disrobed and leap onto his bed in a flurry of athletic achievement. After about twenty minutes of wild sex they both collapse back on the bed in exhaustion. The girl looked admiringly across at the swimmer in the dim light. His beautifully-developed muscles, tanned skin and smooth-shaven scalp glistened with little beads of sweat as he lay beside her. She was very pleased to have met this guy.

At this point the swimmer slowly struggled up from the bed. He fumbled the lid off a bottle on the bedside table, poured himself a small shot in a glass and drank it down in one gulp. Then he stood bolt upright, took a deep breath and, in a surprising energetic motion, dove under the bed, climbing out the other side and beating his chest like a gorilla. Then he vaulted back on top of the girl and commenced a frantic repeat performance.

The Danish girl is very impressed with the gusto of this second encounter. Somehow the Aussie had completely recovered from his previous exhaustion! After nearly half an hour of wild activity in every possible position, the gasping male swimmer again crawled out of bed and swallowed another shot of the mysterious liquid. Once more, he dove under the bed, emerged on the other side, beat his chest and commenced to make love all over again. The girl was just amazed and delighted as the action continued at the same blistering pace as before. In the darkness, she could not properly see what kind of tonic is causing these incredible transformations, but she sure liked the effect!

More than an hour later, after another repeat of the strange drinking ritual on his part, and a whole string of ecstatic multiple orgasms on her part, the Danish girl was now feeling rather faint herself.

"Just a minute, big boy," she whispered to the panting bald-headed Aussie, "I think I need to try some of your tonic!" She rose unsteadily and poured a small shot of the liquid. She braced herself for some sort of medicinal effect, but actually it just tastes like Coca-Cola.

Then she stood up straight, took a deep breath and dove under the bed – only to smash straight into the three other exhausted members of the Australian relay swim team.

• • •

Walking through San Francisco's Chinatown, a tourist from the Midwest was fascinated with all the Chinese restaurants, shops, signs and banners. He turned a comer and saw a building with the sign "Moishe Plotnik's Chinese Laundry." "Moishe Plotnik?" he wondered. "How does that fit in Chinatown?" So he walked into the shop and saw a fairly standard looking Chinese laundry. He could see that the proprietors were clearly aware of the uniqueness of the name as there were baseball hats, T-Shirts and coffee mugs blazoned with the logo "Moishe Plotnik's Chinese Laundry." There was also a fair selection of Chinatown souvenirs, indicating that the name alone had brought many tourists into the shop. The tourist selected a coffee cup as a conversation piece to take back to his office. Behind the counter was a smiling elderly Chinese gentleman who thanked him for his purchase in English, thickly accented with Chinese.

The tourist asked, "Can you tell me how this place got a name like "Moishe Plotnik's Chinese Laundry?"

The old man answered, "Ahh... Everybody ask that. Is name of owner."

Looking around, the tourist asked, "Is he here now?"

"He is right here," replied the old man. "He is me."

"Really? How did you ever get a name like Moishe Plotnik?"

"Is simple," said the old man. "Many, many year ago when I came to this country, I was standing in line at Documentation Center.. Man in front is Jewish gentleman from Poland. Lady look at him and say, 'What your name?"

He say, 'Moishe Plotnik.'

Then she look at me and say, "What your name?'

"I say, 'Sam Ting.'"

• • •

A virile, young Italian soldier was relaxing at his favorite bar in Rome when he managed to attract a spectacular young blonde. Things progressed to the point where he invited her back to his apartment. After some small talk, they made love. After a pleasant interlude he asked with a smile, "So my darlink...you finish?"

She paused for a second, frowned, and replied "No."

Surprised, the young man reached for her; and the lovemaking resumed. This time, she thrashed about wildly; and there were screams of passion. The love making ended; and again, the young man smiled, and asked, "Dis time you finish?" Again, she returned his smile, cuddled closer to him, and softly said, "No."

Stunned, but damned if this woman is going to outlast him, the young man reached for her. Using the last of his strength, he barely managed it; but they climax simultaneously, screaming, clawing and ripping bed sheets. The exhausted man fell onto his back, gasping. Barely able to turn his head, he looked into her eyes, smiled proudly, and asked, "So, you finish?"

"No!" she shouts back, "Stop asking, I no Finish, I Svedish!"

• • •

### Boris and His Vodka Fountain

One night while sitting at a bar in Moscow, Boris accidentally knocked a vodka bottle from on top of the bar counter. Out popped a genie and granted Boris one wish. Boris, who is very drunk, makes a wish... "I wish I could make my own vodka.

The wish was granted instantly.

That night, Boris had to relieve himself. As he is urinating, he noticed that the urine was crystal clear and smelled like vodka. Curious, he tasted the urine, and found it was the very best vodka he has ever tasted. He rushed home to his wife.

"Quick," he yells to his wife, "bring me two glasses."

He unzipped his pants and filled the two glasses.

"Drink!" he declared.

His wife thought he was drunk and had lost his mind, so she just laughed. Boris finally convinced her to drink. After she drank the liquid, she too agreed that it was the best vodka she has ever tasted. Better than Stolichnyia!

The next night Boris returned from work and yelled for two glasses.

Again he filled the two glasses. They both drink and get drunk together.

The same thing happens for the next three nights. On the fourth night Boris yelled for "*one* glass!" His wife was shocked and asked, "What is the matter Boris? Have I done something wrong?"

"Nothing," replied Boris, "Tonight you have the honor of drinking from the fountain my dearest!"

• • •

Barbara Walters was doing a documentary on the customs of Native Americans. While touring a reservation during the documentary she was puzzled as to why the difference in the number of feathers in the headdresses. So she asked a brave who only had one feather in his headdress and his reply was: "Me have only one squaw, me only have one feather."

Feeling the first fellow was only joking she asked another brave. This brave had two feathers in his headdress. And he replied: "Me have two feathers because me sleep with two squaw."

Still not convinced the feathers indicated the number of squaws involved, she decided to interview the Chief. Now the Chief had a headdress full of feathers, which, needless to say, amused Ms Walters.

She asked the Chief, "Why do you have so many feathers in your headdress?"

The Chief proudly pounded his chest and said: "Me Chief, me sleep with 'em all. Big, small, fat and tall, me sleep with 'em all."

Horrified, Ms Walters stated, "You ought to be hung!"

The Chief said: "You damn right, me hung, big like buffalo, long like snake!"

Ms Walters cried, "You don't have to be so hostile!"

The Chief replied: "Hoss-style, dog-style, wolf-style, any style... me sleep with 'em all."

With tears in her eyes, Ms Walters lamented, "Oh, dear!"

The Chief said: "No deer. Ass too high, run too fast."

• • •

Nablus, West Bank. An explosion rocked the office of Yasser Arafat's office in the Palestine Authority headquarters compound. Immediately following the explosion, two aides of Arafat entered the shattered office and found the leader badly shaken, with a bloody face, his checkered kafiya (head scarf) askew, and ringing in his ears.

His aides asked him, "Chairman Arafat, what happened!?"

Responded Arafat, "It was a letter bomb!"

"But Chairman, only your face was injured."

"I was licking the envelope to seal it."

• • •

A Navaho shepherd was herding his flocks in a remote pasture when suddenly a brand new Jeep Cherokee advanced out of a dust cloud towards him. The driver, a young man in a Brioni suit, Gucci shoes, Ray Ban sunglasses and a YSL tie leaned out of the window and asked our shepherd: "If I can tell you exactly how many sheep you have in your flock, will you give me one?"

The shepherd looked at the yuppie, then at his peacefully grazing flock and calmly answered "sure!" The yuppie parked the car, whipped out his notebook, connected it to a cell-phone, surfed to a NASA page on the Internet where he called up a GPS satellite navigation system, scanned the area, opened up a database and some 60 Excel spreadsheets with complex formulas. Finally he printed out a 150-page report on his hi-tech miniaturized printer, turned around to our shepherd and said: "you have here exactly 1586 sheep."

"That is correct. As agreed, you can take one of the sheep," replied the Indian shepherd.

He watched the young man make a selection and bundle it in his Cherokee. Then he said, "If I can tell you exactly what your business is, will you give me my sheep back?"

"Okay, why not" answered the young man.

"You are a consultant," said the shepherd.

## Other Nations, Ethnicities, And Regions As Subjects Of Humor

"This is correct," said the yuppie, how did you guess that?"

"I was no guess, and it was easy" answered the shepherd. "You turned up here although nobody called you. You want to be paid for the answer to a question I already knew the Solution to. And you don't know anything about my business because you took my dog."

• • •

A fellow entered a Chinese restaurant and was shown to a table. Within moments, a waiter appeared and inquired whether the chap would care for a drink before dinner.

"A Stoly with a twist," he replied.

"Once upon a time —"

• • •

It was late fall and the Indians on a remote reservation in British Columbia asked their new chief if the coming winter was going to be cold or mild.

Since he was a chief in a modern society, he had never been taught the old secrets. When he looked at the sky, he couldn't tell what the winter was going to be like. Nevertheless, to be on the safe side, he told his tribal community that the winter was indeed going to be cold and that the members of the village should collect firewood to be prepared. But, being a practical leader, after several days, he got an idea. He went to the phone booth, called the Environment Canada National Weather Service and asked, "Is the coming winter going to be cold?"'

"It looks like this winter is going to be quite cold,"' the meteorologist at the weather service responded.

So the chief went back to his people and told them to collect even more firewood in order to be prepared.

A week later, he called Environment Canada's National Weather Service again. "Does it still look like it is going to be a very cold winter?

"Yes,"' the man at National Weather Service again replied, "it's going to be a very cold winter."

The chief again went back to his people and ordered them to collect every scrap of firewood they could find.

Two weeks later, the chief called Environment Canada's National Weather Service again. "Are you absolutely sure that the winter is going to be very cold?"

"Absolutely," the weatherman replied. "'It's looking more and more like it is going to be one of the coldest winters we've ever seen."

"How can you be so sure?" the chief asked.

The weatherman replied, "The Indians are collecting firewood like crazy."

• • •

These three guys escape from Alcatraz prison. One is British, one is American, and the last one is Turkish.

But now they're bored and so they're wandering around thinking of something to do.

"Let's play golf." The American finally exclaimed.

"I don't know how to play that." The Turk said

"Oh it's easy," answered the Brit, "all you need is a ball, a stick, and a hole."

"I got the ball," said the American.

"I got the stick," says the Brit.

Then the Turk said, "I don't wanna play."

• • •

In Lebanon, men are legally allowed to have sex with animals, but the animals must be female. Having sexual relations with a male animal is punishable by death. (As if that makes sense!)

• • •

OTHER NATIONS, ETHNICITIES, AND REGIONS AS SUBJECTS OF HUMOR

In Cali, Colombia, a woman may only have sex with her husband, and the first time this happens, her mother must be in the room to witness the act.

• • •

There are men in Guam whose full-time job is to travel the countryside and deflower young virgins, who pay them for the privilege of having sex for the first time...Reason: under Guamanians law, it is expressly forbidden for virgins to marry.
   (Let's just think for a minute; is there any job anywhere else in the world that even comes close to this one?)

• • •

In Bahrain, a male doctor may legally examine a woman's genitals, but is prohibited from looking directly at them during the examination. He may only see their reflection in a mirror. (Do they look different reversed?)

• • •

In Hong Kong, a betrayed wife is legally allowed to kill her adulterous husband, but may only do so with her bare hands. The husband's lover, on the other hand, may be killed in any manner desired.

• • •

Muslims are banned from looking at the genitals of a corpse. This also applies to undertakers; the sex organs of the deceased must be covered with a brick or piece of wood at all times.

• • •

The penalty for masturbation in Indonesia is decapitation. (Much worse than "going blind!")

• • •

Topless saleswomen are legal in Liverpool, England - but only in tropical fish stores.

• • •

In Santa Cruz, Bolivia, it is illegal for a man to have sex with a woman and her daughter at the same time. (Let us presume this was such a big enough problem that they had to pass this law?)

• • •

In Maryland, it is illegal to sell condoms from vending machines with one exception: prophylactics may be dispensed from a vending machine only "in places where alcoholic beverages are sold for consumption on the premises."

(Is this a great country or what? But —not as great as Guam!)

• • •

An Alabamian came home and found his house on fire. He rushed next door, telephoned the fire department and shouted, "Hurry over here-muh house is on fahr!"

"OK," replied the fireman, "how do we get there?"

"Shucks, don't you fellers still have those big red trucks?"

• • •

Ida Mae passed away and Bubba called 911. The 911 operator told Bubba that she would send someone out right away.

"Where do you live?" asked the operator.
Bubba replied, "At the end of Eucalyptus Drive."
The operator asked, "Can you spell that for me?"
After a long pause, Bubba said, "How 'bout I drag her over to Oak Street and you pick her up there?"

• • •

Where was the toothbrush invented?
Arkansas. If it were invented anywhere else, it would have been called a teethbrush.

• • •

Did you hear about the $3,000,000 Tennessee State Lottery?
The winner gets $3.00 a year for a million years.

• • •

What do they call reruns of "Hee Haw" in Mississippi?
Documentaries.

• • •

How do you know when you're staying in a Kentucky hotel?
When you call the front desk and say "I've got a leak in my sink," and the person at the front desk says, "Go ahead."

• • •

An Arkansas State trooper pulled over a pickup truck on I-40 and said to the driver, "Got any ID?"
The driver says, "Bout what?"

• • •

Two Mississippians are walking toward each other, and one is carrying a sack. When they meet, one says, "Hey Tommy Ray, whatcha got in th' bag?"

"Jes' some chickens."

"If I guesses how many they is, kin I have one?"

"Shoot, if ya guesses right, I'll give you both of 'em!"

"OK. Ummmmm.five?"

• • •

Why do folks in Kentucky go to R-rated movies in groups of 18 or more?

Because they heard 17 and under aren't admitted.

• • •

Know why they raised the minimum drinking age in Tennessee to 32?

They wanted to keep alcohol out of the high schools.

• • •

A new law was recently passed in South Carolina so that when a couple gets divorced, they're still brother and sister.

• • •

What do a divorce in Alabama, a tornado in Kansas and a hurricane in Florida have in common?

No matter what, somebody's fixin' to lose a trailer!

• • •

A guy went into a store and told the clerk, "I'd like some Polish sausage."

The clerk looks at him and says, "Are you Polish?"

## Other Nations, Ethnicities, And Regions As Subjects Of Humor

The guy, clearly offended, says, "Well, yes I am. But let me ask you something." If I had asked for Italian sausage would you ask me if I was Italian? Or if I had asked for German bratwurst, would you ask me if I was German? Or if I asked for a kosher hot dog would you ask me if I was Jewish? Or if I had asked for a taco would you ask if I was Mexican? Would ya, huh? Would ya?"

The clerk says, "Well, no."

With deep self-righteous indignation, the guy says, "Well, all right then, why did you ask me if I'm Polish just because I ask for Polish sausage?"

The clerk replies, "Because this is Home Depot."

• • •

Vun day, Sven vas valking down da street ven who did he see driving a brand new Chevrolet? It vas Ole. Ole pulled up to him vit a vide smile.

"Ole, vere did you get dat car?" Sven asked.

"Lena gave it to me."

"She gave it to you? I knew she vas sveet on you, but dis?"

"Vell, let me tell you vat happened. Ve ver driving out on county road 6, in da middle of novere. Lena pulled off da road into da woods. She parked, got out of da car, trew off all of her clothes and said, "Ole take vatever you vant."... So I took da car"

"Ole, your such a smart man, dem clothes never voulda fit ya."

• • •

Three Cajuns and three Texans were taking a train to attend a conference. At the station, each Texan bought a ticket, but they noticed that only one Cajun purchased a ticket.

"Don't you all need tickets?" they asked.

"Mais Non," replied the Cajuns, "One is more dan enough, boo."

Once they board the train, the Texans took their seats and noticed that all three Cajuns crammed themselves into a toilet. As the conductor passed through the car, he knocked on the toilet door and said, "Ticket, please."

The door cracked ever so slightly, a hand passed out a ticket, and then the door quickly closed again.

"Ahhh... very clever" think the Texans.

After the conference, the three Cajuns and the three Texans were again at the train station for the return trip. Since the Texans are now so 'money-wise', they smirk as they only purchased one ticket... but then they noticed that the Cajuns don't buy a ticket at all.

"How will you get back without even a single ticket?" they asked.

"Mais, we don' need dat on de back trip!" said one of the Cajuns.

Once they board the train, the three Texans crammed themselves into the largest toilet, and the three Cajuns eased into another toilet. As the train began to move away from the station, one of the Cajuns left the toilet and knocked on the door of the Texans' toilet and says, "Ticket Please."

• • •

### You know you are trailer trash when...

1. The Halloween pumpkin on your porch has more teeth than your spouse.
2. You let your twelve-year-old daughter smoke at the dinner table in front of her kids.
3. You're been married three times and still have the same in-laws.
4. You think a woman who is "out-of-your-league" bowls on a different night.
5. Jack Daniels makes your list of "most admired people."
6. You wonder how service stations keep their restrooms so clean.
7. Anyone in your family ever died right after saying: "Hey, watch this."
8. You think Dom Perignon is a Mafia leader.
9. Your junior prom had a daycare.
10. Your wife's hairdo was once ruined by! a ceiling fan.

11. You think the last words of the Star Spangled Banner are: "Gentlemen, start your engines."
12. You lit a match in the bathroom and your house exploded right off its wheels.
13. The bluebook value of your truck goes up and down, depending on how much gas is in it.
14. You have to go outside to get something from the fridge.
15. One of your kids was born on a pool table.
16. You need one more hole punched in your cards to get a freebie at the House of Tattoos.
17. You can't get married to your sweetheart because there's a law against it.
18. You think "loaded dishwasher" means your wife is drunk.
19. Your toilet paper has page numbers on it.
20. Your front porch collapses and kills more than five dogs.

• • •

**A short history of the French at war.**

Gallic Wars - Lost. In a war whose ending foreshadows the next 2000 years of French history, France is conquered by of all things, an Italian.

Hundred Years War - Mostly lost, saved at last by female schizophrenic who inadvertently creates The First Rule of French Warfare: "France's armies are victorious only when not led by a Frenchman."

Italian Wars - Lost. France becomes the first and only country to ever lose two wars when fighting Italians. Wars of Religion - France goes 0-5-4 against the Huguenots

Thirty Years War - France is technically not a participant, but manages to get invaded anyway. Claims a tie on the basis that eventually the other participants started ignoring her.

War of Devolution - Tied. Frenchmen take to wearing red flowerpots as chapeaux.

The Dutch War – Tied

War of the Augsburg League/King William's War/French and Indian War Lost, but claimed as a tie. Three ties in a row induces deluded Frogophiles the world over, to label the period as the height of French military power.

War of the Spanish Succession - Lost. The War also gave the French their first taste of a Marlborough, which they have loved every since.

American Revolution - In a move that will become quite familiar to future Americans, France claims a win even though the English colonists saw far more action. This is later known as "de Gaulle Syndrome", and leads to the Second Rule of French Warfare: "France only wins when America does most of the fighting."

French Revolution - Won, primarily due the fact that the opponent was also French.

The Napoleonic Wars - Lost. Temporary victories (remember the First Rule!) due to leadership of a Corsican, who ended up being no match for a British footwear designer.

The Franco-Prussian War - Lost. Germany first plays the role of a drunk Frat boy to France's ugly girl home alone on a Saturday night.

World War I - Tied and on the way to losing, France is saved by the United States. Thousands of French women find out what it's like to not only sleep with a winner, but one who doesn't call her "Fraulein." Sadly, widespread use of condoms by American forces forestalls any improvement in the French bloodline.

World War II - Lost. Conquered French liberated by the United States and Britain just as they finish learning the *Horst Wessel Song*.

War in Indochina - Lost. French forces plead sickness, take to bed with the Dien Bien Flu.

Algerian Rebellion - Lost. Loss marks the first defeat of a western army by a Non-Turkic Muslim force since the Crusades, and produces the First Rule of Muslim Warfare: "We can always beat the French." This rule is identical to the First Rules of the Italians, Russians, Germans, English, Dutch, Spanish, Vietnamese and Esquimaux. War on Terrorism – France, keeping in mind its

## Other Nations, Ethnicities, And Regions As Subjects Of Humor

recent history, surrenders to Germans and Muslims just to be safe. Attempts to surrender to Vietnamese ambassador fail after he takes refuge in a McDonald's.

The question for any country silly enough to count on the French should not be "Can we count on the French?" but rather "How long until France surrenders?"

• • •

An Italian walked into a bank in New York City and asked for the loan officer. He told the loan officer that he was going to Italy on business for two weeks and needed to borrow $5,000. The bank officer told him that the bank would need some form of security for the loan, so the Italian handed over the keys to a new Ferrari. The car was parked on the street in front of the bank. The Italian produced the title and everything checked out.

The loan officer agreed to accept the car as collateral for the loan. The bank's president and its officers all enjoyed a good laugh at the Italian for using a $250,000 Ferrari as collateral against a $5,000 loan. An employee of the bank then drove the Ferrari into the bank's underground garage and parked it there. Two weeks later, the Italian returned, repaid the $5,000 and the interest, which came to $15.41. The loan officer remarked, "Sir, we are very happy to have had your business, and this transaction has worked out very nicely, but we are a little puzzled. While you were away, we checked you out and found that you are a multimillionaire. What puzzles us is, why would you bother to borrow $5,000?"

The Italian replied: "Where else in New York City can I park my car for two weeks for only $15.41 and expect it to be there when I return?"

Ah, the Italians!

• • •

## HOW TO IDENTIFY WHERE A DRIVER IS FROM

One hand on wheel, one hand on horn: CHICAGO

One hand on wheel, middle finger out window: NEW YORK

One hand on wheel, middle finger out window, cutting across all lanes of traffic: NEW JERSEY

One hand on wheel, one hand on newspaper, foot solidly on accelerator: BOSTON

One hand on wheel, one hand on nonfat double decaf cappuccino, cradling cell phone, brick on accelerator, gun in lap: LOS ANGELES

Both hands on wheel, eyes shut, both feet on brake, quivering in terror: OHIO, but driving in CALIFORNIA

Both hands in air, gesturing, both feet on accelerator, head turned to talk to someone in back seat: ITALY

One hand on 12oz. double shot latte, one knee on wheel, cradling cell phone, foot on brake, mind on radio game, banging head on steering wheel while stuck in traffic: SEATTLE

One hand on wheel, one hand on hunting rifle, alternating between both feet being on the accelerator and both feet on brake, throwing McDonald's bag out the window: TEXAS

Four-wheel drive pick-up truck, shotgun mounted in rear window, beer cans on floor, squirrel tails attached to antenna: OKLAHOMA

Two hands gripping wheel, blue hair barely visible above windshield, driving 35 on the Interstate in the left lane with the left blinker on: FLORIDA

One hand on the wheel, the other on his sister: ARKANSAS

• • •

### The Bunny and the Snake

Once upon a time (allegedly) in a nice little forest, there lived an orphaned bunny and an orphaned snake. By a surprising coincidence, both were blind from birth.

## Other Nations, Ethnicities, And Regions As Subjects Of Humor

One day, the bunny was hopping through the forest, and the snake was slithering through the woods, when the bunny tripped over the snake and fell down. This, of course, knocked the snake about quite a bit.

"Oh, my," said the bunny, "I'm terribly sorry. I didn't mean to hurt you. I've been blind since birth, so, I can't see where I'm going. In fact, since I'm also an orphan, I don't even know what I am."

"It's quite OK," replied the snake. "Actually, my story is much the same as yours. I, too, have been blind since birth, and also never knew my mother. Tell you what, maybe I could slither all over you, and work out what you are, so at least you'll have that going for you."

"Oh, that would be wonderful" replied the bunny. So the snake slithered all over the bunny, and said, "Well, you're covered with soft fur; you have really long ears; your nose twitches; and you have a soft cottony tail. I'd say that you must be a bunny rabbit."

"Oh, thank you! Thank you," cried the bunny, in obvious excitement.

The bunny suggested to the snake, "Maybe I could feel you all over with my paw, and help you the same way that you've helped me."

So the bunny felt the snake all over, and remarked, "Well, you're smooth and slippery, and you have a forked tongue, no backbone and no balls. I'd say you must be French".

• • •

How can you identify a French war veteran A: He's the one with sunburned armpits.

• • •

An American man was having his coffee, bread, butter and jam at the breakfast table when a Frenchman sat down next to him. The American ignored the Frenchman who, nevertheless, started a conversation.

"You American folk eat the whole bread?" inquired the Frenchman with a large piece of chewing gum in his mouth.

"Of course!"

The Frenchman blew a bubble with his chewing gum, then remarked, "We don't. In France, we only eat what's inside. *We* collect the crusts in containers, recycle them, then transform them into croutons, and sell them to the United States." The Frenchman had a sly smirk on is face.

All the while, the American listened in silence.

"Do ya eat jelly with ze bread?" asked the Frenchman.

"Of course!"

The Frenchman cracked his gum between his teeth and chuckled, "*We* don't. In France, we eat fresh fruit for breakfast and put all peel, seeds and leftovers in containers, recycle them, then transform them into jam, and sell it to the U.S."

"And, what do you Frenchmen do with condoms once you've used them?" asked the American.

"We throw them away, of course," replied the Frenchman, with a dumbfounded look.

The American explained, "*We* don't. In the U.S., we put them in a container, recycle them, then melt them down into chewing gum and sell it to France.

• • •

George W. Bush, Tony Blair and Jacques Chirac were relaxing in a Parisian sauna. Suddenly, there was a distinct beeping sound. President Bush pressed his forearm with his thumb & the beeping stopped. The others looked curiously at him.

Oh, that was just my pager", said George. "I have a microchip embedded under the skin of my forearm."

Two minutes later, the silence was broken by the sound of a phone ringing. Tony Blair lifted the palm of his hand to his ear and the ringing stopped. The Prime Minister explained, "That was my cell phone, chaps. I have a telecom chip implanted in the palm of my hand.

"By this time, French president Jacques Chirac was feeling sort of low-tech. Without saying anything, he quickly scooted out of the sauna, but returned momentarily. When he returned, Bush and Blair both stared at him incredulously. It appeared that a long piece of toilet paper was dangling from the Frenchman's posterior.

When Jacques saw that he had the attention of the other two men, he feigned astonishment: "Marie Sainte! I'm think I'm receiving a fax."

• • •

Three guys, an Englishman, a Frenchman and an American were out walking along the beach together one day. They came across a lantern and a genie popped out of it.

"I will give you each one wish," announced the genie.

The American said, "I am a farmer, my dad was a farmer, and my son will also farm. I want the land to be forever fertile in America."

With a blink of the genie's eye, 'FOOM' - the land in America was forever made fertile for farming.

The Frenchman was amazed, so he said, "I want a wall around France, so that no-one can come into our precious country."

Again, with a blink of the Genie's eye, 'POOF' - there was a huge wall around France.

The Englishman asked, "I'm very curious. Please tell me more about this wall.

The Genie explained, "Well, it's about 150 feet high, 50 feet thick and nothing can get in or out."

The Englishman says, "Fill it up with water."

• • •

Sven and Ole were friends since their early childhood in Norway. Sven was bright and had always had his pick of available buxom blond, blue-eyed girls, whereas Ole, was a bit slower and actually had few belt loops shy of a full waistband. One day, Ole asked Sven why it was that he had always been so popular with the girls, whereas, he, Ole had such trouble meeting eligible lasses. Thinking for a while, Sven rubbed his square chin and opined that it was because most Norwegian girls were as fond of mens' bulges as was any healthy Norwegian man was equally of a girl's smooth curves and bulges. Shrugging his shoulders, Ole asked Sven what he thought he could do to help attract some girls.

"Try putting a sweet-a-potato in your trousers; ja, da girls will certainly notice THAT" said Sven.

About a week later, Ole saw Sven on a beach, absolutely surrounded by curvaceous lovely blond lasses.

"Hey Ole, how's it going; did my advice work?" Inquired Sven.

"Oh Sven" Ole moaned, "It was awful!"

Always a good friend to Ole, Sven asked what had happened to make him so sad.

"Ja, you betcha, I did what you suggested; I put a nice big sweet-a-potato in my breaches, just like you suggested. But when I went down to the beach, all of those fine blond girls just laughed and laughed at me; some even kicked sand in my face!"

Sven asked for a demonstration of how Ole had placed the tuberous root vegetable in his pants and when he was shown, he exclaimed, "Ach, Ole, you fool; you are supposed to put in the front!"

• • •

The newlywed bridegroom from Arkansas showed up at his mother's home on the morning after the wedding.

"What's wrong, son? You should be making love to your new wife," exclaimed his mother.

"Oh Mom," said the young man. "I found out that she's a *virgin*"

"I don't blame you son; if she ain't good enough for HER family, she ain't good enough for *OURS*!"

• • •

"France has neither winter nor summer nor morals. Apart from these drawbacks it is a fine country. France has usually been governed by prostitutes." Mark Twain

"I would rather have a German division in front of me than a French one behind me." General George S. Patton

• • •

"Going to war without France is like going deer hunting without your accordion. All that you lose is some useless, noisy baggage." Gen. Norman Schwartzkopf

• • •

"As far as I'm concerned, war always means failure" Jacques Chirac, President of France
    "As far as France is concerned, you're right." Rush Limbaugh

• • •

"The only time France wants us to go to war is when the German Army is sitting in Paris sipping coffee." Regis Philbin

• • •

"You know, the French remind me a little bit of an aging actress of the 1940s who was still trying to dine out on her looks but doesn't have the face for it." Sen. John McCain

• • •

"I don't know why people are surprised that France didn't help us get Saddam out of Iraq. After all, France wouldn't help us get the Germans out of *France!*" Jay Leno

• • •

How many Frenchmen does it take to change a light bulb? One. He holds the bulb and all of Europe revolves around him. Dave Letterman

• • •

"The last time the French asked for 'more proof' it came marching into Paris under a German flag." Dave Letterman

• • •

### Does this Sound Vaguely Familiar?

This is meant to be read aloud (for the full effect). It's amazing, you will understand what 'Tendjewberrymud' means by the end. This was nominated for best email of 1999. The following is a telephone exchange between a hotel guest and room-service, at a hotel in Asia which was recorded and published in the Far East Economic Review....

Room Service (RS): *"Morny. Ruin sorbees."*
Guest (G): "Sorry, I thought I dialed room-service"
RS: *"Rye..Ruin sorbees..morny! Djewish to odor sunteen??"*
G: "Uh..yes..I'd like some bacon and eggs"
RS: *"Ow July den?"*
G: "What??"
RS: *"Ow July den?...pry, boy, pooch?"*
G : "Oh, the eggs! How do I like them? Sorry, ... scrambled please."
RS: "Ow July dee bayhcem...crease?"
G: "Crisp will be fine."
RS : *"Hokay. An San tos?"*
G: "What?"
RS:*"San tos. July San tos?"*
G: "I don't think so"
RS: *"No? Judo one toes??"*
G: "I feel really bad about this, but I don't know what 'judo one toes' means."

RS: *"Toes! toes!...why djew Don Juan toes? Ow bow singlish mopping we  bother?"*

G: "English muffin!! I've got it! You were saying 'Toast.' Fine. Yes, an English muffin will be fine."

RS: *"We bother?"*

G: "No...just put the bother on the side."

RS: *"Wad?"*

G: "I mean butter...just put it on the side."

RS: *"Copy?"*

G: "Sorry?"

RS: *"Copy...tea...mill?"*

G: "Yes. Coffee please, and that's all."

RS: *"One Minnie. Ass ruin torino fee, strangle ache, crease baychem, tossy singlish mopping we bother honey sigh, and copy.... rye??"*

G: "Whatever you say"

RS: *"Tendjewberrymud"*

G: "You're welcome"

• • •

Ole's wife, Lena, was pregnant. So, he brought her to the doctor. The doctor delivered the baby, a little boy, and the doctor looked over at Ole and said, "Hey Ole, You just had a son!"

Ole got excited by this, but just then the Doctor spoke up and said, "Hold on! We ain't finished yet!" The doctor then delivered a little girl. He said, "Yumpin yimminy! Ole, yous gots a daughter too!"

Ole was a bit puzzled by this, and then the doctor said, "Hold on, we ain't finished yet!" The doctor then delivered another boy. He said, "Ole, you bugger... you just had anudder boy! But Dats it!"

Later, Ole and his wife went home with the three children. When they got home, they began talking. Ole said, "Lena...you remember dat night? We ran out of Vaseline and had ta use dat 3-in-1 Oil."

She said, "Oh-yaa!" He said, "By cripes, it's a good ting we didn't use dat WD-40!"

• • •

A Texan, a Californian, and Oregonian are out riding horses. The Texan pulled out an expensive bottle of whiskey, took a long draught, then another and suddenly threw the bottle into the air, pulled out his gun and shot the bottle in midair.

The Californian looked at him and said, "What are you doing? That was a perfectly good bottle of whiskey!"

The Texan says, "In Texas, there is plenty of whiskey and the bottles are cheap."

A while later, not wanting to be outdone, the Californian pulled out a bottle of champagne, took a few swigs, threw the champagne bottle into the air, pulled out his gun and shot it in midair. The Oregonian couldn't believe his eyes,

"What the heck did you do that for? That was a perfectly good bottle of champagne!"

The Californian replied, "In California, we have plenty of champagne and bottles are cheap."

So, awhile later, the Oregonian pulled out a bottle of Widmer Hefeweizen.beer. He opened it took a sip, and then chugs the whole bottle. He then put the bottle in his saddlebag, pulled out his gun, and shot the Californian.

The Texan, shocked, says, "Why the hell did you do that?"

The Oregonian replies, "In Oregon, we have plenty of Californians and the bottles are worth a nickel.

• • •

Two rednecks, Bubba and Earl, were driving down the road drinking a couple of bottles of Bud. The passenger, Bubba, said, "Lookey thar up ahead, Earl, it's a po-lice roadblock! We're gonna get busted fer drinkin' these here beers!!"

"Don't worry, Bubba," Earl said. "We'll just pull over and finish drinkin' these beers, peel off the label and stick it on our foreheads, and throw the bottles under the seat."

"What fer?" asked Bubba.

"Just let me do the talkin', OK?" said Earl.

Well, they finished their beers, threw the empty bottles under the seat, and each put a label on their forehead.

When they reached the roadblock, the sheriff said, "You boys been drinkin'?"

"No sir," Earl said. "We're on the patch."

• • •

Two delicate flowers of Southern womanhood, one from Texas, the other from Alabama, were conversing on the porch swing of a large pillared mansion.

The Texas lady said, "When my first child was born, my husband built this beautiful mansion for me."

The lady from Alabama commented. "Well, isn't that nice?"

The first woman continued, "When my second child was born, my husband bought me that fine Cadillac you see parked in the drive over there."

Again the Alabama belle commented, "Well, isn't that nice?"

The first woman boasted again. "Then when my third child was born, my darling husband bought me this exquisite diamond bracelet."

Yet again the second lady commented, "Well isn't that nice"

The Texan, not getting the hoped for jealous reaction, asked the other woman, "What did your husband buy for you when you had your first child?"

"My husband sent me to charm school," replied the Alabama Belle.

"Charm School! "The first woman cried. Is that all? Land sakes, what on earth for?"

The Alabama lady responded, "So that I could learn to say, 'Isn't that nice,' instead of 'Who gives a shit!'"

A guy walked into a bar down in the Deep South and ordered a Grape Nehi. Surprised, the bartender looks around and says "You ain't from around here... where you from, boy?"

The guy answered, "I'm from Pennsylvania."

The bartender asked, "What do you do up in Pennsylvania?"

The guy responds, "I'm a taxidermist."

The bartender inquired, "A taxidermist... what the hell is a taxidermist?"

The guy replied, "I mount dead animals."

The bartender smiled and shouted to the whole bar, "It's OK boys, he's one of us."

• • •

### Auburn, FL, TN and Georgia Tech Engineering Exam

Calculate the smallest limb diameter on a persimmon tree that will support a 10-pound possum.

Which of the following cars will rust out the quickest when placed on blocks in your front yard? 66 Ford Fairlane, 69 Chevrolet Chevelle, 64 Pontiac GTO.

If your uncle builds a still that operates at a capacity of 20 gallons of 'shine per hour, how many car radiators are necessary to condense the product?

A front porch is constructed of 2x8 pine on 24-inch centers with a field rock foundation. The span is 8 feet and the porch length is 16 feet. The porch floor is 1-inch rough sawn pine. When the porch collapses, how many hound dogs will be killed?

A man owns a house and 3.7 acres of land in a hollow with an average slope of 15%. The man has 5 children. Can each of the children place a mobile home on the man's land?

A 2-ton pulpwood truck is overloaded and proceeding 900 yards down a steep grade on a secondary road at 45 mph. The brakes fail. Given the average traffic loading of secondary roads, what are the chances that it will strike a vehicle that has a muffler?

• • •

A redneck woman went to the school to register her boys. The office worker asked her, "How many children do you have?"

"Ten," she replied.

"And what are their names?" he asked.

"Bob, Bob, Bob, Bob, Bob, Bob, Bob, Bob, Bob, and Bob."

"They're ALL named Bob?" he asked. "What if you want them to come in from playing outside?"

"Oh, that's easy," she explained, "I just call 'Bob,' and they all come running inside."

"And if you want them to come to the table for dinner?"

"I just say, 'Bob, come eat your dinner,' and they do." She answered.

"But what if you want just ONE of them to do something?" he asked. "Oh, that's easy," she said. "I just use their last name."

• • •

### Italian Pasta Diet – It Really Works !!

1. You walka pasta da bakery.
2. You walka pasta da candy store.
3. You walka pasta da Ice Cream shop.
4. You walka pasta da table and fridge.

You *will* lose weight!

• • •

The Israelis and Arabs finally realized that if they continued fighting, they would some day end up destroying the world.

So they sat down and decided to settle the whole dispute with a dogfight. The negotiators agreed that each country would take five years to develop the best fighting dog they could. The dog that won the fight would earn its country the right to rule the disputed areas. The losing side would have to lay down its arms.

The Arabs found the biggest, meanest Dobermans, Pit-bulls, Rottweilers and Mastiffs in the world. They bred them together and then crossed their offspring with the meanest Siberian wolves. They selected only the biggest, strongest puppy from each litter, killed all the other puppies and fed them the best food. They used steroids and trainers in their quest for the perfect and efficient killing machine.

After the five years were up, they had a dog that needed high-strength steel prison bars on its cage. Only the trainers could handle this beast.

When the day of the big fight arrived, the Israelis showed up with a strange animal. It was a nine-foot-long Dachshund. Everyone felt sorry for the Israelis. No one else thought this weird animal stood a chance against the growling beast in the Arab camp. The bookies predicted the Arabs would win in less than a minute.

The cages were opened. The Dachshund waddled toward the center of the ring. The Arab dog leapt from his cage and charged the giant wiener-dog. As he got to within an inch of the Israeli dog, the Dachshund opened its jaws and swallowed the Arab beast in one bite. There was nothing left but a small bit of fur from the killer dog's tail.

The Arabs approached the Israelis, shaking their heads in disbelief. "We do not understand. Our top scientists and breeders worked for five years with the meanest, biggest Doberman Pinschers, Pit-bulls, Rottweilers, and Mastiffs. They developed a killing machine."

"Really?" the Israelis replied. "We had our top plastic surgeons working for five years to make a crocodile look like a Dachshund."

• • •

A gas station owner in Arkansas was trying to increase his sales, so he put up a sign that read, "Free Sex with Fill-Up."

## OTHER NATIONS, ETHNICITIES, AND REGIONS AS SUBJECTS OF HUMOR

Soon a local redneck pulled in, filled his tank and asked for his free sex. The owner told him to pick a number from 1 to 10. If he guessed correctly he would get his free sex.

The redneck guessed 8, and the proprietor said, "You were close. The number was 7. Sorry. No sex this time."

A week later, the same redneck, along with a buddy, Bubba, pulled in for another fill-up. Again he asked for his free sex. The proprietor again asked him to guess the correct number. The redneck guessed 2 this time. The proprietor said, "Sorry, it was 3. You were close, but no free sex this time."

As they were driving away, the redneck said to his buddy, "I think that game is rigged and he doesn't really give away free sex."

Bubba replied, "No, it ain't rigged. My wife won twice last week."

• • •

An Italian grandmother is giving directions to her grown grandson who is coming to visit with his wife.

"'You comma to de front door of the apartamenta. I am inna apartamenta 301. There issa bigga panel at the front door. With you elbow, pusha button 301. I will buzza you in. Come inside, the elevator is on the right. Get in, and with you elbow, pusha 3. When you get out, I'mma on the left. With you elbow, hit my doorbell.'"

"Grandma, that sounds easy, but, why am I hitting all these buttons with my elbow?

"Whata . . . You coming empty handed?"

• • •

### How to get to Heaven from Ireland

I was testing children in my Dublin Sunday school class to see if they understood the concept of getting to heaven.

I asked them, "If I sold my house and my car, had a big garage sale and gave all my money to the church, would that get me into heaven?"

"NO!" the children answered.

"If I cleaned the church every day, mowed the garden, and kept everything tidy, would that get me into heaven?"

Again, the answer was "NO!" By now I was starting to smile.

"Well, then, if I was kind to animals and gave sweets to all the children, and loved my husband, would that get me into heaven?"

Again, they all answered "NO!" I was just bursting with pride for them.

I continued, "Then how can I get into heaven?"

A six year-old boy shouted out: *"YUV GOTTA BE FOOKN' DEAD !"*

• • •

An old Native American grampa sat in his lodge on the reservation, smoking a ceremonial pipe and eying two US government officials sent to interview him.

"Chief Two Eagles, you have observed the white man for 90 years. You've seen his wars and his technological advances. You've seen his progress, and the damage he's done."

The Chief nodded in agreement.

The official continued, "Considering all these events, in your opinion, where did the white man go wrong?"

The Chief stared at the government officials for a minute and then calmly replied, "When white man found the land, Indians were living here. No tax, no debt, plenty buffalo, plenty beaver, women did all the work, Medicine Man free, Indian man spent all day hunting and fishing, All night having sex." Then the chief leaned back and smiled... "Only white man dumb enough to think he could improve system like that."

• • •

# Other Nations, Ethnicities, And Regions As Subjects Of Humor

"It's a curious race, the Irish."

—Oscar Wilde

• • •

Brian and Colin were walking down a street in London. Brian happened to look in one of the shop windows and saw a sign that caught his eye. The sign said: "Suits £5.00 each, Shirts £2.00 each, Trousers £2.50 per pair".

Brian says to his pal, "Colin, look! We could buy a whole lot of dose, and when we get back to Ireland, we could make a fortune. Now when we go into the shop, you be quiet, OK?" Just let me do all the talking, cause if they hear our accent, they might not be nice to us. I'll speak in my best English accent."

"Roight y'are, Brian, I'll keep me mouth shut, so I will," replies Colin.

They go in and Brian says, "I'll take 50 suits at £5.00 each, 100 shirts at £2.00 each, and 50 pairs of trousers at £2.50 each. I'll back up my van and…"

The owner of the shop interrupts. "You're from Ireland, aren't you?"

"Well… Yes," says a surprised Brian. "How de hell d'ye know dat?"

The owner replied, "This is a dry cleaners".

• • •

A man owned a small farm in Saskatchewan. The Saskatchewan Provincial Wage and Hours Department claimed he was not paying proper wages to his help and sent an agent out to interview him.

"I need a list of your employees and how much you pay them," demanded the agent.

"Well," replied the farmer, "there's my farm hand who's been with me for 3 years. pay him $200 a week plus free room and board. The cook has been here for 18 months, and I pay her $150 per week plus free room and board. Then there's the half- wit. He works about 18 hours every day and does about 90% of all the work around here. He makes about $10 per week, pays his own room and board, and I buy him a bottle of bourbon every Saturday night. He also sleeps with my wife occasionally."

"That's the guy I want to talk to ... the half-wit," says the agent.

"That would be me," replied the farmer.

• • •

An old Italian Mafia Don is dying and he calls for his grandson to approach the bed, *"Lissin a me. I wanna for you to taka my chrome-plated. 38-caliber revolver so you will always remember me."*

The grandson smiled weakly and replies,*"But Grandpa, I really doana lika guns. Howzabout you leava me you ROLEX watch instead?"*

Gasping for air, the old man answered with a snarl in his voice, *"Shuddup an lissin. Somma day you gonna runna da business. You gonna have a beautifula wife, lotsa money, a biga home, and may-bea a couple of bambinos."*

After a slight pause to catch his breath he continued, *"Somma day you gonna comma home and maybe find you wife inna bed with another man. Whadda you gonna do then...pointa to your watch and say 'Time's up?'"*

• • •

Jose' and Pedro worked together and both were laid; off so they went to the unemployment office.

When asked his occupation, Jose' answered, "Panty Stitcher. I sew da elastic on da ladies' cotton panties." The clerk looked up "Panty Stitcher." Finding it classified as "unskilled labor," she gave him $300 a week unemployment pay.

Pedro was asked his occupation. "Diesel Fitter," he replied. Since "Diesel Fitter" was a "skilled" job, the clerk gave Pedro $600 a week.

When Jose' found out, he was furious. He stormed back into the office to ask why his friend and co-worker was collecting double his pay.

The clerk explained, "Panty Stitchers" are "unskilled labor," but "Diesel Fitters" are "skilled."

"What skill?" yelled Jose'. "I sew da elastic on da panties, then Pedro puts dem over his head and says, "Yeah, diesel fitter."

• • •

A scouser from Liverpool, was on holiday in Arizona, USA. He was staying in a remote frontier type town and walked into a bar. He ordered his drink and sat down at the bar when he noticed a native American Indian, dressed in full regalia, feathered head dress, tomahawk, yew wood bow and arrows, the lot, sitting in the corner under a sign saying *"Ask me anything."*

The scouser was intrigued and asked the barman about him.

"Oh, we call him the memory man, he knows everything," replied the barman.

"What do you mean he knows everything?" inquired the scouser.

"Well, he knows every fact there is to know and he never, ever forgets anything."

"Yeah right," mocked the scouser.

"If you don't believe me, try him out. Ask him anything, and he'll know the answer."

"Alright" said the scouser and walked up to the Memory Man.

"Where am I from?"

"Knotty Ash, Liverpool, England" replied the Red Indian. And he was right.

"Alright" says the scouser, "That was easy you probably recognised my accent. Who won the 1965 FA Cup Final?"

"Liverpool" exclaimed the memory man quick as a flash.

"Yes and who did they play?"

"Leeds United," again without blinking

"And the score?"

"2-1" says the memory man without hesitation.

"Pretty good, but I bet you don't know who scored the winning goal?"

"Ian St John" replied the Indian in an instant.

Flabbergasted the tourist continues on his holiday and on his return to Birken- head told all and sundry about the amazing Memory Man. He just couldn't get him out of his mind and so he vowed to return and find him again and pay him his due respect.

He saves his dole money for years and finally twelve years later he has saved enough and returned to the 'states in search of the memory man. He searched high and low for him. And after two weeks of trying virtually every bar and town in Arizona he found him sitting in a cave in the mountains, older, greyer and more wrinkled than before but still resplendent in his war-paint and full regalia.

The scouser, duly humbled approached him and decided to greet him in the traditional manner

"How"

The memory man squints at the scouser.

"Flying header in the six yard box."

• • •

### A Jew Takes a Train Trip

After months of negotiation with the Soviet authorities, a Jewish scholar from Odessa was finally granted permission to visit Moscow. He boarded the train and found an empty seat. At the next stop, a young man got on and sat next to him. The scholar looked at the young man and thought, "This fellow doesn't look like a peasant, so if he is no peasant he probably comes from this district. If he comes from this district, then he must be Jewish because this is, after all, a Jewish district. But, on the other hand, if he is a Jew, where could he be going? I'm the only Jew in this district who has permission to travel to Moscow. Aahh, wait! Just outside Moscow there is a little village called Samvet, and Jews don't need special permission to go to Samvet. But why would he travel to Samvet? He is surely going to visit one of the Jewish families there. But how many Jewish families are there in Samvet? Aha, only two - the Bernsteins and the Steinbergs. But since the Bernsteins are a low, terrible, family, such a nice looking fellow as this young man must be visiting the Steinbergs. But why is he going to the Steinbergs in Samvet? The Steinbergs have only daughters, two of them, so maybe he's their son-in-law. But if he is, then which daughter did he marry? They say that Sarah Steinberg married a nice lawyer from Budapest, and Esther married a business-man from Zhitomer, so this must be Sarah's husband. Which means that his name is Alexander Cohen, if I'm not mistaken. "But if he came from Budapest, with all the anti-Semitism they have there, he must have changed his name. What's the Hungarian equivalent of Cohen? It is Kovacs. But since they allowed him to change his name, he must have special status to change it. What could it be? He must have a doctorate from the University. Nothing less would do."

At this point, therefore, the scholar turned to the young man and said, "Excuse me. Do you mind if I open the window, Dr. Kovacs?"

"Not at all," answered the startled fellow passenger. "But how is it that you know my name?"

"Ahhh," replies the Talmudist, "It was obvious."

• • •

Mrs. Yetta Rosenberg got off the plane in Miami and, being tired from the flight, went to the first hotel she saw in order to get a room. She walked up to the desk and told the clerk, "I'm Mrs. Yetta Rosenboig, and I desire a room for de night."

The clerk looked disdainfully at her and coldly replied, "I'm sorry, madam, but our hotel is "completely booked."

Just then, a man with his suitcase in hand, dropped his key and a check at the desk, and headed for the door.

"Oy, vot luck, says Mrs. Rosenberg. "I can take 'his' room."

"I'm sorry, madam," said the clerk, "but I thought you understood my meaning. To be blunt, we do not cater to Jews."

"Jews?" exclaimed Mrs. Rosenberg. "So, who's a Jew? I'm a Cat'lic."

In obvious disblief, the clerk asked her, "If you're a Catholic, then answer this question: Who is the Son of God?"

"Dot's easy," says Mrs. Rosenberg, "Jesus Christ."

The clerk, still not convinced, then askeds, "Who was Jesus' mother and father?"

"Mary and Joseph," replies Mrs. Rosenberg, testily.

Then the clerk asks, "And where was Jesus born?"

"In a manger in a barn," answers Mrs. Rosenberg, becoming agitated.

"And why was Jesus born in a manger in a barn?" asks the clerk.

"Cause a shmuck like you vouldn't rent a room to Jews!!!"

• • •

### You can retire to Phoenix, Arizona, where...

1. You are willing to park 3 blocks away because you found shade.
2. You've experienced condensation on your butt from the hot water in the toilet bowl.
3. You can drive for 4 hours in one direction and never leave town.
4. You have over 100 recipes for Mexican food.
5. You know that "dry heat" is comparable to what hits you in the face when you open your oven door.
6. The 4 seasons are: tolerable, hot, really hot, and ARE YOU KIDDING ME??!

• • •

### You can retire to California where...

1. You make over $250,000 and you still can't afford to buy a house.
2. The fastest part of your commute is going down your driveway.
3. You know how to eat an artichoke.

## Other Nations, Ethnicities, And Regions As Subjects Of Humor

4. You drive your rented Mercedes to your neighborhood block party.
5. When someone asks you how far something is, you tell them how long it will take to get there rather than how many miles away it is.
6. The 4 seasons are: Fire, Flood, Mud, and Drought.

• • •

### You can retire to New York City where...

1. You say "the city" and expect everyone to know you mean Manhattan
2. You can get into a four-hour argument about how to get from Columbus Circle to Battery Park, but can't find Wisconsin on a map.
3. You think Central Park is "nature."
4. You believe that being able to swear at people in their own language makes you multi-lingual.
5. You've worn out a car horn. (Editor's note: if you have a car)

### You can retire to Maine where —

1. You only have four spices: salt, pepper, ketchup, and Tabasco.
2. Halloween costumes fit over parkas.
3. You have more than one recipe for moose.
4. Sexy lingerie is anything flannel with less than eight buttons.
5. The four seasons are: winter, still winter, almost winter, and construction.

### You can retire to the Deep South where...

1. You can rent a movie and buy bait in the same store.
2. "Y'all" is singular and "all y'all" is plural.
3. "He needed killin'" is a valid defense.

4. Everyone has 2 first names: Billy Bob, Jim Bob, Jimmy Joe, Betty Jean, Mary Beth, etc.
5. Everything is either "in yonder," "over yonder" or "out yonder." It's important to know the difference, too.

### You can retire to Colorado where...

1. You carry your $3,000 mountain bike atop your $500 car.
2. You tell your husband to pick up Granola on his way home and so he stops at the day care center to get her.
3. A pass does not involve a football or dating.
4. The top of your head is bald, but you still have a pony tail.
5. Your feet are frozen, but your face is sun burnt.

### You can retire to the Midwest where...

1. You've never met any celebrities, but the mayor knows your name.
2. Your idea of a traffic jam is ten cars waiting to pass a tractor.
3. You have had to switch from "heat" to "A/C" on the same day.
4. You end sentences with a preposition: "Where's my coat at?"
5. When asked how your trip was to any exotic place, you say, "It was different!"

### or– You can retire to Florida where...

1. You eat dinner at 3:15 in the afternoon.
2. All purchases include a coupon of some kind – even houses and cars.
3. Everyone can recommend an excellent dermatologist.
4. Road construction never ends anywhere in the state.
5. Humidity can necessitate a shower if you've walked from your front door to the car.
6. Cars in front of you often appear to be driven by headless people.

• • •

# Other Nations, Ethnicities, And Regions As Subjects Of Humor

Bruce, an Australian who was working on contract for 3 months in Dublin was drinking in O'Donoghue's pub in Merrion Row when he got a call on his mobile phone. He hangs up grinning from ear to ear, orders a round of drinks for everyone in the bar, because, he announced his wife back home had just produced a typical baby boy weighing 25 pounds.

Nobody can believe that any baby can weigh in at 25 pounds but Bruce just shrugs,

"That's about average in Oz. Like I said my boy is a typical Australian baby boy.

Congratulations showered him from all around and many exclamations were heard. One woman even fainted due to sympathy pains.

Two weeks later Bruce returns to the bar. Greg, the bartender says "You're the father of that typical Australian baby that weighed 25 pounds at birth. Everybody's been having bets about how big he'd be in 2 weeks, we were going to call you. So how much does he weigh now?"

The proud father answers "17 pounds"

Greg is puzzled and concerned.

"What happened? He weighed 25 pounds the day he was born."

Bruce takes a long s-l-o-w swig from his beer, wipes his lips on his shirt sleeve, leaned onto the bar and proudly replied .... "Had him circumcised mate"

• • •

A young Japanese girl had been taught all her life that when she married she was to please her husband and never upset him. So the first morning of her honey-moon the young Japanese bride crawled out of bed after making love, stooped down to pick up her husband's clothes and accidentally let out a big fart. She looked up and said: "Aww so sowwy ... excuse prease, front hole so happy back hole laugh out loud."

• • •

After their third child, an Alabama couple decided that was enough, as they could not afford a larger bed.

So the husband went to his veterinarian and told him that he and his cousin didn't want to have more children.

The good doctor told them that there was a surgical procedure called a vasectomy that could fix the problem but that it was pretty expensive. "A less costly alternative," said the doctor, "is to go home, get a cherry bomb" (fireworks are legal in Alabama) and put it in an empty beer can and hold it up to your, and count to 10."

So the Alabaman said to the vet, "I may not be the smartest tool in the shed, Doc, but I don't see how puttin' a cherry bomb in a beer can next to my ear is going to help me."

"Trust me." Replied the learned veterinarian.

So the Alabaman went home, put a lit cherry bomb into an empty beer can, put it up to his ear and began to count:

"1, 2, 3, 4, 5," at which point he paused placed the beer can between his legs and resumed the count on his other hand.

This procedure works well in Kentucky, Arkansas, Tennessee, Mississippi, West Virginia, Louisiana, Texas, North and South Carolina and Georgia

• • •

The European Commission has just announced an agreement whereby English will be the official language of the European Union rather than German, which was the other possibility.

As part of the negotiations, the British Government conceded that English spelling had some room for improvement and has accepted a 5- year phase-in plan that would become known as "Euro-English."

In the first year, "s" will replace the soft "c." Sertainly, this will make the sivil servants jump with joy. The hard "c" will be dropped in favour of "k." This should klear up konfusion, and keyboards kan have one less letter. There will be growing publik enthusiasm in the sekond year when the troublesome "ph" will be replaced with "f." This will make words like fotograf 20% shorter.

In the 3rd year, publik akseptanse of the new spelling kan be expekted to reach the stage where more komplikated changes are possible. Governments will enkourage the removal of double letters which have always ben a deterent to akurate speling. Also, al wil agre that the horibl mes of the silent "e" in the languag is disgrasful and it should go away.

By the 4th yer people wil be reseptiv to steps such as replasing "th" with "z" and "w"with "v."

During ze fifz yer, ze unesesary "o" kan be dropd from vords kontaining "ou" and after ziz fifz yer, ve vil hav a reil sensi bl riten styl. Zer vil be no mor trubl or difikultis und evrivun vil find it ezi tu understand ech oza. Ze drem of a united urop vil finali kum tru. Und efter ze fifz yer, ve vil al be speking German like zey vunted in ze vorst plas If zis mad you smil, pleas pas on to oza pepl.

• • •

Three strangers strike up a conversation in the airport passenger lounge in Bozeman, Montana, while awaiting their respective flights. One is an American Indian passing through from Lame Deer. Another is a Cowboy on his way to Billings for a livestock show and the third passenger is a fundamentalist Arab student, newly arrived at Montana State University from the Middle East.

Their discussion drifts to their diverse cultures. Soon, the two Westerners learn that the Arab is a devout, radical Muslim and the conversation fell into an uneasy lull.

The cowboy leaned back in his chair, crossed his boots on a magazine table and tipped his big sweat-stained hat forward over his face. The wind outside was blowing tumbleweeds around, and the old windsock was flapping; but still no plane came.

Finally, the American Indian cleared his throat and softly he spoke, "At one time here, my people were many, but sadly, now we are few."

The Muslim student raised an eyebrow and leaned forward, "Once my people were few," he sneers, "and now we are many. Why do you suppose that is?"

The Montana cowboy shifted his toothpick to one side of his mouth and from the darkness beneath his Stetson intoned in a smooth drawl, "That's 'cause America ain't played Cowboys and Muslims yet, but I do believe it's a-comin'."

• • •

The mayor of Houston Texas was very worried about a plague of pigeons in Houston. The mayor could not remove the pigeons from the city. All of Houston was full of pigeon poop. The people of Houston couldn't walk on the sidewalks or drive on the roads. It was costing a fortune to try to keep the streets and sidewalks clean.

One day a man came to City Hall and offered the Mayor a proposition. "I can rid your beautiful city of its plague of pigeons without cost to the city. But, you must promise not to ask me any questions. Or, you can pay me five million dollars and ask *one* question."

The mayor considered the offer briefly and accepted the free proposition.

The next day the man climbed to the top of City Hall, opened his coat, and released a red pigeon. The red pigeon circled in the air and flew up into the bright blue Texas sky. All the pigeons in Houston saw the red pigeon. They gathered up behind the red pigeon. The Houston pigeons followed the red pigeon as she flew eastward out of the city.

The next day the red pigeon returned completely alone to the man atop City Hall. The Mayor was very impressed. He thought the man and the red pigeon had performed a wonderful miraculous feat to rid Houston of the plague of pigeons.

## Other Nations, Ethnicities, And Regions As Subjects Of Humor

Even though the man with the pigeon had charged nothing, the mayor presented him with a check for 5 million dollars and told the man that, indeed, he did have a question to ask and even though they had agreed to no fee and the man had rid the city of pigeons, he decided to pay the 5 million just to get to ask *one* question.

The man accepted the money and told the mayor to ask his question.

The mayor asked: "Do you have any red Mexicans?

• • •

The first Texan says, "My name is Roger. I own 50,000 acres. I have 1,000 head of cattle and they call my place The Jolly Roger."

The second Texan says, "My name is John. I own 250,000 acres. I have 5,000 head of cattle and they call my place Big John's Ranchero."

They both look down at the Jewish man who said, "My name is Irving and I own 40 acres."

Roger looked down at him and said, "40 Acres? What do you raise?"

"Nothing" Irving replied.

"Well then, what do you call it?" asked John.

The little old Jewish man answered, "Downtown Dallas."

• • •

"Only thing worse than a Frenchman is a Frenchman who lives in Canada." Ted Nugent

• • •

"War without France would be like ….. World War II." Unknown

• • •

"What do you expect from a culture and a nation that exerted more of its national will fighting against Disney World and Big Macs than the Nazis?" Dennis Miller

• • •

"It is important to remember that the French have always been there when they needed us." Alan Kent

• • •

"They've taken their own precautions against al-Qa'eda. To prepare for an attack, each Frenchman is urged to keep duct tape, a white flag, and a three-day supply of mistresses in the house." Argus Hamilton

• • •

"Somebody was telling me about the French Army rifle that was being advertised on eBay the other day – the description was, 'Never shot. Dropped once.'" Roy Blunt, Missouri

• • •

"The French will only agree to go to war when we've proven we've found truffles in Iraq." Dennis Miller

• • •

"Raise your right hand if you like the French, … raise both hands if you are French." Unknown

• • •

## Other Nations, Ethnicities, And Regions As Subjects Of Humor

Q. What did the mayor of Paris say to the German Army as they entered the city in WWII? A. Table for 100,000 m'sieur?

• • •

"Do you know how many Frenchmen it takes to defend Paris? It's not known, it's never been tried." Roy Blunt, Missouri

• • •

"Do you know it only took Germany three days to conquer France in WWII? And that's because it was raining." John Xereas, Manager, DC Improv

• • •

The AP and UPI reported that the French Government announced after the London bombings that it had raised its terror alert level from *Run* to *Hide*. The only two higher levels in France are *Surrender* and *Collaborate*. The rise in the alert level was precipitated by a recent fire which destroyed France's white flag factory, effectively disabling their military.

• • •

French Ban Fireworks at Euro Disney (AP), Paris, March 5, 2003
The French Government announced today that it was imposing a ban on the use of fireworks at Euro Disney. The decision comes the day after a nightly fireworks display at the park, located just 30 miles outside of Paris, caused the soldiers at a nearby French Army garrison to surrender to a group of Czech tourists.

• • •

Jacques Chirac, The French Prime Minister, was sitting in his office wondering what kind of mischief he could perpetrate against the United States when his telephone rang. "Hallo, Mr. Chirac!," a heavily accented voice said. "This is Paddy down at the Harp Pub in County Sligo, Ireland. I am ringing to inform ya that we are officially declaring war on ya!"

"Well, Paddy," Chirac replied, "This is indeed important news! How big is your army?"

"Right now," said Paddy after a moment's calculation, "there's meself, me cousin Sean, me next door neighbor Seamus, and the entire dart team from the pub. That makes eight!"

Chirac paused. "I must tell you, Paddy that I have one hundred thousand men in my army waiting to move on my command."

"Begorra!" said Paddy. "I'll have ta ring ya back!"

Sure enough, the next day, Paddy called again.

"Mr. Chirac, the war is still on. We have managed ta get us some infantry equip- ment!"

"And what equipment would that be, Paddy" Chirac asked.

"Well, we have two combines, a bulldozer, and Murphy's farm tractor."

Chirac sighed, amused. "I must tell you, Paddy, that I have 6,000 tanks and 5,000 armored personnel carriers. Also, I've increased my army to one hundred fifty thousand since we last spoke."

"Saints preserve us!" said Paddy. "I'll have ta get back to ya."

Sure enough, Paddy rang again the next day.

"Mr. Chirac, the war is still on! We have managed ta get ourselves airborne! We've modified Jackie McLaughlin's ultra-light with a couple o' shotguns in the cockpit, and four boys from Aidan Kelly's Shamrock Pub have joined us as well!"

Chirac was silent for a minute and then cleared his throat. "I must tell you, Paddy, that I have 100 bombers and 200 fighter planes. My military complex is surrounded by laser-guided, surface-to-air missile sites. And since we last spoke, I've increased my army to two hundred thousand!"

## OTHER NATIONS, ETHNICITIES, AND REGIONS AS SUBJECTS OF HUMOR

"Jesus, Mary, and Joseph!" said Paddy, "I'll have ta ring ya back."

Sure enough, Paddy called again the next day.

"Top o' the mornin', Mr. Chirac, I am sorry ta tell ya that we have had ta call off the war."

"I'm sorry to hear that," said Chirac. "Why the sudden change of heart?"

"Well," said Paddy, "We've all had a long chat over a bunch o' pints, and decided there's no fookin way we can feed two hunerd tousand prisoners."

• • •

When George Burns was 97 years old he was interviewed by Oprah Winfrey. Oprah asked, "Mr. Burns, how do you carry so much energy with you? You are always working and at your age I think that is remarkable."

George Burns replied," I just take good care of myself and enjoy what I do when I do it."

Oprah said," I understand you still do the sex thing, even at your age."

George said, "Of course I still do the sex thing, and I am quite good at it."

Oprah said, "I have never been with an older man, would you do it with me?" So they had sex and when they finished Oprah said, "I just don't believe I have ever been so satisfied, you are a remarkable man.

George said, "The second time is even better than the first time."

Oprah said, "You can really do it again at your age?"

George said, "Just let me sleep for 1/2 hour. You hold my testicles in your left hand and my penis in your right hand and wake me up in thirty minutes."

When she woke him up, they again had great sex, and Oprah was beside herself with joy. She said, "Oh Mr. Burns, I am astounded that you could do a repeat performance and have it be better than the first time. At your age, Oh My, Oh My!!!"

George said that the third time would be even better. "You just hold my testicles in your left hand and my penis in your right hand and call me in thirty minutes."

Oprah said, "Does me holding you like that kind of recharge your batteries?"

George said, "No, but the last time I had sex with a black woman she stole my wallet."

• • •

This one, 'says it all', about the basic philosophy of our country and what it is all about, and how we are received around the world.

At the Charles De Gaul Airport....A group of American retired teachers recently went to France on a tour. Robert Whiting, an elderly gentleman of 83, was part of the tour group. At French Customs, he took a few minutes to locate his passport in his carry-on.

"You have been to France before, monsieur?" the customs officer asked sarcastically.

Mr. Whiting admitted that he had been to France, previously.

"Then you should know enough to have your passport ready."

The American said, "The last time I was here, I didn't have to show it."

"Impossible!" barked the officer. "Americans always have to show their passports on arrival in France."

The American senior gave the Frenchman a long hard look. Then he quietly explained: "Well, when I came ashore at Omaha Beach on D-Day in June, 1944 to help liberate this country, I couldn't find any Frenchmen to show it to."

• • •

Seamus was in court for a double murder and the judge said, "You are charged with beating your wife to death with a spanner wrench."

A voice at the back of the courtroom yelled out, "You bastard!"

The judge continued, "You are also charged with beating your daughter to death with a spanner."

Again, the voice at the back of the courtroom yelled out, "You fucking bastard!"

The judge stopped, looked at the man in the back of the courtroom, and said, "Paddy, I can understand your anger and frustration at this crime, but I will not have any more of these outbursts from you or I shall charge you with contempt! Now what is the problem?"

Paddy, at the back of the court stood up and responded, "For fifteen years I lived next door to that bastard. And every time I asked to borrow a fucking spanner, he said he didn't have one!"

• • •

Mick died in a fire and was burnt pretty badly. So the morgue needed someone to identify the body. His two best friends, Seamus and Colin were sent for. Seamus went in and the mortician pulled back the sheet.

Seamus said "Yup, he's burnt pretty bad. Roll him over."

So the mortician rolled him over.

Seamus looked and said "Nope, it ain't Mick."

The mortician thought that was rather strange and then he brought Colin in to identify the body. Colin took a look at him and said, "Yup, he's burnt real bad, roll him over."

The mortician rolled him over and Sean looked down and said, "No, it ain't Mick."

The mortician asked, "How can you tell?"

Colin said, "Well, Mick had two arseholes."

"What, he had *two* arseholes?" inquired the mortician.

"Yup, everyone knew he had two arseholes. Every time we went into town, folks would say, "Here comes Paddy with them two arseholes...."

• • •

Five Englishmen in an Audi Quattro arrived at an Irish border checkpoint.

Sean the officer stops them and tells them: "It is illegal to put 5 people in a Quattro; Quattro means four"

"Quattro is just the name of the automobile," the Englishman retorted disbelievingly. "Look at the papers: this car is designed to carry five persons."

"You cannot pull that one on me," replied Sean, "Quattro means four You have five people in your car and you are therefore breaking the law.

The Englishmen replied angrily, "You idiot! Call your supervisor over; I want to speak to someone with more intelligence!"

Sorry," responds Sean, "Murphy is busy with 2 guys in a Fiat Uno."

• • •

A Polish immigrant went to the DMV to apply for a driver's license. First, of course, he had to take an eye sight test. The technician showed him a card with the letters: 'C Z W I X N O S T A C Z.'

"Can you read this?" the technician asked.

"Read it?" the Polish immigrant replied, "I know the man."

• • •

Two partners, Sol and Abe, in the *schmata* (retail inexpensive clothing) business in New York's Garment District have done very well.

One day Abe says to Sol, "Solly, we've worked hard and done very well. I think we should take a really exotic vacation"

They think about it and decide to go on a safari. The next thing you know they're at Abercrombie & Fitch getting outfitted for a trip to Africa.

On their second day in Africa they're following their guide through the tall grass when Sol feels something pushing him in the back.

Frozen with fear, he says to his partner, "Abe! Something is nudging me in the back. Take a look and tell me is it a Tiger or a Leopard?"

To this his partner replies "What am I? A furrier?"

• • •

Solomon and Sadie were married for just a little less than fifty years when suddenly, Solomon died. Of course, Sadie was bereft and tended to let herself "go" a bit. However, after a while, one of her friends convinced Sadie to get back into living a more or less normal life. First, her friend suggested, get another hair style and some new clothes that showed her figure to its best. Then, her friend advised, contact an escort service to find a younger man to take her out; someone who knew how to order dinner from a fancy menu; which fine wine to pair with a particular menu item; someone who could dance well.

Well, Sadie did just that. She contacted an escort service and requested that they send a chap who could take her to a fine dinner, order from a grand menu, liked fine wines, and who could dance well.

Soon, Sadie's doorbell rang. She rushed to open her door and there, standing smartly dressed in a Brooks Brothers suit was a tall, well-built, handsome black fellow, Leroy Jackson.

To make a lengthy story a bit shorter, Leroy was absolutely perfect. He knew just the restaurants to which the couple should visit; which wines to order that best suited a particular menu item; and, he danced perfectly, knowing all of the newest dances.

Sadie was so pleased that she booked Leroy for the next six weeks. On the sixth "date" she invited Leroy in for a nightcap after they had dined and danced the evening through. Without much ado, Sadie invited Leroy to her bedroom. Her invitation was accepted and she was ever so satisfied. A few days later, Sadie visited her gynecologist for her annual routine examination.

The physician found everything perfectly normal and, as was his custom, he asked Sadie to come into his private office to discuss his findings and answer any questions that she might have. Amongst his comments was that he found Sadie seemingly happier than he had seen her in years. Also, he commented that her vagina was cleaner than he had ever found it. How did she account for that?

"*Vell,*" Sadie replied, "*I have a schwartza come in once a week,*"

• • •

Everyone seems to be wondering why Muslim terrorists are so quick to commit suicide. Let's have a look at the evidence:

- No Christmas
- No television
- No nude women
- No football
- No pork chops
- No hot dogs
- No burgers
- No beer
- No bacon
- Rags for clothes
- Towels for hats
- Constant wailing from some idiot in a tower
- More than one wife
- More than one mother in law
- You can't shave

- Your wife can't shave
- You can't wash off the smell of donkey
- You wipe your ass with your left hand
- You cook over burning camel shit
- Your wife is picked by someone else for you
- and your wife smells worse than your donkey

Then they tell you that "when you die, it all gets better"??
Well no shit Sherlock!.... It's not like it could get much worse

• • •

The bottom line: The Arabs **aren't** happy!

They're not happy in Gaza.
They're not happy in Egypt.
They're not happy in Libya.
They're not happy in Morocco.
They're not happy in Iran.
They're not happy in Iraq.
They're not happy in Yemen.
They're not happy in Afghanistan.
They're not happy in Pakistan.
They're not happy in Syria.
They're not happy in Lebanon.
They're not happy in Sudan.
They're not happy in Somalia
They're not happy in Nigeria

HOWEVER –

And where **are** they happy?

They're happy in Canada.
They're happy in England.

They're happy in France.
They're happy in Italy.
They're happy in Germany.
They're happy in Sweden.
They're happy in Norway.
They're happy in Denmark
They're happy in the USA.
They're happy in Australia.
They're happy in New Zealand.

They're happy in every country that is not Muslim.
And **who** do they blame?

Not Islam.
Not their leadership.
Not themselves.

THEY BLAME THE COUNTRIES IN WHICH THEY **ARE** HAPPY.

• • •

Paddy had been drinking at his local Dublin pub all day and most of the night.

Brian, the bartender, said "You'll not be drinking any more tonight, Paddy." Paddy replied "OK Brian, me man, I'll be on my way then."

Paddy spun around on his stool and stepped off. He fell flat on his face. "What the...." he said and pulled himself up by the stool and dusted himself off. He took a step toward the door and fell flat on his face again. "Damn!" he said. He looked to the doorway and thought that if he can just get to the door and got some fresh air he'd be fine. He belly crawled to the door and shimmied up the door frame. He stuck his head outside and took a deep breath of fresh air, felt much better and took a step out onto the pavement and fell flat on his face.

"Bi' Jesus... I'm soused," he said. He can see his house just a few doors down, and decided to try for it. He crawled down the street and shimmied up the door frame, opened the door and looked inside. He took a look up the stairs and said, "No fookin' way."

But he somehow crawled up the stairs to his bedroom door and thought, "I think I can make it to the bed." He took a step into the room and fell flat on his face again. He exclaimed, "This is hell. I gotta stop drinking," but managed to crawl to the bed and fall in.

The next morning, his wife came into the room carrying a cup of coffee and said, "Get up Paddy. Did you have a wee bit to drink last night?"

Paddy replied, "I did Jess. I was totally pissfaced. But how'd you know?"

"Brian called. You left your wheelchair at the pub."

• • •

Two paddies, Ryan and Flynn, were working for the city public works department. One would dig a hole and the other would follow behind him and fill the hole in. They worked up one side of the street, then down the other, then moved on to the next street, working furiously all day without rest, one man digging a hole, the other filling it in again.

An onlooker was amazed at their hard work, but couldn't understand what they were doing. So he asked the hole-digger, "I'm impressed by the effort you two are putting into your work, but I don't get it: why do you dig a hole, only to have your partner follow behind and fill it up again?"

The hole digger wiped his brow and sighed, "Well, I suppose it probably looks odd because we're normally a three-person team. But today the lad who plants the trees called in sick."

• • •

A woman from New York was driving through a remote part of Arizona when her car broke down.

A Navaho on horseback came along and offered her a ride to a nearby town.

She climbed up behind him on the horse and they rode off. The ride was uneventful, except that every few minutes the Indian would let out a Ye-e-e-e-h-a-a-a-a' so loud that it echoed from the surrounding hills.

When they arrived in town, he let her off at the local service station, yelled one final 'Ye-e-e-e-h-a-a-a-a!' and rode off.

"'What did you do to get that Indian so excited?" asked the service-station attendant.

"Nothing, the woman answered. "I merely sat behind him on the horse, put my arms around his waist, and held onto the saddle pommel so I wouldn't fall off.'

"Lady," the attendant said, 'Indians don't use saddles'

• • •

### Chinese Call Center

Caller: Hello, can I speak to Annie Wan?

Operator: *Yes, you can speak to me..*

Caller: No, I want to speak to Annie Wan!

Operator: *Yes I understand you want to speak to anyone. You can speak to me.. Who is this?*

Caller: I'm Sam Wan: And I need to talk to Annie Wan! It's urgent.

Operator*: I know you are someone and you want to talk to anyone, but what's this urgent matter about?*

Caller: Well just tell my sister Annie Wan that our brother Noe Wan was involved in an accident. Noe Wan got injured and now Noe Wan is being sent to the hospital.

Right now, Avery Wan is on his way to the hospital.

Operator: *Look, if no one was injured and no one was sent to the hospital, then the accident isn't an urgent matter! You may find this hilarious but I don't have time for this!*

## Other Nations, Ethnicities, And Regions As Subjects Of Humor

Caller: You are so rude! Who are you?
Operator: *I'm Saw Ree ..*
Caller: Yes! You should be sorry. Now give me your name!!
Operator: *That's what I said. I'm Saw Ree ..*
Caller: Oh God.

• • •

Rajesh wanted to have sex with a girl in his office, but she belonged to someone else. One day, Rajesh got so frustrated that he went up to her and said, "I'll give you a 100 Rupees if you let me shag you.

But the girl said "No, never!"

Rajesh said, "I'll be fast. I'll throw the money on the floor, you bend down, and I'll be finished by the time you pick it up."

She thought for a moment and said that she would have to consult her boyfriend. So she called her boyfriend and told him the story.

Her boyfriend replied, "Ask him for R200, pick up the money very fast, he won't even be able to get his pants down."

So she agreed and accepted the proposal. Half an hour went by, and the boy- friend was waiting for his girlfriend to call. Finally, after 45 minutes, the boyfriend called and asked what happened.

She responded, "The bastard used *coins!*"

Management lesson: When dealing with anyone, *Always* consider a business proposal in its entirety before agreeing to it and getting screwed!

• • •

**Consider The Difference When You Marry a Scottish Girl:**

Three friends married women from different parts of the UK. The first man married a woman from Wales. He told her that she was to do the dishes and house cleaning. It took a couple of days, but on the third day, he came home to see a clean house and dishes washed and put away.

The second man married a woman from England. He gave his wife orders that she was to do all the cleaning, dishes and the cooking. The first day he didn't see any results, but the next day he saw it was better. By the third day, he saw his house was clean, the dishes were done, and there was a huge dinner on the table.

The third man married a girl from Scotland. He ordered her to keep the house cleaned, dishes washed, lawn mowed, laundry washed, and hot meals on the table for every meal. He said the first day he didn't see anything, the second day he didn't see anything but by the third day, some of the swelling had gone down and he could see a little out of his left eye, and his arm was healed enough that he could fix himself a sandwich and load the dishwasher. He still has some difficulty when he pees.

• • •

### Irish Burial at Sea

Seamus and Kilkenny had promised their Uncle Flynn, who had been a sea-faring gent all his life, to bury him at sea when he died. Of course, in due time, he *did* pass away and the boys kept their promise.

They set off with Uncle Simon all stitched up in a burial bag and loaded it onto their rowboat. After a while Seamus said, 'Do yer think this is fer enuff out, Kilkenny?'

Without a word Kilkenny slipped over the side only to find himself standing in water up to his knees. "This'll never do, Seamus. Let's row some more."

After a bit more rowing Kilkenny slipped over the side again, but the water was still only up to his belly, so they rowed on.

Again Seamus asked Kilkenny, "Do yer think this is fer enuff out?"

Once again Seamus slipped over the side and almost immediately said, 'No this'll neva do.' The water was only up to his chest.

So on they row and row and row and finally Kilkenny slipped over the side and disappeared. Quite a bit of time went by and poor Seamus was really getting himself into a state when suddenly Kilkenny broke the surface gasping for breath.

'Well is it deep enuff yet, Paddy?'

Aye "tis, NOW hand me that fookin' shovel."

• • •

### Yossell the Putz

Yossell the Hassid was in London on business. It was now one hour until *shabbos* (Sabbath) and he was all dressed up in his shabbos clothes ready to go to a local synagogue.

He took the lift to the ground floor and walked towards the exit, as he reached the reception area he saw a stunning British Airways hostess with blond hair and a face and figure you could die for. She had just checked in. As soon as she spied Yossell, she stopped in her tracks and walked quickly over to him.

"Hello," she said to him.

"Hello to you, too," he replied.

"I have a confession to make," she said.

"What is it?" he inquired.

"I have a sexual fantasy," she confessed.

"Nu, so go on," he said.

"I've always wanted to be with a Hassidic man. I want to run my hands up and down his white silk socks, run my hands over his *tzitzis* and my fingers through his beard, play with his *peyess*, eat *kichel* with him, poke my finger in his *puppik*, remove his *gatkes*, play with his *schlong* and then *shtup*. So, I want you to join me now? I have a room upstairs just waiting for us. What do you say?"

Yossell looked at her thoughtfully and asked, "And so, what's in it for me?"

### The Arab and the Scotsman

An Arab Sheik was admitted to St Vincent's Hospital for heart surgery, but prior to the surgery, the doctors decided to store his blood in case the need arose. As the gentleman had a rare type of blood, it couldn't be found locally, so, the call went out to all the states. Finally a Scot was located who had a similar blood type. The Scot willingly donated his blood for the Arab.

After the surgery, the Arab sent the Scotsman as appreciation for giving his blood, a new BMW, diamonds and US dollars.

A couple of days later, once again, the Arab had to go through a corrective surgery. His doctor telephoned the Scotsman who was more than happy to donate his blood again.

After the second surgery, the Arab sent the Scotsman a Thank-You card and a jar of candies.

The Scotsman was shocked that the Arab this time did not reciprocate his kind gesture as he had anticipated. He phoned the Arab and asked him, "I thought you would be generous again, that you would give me a BMW, diamonds and money, but you only gave me a thank-you card and a jar of candies".

To this the Arab replied: "Aye, but I now have Scottish blood in my veins".

• • •

Mrs. Murphy and Mrs. Cohen had been longtime close friends. But, being old-fashioned, each went to a retirement home of their own respective religion. It was not long before Mrs. Murphy felt lonesome for Mrs. Cohen, so one day she asked to be driven to the Jewish Home to visit her old friend. When she arrived she was greeted with open arms, hugs and kisses.

Mrs. Murphy said, "Don't be holding back, Mrs. Cohen, how do you like it here?"

Mrs. Cohen went on and on about the wonderful food, the facility and the care-takers. Then, with a twinkle in her eye she said, "But the best thing is that I now have a boyfriend."

Mrs. Murphy said, "Now isn't that wonderful! Tell me all about him."

Mrs. Cohen said, "After lunch, we go up to my room and sit on the edge of the bed. I let him touch me on the top, and then on the bottom, and then we sing Jewish songs."

Mrs. Murphy said, "For sure it's surely a blessing. I'm so glad for you, Mrs. Cohen."

Mrs. Cohen said, "And how is it with you, Mrs. Murphy?"

Mrs. Murphy said it was also wonderful at her new facility, and that she too now has a boyfriend. "We also go up to my room after lunch and sit on the edge of the bed. Like you, I let him touch me on top, and then I let him touch me down below."

Mrs. Cohen said, "Yes? And then what happens?"

Mrs. Murphy said, "Well, since we don't know any Jewish songs, we fuck."

• • •

Brendan O'Leary went to the vet with his goldfish.
"I think it's got epilepsy" he tells the vet.
The vet takes a look and says "It seems calm enough to me".
Brendan says, "I haven't taken it out of the bowl yet".

• • •

### Things I learned in the South

A possum is a flat animal that sleeps in the middle of the road.
There are 5,000 types of snakes and 4,998 of them live in the South.
There are 10,000 types of spiders. All 10,000 of them live in the South, plus a couple no one's seen before.

If it grows, it'll stick ya. If it crawls, it'll bite cha.
Onced and Twiced are words.
It is not a shopping cart, it is a buggy!
Jawl-P? Means, did you all go to the bathroom?
People actually grow, eat and like okra.
Fixinto is one word. It means I'm going to do that.

There is no such thing as lunch. There is only dinner and then there's supper.

Iced tea is appropriate for all meals and you start drinking it when you're two.

We do like a little tea with our sugar. It is referred to as the Wine of the South.

Backwards and forwards means I know everything about you.

The word jeet is actually a question meaning, 'Did you eat?'

You don't have to wear a watch, because it doesn't matter what time it is,

You work until you're done or it's too dark to see.

You don't PUSH buttons, you MASH em.

Ya'll is singular. All ya'll is plural.

All the festivals across the state are named after a fruit, vegetable, grain, insect, or animal.

You carry jumper cables in your car - for your *OWN* car.

You only own six spices: salt, pepper, garlic, mustard, Tabasco and ketchup.

The local papers cover national and international news on one page, but require 6 pages for local high school sports, the motor sports, and gossip.

You think that the first day of deer season should be a national holiday.

You know what a hissyfit is.

Fried catfish is the other white meat.

We don't need no dang Driver's Ed. If our mama says we can drive, we can drive!!!

• • •

## Other Nations, Ethnicities, And Regions As Subjects Of Humor

Paddy spied a letter lying on his doormat. It read on the envelope "DO NOT BEND. "

Paddy spends the next 2 hours trying to figure out how to pick up the bloody thing.

• • •

Ryan shouted frantically into the phone "My wife is pregnant and her contractions are only two minutes apart!"

"Is this her first child?" asks the Doctor.

"No", shouts Ryan, "This is her husband!"

• • •

Finnegan was driving home, drunk as a skunk, suddenly he had to swerve to avoid a tree, then another, then another.

A cop car pulled him over as he veered about all over the road.

Finnegan told the cop about all the trees in the road.

Cop says "For God's sake Finnegan, that's your air freshener swinging about!"

• • •

An old Irish farmer's dog went missing and he was inconsolable.

His wife said "Why don't you put an advert in the paper?"

He did, but two weeks later the dog was still missing.

"What did you put in the paper?" his wife asked.

"Here boy" he replied.

• • •

O'Shaunacy was in jail. The guard looked in his cell and sees him hanging by his feet.

"What the hell you doing?" he asked.

"Hanging meself," O'Shaunacy replied.

"It should be around your neck" says the Guard.

"I know" says O'Shaunacy "I tried that but I couldn't breathe".

• • •

An American tourist asked an Irishman: "Why do Scuba divers always fall backwards off their boats?"

To which the Irishman replies: "If they fell forwards, they'd still be in the bloody boat."

• • •

A short time ago, Iran's Supreme Leader Grand Ayatollah Ali urged the Muslim World to boycott anything and everything that originates with the Jewish people. In response, Meyer M. Treinkman, a pharmacist, out of the kindness of his heart, offered to assist them in their boycott as follows:

"Any Muslim who has Syphilis must not be cured by Salvarsan discovered by a Jew, Dr. Ehrlich. He should not even try to find out whether he has Syphilis, because the Wasserman Test is the discovery of a Jew. If a Muslim suspects that he has Gonorrhea, he must not seek diagnosis, because he will be using the method of a Jew named Neissner."

"A Muslim who has heart disease must not use digitalis, a discovery by a Jew, Ludwig Traube."

"Should he suffer with a toothache, he must not use novocaine, a discovery of the Jews, Widal and Weil."

"If a Muslim has diabetes, he must not use Insulin, the result of research by Minkowsky, a Jew. If one has a headache, he must shun pyramidon and antypyrin, due to the Jews, Spiro and Ellege."

"Muslims with convulsions must put up with them because it was a Jew, Oscar Leibreich, who proposed the use of chloral hydrate."

"Arabs must do likewise with their psychic ailments because Freud, father of psychoanalysis, was a Jew."

"Should a Muslim child contract diphtheria, he must refrain from the "Schick" reaction which was invented by the Jew, Bella Schick."

"Muslims should be ready to die in great numbers and must not permit treatment of ear and brain damage, work of Nobel Prize winner, Robert Baram."

"They should continue to die or remain crippled by infantile paralysis (Polio) because the discoverer of the anti-polio vaccine is a Jew, Jonas Salk. Yet another polio vaccine was developed by another Jew, Dr. Sabin."

"Muslims must refuse to use streptomycin and continue to die of tuberculosis because a Jew, Zalman Waxman, invented the wonder drug against this killing disease.

"Muslim doctors must discard all discoveries and improvements by dermatologist Judas Sehn Benedict, or the lung specialist, Frawnkel, and of many other world renowned Jewish scientists and medical experts."

"In short, good and loyal Muslims properly and fittingly should remain afflicted with syphilis, gonorrhea, heart disease, headaches, typhus, diabetes, mental disorders, polio, convulsions and tuberculosis and be proud to obey the Islamic boycott."

"Meanwhile I ask, what equivalent medical contributions to the world have the Muslims made?"

• • •

### New British Destroyer

*A press release to coincide with the introduction of the new Type 45 Destroyers.*

Details have been released regarding Britain's introduction of the next generation of fighting ships. The Royal Navy is proud of the cutting edge capability of the fleet of Type 45 destroyers.

## Politicians & Diapers Should Be Changed Frequently

Costing £750 million, they have been designed to meet the needs of the 21st century; in addition to state of the art technology, weaponry, and guidance systems, the ships will comply with the very latest employment, equality, health & safety and human rights legislation.

They will be able to remain at sea for several months and positively bristle with facilities. For instance, the new user friendly crow's nest comes equipped with wheel-chair access. Live ammunition has been replaced with paintballs to reduce the risk of anyone getting hurt and to cut down on the number of compensation claims. Stress councilors and lawyers will be on duty 24hrs a day, and each ship will have its own onboard industrial tribunal.

The crew will be 50/50 men and women, and balanced in accordance with the latest Home Office directives on race, gender, sexuality, and disability. Sailors will only have to work a maximum of 37hrs per week in line with Brussels Health & Safety rules even in wartime! All bunks will be double occupancy, and the destroyers will all come equipped with a maternity ward situated on the same deck as the Gay Disco. Tobacco will be banned throughout the ship, but cannabis will be allowed in the Officer's Ward-room. The Royal Navy is eager to shed its traditional reputation for "Rum, Sodomy, and the Lash". Out goes the occasional rum ration which is to be replaced by Perrier water, although sodomy remains, this has now been extended to include all ratings under 18. The lash will still be available but only by request.

Saluting officers has been abolished because it is elitist; it is to be replaced by the more informal "Hello Sailor." All notices on boards will be printed in 37 different languages and Braille. Crew members will no longer be required to ask permission to grow beards or moustaches, even the women. The MOD is working on a new "Non specific" flag based on the controversial British Airways "Ethnic" tailfin design, because the White Ensign is considered to be offensive to minorities. The ship is due to be launched soon in a ceremony conducted by Captain Hook from the Finsbury Park Mosque who will break a petrol bomb over the hull. The ship will gently slide into the water to the tune of "In the Navy" by the Village People played by the band of Her Majesty's Royal Marines.

Sea Trials are expected to take place, when the first of the new destroyers HMS *Cautious*, sets out on her maiden mission. It will be escorting boat loads of illegal immigrants across the channel to ports on the south coast. The Prime Minister said that "While the ships reflected the very latest of modern thinking they were also capable of being up-graded to comply with any new legislation". His final words were "Britain never, never waives the rules!"

• • •

## Black Robbers
(A True Story)

For anyone who didn't see the episode of David Letterman's show where this story was told, read this (And remember it's a *true* story...):

On a recent weekend in Atlantic City, a woman won a bucketful of quarters at a slot machine. She took a break from the slots for dinner with her husband in the hotel dining room. But first she wanted to stash the quarters in her room.

'I'll be right back and we'll go to eat' she told her husband and carried the coin-laden bucket to the elevator. As she was about to walk into the elevator she noticed two men already aboard. Both were black. One of them was very tall and had an intimidating figure. The woman froze. Her first thought was: "These two are going to rob me."

Her next thought was: "Don't be a bigot, they look like perfectly nice gentlemen." But racial stereotypes are powerful, and fear immobilized her. Avoiding eye contact, she turned around stiffly and faced the elevator doors as they closed.

A second passed, and then another second, and then another. Her fear increased! The elevator didn't move. Panic consumed her. "My God" she thought, "I'm trapped and about to be robbed!" Her heart pounded. Perspiration poured from every pore.

Then one of the men said, "Hit the floor."

Instinct told her to do what they told her. The bucket of quarters flew upwards as she threw out her arms and collapsed on the elevator floor. A shower of coins rained down on her. "Take my money and spare me," she prayed.

More seconds passed. She heard one of the men say politely, "Ma'am, if you'll just tell us what floor you're going to, we'll push the button."

The one who said it had a little trouble getting the words out. He was trying mightily to hold in a belly laugh.

The woman lifted her head and looked up at the two men. They reached down to help her up. Confused, she struggled to her feet.

"When I told my friend here to hit the floor," said the average sized one, "I meant that he should hit the elevator button for our floor; I didn't mean for you to hit the floor, ma'am." He spoke genially. He bit his lip. It was obvious he was having a hard time not laughing.

The woman thought: "My God, what a spectacle I've made of myself." She was too humiliated to speak.

The three of them gathered up the strewn quarters and refilled her bucket.

When the elevator arrived at her floor they then insisted on walking her to her room. She seemed a little unsteady on her feet, and they were afraid she might not make it down the corridor. At her door they bid her a good evening. As she slipped into her room she could hear them roaring with laughter as they walked back to the elevator.

The woman brushed herself off. She pulled herself together and went downstairs for dinner with her husband.

The next morning flowers were delivered to her room; a dozen roses. Attached to EACH rose was a crisp one hundred-dollar bill. The card said: 'Thanks for the best laugh we've had in years.
It was signed: Eddie Murphy & Michael Jordan.

• • •

Hung Chow called into work and said, "Hey, I no come work today, I really sick. Got headache, stomach ache and legs hurt, I no come work."

The boss John said, "You know something, Hung Chow, I really need you today. When I feel sick like you do, I go to my wife and tell her to give me sex. That makes everything better and I go to work. You try that."

Two hours later Hung Chow calls again. "I do what you say and I feel great. I be at work soon....You got nice house"

• • •

### The Irish Firefighter

Paddy, was walking along the street during his once-in-a-lifetime visit to New York when he rounds a corner and there's a high rise building on fire. Paddy, ever the kind-hearted and resourceful Irishman, ran up to the building to see if he can help, and noticed people trapped five stories up.

Paddy yelled to the people: "I'm Patrick Sean Michael Fitzpatrick, the Irish Rugby Union fullback! If you jump, I'll catch you, I've only had 6 pints to drink all today!"

One lady, in desperation, jumped and sure enough Paddy caught her. Then a man saw that Paddy caught the women and he jumped.

Sure enough, Paddy caught him also.

Then a black man jumped out and crashed to the sidewalk.

Paddy didn't even attempt to catch him.

Paddy looked up and yelled: "Don't be throwin' out the burnt ones!"

• • •

On holiday recently in Spain I saw a sign saying 'English speaking Doctor'. I thought; "What a good idea, why don't we have them in our country."

• • •

I was walking past a block of flats this morning. One of the tenants was leaning over the balcony shaking a carpet.

I shouted, "What's up, Abdul, can't you get it started?"

• • •

Recently, a world-wide survey was conducted by the UN. The only question asked was: "Would you please give your honest opinion about solutions to the food shortage in the rest of the world?" The survey was a huge failure because of the following:

In Eastern Europe they didn't know what "honest" meant.
In Western Europe they didn't know what "shortage" meant.
In Africa they didn't know what "food" meant.
In China they didn't know what "opinion" meant.
In the Middle East they didn't know what "solution" meant.
In South Africa they didn't know what "please" meant.
In the USA they didn't know what "the rest of the world" meant.
In Australia they hung up as soon as they heard the Indian accent.

• • •

### Ole & Sven working at the Airport

Ole and Sven were drinking buddies who worked as aircraft mechanics in Minneapolis and one day the airport was fogged in and they were stuck in the hangar with nothing to do.

Ole said, "I vish ve had somethin ta drink!"

Sven says, "Me too. Y'know, I hear ya can drink dat jet fuel and get a buzz. Ya vanna try it?"

So they pour themselves a couple of glasses of high octane hooch and got completely smashed.

Next morning Ole woke up and is surprised at how good he feels. In fact he feels GREAT! NO hangover! NO bad side effects. Nothing!

The phone rang. It was Sven who asks "How iss you feelin dis mornin?"

Ole says, "I feel great. How 'bout you?"

Sven says, "I feel great, too. Ya don't have no hangover?"

Ole says, "No dat jet fuel iss great stuff – no hangover, nothin. Ve oughta do dis more often."

Sven agreed, "Yeah, vell, but dere's yust vun ting."

Ole asked, "Vat's dat?"

Sven questioned, "Haff you farted yet?"

Ole stopped to think. "No "

"Vell, *DON'T*, 'cause I'm in Bahrain.

• • •

Sorry for not calling you on New Years, I just got out of jail. I got locked up for punching the stuffing out of this idiot at a party. In my defense...when you hear an Arab counting down from 10, your instincts kick in.

• • •

Two maintenance engineers, Sven & Ole were standing at the base of a flagpole, looking up. A woman walked by and asked what they were doing.

"We're supposed to find the height of this flagpole, said Sven, "but we don't have a ladder."

The woman took a wrench from her purse, loosened a couple bolts, and laid the pole down on the ground. Then she took a tape measure from her pocketbook, took a measurement, announced, "Twenty-one feet, six inches," and walked away.

Ole shook his head and laughed. "Ain't that just like a woman! We ask for the height and she gives us the length!"

Sven and Ole have since quit their engineering jobs and are currently serving in the United States House of Representatives.

• • •

A twin-engine passenger plane had an engine failure and the altitude and speed were decreasing rapidly. The pilot announced over the intercom: *"I'm sorry it has come to this ladies and gentlemen, but unfortunately we are going to have to jettison the luggage in order for the aircraft to remain airborne."*

Baggage is thrown out but still the plane's altitude continues to decrease.

Once again the pilot gets on the intercom, *"I hate to do this folks but in order to save the majority we are going to have to start off-loading some passengers. The only fair way is to do this alphabetically, so we'll start with the letter 'A' Africans? Are there any Africans on board?"*

There was no answer so the pilot calls, *"The next letter is *B* for 'Black people', are there any black people on board?"*

Again silence. *"Next letter is "C" - coloured people? Are there any colored people on board?"*

Still there is silence.

A little black boy sitting near the rear of the plane turned to his mother and said, "Mum, ain't we African? Ain't we black? Ain't we coloured?"

She replied, "Yes, son but, for the moment we is Negroes. Let them do the Muslims first. If that don't work, we is Zulus!

• • •

I saw a billboard sign that read:
**NEED HELP, CALL JESUS 1-800-005-3787**
Out of curiosity, I called the number.
A Mexican showed up with a lawnmower.

• • •

Aidan met Sean in the street and said, "Sean, in future you should draw your bedroom curtains before making love to your wife!"

"'Why?" Sean asked.

"Because lad," said Aidan, "all the street was sniggering when they saw you two making love yesterday afternoon."

Sean replied, "Nosey buggers, well, the laugh's on them; I wasn't home yesterday afternoon."

• • •

A hunter walking through the rain forest found a huge dead rhinoceros with a pigmy standing beside it.

Amazed, he asked: "Did you kill this great beast?"

The pigmy said "Yes."

The hunter asked, "How could a little bloke like you kill a huge beast like that?"

Replied the pigmy: "I killed it with my club."

The astonished hunter asked: "Heavens, how big is your club?"

The pigmy replied: "Oh, there's about 600 of us."

• • •

An Irishman was walking home late at night and saw a woman lurking in the shadows. "Twenty dollars," she whispered.

Paddy had never had a hooker before, but decided what the hell, it's only twenty bucks. So they hide in the bushes. They're going at it for a couple of minutes when, all of a sudden, a light flashes on them. It's a police officer.

"What's going on here, people? Demanded the officer. "Oh, I'm making love to me wife," the Irishman answered, sounding annoyed.

"Oh, I'm so sorry," said the cop, "I didn't know."

"Well, needer did I," says Paddy, 'til ya shoined dat bloody light in her face!!!

• • •

Some guy just knocked on my door selling raffle tickets for poor black orphans. I said, "Fuck that – knowing my luck, I'd win one!"

• • •

### Coffee Table Politics

What happens when a fly falls into a coffee cup?
The Italian-throws the cup and walks away in a fit of rage.
The Frenchman-takes out the fly, and drinks the coffee.
The Chinese - eats the fly and throws away the coffee.
The Russian - Drinks the coffee with the fly, since it was extra with no charge.
The Israeli - sells the coffee to the Frenchman, the fly to the Chinese, buys himself a new cup of coffee and uses the extra money to invent a device that prevents flies from falling into coffee.
The Palestinian - blames the Israeli for the fly falling in his coffee, protests the act of aggression to the UN, takes a loan from the European Union to buy a new cup of coffee, uses the money to purchase explosives and then blows up the coffee house where the Italian, the Frenchman, the Chinese, and the Russian are all trying to explain to the Israeli that he should give away his cup of coffee to the Palestinian.

• • •

### Vus Titzuch?

President George W. Bush called the Head of the CIA and asked, "How come the Jews know everything before we do?"

The CIA chief replied, 'The Jews have this expression: *'Vus titzuch?'* '

The President asked, "What does that mean?"

"Well, Mr. President," replied the CIA chief, "it's a Yiddish expression that roughly translates to "what's happening?" They just ask each other and they find out and, inevitably, they know everything."

The President decided to go undercover to determine if this is true.

He dressed up as an Orthodox Jew. Wearing the traditional black hat, beard, long black coat–the whole schtick. The President was secretly flown in an unmarked plane to New York, picked up in an unmarked car, and dropped off in Crown Heights, Brooklyn's *most* Jewish neighborhood.

Soon a little old man came shuffling along.

The President stopped him and whispered, "Vus titzuch?"

The old guy whispered back, "That shmuck Bush is in Brooklyn!"

• • •

A man walked into the Lingerie Department of Macy's in New York City. He told the saleslady, "I would like a Jewish bra for my wife, size 34B."

With a quizzical look the saleslady asked, "What kind of bra?"

"A Jewish bra. She said to tell you that she wanted a Jewish bra, and that you would know what she wanted."

"Ah, now I remember," said the saleslady. "We don't get as many requests for them as we used to. Mostly our customers lately want the Catholic bra, or the Salvation Army bra, or the Presbyterian bra."

Confused, and a little flustered, the man asked, "So, what are the differences?"

"It is all really quite simple. The Catholic bra supports the masses. The Salvation Army lifts up the fallen, and the Presbyterian bra keeps them staunch and upright."

He mused on that information for a minute and said, "Hmmm. I know I'll regret asking, but what does the Jewish bra do?"

"A Jewish bra," she replied, "makes mountains out of molehills."

• • •

A Jewish woman goes to see her Rabbi. " Jack and Joe are both in love with me," she says. "Who will be the lucky one?"

The wise old Rabbi answered: "Jack will marry you. Joe will be the lucky one."

• • •

If a married Jewish man is walking alone in a park and expresses an opinion without anybody hearing him, is he still wrong?

• • •

My father said, "Marry a girl who has the same belief as the family."

I said, "Dad, why would I marry a girl who thinks I'm a schmuck?"

• • •

Jewish Marriage advice "Don't marry a beautiful person. They may leave you. Of course, an ugly person may leave you too. But who cares?"

• • •

A hippie gets on a bus and spies a pretty young nun. He sits down next to her, and asks her: "Can we have sex?"

"No," she replies, "I'm married to God." She stands up, and gets off at the next stop. The bus driver, who overheard, turns to the hippie and says: "I can tell you how to get to have sex with her!"

"Yeah?", says the hippie.

"Yeah!", say the bus driver. "She goes to the cemetery every Tuesday night at midnight to pray, so all you have to do is dress up in a robe with a hood, put' some of that luminous powder stuff in your beard, and pop up in the cemetery claiming to be God."

The hippie decides to give it a try, and arrives in the cemetery dressed as suggested on the next Tuesday night.

"I am God," he declares to the nun, Keeping the hood low about his Face.

"Have sex with me."

The nun agrees without question, but begs him to restrict himself to anal sex, as she is desperate not to lose her virginity.

'God' agrees, and promptly has his wicked way with her. As he finishes, he jumps up and throws back his hood with a flourish.

"Ha-ha," he cries. "I'm the hippie!"

"Ha-ha," cries the nun. "I'm the bus driver!

• • •

Morris, went to his rabbi for some needed advice. "Rabbi, tell me is it proper for one man to profit from another man's mistakes?"

"No, Morris, a man should not profit from another man's mistakes" answered the rabbi.

"Are you sure Rabbi?"

"Of course, I'm sure, in fact I'm positive" exclaimed the Rabbi.

"OK, Rabbi, if you are so sure, how about returning the two hundred dollars I gave you for marrying me to my wife?"

• • •

The Italian says, "I'm tired and thirsty. I must have wine."
　　The Frenchman says, "I'm tired and thirsty. I must have cognac."
　　The Russian says, "I'm tired and thirsty. I must have vodka."
　　The German says, "I'm tired and thirsty. I must have beer."
　　The Mexican says, "I'm tired and thirsty. I must have tequila."
　　The Jew says, "I'm tired and thirsty. I must have diabetes."

• • •

A Jewish man spotted a friend reading an Arabic newspaper said, "Moshe, have you lost your mind?"

"Well, I used to read the Jewish papers, but what did I find?" Moshe replied. "Jews being persecuted, Israel being attacked, Jews disappearing through assimilation, Jews living in poverty. So I switched to an Arab newspaper. Now what do I find? Jews own the banks, Jews control the media, Jews are all rich and powerful, Jews rule the world. The news is **so** much better!"

• • •

A devout Arab Muslim entered a black cab in London. He curtly asked the cabbie to turn off the radio because as decreed by his religious teaching, he must not listen to music because in the time of the prophet there was no music, especially Western music which is the music of the infidel.

The cab driver politely switched off the radio, stopped the cab and opened the door.

The Arab asked him, "What are you doing?"

The cabbie answered, "In the time of the prophet there were no taxis, so fuck off and wait for a camel!!"

• • •

Vinny and Guido were out in the woods hunting when suddenly Guido grabbed his chest and falls to the ground. He didn't seem to be breathing; his eyes were rolled back in his head.

Vinny whipped out his cell phone and called 911. He gasped to the operator, "I think Sal is dead! What should I do?"

The operator, in a calm soothing voice says, "Just take it easy and follow my instructions. First, let's make sure he's dead."

There is a silence. And then a gun shot is heard.

Vinny's voice came back on the line, "Okay... Now what?"

## The Official Texas Sheriff's Exam

A young Texan grew up wanting to be a lawman. He grew up big, 6' 2", strong as a longhorn and fast as a mustang. He could shoot a bottle cap tossed in the air at 40 paces. When he finally came of age, he applied to where he had only dreamed of working: the West Texas Sheriff's Department.

After a series of tests and interviews, the Chief Deputy finally called him into his office for the young man's last interview. The Chief Deputy said, "You're a big strong kid and you can really shoot. So far your qualifications all look good, but we have, what you might call, an *'Attitude Suitability Test,'* that you must take before you can be accepted. We just don't let anyone carry our badge, son."

Then, sliding a service pistol and a box of ammo across the desk, the Chief said, "Take this pistol and go out and shoot the following:

> six illegal aliens,
> six lawyers,
> six meth dealers,
> six Muslim extremists,
> six Democrats,
> and a rabbit."

"Why the rabbit?" queried the applicant.
"You pass," said the Chief Deputy. "When can you start?"

• • •

Flynn and Murphy fancied a pint or two but didn't have a lot of money between them; they could only raise the staggering sum of one Euro.

Murphy said "Hang on, I have an idea." He went next door to the butcher's shop and came out with one large sausage.

Flynn said "Are you crazy? Now we don't have any money at all!"

Murphy replied, "Don't worry - just follow me." He went into the pub where he immediately ordered two pints of Guinness and two glasses of Jamieson Whisky.

Flynn said "Now you've lost it. Do you know how much trouble we will be in? We haven't got any money!!"

Murphy replied, with a smile. "Don't worry; I have a plan, Cheers!"

They downed their drinks. Murphy said, "OK, I'll stick the sausage through my zipper and you go on your knees and put it in your mouth."

The barman noticed them, went berserk, and threw them out.

They continued this, pub after pub, getting more and more drunk, all for free.

At the tenth pub Flynn said "Murphy - I don't think I can do any more of this. I'm drunk and me knees are killing me!"

Murphy said, "How do you think I feel? I can't even remember which pub I lost the sausage in."

• • •

Q: What is a Jewish ménage-a-trois?
A: Two headaches and an erection.

• • •

Q: Why did Adam and Eve have a *perfect* marriage?
A: He didn't have to hear about all the men she could have married, and she didn't have to hear about the way his mother cooked.

• • •

Q: What business is a yenta in?
A: Yours.

• • •

## OTHER NATIONS, ETHNICITIES, AND REGIONS AS SUBJECTS OF HUMOR

A man was walking down the street when a very beautiful woman appeared out of nowhere, right in front of him. She was stunning, completely nude, and has green skin.

Astonished, the man started to speak to her. "Excuse me, but you just popped out of thin air. How did you do that?"

"Oh," replied the woman, "I'm from Andromeda, in what you call 'outer space'"

"Andromeda?" said the man, "Wow! Are all the women on Andromeda as beautiful as you, and do you all have green skin?"

"Yes, we are all beautiful," replied the woman, "and everyone is green on Andromeda."

The man continued to stare and speak. "Excuse me for asking, but I can't help noticing that you have 12 toes on each foot. Here on Earth we all have five toes on each foot. Do all Andromedan people have 12 toes on each foot?"

"Yes, they do," replied the woman.

"Please, may I ask you one more question?" The woman nodded her assent"

I also can't help noticing that on each of your hands you have seven fingers, and on each finger is a very large diamond. Here on Earth, diamonds are very rare and valuable. Do all Andromedan women have large diamonds on their fingers?"

"Well, no," the woman answers, "not the *Shiksas*." (Gentile women)

• • •

### UK Headlines from the Year 2040

Ozone created by electric cars now killing millions.

White minorities still trying to have English recognized as the UK's third language.

Children from two-parent, married, heterosexual families bullied in schools for being 'different'. Tolerance urged.

Manchester schoolgirl expelled for not wearing a Burqa.

Japan announces that they will no longer consume whale meat as whales are now extinct, and the scientific research fleet are unemployed.

UK Government has told the Japanese that Grey Squirrels taste like whale meat.

Britain now has ten Universities of Political Correctness. Professor Goldman of LSPC says there is still a long way to go in the fight to stop people saying what they think.

Britain's deficit £15 trillion and rising. Government declares return to surplus in 100 years which is 300 years ahead of time. Prime Minister Mohammed Yousuf claims increased growth through more immigration is the secret to success.

Baby conceived naturally. Scientists stumped.

Iran still isolated. Physicists estimate at least ten more years before radioactivity decreases to safe levels.

France pleads for global help after being taken over by Islamic countries. No other country comes forward.

Jose Manuel Rodrigez Bush says he will run for second term as US President in 2042.

Post Office raises price of stamps to £28 and reduces mail delivery to Wednesdays only.

After a ten-year, £75.8 billion study commissioned by the Labour Party, scientists prove diet and exercise is the key to weight loss.

Average weight of a British male drops to 18 stone.

Japanese scientists have created a camera with such a fast shutter speed they can now photograph a woman with her mouth shut.

Supreme Court rules punishment of criminals violates their civil and human rights. Victims to be held partly responsible for crime.

Average height of professional basketball players is now nine feet, seven inches.

New law requires that all nail clippers, screwdrivers, fly swatters and rolled-up newspapers must be registered by January 2045 as lethal weapons.

Inland Revenue sets lowest tax rate in decades at 75 per cent.

Bradford win FA Cup Final, beating Hindu Hornets 4-1.

• • •

## Who's Yo Daddy?

The following are all replies that Detroit women have written on Child Support Agency Forms in the section for listing 'father's details;' or putting it another way..... Who's yo Daddy? These are *genuine* excerpts from the forms. Be sure to check out #11. It takes 1st prize and #3 is runner-up.

1. Regarding the identity of the father of my twins, Makeeshia was fathered by Maclearndon McKinley. I am unsure as to the identity of the father of Marlinda, but I believe that she was conceived on the same night.
2. I am unsure, as to the identity of the father of my child as I was being sick out of a window when taken unexpectedly from behind. I can provide you with a list of names of men that I think were at the party if this helps.
3. I do not know the name of the father of my little girl. She was conceived at a party at 3600 East Grand Boulevard where I had sex with a man I met that night. I do remember that the sex was so good that I fainted. If you do manage to track down the father, can you please send me his phone number? Thanks.
4. I don't know the identity of the father of my daughter. He drives a BMW that now has a hole made by my stiletto in one of the door panels. Perhaps you can contact BMW service stations in this area and see if he's had it replaced.
5. I have never had sex with a man. I am still a Virginian. I am awaiting a letter from the Pope confirming that my son's conception was ejaculate and that he is the Saver risen again.
6. I cannot tell you the name of Alleshia's dad as he informs me that to do so would blow his cover and that would have cataclysmic

implications for the economy. I am torn between doing right by you and right by the country. Please advise.
7. I do not know who the father of my child was as they all look the same to me.
8. Tyrone Hairston is the father of child A. If you do catch up with him, can you ask him what he did with my AC/DC CDs? Child B who was also borned at the same time.... Well, I don't have clue.
9. From the dates it seems that my daughter was conceived at Disney World; maybe it really is the Magic Kingdom.
10. So much about that night is a blur. The only thing that I remember for sure is Delia Smith did a program about eggs earlier in the evening. If I had stayed in and watched more TV rather than going to the party at 8956 Miller Ave, mine might have remained unfertilized.
11. I am unsure as to the identity of the father of my baby, after all, like when you eat a can of beans you can't be sure which one made you fart.

• • •

A little black boy was asking his father some questions one day. He asked, "Father, why do we have such curly hair?"

His father replied, "Son, we are the hunters of Africa. Our hair is short and curly so that it doesn't get caught in the thorn bushes and trap us while we are hunting lions."

The little boy pondered awhile, and asked "Father, why do we have such flat noses and big nostrils?

His father replied, "Son, we are the hunters of Africa. Our noses are like that so that we can breathe silently and detect the subtlest of scents while we are tracking the great Kudu for food."

The little boy then asked, "Father, why do we have such big, flat feet?" His father answered, "Son, we are the hunters of Africa. We have such big flat feet so that we can walk so silently over the jungle floor that nothing can hear us."

OTHER NATIONS, ETHNICITIES, AND REGIONS AS SUBJECTS OF HUMOR

The little boy contemplated these answers for a long while, then asked, "Father, if we are the hunters of Africa ... why are we living in Detroit?"

• • •

### You know you're a redneck when

1. You take your dog for a walk and you both use the same tree.
2. You can entertain yourself for more than 15 minutes with a fly swatter.
3. Your boat has not left the driveway in 15 years.
4. You burn your yard rather than mow it.
5. You think "The Nutcracker" is something you do off the high dive.
6. The Salvation Army declines your furniture.
7. You offer to give someone the shirt off your back and they don't want it.
8. You have the local taxidermist on speed dial.
9. You come back from the dump with more than you took.
10. You keep a can of Raid on the kitchen table.
11. Your wife can climb a tree faster than your cat.
12. Your grandmother has "ammo" on her Christmas list.
13. You keep flea and tick soap in the shower.
14. You've been involved in a custody fight over a hunting dog.
15. You go to the stock car races and don't need a program.
16. You know how many bales of hay your car will hold.
17. You have a rag for a gas cap.
18. Your house doesn't have curtains, but your truck does.
19. You wonder how service stations keep their rest-room's so clean.
20. You can spit without opening your mouth.
21. You consider your license plate personalized because your father made it.
22. Your lifetime goal is to own a fireworks stand.
23. You have a complete set of salad bowls and they all say "Cool Whip" on the side.

24. The biggest city you've ever been to is Wal-Mart.
25. Your working TV sits on top of your non-working TV.
26. You've used your ironing board as a buffet table.
27. A tornado hits your neighborhood and does $100,000 worth of improvements.
28. You've used a toilet brush to scratch your back.
29. You missed your 5th grade graduation because you were on jury duty.
30. You think fast food is hitting a deer at 65 m.p.h..

• • •

### Fred Boudreaux Moves to Arkansas

The Cajun, Boudreaux left the bayou and moved to Arkansas where he bought himself a donkey from an old farmer for $100. The farmer agreed to deliver the donkey the next day.

The next day, the farmer drove up and said, "I'm sorry, but I have some bad news...the donkey died last night."

"Well den," said Boudreaux, "Jus' give me my money back, yeah."

"I can't do that sir. I went and spent it already."

"OK, den, jus' unload dat donkey."

"What are you gonna do wit' him?"

"I'm gon-to raffle him off."

"You can't raffle off a dead donkey, you dumb coon-ass!"

"Well, dat's where you wrong! You wait an' you learn how smart we Cajuns are!"

A month later, the farmer ran into the Cajun and asked, "What happened with that dead donkey?"

"I raffled dat donkey off. I sold 500 tickets at two dollars apiece and made me $898."

"Didn't anyone complain?"

"Jus' dat guy who won. So I gave him his two dollars back."

• • •

## Other Nations, Ethnicities, And Regions As Subjects Of Humor

Mohammad Rashid and Ahmed Fawzi both immigrated to the U.S at the same time. Both men lived and worked in the same Working Class suburb of Detroit, Michigan, but almost never saw each other because they were so busy with growing their family businesses. Both were extremely industrious, hard working men who toiled to establish and expand their respective enterprises. Mohammad had a successful gas station with a *bodega* / snack bar, selling the usual chips, high-energy drinks, gum, tobacco products, beer, inexpensive wine, automotive accessories, condoms, and many, many lotto tickets.

Ahmed purchased and - then expanded - a motel where the tourists kept his business going, but not very exuberantly. Because the two men were so busy, they drifted away from each other. However, very shortly after they arrived in the United States, they made a solemn pact to meet in twenty years to compare notes on how they had prospered and well they had become assimilated during the intervening two decades since their arrival in America.

When their anniversary of the twenty year period arrived, the two met for lunch at a fancy restaurant. Over iced tea, and a good meal of roasted lamb, chickpeas and rice, the two began their comparisons. Mohammad began with, "I am married to Fatima, whom my parents selected for me, and we have two sons and a daughter. Fatima is a corporate attorney in a large multinational petroleum firm based in Houston but works from her office in our home in Larchmont, the gated community in the Lake District. She is considering running for election to Congress from our district. My eldest son, Mohammad, graduated Phi Beta Kappa, and was his class's valedictorian. He won a full scholarship to Harvard and has plans to become a cardiovascular surgeon when he graduates from Medical School. My younger son, Abdul, has a full football scholarship to Ohio State University, and, upon graduation, will be applying to NASA for astronaut training. My daughter, Jasmin, is a brownie scout and plans to be a librarian when she grows up. My business, Praised be to Allah, is thriving and I hope to sell it and retire later this year."

Ahmed Fawzi was listening gravely to all of this good news, but saying not a word. When their lunch was just about completed, Mohammad mentioned to Ahmed that he was going to stop by

Baskin & Robbins for some ice cream for his family's supper dessert that evening and inquired whether Ahmed would care to have him pick up some for Ahmed's family's dinner.

Ahmed, at long last, opened his mouth and said, "Fuck you, Towel Head!"

• • •

Mujibar was trying to get a job in India. The Personnel Manager said, "Mujibar, you have passed all the tests, except one. Unless you pass it you cannot qualify for this job."

Mujibar said, "I am ready, Sahib."

The manager said, "Make a sentence using the words Yellow, Pink and Green."

Mujibar thought for a few minutes and said, "Sahib manager, I am ready."

The manager said, "Go ahead."

Mujibar said, "The telephone goes green, green, green, and I pink it up, and say, 'Yellow, this is Mujibar.'"

Mujibar now works as a technician at a Microsoft call center for computer problems. No doubt you have spoken to him.

• • •

A couple flew to France to celebrate their fiftieth wedding anniversary. Sadly, the wife died two days after their arrival in Paris. The bereaved widower hurried to complete the funeral arrangements and for the return of his wife's remains to the U.S. He checked his wardrobe and found that although he had packed a black suit, black tie, and black shoes for some formal dinners that he had anticipated, he did not have a black hat.

Although he had a passing acquaintance with conversational French, he was hardly fluent.

After returning to the hotel's lobby from his room upstairs, he inquired of a bellhop where he could purchase a black hat. Rather than asking the bellman in English, he used his own pidgin form of Franglish and inquired, *"Pardon moi, mon ami, do you know where I could purchase un capo noire?"*

In French, a chapeaux is a hat but a "capo" is a slang word for a condom. The bellman, not aware that the hotel's guest had just lost his wife of many years, nodded his head, *"Oui monsieur"* and indicated that he should walk a few paces and inquire at the local pharmacy.

Thinking it strange that he might be able to purchase a black hat at a druggist's establishment, he figured that at the very least, the pharmacist might speak English fluently.

Entering the apothecary shop, he walked up and asked the pharmacist whether he could purchase a *capo noire.*

*"Oui, oui monsieur,"* replied the druggist as he searched below the counter and produced the desired item. As he handed the packet to the startled man, he asked in English, "Sir, certainly we carry many such items in our store. But, I am curious, why a black one?"

The bereaved man replied, "Oh, because my wife just died."

The pharmacist shook his head gravely and replied, *"Oh monsieur, quelle sentiment!"*

• • •

### Dining in the UK in the Nineteen Fifties

(contributed by one of my UK-based esteemed veterinarian colleagues, Derek Lyon)

* Pasta had not been invented.
* Curry was an unknown entity.
* Olive oil was kept in the medicine cabinet
* Spices came from the Middle East where we believed that they were used for embalming
* Herbs were used to make rather dodgy medicine.
* A takeaway was a mathematical problem.
* A pizza was something to do with a leaning tower.
* Bananas and oranges only appeared at Christmas time.

* The only vegetables known to us were spuds, peas, carrots and cabbage, anything else was regarded as being a bit suspicious.

* All crisps were plain; the only choice we had was whether to put the salt on or not.

* Condiments consisted of salt, pepper, vinegar and brown sauce if we were lucky.

* Soft drinks were called pop.

* Coke was something that we mixed with coal to make it last longer.

* A Chinese chippy was a foreign carpenter.

* Rice was a milk pudding, and never, ever part of our dinner.

* A Big Mac was what we wore when it was raining.

* A Pizza Hut was an Italian shed.

* A microwave was something out of a science fiction movie.

* Brown bread was something only poor people ate.

* Oil was for lubricating your bike not for cooking, fat was for cooking

* Bread and jam was a treat.

* Tea was made in a teapot using tea leaves, not bags.

* The tea cozy was the forerunner of all the energy saving devices that we hear so much about today.

* Tea had only one colour, black. Green tea was not British.

* Coffee was only drunk when we had no tea….. and then it was Camp, and came in a bottle.

* Cubed sugar was regarded as posh.

* Figs and dates appeared every Christmas, but no one ever ate them.

* Sweets and confectionery were called toffees.

* Coconuts only appeared when the fair came to town.

* Jellied eels were peculiar to Londoners.

* Salad cream was a dressing for salads, mayonnaise did not exist

* Hors d'oeuvre was a spelling mistake.

* The starter was our main meal.

* Soup was a main meal..

* The menu consisted of what we were given, and was set in stone.
* Only Heinz made beans, any others were impostors.
* Leftovers went in the dog.
* Special food for dogs and cats was unheard of.
* Sauce was either brown or red.
* Fish was only eaten on Fridays.
* Fish didn't have fingers in those days.
* Eating raw fish was called poverty, not sushi.
* Ready meals only came from the fish and chip shop.
* For the best taste fish and chips had to be eaten out of old newspapers.
* Frozen food was called ice cream.
* Nothing ever went off in the fridge because we never had one.
* Ice cream only came in one colour and one flavour.
* None of us had ever heard of yoghurt.
* Jelly and blancmange was only eaten at parties.
* If we said that we were on a diet, we simply got less.
* Healthy food consisted of anything edible.
* Healthy food had to have the ability to stick to your ribs.
* Calories were mentioned but they had nothing at all to do with food.
* The only criteria concerning the food that we ate were ... did we like it and could we afford it.
* People who didn't peel potatoes were regarded as lazy so and so's.
* Indian restaurants were only found in India
* A seven course meal had to last a week.
* Brunch was not a meal.
* Cheese only came in a hard lump.
* If we had eaten bacon lettuce and tomato in the same sandwich we would have been certified
* A bun was a small cake back then.
* A tart was a fruit filled pastry, not a lady of horizontal pleasure.
* The word" Barbie" was not associated with anything to do with food.
* Eating outside was called a picnic.

* Cooking outside was called camping.
* Seaweed was not a recognized food.
* Offal was only eaten when we could afford it.
* Eggs only came fried or boiled.
* Hot cross buns were only eaten at Easter time.
* Pancakes were only eaten on Pancake Tuesday - in fact in those days it was compulsory.
* "Kebab" was not even a word never mind a food.
* Hot dogs were a type of sausage that only the Americans ate.
* Cornflakes had arrived from America but it was obvious that they would never catch on.
* The phrase "boil in the bag" would have been beyond our realms of comprehension.
* The idea of "oven chips" would not have made any sense at all to us.
* The world had not yet benefited from weird and wonderful things like Pot Noodles, Instant Mash and Pop Tarts.
* We bought milk and cream at the same time in the same bottle.
* Sugar enjoyed a good press in those days, and was regarded as being white gold.
* Lettuce and tomatoes in winter were just a rumour.
* Most soft fruits were seasonal except perhaps at Christmas.
* Prunes were medicinal.
* Surprisingly muesli was readily available in those days, it was called cattle feed.
* Turkeys were definitely seasonal.
* Pineapples came in chunks in a tin; we had only ever seen a picture of a real one.
* We didn't eat croissants in those days because we couldn't pronounce them, we couldn't spell them and we didn't know what they were.
* We thought that baguettes were a serious problem the French needed to deal with.
* Garlic was used to ward off vampires, but never used to flavour bread.

\* Water came out of the tap, if someone had suggested bottling it and charging treble for it they would have become a laughing stock.

\* Food hygiene was all about washing your hands before meals.

\* *Campylobacter, Salmonella, E..coli, Listeria*, and Botulism were all called "food poisoning."

\* The one thing that we never ever had on our table in the fifties .... elbows.

• • •

### Spanish Computer

A Spanish teacher was explaining to her class that in Spanish, unlike English, nouns are designated as either masculine or feminine.

"'House' for instance, is feminine: 'la casa.' 'Pencil,' however, is masculine: 'el lapiz.'

A student asked, 'What gender is 'computer'?'

Instead of giving the answer, the teacher split the class into two groups, male and female, and asked them to decide for themselves whether computer' should be a masculine or a feminine noun. Each group was asked to give four reasons for its recommendation.

The men's group decided that 'computer' should definitely be of the feminine gender ('la computadora'), because:

1. No one but their creator understands their internal logic.
2. The native language they use to communicate with other computers is incomprehensible to everyone else.
3. Even the smallest mistakes are stored in long term memory for possible later retrieval; and –
4. As soon as you make a commitment to one, you find yourself spending half your paycheck on accessories for it.

The women's group, however, concluded that computers should be masculine ('el computador'), because:

1. In order to do anything with them, you have to turn them on.
2. They have a lot of data but still can't think for themselves.

3. They are supposed to help you solve problems, but half the time they *are* the problem; and
4. As soon as you commit to one, you realize that if you had waited a little longer, you could have gotten a better model.

The women won.

• • •

A rich man living in Darwin, Australia, said that he wanted to throw a party and invited all of his buddies and neighbors. He also invited Colin, the only aborigine in the neighborhood. He held the party around the pool in the backyard of his mansion.

Everyone was having a good time drinking, dancing, eating prawns, oysters, from the BBQ and flirting.

At the height of the party, the host said, "I have a 15 foot man-eating crocodile in my pool and I'll give a million dollars to anyone who has the balls to jump in."

The words were barely out of his mouth when there was a loud splash and everyone turned around and saw Colin in the pool fighting the croc, jabbing the croc in the eyes with his thumbs, throwing punches, doing all kinds of stuff like head butts and choke holds, biting the croc on the tail and flipping the croc through the air like some kind of Judo Instructor.

The water was churning and splashing everywhere. Both Colin and the croc were screaming and raising hell... Finally Colin strangled the croc and let it float to the top like a dead goldfish.

Colin then slowly climbed out of the pool.

Everybody was just staring at him in disbelief.

The host said, "Well, Colin, I reckon I owe you a million dollars."

'Nah, you all right boss, I don't want it,' said Colin.

The rich man said, "Man, I have to give you something. You won the bet. How about half a million bucks then?"

'No thanks... I don't want it,' answered Colin.

The host said, "Come on, I insist on giving you something. That was amazing. How about a new Porsche AND a Rolex AND some stock options?"

Again, Colin said "No."
Confused, the rich man asked, 'Well Colin, then what do you want?
Colin said, "All I want is the bastard who pushed me in."

• • •

An Irish daughter had not been home for over three years. Upon her return, her father yelled at her, "Where have ye been all this time?

Why did ye not write to us? Not even a line. Why didn't ye call? Can ye not understand what ye put yer old Mother thru?"

The girl, crying, replied, Sniff, sniff...."Dad.....I was too embarrassed, I became a prostitute."

"Ye did what!!? Get out of here, ye shameless hussy! Sinner! You're a disgrace to this Catholic family!"

"OK, Daddy...as ye wish..."

"I just came back to give Mammy this luxurious fur coat, a title deed to a eight bedroom mansion plus a cheque for $5 million.

For me little brother Seamus, this gold Rolex.

And for ye Daddy, the sparkling new Mercedes limited edition convertible that's parked outside, plus a membership to the Limerick Country Club.

She took a breath and continued, "And an invitation for ye all to spend New Years Eve on board my new yacht in the Caribbean."

"Now what was it ye said ye had become?" says Daddy

Girl, crying again, Sniff, sniff.... "A prostitute Daddy!" Sniff, sniff.

"Oh! Be Jesus! Ye scared me half to death girl! Come, giv your old dad a hug!. I thought ye said a Protestant.

• • •

It isn't widely known, but the first toilet seat was invented by a Polish scientist in the 18th century.

The invention was later modified in the 19th century by a Jewish inventor who added a hole in the center.

• • •

An 18-year-old suicide bomber blew himself up and appeared before Allah. He said, "Oh, Allah, most merciful, I did your bidding, but I have a request. Since I'm only 18 and spent all my time in terrorist training school, I have never been with a woman. So, instead of 72 virgins, who also won't know what to do sexually, can I have 72 prostitutes?"

Allah regarded him for a moment, then replied, "Actually, the 72 virgins are here in heaven because assholes like you murdered them before they could experience the pleasure of sex. So you're here to service them. Since they're virgins, they're quite sexually ravenous; and, frankly, you'll be on constant, exhausting duty."

The bomber responded, "Well, I guess I can live with that. How hard can it be to keep 72 women satisfied for all eternity?"

And Allah replied, "Who said they were *women*?"

• • •

A man went to a public golf course. He approached the man behind the counter in the pro shop and said, "I would like 18 holes of golf and a caddie."

The man behind the counter replied, "The 18 holes of golf is no problem, but all of the caddies are out on the course. What I will do for you is this: We just received 8 brand new robot golf caddies. If you're willing to take one with you out on the course and come back and tell me how well it works, your round of golf is on me today."

The golfer obviously accepted the man's offer. He approached the first tee, looked at the fairway and murmured to himself, "I think my driver will do the job."

The robot caddie turned to the man and said, "No sir. Use your 3 wood. A driver is far too much club for this hole."

Hesitantly, the golfer pulled out his 3 wood, made good contact with the ball, and the ball landed about 10 feet to the right front of the hole on the green. The golfer, delighted, turned to the robot and thanked him for his assistance. As the golfer pulled out his putter he said, "I think this green is gonna break left to right."

The robot then again spoke up and said, "No sir. I do believe this green will break right to left."

Thinking about the last time the robot corrected his prediction, the golfer decided again to listen to the machine. He made his putt and birdied the hole thanks to the robot and his advice. But his luck didn't end there. His entire game was the best game he ever played, thanks to the assistance of the new robot golf caddie.

Upon returning to the clubhouse, the man behind the counter asked, "How was your game?"

The golfer stated, "It was, by far, the BEST game I ever played. Thank you very much for letting me take one of your robots. See you next week."

The week passed, and excited, the golfer returned to the pro shop. Upon entering, he turned to the man behind the counter and said, "I would like 18 holes of golf and one of those robot golf caddies, please."

The gentleman from behind the counter turned to the man and said, "Well the 18 holes is no problem. However, we had to get rid of the robots. We had too many complaints."

"*Complaints?* Who in the hell could've complained about those robots? They were incredible."

The man sighed and said, "Well, it wasn't their performance. It was that they were made of shiny silver metal, and the sun reflecting off them was blinding to other golfers on the fairway."

The golfer said, "So then why didn't you just paint them black?"

The man nodded sadly and replied, "We did. Then four of 'em didn't show up for work, two filed for welfare, one of them robbed the pro shop, and the other thinks he's the President."

• • •

# GOLF AND GOLFERS

Long ago when men cursed and beat the ground with sticks, it was called witchcraft..... Today, it's called golf.

• • •

Two golfers were ruminating about their best and worst games that they ever played. One remarked that the best two balls that he ever hit was when he stepped on a rake.

• • •

A woman complained to the pro at the golf course that she had been stung by a bee.
 "Where did the sting occur?" asked the pro.
 "Between the first and second holes." she responded the woman.
 'Lady, your stance is too wide!" exclaimed the pro.

• • •

An avid golfer entered the pro shop and asked the manager for a caddie with excellent eye sight because his was failing a bit as he grew older.
 The pro shop manager assigned him to an eight-five year old caddie.

Hey, wait a minute, I said that I wanted a caddie with better than average eye sight.

"Oh, don't be concerned," the manager assured him, this guy can see like a peregrine falcon."

Immediately following his very first drive down the fairway, the golfer inquired,

"Did you see where my ball landed?"

"Yes," replied the caddie.

"Where did it land?" asked the golfer.

"I forgot," said the caddie.

• • •

### Newest Golf Lingo

A 'Rock Hudson ' - a putt that looked straight, but wasn't.
A 'Saddam Hussein' - from one bunker into another.
A 'Yasser Arafat' - butt ugly and in the sand.
A 'John Kennedy Jr.' - didn't quite make it over the water.
A 'Rodney King' - over-clubbed.
An 'O.J.'- got away with one.
A 'Princess Grace' - should have used a driver.
A 'Princess Di' - shouldn't have used the driver.
A 'Rush Limbaugh' - way right.
A 'Nancy Pelosi' - Way to the left and out of bounds.
A 'James Joyce' - a putt that's impossible to read.
A 'Ted Kennedy' - goes in the water and jumps out.
A 'Sonny Bono' - straight into the trees.
A `Tiger Woods' - Wrong Hole

• • •

### Posted at a Local Golf Club

Back straight, knees bent, feet should width apart.

Form a loose grip.
Keep you head down.
Avoid a quick backswing
Stay out of the water.
Try not to hit anyone.
If you are taking too long, please let others go ahead of you.
Don't stand directly in front of others.
Quiet please...while others are preparing to go.
Don't take extra strokes.

*VERY GOOD. NOW FLUSH THE URINAL, GO OUTSIDE, AND TEE OFF*

• • •

A man took a day off from work and decided to play golf. He was on the second hole ready to tee off, when he noticed a frog sitting next to the green. He thought nothing of it and was about to swing his club when he heard, "*Ribbit ... 9 iron.*"

The fellow looked around and didn't see anyone.

"*Ribbit ... 9 iron.*"

He spied the frog and decided to prove the frog wrong, and put his other club away, and grabbed a 9 iron. Wham; he hit the ball 10 inches from the cup! He was absolutely shocked and said to the frog, "Wow! That's amazing. You must be a lucky frog, eh?"

The frog replied "*Ribbit; lucky frog.*"

The golfer decided to take the frog with him to the next hole.

"What do you think, froggie?" the man asked.

"*Ribbit; 3 wood.*"

So the golfer removed a three wood from his bag; teed up the ball, and stroked a hole-in-one. By the end of the day, he had played the best round of golf in his life and asked the frog, "OK Froggie, where to next?"

The frog replied, "*Ribbit; Las Vegas.*"

So, the grateful golfer took his green amphibian friend to Las Vegas and upon arrival, he inquired, "OK Frog, now what?"

The frog responded, *"Ribbit, roulette."*

Upon approaching the roulette table, the golfer asked, "What do you think I should bet?"

*"Ribit ...three grand on black 6."*

This was a million-to-one shot to win, but after the fantastic golf game, the chap figured what the hell, and placed a bet on black six.

Boom! Tons of cash comes sliding across the table to his position. The lucky man took his winnings and booked the best room in the hotel. He placed the frog on the coffee table in front of the couch and said, "Frog, I don't know how to repay you. You've won me all of this money and I am forever grateful."

The frog replied, *"Ribbit, kiss me!"*

The happy golfer thought to himself, "What the hell, after all, if that's what the frog wants, it deserves a kiss."

With a kiss, the frog turned into a gorgeous, 15 year-old girl.

"And that, your honor, is how the girl happened to be in my room!"

• • •

A blonde was standing by the first tee, waiting for her golf lesson from the resident professional. A foursome was in process of teeing off. The first golfer addressed the ball and swung his club, hitting the ball 230 yards straight down the middle of the fairway.

"That was a good shot," said the blonde.

"Not bad considering my impediment," said the golfer.

"What do you mean?" said the blonde.

"I have a glass eye," said the golfer.

"I don't believe you, show me," said the blonde.

He popped his eye out and showed her.

The next golfer addressed the ball and swung, hitting his ball 240 yards straight down the middle of the fairway.

"That was a good shot," said the blonde.

"Not bad considering my impediment," said the golfer.

"What's wrong with you?" said the blonde. "I have a prosthetic arm." Said the golfer.

"I don't believe you, show me" said the blonde, so he screwed his arm off and showed her.

The next golfer addressed his golf ball and swung, hitting it 250 yards straight down the middle of the fairway.

"That was a good shot," said the blonde.

"Not bad considering my impediment," said the golfer.

"What's wrong with you?" said the blonde.

"I have prosthetic leg," replied the golfer.

"I don't believe you, show me" said the blonde, so he unscrewed his leg and showed her.

The fourth golfer addressed his ball and swung, hitting it 280 yards straight down the middle of the fairway.

"That was a wonderful shot," exclaimed the blonde.

"Not bad considering my impediment," replied the golfer.

"What's wrong with you?" said the blonde. "I have an artificial heart," said the golfer.

"I don't believe you, show me" said the blonde.

"I can't show you out here in the open," said the golfer, "come around here behind the Pro Shop."

As they had not returned within five minutes, his golfing buddies decided to go and see what was holding them up.

As they turned the corner behind the Pro Shop, sure enough, there he was screwing his heart out.

• • •

A foursome is waiting at the men's tee when another foursome of ladies were hitting from the ladies tee. The ladies are taking their time and when finally the last one was ready to hit the ball she hacked it about 10 feet, went over to it, hacked it another ten feet and looked up at the men waiting and said apologetically: "I guess all those fucking lessons that I took this winter didn't help"

One of the men immediately replied: "No, you see that's your problem. You should have been taking golf lessons instead"

• • •

A group of male lawyers lived and died for their Saturday morning round of golf. One transferred to another city. It wasn't the same without him. A new woman lawyer joined their law firm. She overheard the guys talking about their golf round. She said, "You know, I used to play on my golf team in college and I was pretty good. Would you mind if I joined you next week?"

The three guys looked at each other. Not one of them wanted to say 'yes', but she had them on the spot. Finally, one man said it would be okay, but they would be starting early – at 6:30 am.

He figured the early tee-time would discourage her. The woman said this may be a problem, and asked if she could be up to 15 minutes late. They rolled their eyes, but said okay. She smiled and said, "Good, I'll be there at 6:30 or 6:45."

She showed up at 6:30 sharp, and beat all three of them with an eye-opening 2-under par round. She was fun and pleasant person, and the guys were impressed. Back at the clubhouse, they congratulated her and invited her back the next week. She smiled, and said, "I'll be there at 6:30 or 6:45."

The next week she again showed up at 6:30 sharp. Only this time, she played left-handed. The three lawyers were incredulous as she still beat them with an even par round, despite playing with her off-hand. They were totally amazed, but wondered if she was trying to make them look bad by beating them left-handed.

They couldn't figure her out. She was again very pleasant and didn't seem to be purposely showing them up. They invited her back again, but each man harbored a burning desire to beat her game.

The third week, the guys had their game faces on. But this time, she was 15 minutes late, which made the guys irritable. This week the lady lawyer played right-handed, and narrowly beat all three of them.

The men mused that her late arrival was due to petty gamesmanship on her part. However, she was so gracious and so complimentary of their strong play, they couldn't hold a grudge.

Back in the clubhouse, all three guys were shaking their heads. This woman was a riddle no one could figure out. They had a couple of beers, and finally, one of the men asked her point blank, "How do you decide if you're going to golf right-handed or left-handed?"

The lady blushed, and grinned. "That's easy," she said. "When my Dad taught me to play golf, I learned I was ambidextrous. I like to switch back and forth. When I got married in college, I discovered my husband always sleeps in the nude. From then on, I developed a silly habit. Right before I left in the morning for golf practice, I would pull the covers off him. If his you-know-what was pointing to the right, I golfed right-handed; if it was pointed to the left, I golfed left-handed. Right before I left in the morning for golf practice, I would pull the covers off him. If his you-know-what was pointing to the right, I golfed right-handed; if it was pointed to the left, I golfed left-handed.

The guys on the team thought this was hysterical. Astonished at this bizarre information, one of the guys shot back, "But what if it's pointing straight up in the air?"

She said, "Then, I'm fifteen minutes late."

• • •

A couple was on their honeymoon, lying in bed, about ready consummate their marriage, when the new bride said to the husband, "I have a confession to make, I'm not a virgin."

The husband replied, "That's no big thing in this day and age."
The wife continued, "Yeah, I've been with one guy.
"Oh yeah? Who was the guy?"
"Tiger Woods."
"Tiger Woods, the golfer?"
"Yeah."
"Well, he's rich, famous, and handsome. I can see why you went to bed with him"

The husband and wife then made passionate love. When they were done, the husband got and walked to the telephone. "What are you doing?" asked the wife.

The husband answered, "I'm hungry, I was going to call room service and get something to eat."

"Tiger wouldn't do that."

"Oh yeah? What would Tiger do?"

"He'd come back to bed and do it a second time."

The husband put down the phone and got back to bed to make love a second time. When they finished, he got up and went over to the phone.

"Now what are you doing now?" She asked.

The husband said, "I'm still hungry so I was going to get room service to get something to eat."

"Tiger wouldn't do that."

"Oh yeah? What would Tiger do?"

"He'd come back to bed and do it again."

The guy slammed down the phone, went back to bed, and made love one more time.

When they finished he was tired and beat. He dragged himself over to the phone and started to dial.

The wife asked, "Are you calling room service?"

"No! I'm calling Tiger Woods, to find out what's par for this damn hole!"

• • •

### Golfer's Honeymoon

A guy out on the golf course takes a high speed ball right in the crotch. Writhing in agony, he falls to the ground. As soon as he could manage, he took himself to the doctor.

He said "How bad is it doc? I'm going on my honeymoon next week and my fiancée is still a virgin in every way"

## Politicians & Diapers Should Be Changed Frequently

The doctor told him, "I'll have to put your willie in a splint to let it heal and keep it straight; it should be okay next week."

He took four tongue depressors and formed a neat little 4 sided splint, and taped it all together; an impressive work of art.

The guy mentions none of this to his fiancée,' marries her, and goes on their honeymoon. That night in the motel room, she rips open her blouse to reveal her beautiful breasts. She said, "You're the first; no one has **ever** touched these."

He immediately dropped his pants and replied "Look at this, still in the crate!"

• • •

A bum, who obviously had seen more than his share of hard times, approached A well dressed gentleman on the street.

"Hey, Buddy, can you spare two dollars?"

The gentleman responded, "You are not going to spend in on liquor are you'?"

"No, sir, I don't drink," retorted the bum.

"You are not going to throw it away in some crap game, are you?" asked the gentleman.

"No way, I don't gamble," answered the bum.

"You wouldn't waste the money at a golf course for greens fees, would you?" asked the man.

"Never" says the bum, "I don't play golf."

The man asked the bum if he would like to come home with him for a home cooked meal. The bum accepted eagerly. While they are heading for the man's house, the bum's curiosity got the better of him. "Isn't your wife going to be angry when she see a guy like me at your table?"

"Probably," says the man, "but it will be worth it. I want her to see what happens to a guy who doesn't drink, gamble or play golf."

## Catholic Golf.

A nun walks into Mother Superior's office and plunked down into a chair. She let out a sigh heavy with frustration.

"What troubles you, Sister?" asked the Mother Superior. "I thought this was the day you spent with your family."

"It was," sighed the Sister. "And I went to play golf with my brother. We try to play golf as often as we can. You know I was quite a talented golfer before I devoted my life to the church."

"I seem to recall that," the Mother Superior agreed. "So I take it your day of recreation was not relaxing?"

"Far from it," snorted the Sister. "In fact, I even took the Lord's name in vain today!"

"Goodness, Sister!" gasped the Mother Superior, astonished. "You must tell me all about it!"

"Well, we were on the fifth tee...and this hole is a monster Mother...540 yard Par five, with a nasty dogleg left and a hidden green...and I hit the drive of my life. I creamed it. The sweetest swing I ever made.

And it's flying straight and true, right along the line I wanted... and it hits a bird in mid-flight!"

"Oh my!" commiserated the Mother. "How unfortunate! But surely that didn't make you blaspheme, Sister!"

"No, that wasn't it," admitted Sister. "While I was still trying to fathom what had happened, this squirrel ran out of the woods, grabbed my ball and scurried off down the fairway!"

"Oh, that would have made me blaspheme!" sympathized the Mother.

"But I didn't, Mother!" sobbed the Sister. "And I was so proud of myself! And while I was pondering whether this was a sign from God, this hawk swooped out of the sky and grabbed the squirrel and flew off, with my ball still clutched in his paws!"

"So that's when you cursed," said the Mother with a knowing smile.

"Nope, that wasn't it either," cried the Sister, anguished, "because as the hawk started to fly out of sight, the squirrel started struggling, and the hawk dropped him right there on the green, and the ball popped out of his paws and rolled to about 18 inches from the cup!"

Mother Superior sat back in her chair, folded her arms across her chest, fixed the Sister with a baleful stare and said, "You missed the fucking putt, didn't you?

• • •

## Catholic Golf
(Another version)

A Catholic priest and a nun were taking a rare afternoon off and enjoying a round of golf.

The priest stepped up to the first tee and took a mighty swing. He missed the ball entirely and said "Shit, I missed."

The good Sister told him to watch his language.

On his next swing, he missed again. "Shit, I missed."

"Father, I'm not going to play with you if you keep swearing," the nun said tartly.

The priest promised to do better and the round continued.

However, on the 4th tee, he misses again. The usual comment followed.

Sister was really angry now and said, "Father John, God is going to strike you dead if you keep swearing like that."

On the next tee, Father John swings and misses again.

"Shit, I missed."

A terrible rumble was heard and a gigantic bolt of lightning came out of the sky and struck Sister Marie dead in her tracks.

And from the sky came a booming voice

"Shit, I missed."

• • •

During my physical, my doctor asked me about my daily activity level. So I described a typical day this way:

"Well, yesterday afternoon, I waded along the edge of a lake, escaped from wild dogs in the heavy brush, marched up and down several rocky hills, stood in a patch of poison ivy, crawled out of quicksand, and jumped away from an aggressive rattlesnake."

Inspired by my story, the doctor said, "You must be some outdoorsman!"

"No," I replied, "I'm just a Shitty golfer."

• • •

A golfer is in a competitive match with a friend, who is ahead by a couple of strokes. "Boy, I'd give anything to sink this putt," the golfer mumbles to himself.

Just then, a stranger walked up beside him and whispered, "Would you be willing To give up one-fourth of your sex life?"

Thinking the man is crazy and his answer will be meaningless, the golfer also felt that maybe this is a good omen so he said, "Sure," and sinks the putt.

Two holes later, he mumbles to himself again, "Gee, I sure would like to get an eagle on this one."

The same stranger is at his side again and whispered, "Would it be worth giving up another fourth of your sex life?"

Shrugging, the golfer replied, "Okay" And he makes an eagle.

On the final hole, the golfer needed another eagle to win. Without waiting for him to say anything, the stranger quickly moved to his side and said, "Would winning this match be worth giving up the rest of your sex life?"

"Definitely," the golfer replied, and he made the eagle.

As the golfer was walking to the club house, the stranger walked alongside him and said, "I haven't really been fair with you because you don't know who I am. I'm the devil, and from this day forward you will have no sex life."

"Nice to meet you," the golfer replied, "I'm Father O'Malley."

• • •

Four men went golfing one day. Three of them headed to the first tee and the fourth went into the clubhouse to take care of the bill. The three men started talking and bragging about their sons.

The first man told the others, "My son is a home builder, and he is so successful that he gave a friend a new home for free.

The second man said, "My son was a car salesman, and now he owns a multi-line dealership. He's so successful that he gave a friend a new Mercedes, fully loaded.

The third man, not wanting to be outdone, bragged, "My son is a stockbroker, and he's doing so well that he gave a friend an entire portfolio.

The fourth man joined them on the tee after a few minutes of taking care of business. The first man mentioned, "We are just talking about our sons, how is yours doing?

The fourth man replied, "Well, my son is gay and go-go dances in a gay bar."

The other three men grew silent, as he continued, "I'm not totally thrilled about the dancing, but he must be doing well. His last three boyfriends gave him, a house, a brand new Mercedes and a stock portfolio.

• • •

Four men were out golfing and discussing how each convinced their wife to let them play golf every morning.

1st guy: I had to buy my wife a BMW to let me play golf daily.

2nd guy: You got off cheap! I had to buy my wife a BMW and a mink coat.

3rd guy: You both got off dirt cheap! I had to buy my wife the BMW, mink coat and a diamond necklace.

4th guy: Ha! I didn't have to buy my wife a single thing! Every morning when I wake up, I lean over in bed, nudge my wife and ask, "Intercourse or golf course?" She instantly replies, "Don't forget to take your sweater."

• • •

A man staggered into an emergency room with a concussion, multiple bruises, two black eyes and a five iron wrapped tightly around his throat. Naturally, the doctor asked him what happened.

"Well, it was like this", said the man. "I was having a quiet round of golf with my wife, when at a difficult hole. We both sliced our balls into a pasture of cows. We went to look for them, and while I was rooting around noticed one of the cows had something white at its rear end. I walked over and lifted up the tail, and sure enough, there was a golf ball with my wife's monogram on it – stuck right in the middle of the cow's anus! That's when I made my big mistake."

What did you do?" asked the doctor.

"Well, I lifted the cow's tail and yelled to my wife, 'Hey, this looks like yours!' I don't remember much after that."

• • •

Toward the end of the golf course, Dave somehow managed to hit his ball into the woods, finding it in a patch of pretty yellow buttercups. Trying to get his ball back in play, he ended up thrashing just about every buttercup in the patch.

All of a sudden...POOF!! In a flash and puff of smoke, a little old woman appeared. She said, "I'm Mother Nature! Do you know how long it took me to make those buttercups? Just for that, you won't have any butter for your popcorn for the rest of your life; better still, you won't have any butter for your toast for the rest of your life. As a matter of fact, you won't have any butter for anything the rest of your life!" THEN, POOF...there she was ... gone.

After Dave got hold of himself, he hollered for his friend, Fred. "Fred, where are you?"

Fred yelled back, "I'm over here, in the pussy willows."

Dave yelled back, "DON'T SWING, FRED!! For the love of God, DON'T SWING!!"

• • •

A fellow, who had been stranded on a desert island all alone for ten years, saw an unusual speck on the horizon. "It's certainly not a ship," he thinks to himself. And as the speck got closer arid closer, he begins to rule out the possibilities of a small boat, then even a raft.

Suddenly, emerging from the surf came a drop-dead gorgeous blonde woman wearing a wet suit and scuba gear. She approached the stunned fellow and asked, "How long has it been since you had a cigarette?"

"Ten years!" he says.

She reached over and unzipped a waterproof pocket on her left sleeve and pulled out a pocket of fresh cigarettes. He took one, lit it, and took a long drag, and said, "Man, oh man, is that ever good?"

She then asked him, "How long has it been since you've had a sip of bourbon?" Trembling with expectation, he replied, "Ten years!"

She then reached over, unzipped her waterproof pocket on the right sleeve, extracted a flask, and handed it to him.

He opened the flask, takes a long swig, and said, "Wow, that's absolutely fantastic!"

Then, she started slowly unzipping the long zipper that ran down the front of her wet suit, looked at him seductively, and asked, "How long has it been since you've played around?"

The guy, with tears welling from his eyes and running down his tanned cheeks, replied, "Oh sweet Jesus, don't tell me you've got a set of golf clubs in there!"

• • •

A husband and wife loved to golf together, but neither of them were playing like they really wanted to, so they decided to take private lessons. The husband had his lesson first. After the pro witnessed his swing, he said, "No, no, no, you're gripping the club way too hard!"

"Well, what should I do?" asked the man.

"Hold the club gently," the pro replied, "Just like you'd hold your wife's breast." Taking the advice, he took a swing, and POW! He hits the ball 250 yards straight up the fairway. The man went back to his wife with the good news and the wife couldn't wait for her lesson.

The next day the wife went to the pro for her lesson. The pro watched her swing and says, "No, no, no, you're gripping the club way too hard."

"What can I do?" asks the wife.

"Hold the club gently just like you'd hold your husband's penis."

The wife listens carefully to the pro's advice, takes a swing and THUMP. The ball goes straight down the fairway about 15 feet.

"That was great," the pro says. "Now, take the club out of your mouth and swing it like you're supposed to!"

• • •

**Rules of Bedroom Golf**

1. Each player shall furnish his own equipment, normally one club and two balls.
2. Play on a course must be approved by the owner of the holes.
3. Owner of the course must approve the equipment before play may begin.
4. For most effective play, the club must have a firm shaft. Course owners are permitted to check the shaft stiffness before play begins.
5. Course owners reserve the right to restrict the shaft length to avoid any damage to the course .

6. Unlike outdoor golf, the goal is to get the club in the hole, while keeping the balls out.
7. The object of the game is to take as many strokes as deemed needed necessary until the course owner is satisfied that play is complete. Failure to do so may result in being denied permission to play the course in the future.
8. It is considered bad form to begin playing the hole immediately upon arrival at the course. The experienced player will normally take time to admire the entire course, with special attention being given to the well formed bunkers.
9. Players are cautioned not to mention other courses they may have played or are currently playing to the owner of the course being played. Upset course owners have been known to damage a players equipment for this reason.
10. Players should assure themselves that their match has been properly scheduled, particularly when a new course is being played for the first time.
11. Players should not assume a course is in shape for play at all times. Some players may embarrassed if they find the course to be temporarily under repair. Players are advised to be extremely tactful in this situation. More advanced players will find alternate means of play when this is the case. Players are encouraged to have proper rain gear along, just in case.
12. Players are advised to obtain the course owners permission before attempting to play the back nine.
13. Slow play is encouraged, however, players should be prepared to proceed at a quicker pace, at least temporarily, at the request of the course owner.
14. It is considered outstanding performance, time permitting, to play the same hole several times in one match.
15. The course owner will be the sole judge as to who is the best player.
16. Players are advised to think twice before considering a membership at a given course. Additional assessments may be levied by the course owner, and they are subject to change. For this

reason many players prefer to continue to play several different courses.

• • •

An 80-year old Italian man goes to the doctor for a check-up. The doctor is amazed at what good shape the guy is in and asks, "How do you stay in such great physical condition?"

I'm Italian and I am a golfer," says the old guy, "and that's why I'm in such good shape." I'm up well before daylight and out golfing up and down the fairways. Have a glass of vino, and all is well."

"Well," says the doctor, "I'm sure that helps, but there's got to be more to it. How old was your Dad when he died?"

"Who said my Dad's dead?"

The doctor is amazed. "You mean you're 80 years old and your Dad's still alive. How old is he?"

"He's 100 years old," replied the old Italian golfer. "In fact he golfed with me this morning, and then we went to the topless beach for a walk, that's why he's still a live ... he's Italian and he's a golfer too."

"Well," the doctor says, "that's great, but I'm sure there's more to it than that. How about your Dad's Dad? How old was he when he died?"

"Who said my grandpa's dead? He's still a' kick'n."

Stunned, the doctor asks, "You mean you're 80 years old and your grandfather's still living! Incredible, how old is he?"

"He's 118 years old," replied the old Italian golfer. The doctor was getting frustrated at this point, "So, I guess he went golfing with you this morning too?"

"No. Grandpa couldn't go this morning because he's getting married today."

At this point the doctor was close to losing it. "Getting married!! Why would a 118 year-old guy want to get married?"

"Who said he wanted to?"

• • •

One day, a man came home and was greeted by his wife dressed in a very sexy nightie.

"Tie me up," she purred, "and you can do anything you want."

So he tied her up and went golfing.

• • •

Ed and Dorothy met while on a singles cruise and Ed fell head over heels for her. When they discovered they lived in the same city only a few miles apart Ed was ecstatic. He immediately started asking her out when they got home.

Within a couple of weeks, Ed had taken Dorothy to dance clubs, restaurants, concerts, movies, and museums. Ed became convinced that Dorothy was indeed his soul mate and true love. Every date seemed better than the last. On the one-month anniversary of their first dinner on the cruise ship, Ed took Dorothy to a fine restaurant.

While having cocktails and waiting for their salad, Ed said, "I guess you can tell I'm very much in love with you. I'd like a little serious talk before our relationship continues to the next stage. So, before I get a box out of my jacket and ask you a life changing question, it's only fair to warn you, I'm a total golf nut. I play golf, I read about golf, I watch golf on TV. In short, I eat, sleep, and breathe golf. If that's going to be a problem, for us, you'd better say so now!"

Dorothy took a deep breath and responded, "Ed, that certainly won't be a problem. I love you as you are and I love golf too; but, since we're being totally honest with each other, you need to know that for the last five years I've been a hooker."

"Oh wow! I see," Ed replied. He looked down at the table, and was quiet for a moment, deep in serious thought then he added, "You know, it's probably because you're not keeping your wrists straight when you hit the ball."

• • •

A Catholic Priest, an Indian Doctor, a rich Chinese Businessman and an Aussie were waiting one morning for a particularly slow group of golfers in front of them.

The Aussie fumed, "What's with those blokes? We must have been waiting for fifteen minutes!"

The Indian Doctor chimed in, "I don't know, but I've never seen such poor golf!"

The Chinese Businessman called out "Move it, time is money"

The Catholic Priest said, "Here comes George the greens keeper. Let's have a word with him."

"Hello, George!" said the Catholic Priest, "What's wrong with that group ahead of us? They're rather slow, aren't they?"

George the greens keeper replied, "Oh, yes, that's a group of blind fire fighters. They lost their sight saving our clubhouse from a fire last year, so we always let them play for free anytime."

The group fell silent for a moment.

The Catholic Priest said, "That's so sad. I think I will say a special prayer for them tonight."

The Indian Doctor said, "Good idea. I'm going to contact my ophthalmologist colleague and see if there's anything he can do for them."

The Chinese Businessman replied, "I think I'll donate $50,000 to the fire-fighters in honour of these brave souls."

The Aussie said, "Why can't they play at night?"

• • •

A father put his 3-year-old daughter to bed, told her a story & listened to her prayers, which ended by saying: "God bless Mommy, God bless Daddy, and God bless Gandma & good-bye Grandpa."

The father asked, "Why did you say good-bye grandpa?"

The little girl said, "I don't know daddy, it just seemed like the thing to do."

The next day grandpa died. The father thought it was a strange coincidence.

A few months later the father put the girl to bed & listened to her prayers which went like this: "God bless Mommy, God Bless Daddy & good-bye Grandma."

The next day the grandmother died.

Oh my gosh, thought the father, this kid is in contact with the other side.

Several weeks later when the girl was going to bed the dad heard her say: "God bless Mommy & good-bye Daddy."

He practically went into shock. He couldn't sleep all night & got up at the crack of dawn to go to his office. He was nervous as a cat all day, had lunch & watched the clock. He figured if he could get by until midnight he would be okay. He felt safe in the office, so instead of going home at the end of the day he stayed there, drinking coffee, looking at his watch & jumping at every sound. Finally midnight arrived, he breathed a sigh of relief & went home. When he got home his wife said, "I've never seen you work so late, what's the matter?"

He said "I don't want to talk about it, I've just spent the worst day of my life."

She said, "You think you had a bad day, you'll never believe what happened to me. This morning my golf pro dropped dead in the middle of my lesson!"

• • •

Tiger Woods & Stevie Wonder were in a bar. Tiger turns to Stevie and said, "How's the singing career going?"

Stevie replies, "Not too bad. How's the golf?"

Woods replies, "Not too bad, I've had some problems with my swing, but I think I've got that right, now."

Stevie said, "I always find that when my swing goes wrong, I need to stop playing for a while and not think about it. Then, the next play, it seems to be all right."

Incredulous, Tiger says, "You play GOLF?"

Stevie says, "Yes, I've been playing for years."

Tiger replies, "But – you're blind! How can you play golf if you can't see?"

Stevie Wonder replies, "Well, I get my caddy to stand in the middle of the fairway and call to me. I listen for the sound of his voice and play the ball towards him. Then, when I get to where the ball lands, the caddy moves to the green or farther down the fairway and again I play the ball towards his voice."

But, "how do you putt" asks Tiger.

"Well", says Stevie, "I get my caddy to lean down in front of the hole and call to me with his head on the ground and I just play the ball toward his voice."

Tiger asks, "What's your handicap?"

Stevie says, "Well, actually – I'm a scratch golfer."

Woods, incredulous again, says to Stevie, "We've got to play a round sometime."

Stevie replied, "Well, people don't take me seriously, so I only play for money, and never play for less than $10,000 a hole. Is that a problem?"

Woods thinks about it and says, "I can afford that; OK, I'm game for that. $10,000 a hole is fine with me. When would you like to play?"

Stevie Wonder says. "Pick a night."

• • •

A crusty old golfer came in from a round of golf at a new course and headed into the grill room. As he passed through the swinging doors he saw a sign hanging over the bar:

| | |
|---|---|
| COLD BEER: | $2.00 |
| HAMBURGER: | $2.25 |
| CHEESEBURGER: | $2.50 |
| CHICKEN SANDWICH: | $3.50 |
| HAND JOB: | $50.00 |

Checking his wallet to be sure he has the necessary payment, the old golfer walked up to the bar and beckoned to the exceptionally attractive female bartender who was serving drinks to a couple of sun-wrinkled golfers. She glided down behind the bar to the old golfer.

"Yes?" she inquired with a wide, knowing smile, "May I help you?"

The old golfer leaned over the bar and whispered, "I was wondering, young lady, are you the one who gives the hand-jobs?"

She looked into his eyes with that wide smile and purred: "Yes Sir, I sure am"

The old golfer leaned closer and into her left ear and said softly, "Well, wash your hands real good, 'cause I want a cheeseburger."

• • •

A guy was getting ready to tee off on the first hole when a second golfer approached and asked if he could join him The first said that he usually played alone, but agreed to the twosome.

They were even after the first few holes. The second fellow said, "We're about evenly matched, how about playing for five bucks a hole?"

The first guy said that he wasn't much for betting, but agreed to the terms.

The second guy won the remaining sixteen holes with ease.

As they were walking off number eighteen, the second golfer was busy counting his $80.00. He confessed that he was the pro at a neighboring course and liked to pick on suckers.

The first fellow revealed that he was the Parish Priest.

The pro was flustered and apologetic, offering to return the money.

The Priest said, "You won fair and square and I was foolish to bet with you. You keep your winnings."

The pro said, "Is there anything I can do to make it up to you?"

The Priest said, "Well, you could come to Mass on Sunday and make a donation. And, if you want to bring your mother and father along, I'll marry them.

• • •

## Golfing Wit and Wisdom

When I die, bury me on the golf course, so my husband will visit. Author Unknown

I don't say my golf game is bad, but if I grew tomatoes they'd come up sliced. Author Unknown

I've spent most of my life golfing. The rest I've just wasted. Author Unknown

They call it golf because all the other four-letter words were taken. Raymond Floyd

The ardent golfer would play Mount Everest if somebody would put a flag stick on top. Pete Dye (His golf courses reflect this defy belief)

Golf is played by twenty million mature American men whose wives think they are out having fun. Jim Bishop

It took me seventeen years to get three thousand hits in baseball. I did it in one afternoon on the golf course. Hank Aaron

Golf is a game in which you yell "fore," shoot six, and write down five. Paul Harvey

Give me golf clubs, fresh air and a beautiful partner, and you can keep the clubs and the fresh air. Jack Benny

Have you ever noticed what golf spells backwards? Al Boliska

The only time my prayers are never answered is on the golf course. Billy Graham

Reverse every natural instinct and do the opposite of what you are inclined to do, and you will probably come very close to having a perfect golf swing. Ben Hogan

Go play golf. Go to the golf course. Hit the ball. Find the ball. Repeat until the ball is in the hole. Have fun. The end. Chuck Hogan

If you think it's hard to meet new people, try picking up the wrong golf ball. Jack Lemmon

It's good sportsmanship to not pick up lost golf balls while they are still rolling. Mark Twain

Don't play too much golf. Two rounds a day are plenty. Harry Vardon

Golf is a game in which one endeavors to control a ball with implements ill adapted for the purpose. Woodrow Wilson

A golfer's diet: live on greens as much as possible. Author Unknown

Gone golfin' ... be back about dark thirty. Author Unknown

Born to golf. Forced to work. Author Unknown

My body is here, but my mind has already teed off. Author Unknown

Golf and sex are the only things you can enjoy without being good at them. Jimmy DeMaret

May thy ball lie in green pastures .... and not in still waters. Author Unknown

If I hit it right, it's a slice. If I hit it left, it's a hook. If I hit it straight, it's a miracle. Author Unknown

The difference in golf and government is that in golf you can't improve your lie. George Deukmejian

Golf is a game invented by the same people who think music comes out of bagpipes. Author Unknown

• • •

All golfers should live so long as to be this kind of old man! Toward the end of the Sunday service, the Minister asked, "How many of you have forgiven your enemies?"

Eighty percent held up their hands.

The Minister then repeated his question. All responded this time, except one man, Walter Barnes, who attended church only when the weather was bad.

"Mr. Barnes, it's obviously not a good morning for golf. It's good to see you here today. Are you not willing to forgive your enemies?"

"I don't have any," he replied gruffly.

"Mr. Barnes, that is very unusual. How old are you?"

"Ninety-eight," he replied. The congregation stood up and clapped their hands.

"Oh, Mr. Barnes, would you please come down in front and tell us all how a person can live ninety-eight years and not have an enemy in the world?"

The old golfer tottered down the aisle, stopped in front of the pulpit, turned around, faced the congregation, and said simply, "I outlived all them assholes" - and he calmly returned to his seat.

• • •

### Murphy's Laws of Golf

A two-foot putt counts the same as a two-foot drive.
Never wash your ball on the tee of a water hole.
There is no such thing as a friendly wager.
The stages of golf are Sudden Collapse, Radical Change, Complete Frustration, Slow Improvement, Brief Mastery, and Sudden Collapse.
The only sure way to get a par is to leave a four-foot birdie putt two inches short of the hole.
Don't play with anyone who would question a 7.
It's as easy to lower your handicap as it is to reduce your hat size.
If you really want to be better at golf, go back and take it up at a much earlier age.
If your driver is hot, your putter will be ice cold; if you can hit your irons, you will top your woods; if you are keeping your right elbow tucked in, your head will come up.
Progress in golf consists of two steps forward and ten miles backward.
One good shank deserves another.
It takes 17 holes to really get warmed up.
No golfer ever swung too slowly.
No golfer ever played too fast.
One birdie is a hot streak.
No matter how badly you are playing, it's always possible to play worse.
Whatever you think you're doing wrong is the one thing you're doing right.
Any change works for three holes.

The odds of hitting a duffed shot increase by the square of the number of people watching.

Never teach golf to your wife.

Never play your son for money.

Never try to keep more than 300 separate thoughts in your mind during your swing.

The less skilled the player, the more likely he is to share his ideas about the golf swing.

I's surprisingly easy to hole a 50-foot putt when you lie 10.

The statute of limitation on forgotten strokes is two holes.

Bets lengthen putts and shorten drives.

Confidence evaporates in the presence of fairway water.

It takes considerable pressure to make a penalty stroke adhere to a scorecard.

It's not a gimme if you're still away.

The more your opponent quotes the rules, the greater the certainty that he cheats.

Always limp with the same leg for the whole round.

The rake is always in the other trap.

The wind is in your face on 16 of the 18 holes.

Nothing straightens out a nasty slice quicker than a sharp dog-leg to the right.

The rough will be mowed tomorrow.

The ball always lands where the pin was yesterday.

It always takes at least five holes to notice that a club is missing.

The nearest sprinkler head will be blank.

Every time a golfer makes a birdie, he must subsequently make two triple bogeys to restore the fundamental equilibrium of the universe.

You can hit a 2-acre fairway 10% of the time and a two inch branch 90% of the time.

Out of bounds is always on the right, for right-handed golfers.

The practice green is either half as fast or twice as fast as all the other greens.

No one with funny head covers ever broke par (except for Tiger Woods).

The lowest numbered iron in your bag will always be impossible to hit.

Your straightest iron shot of the day will be exactly one club short.

No matter how far its shaft extends, a ball retriever is always a foot too short to reach the ball.

If you seem to be hitting your shots straight on the driving range, it's probably because you're not aiming at anything.

A ball you can see in the rough from 50 yards away is not yours.

The only thing you can learn from golf books is that you can't learn anything from golf books, but you have to read an awful lot of golf books to learn it.

• • •

A husband reluctantly agreed to play in the couples' alternate shot tournament at his club. He teed off on the first hole, a par four, and blistered a drive 300 yards down the middle of the fairway. Upon reaching the ball, the husband said to his wife, "Just hit it toward the green, anywhere around there will be fine."

The wife proceeded to shank the ball deep into the woods. Undaunted, the husband said "That's OK, Sweetheart" and spent the full five minutes looking for the ball. He found it just in time but in a horrible position. He played the shot of his life to get the ball within two feet of the hole. He told his wife to knock the ball in.

His wife then proceeded to knock the ball off the green and into a bunker.

Still maintaining composure, the husband summoned all of his skill and holed the shot from the bunker.

He took the ball out of the hole and, while walking off the green, put his arm around his wife and calmly said, "Honey, that was a bogey five and that's OK, but I think we can do better on the next hole".

To which she replied, "Listen asshole, don't bitch at me, only 2 of those 5 shots were mine."

• • •

In 1923, Who Was:

1. President of the largest steel company?
2. President of the largest gas company?
3. President of the New York stock Exchange?
4. Greatest wheat speculator?
5. President of the Bank of International Settlement?
6. The Great Bear of Wall Street?

These men were considered some of the worlds most successful of their days.

Now, 90 years later, the history book asks us, if we know what ultimately became of them.

The Answers:

1. The president of the largest steel company. Charles Schwab, died a pauper.
2. The president of the largest gas company, Edward Hopson, went insane.
3. The president of the NYSE, Richard Whitney, was released from prison to die at home.
4. The greatest wheat speculator, Arthur Cooger, died abroad, penniless.
5. The president of the Bank of International Settlement, shot himself.
6. The Great Bear of Wall Street, Cosabee Livermore, also committed suicide.

However, in that same year, 1923, the PGA Champion and the winner of the most important golf tournament, the US Open, was Gene Sarazen. What became of him?

He played golf until he was 92 and died in 1999 at the age of 95. He was financially secure at the time of his death.

The Moral: Screw work; Play golf.

• • •

A particularly skilled golfer was in a terrible accident during which he lost his right arm. At the emergency hospital, he fell into a bit of very good luck: A surgeon on the staff was able to locate a donor arm which he could transplant on the shoulder of the unfortunate golfer. The only problem was that, although the tissue match was fairly close to his own genomic endowment, the donor was a young woman who had lost her life in a terrible accident.

Several months after the transplantation, the golfer was on the golf course and noticed that the foursome who were just ahead of his small group included the surgeon who had so helped him in his time of need.

The surgeon noticed his patient and excused himself from his friends for a moment to chat with the transplant recipient.

"How is it going?"

His patient replied, "Oh, *really* great doctor. My putting is actually more accurate because I put a little less force on the club and, thus the ball runs straighter toward the cup. My drives are not as lengthy, but they are more accurate and I slice the ball much less often. My handwriting is much more legible, and I can now place cut flowers in very nice arrangements. My only problem is that when I get an erection, I simultaneously get a headache!"

• • •

A husband and wife are on the 9th green when suddenly she collapsed from a heart attack! "Help me dear," she groans to her husband.

The husband called 911 on his cell phone, talked for a few minutes, picked up his putter, and lined up his putt.

His wife raised her head off the green and stared at him. "I'm dying here and you're putting?"

"Don't worry dear," said the husband calmly, "they found a cardiologist on the second hole and he's coming to help you."

"Well, how long will it take for him to get here?" she asks feebly.

"No time at all," says her husband. "Everybody's already agreed to let him play through."

• • •

A gushy reporter told Phil Mickelson, "You are spectacular, your name is synonymous with the game of golf. You really know your way around the course. What's your secret?"

Mickelson replied, "The holes are numbered."

• • •

A young man and a priest are playing together. At a short par-3 the priest asks, "What are you going to use on this hole, my son?"

The young man says, "An 8-iron, Father. How about you?"

The priest says, "I'm going to hit a soft seven and pray."

The young man hit his 8-iron and putted the ball onto the green. The priest topped his 7-iron and dribbled the ball out a few yards.

The young man exclaimed, "I don't know about you, Father, but in my church, when we pray, we keep our head down."

• • •

Police were called to an apartment and found a woman, holding a bloody 5-iron, standing over a lifeless man.

The detective asked, "Ma'am, is that your husband?"

"Yes" says the woman.

"Did you hit him with that golf club?"

"Yes, yes, I did." The woman began to sob, dropped the club, and put her hands to her face.

"How many times did you hit him?"

"I don't know – five, six, maybe seven times – just put me down for a five."

• • •

A golfer teed up his ball on the first tee, took a mighty swing and hit his ball into a clump of trees. He found his ball and saw an opening between two trees he thought he could hit through. Taking out his 3-wood, he took a mighty swing. The ball hit a tree, bounced back, hit him in the forehead and killed him. As he approached the gates of Heaven, St. Peter asked, "Are you a good golfer?"

The man replied: "Got here in two, didn't I?"

• • •

The bride was escorted down the aisle and when she reached the altar, the groom was standing there with his golf bag and clubs at his side.
She said: "What are your golf clubs doing here?"
He looked her right in the eye and said, "This isn't going to take all day, is it?"

• • •

## Dave Feherty CBS Golf Announcer

Feherty is a CBS and Golf Channel announcer, who finds very unique, colorful and uninhibited ways of explaining or describing whatever is on his mind ... (probably always on time delay these days).

He said one day, "It would be easier to pick a broken nose, than a winner in that group."
"Fortunately, Rory is 22 years old so his right wrist should be the strongest muscle in his body."
"That ball is so far left, Lassie couldn't find it if it was wrapped in bacon."
"I am sorry Nick Faldo couldn't be here this week. He is attending the birth of his next wife."
Jim Furyk's swing "looks like an octopus falling out of a tree."

Describing VJ Singh's prodigious practice regime, "VJ hits more balls than Elton John's chin." (Thought I was going to hurt myself laughing at this one.)

"That's a great shot with that swing." "It's OK - the bunker stopped it."

At Augusta 2011 - "It's just a glorious day. The only way to ruin a day like this would be to play golf on it."

"That was a great shot - if they'd have put the pin there today."

"Watching Phil Mickelson play golf is like watching a drunk chasing a balloon near the edge of a cliff."

"That green appears smaller than a Pygmy's nipple".

• • •

A Scottish Jew decided to retire and take up golf, so he applied for membership at a local golf club. About a week later he received a letter that his application has been rejected.

He went immediately to the club to inquire as to why.

Secretary: You are aware that this is a Scottish golf club?

Scot: Aye, but I am as Scottish as you are, ma'am, my name is Ian MacTavish.

Secretary: Do you know that on formal occasions we wear a kilt?

Scot: Aye, I do know, and I wear a kilt too.

Secretary: You are also aware, that we wear nothing under the kilt?

Scot: Aye, and neither do I.

Secretary: Are you also aware, that the members sit naked in the steam room?

Scot: Aye, I also do the same.

Secretary: But you are a Jew?

Scot: Aye, I be that.

Secretary: So, being Jewish, you are circumcised, is that correct?

Scot: Aye, I be that, too.

Secretary: I am terribly sorry, but the members just would not feel comfortable sitting in the steam room with you, since your privates are different from theirs.

Scot: Ach, I know that you have to be a Protestant to march with the Orangemen. And I know that you have to be a Catholic to join the Knights of Columbus. But this is the first time I've heard that you have to be a complete prick to join a golf club!

• • •

Some canny duffers have coined their own terms for mild mishaps whilst driving and putting. Here are two:

An "Adolph Hitler" is defined as *two shots in a bunker*.

A "Junior Prom" is defined as *all lip, but no hole*.

• • •

During a physical examination, the doctor asked Howard about his physical activity level. He described a typical day this way:

"Well, in the afternoon, I take a five hour walk about 4 miles through some pretty rough terrain. I waded along the edge of a lake. I pushed my way through brambles. I got sand in my shoes, eyes and hair. Avoided standing on a snake. I climbed several steep hills. I took a few leaks behind some big trees. At the end of it all, I drank four beers.

Impressed by the story, the doctor said, "You must be one hell of an outdoors man!"

"No, I am just a shitty golfer," he replied.

• • •

The Pope met with his cardinals to discuss a proposal from Benjamin Netanyahu, the leader of Israel. "Your Holiness", said one of his Cardinals, Mr. Netanyahu wants to challenge you to a game of golf to show the friendship and ecumenical spirit shared the Jewish and Catholic faiths."

The Pope thought this was a good idea, but he had never held a golf club in his hand. "Don't we have a cardinal to represent me?" He asked.

"None who plays very well," a cardinal replied. "But," he added, there is a man named Jack Nicklaus, an American golfer who is a devout Catholic. We can offer to make him a cardinal, then ask him to play Mr. Netanyahu as your personal representative. In addition, to showing our spirit of cooperation, we'll also win the match."

Everyone agreed it was a good idea. The call was made. Of course, Nicklaus was honored and agreed to play. The day after the match, Nicklaus reported to the Vatican to inform the Pope of the result. "I have some good news and some bad news, your Holiness," said the golfer.

"Tell me the good news first, Cardinal Nicklaus," said the Pope.

"Well your Holiness, I don't like to brag, but even though I've played some pretty terrific rounds of golf in my life, this was best I have ever played, by far. I must have been inspired from above. My drives were long and true, my irons were accurate and purposeful, and my putting was perfect. With all due respect, my play was truly miraculous.

"There's bad news?" the Pope asked.

"Nicklaus sighed. "I lost to Rabbi Tiger Woods by three strokes."

• • •

# BODY PARTS

A slave call girl from Sardinia named Gedophamee was attending a great but as yet unnamed athletic festival 2500 years ago in Greece. In those days, believe it or not, the athletes performed naked. To prevent unwanted arousal while competing, the men imbibed freely on a drink containing saltpeter before and throughout the variety of athletic events.

At the opening ceremonial parade, Gedophamee observed the first wave of naked magnificent males marching toward her and she exclaimed: "OH!! Limp pricks!"

Over the next two and a half millennia that morphed into "Olympics."

• • •

### The difference between Officers and NCOs

A young Army officer was severely wounded in the head by a grenade, but the only visible, permanent injury was that both of his ears were amputated.

Since his remaining hearing was sufficient, he remained in the Army.

Many years later he eventually rose to the rank of Major General. He was, however, very sensitive about his appearance.

One day the General was interviewing three servicemen who were candidates for his headquarters staff.

The first was a Captain, a tactical helicopter pilot, and it was a great interview. At the end of the interview the General asked him, 'Do you notice anything different about me?' The young officer answered, 'Why, yes, Sir, I couldn't help but notice that you have no ears.'

The general was displeased with his lack of tact and threw him out.

The second interview was with a Navy Lieutenant, and he was even better. The General then asked him the same question, 'Do you notice anything different about me?' He replied sheepishly, 'Well, sir, you have no ears.' The General threw him out also.

The third interview was with an old Sergeant Major, an Infantryman and staff-trained NCO. He was smart, articulate, fit, looked sharp, and seemed to know more than the two officers combined.

The General really liked this guy, and went ahead with the same question, 'Do you notice anything different about me?' To his surprise the Sergeant Major said, 'Yes, sir, you wear contact lenses.'

The General was very impressed and thought, 'What an incredibly observant NCO, and he didn't mention my ears.' He asked, 'Sergeant Major, how do you know I wear contacts?'

'Well, sir,' the soldier replied, 'it's pretty hard to wear glasses with no fucking ears.'

• • •

A little boy went shopping with his mother and was waiting right outside of the ladies dressing room for his Mom to come out. While waiting the little boy gets bored and just when his mom came walking out, she saw her son sliding his hand up a mannequin's skirt.

"Get your hand out of there!" she shouted. "Don't you know that women have teeth down there?"

The little boy quickly snatched his hand away and thanked his lucky stars he didn't get bitten.

For the next ten years, the boy grew up believing all women have teeth between their legs. When he was 16, he got a girlfriend. One night, while her parents are out of town, she invited him over for a little action.

After an hour of making out and grinding on the sofa, she said, "You know,
could go a little further if you want."

"What do you mean?" he asked.

"Well, why don't you put your hand down there?" she suggested, pointing to her crotch.

"HELL NO," he cried, "you've got teeth down there!"

"Don't be ridiculous," she responded, "there's no such thing as teeth down there!"

"Yes, there are," he argued, "my Mom told me so."

"No, there aren't," she insisted. "Here, look for yourself." With that, she pulled down her pants and gave him a little peek.

"No, I'm sorry" he said. "My Mom already told me that all women have teeth down there."

"Oh for crying out loud!" she cried. She whipped off her panties, threw her legs behind her head and says, "LOOK, I DON'T have any teeth down there."

The lad took a good long look and replied, "Well, after seeing the condition of those gums, I'm not surprised!"

• • •

Have you heard about the latest Chinese pornographic film? It's title is "Mid Throat."

• • •

The doctor replied 'Of course I won't laugh, I'm a professional. In over twenty years I've never laughed at a patient.'

'Okay then,' Bob said, and proceeded to drop his trousers, revealing the tiniest penis the doctor had ever seen. It couldn't have been bigger than the size of a AAA battery.

Unable to control himself, the doctor started giggling, then fell laughing to the floor. Ten minutes later he was able to struggle to his feet and regain his composure. 'I'm so sorry,' said the doctor. 'I really am. I don't know what came over me. On my honor as a doctor and a gentleman, I promise it won't happen again.

Now, what seems to be the problem?'

'It's swollen,' Bob replied.

• • •

### The Refreshing Swim

The weather was very hot, so this fellow wanted desperately to take a dip in the nearby lake. He didn't bring his swimming outfit, but since he was all alone, he didn't care. He undressed and got into the water.

After some delightful minutes of cool swimming, a pair of old ladies walked onto the shore in his direction. He panicked, got out of the water and grabbed a bucket, which was lying on the sandy beach. He held the bucket in front of his private parts and sighed with relief.

The ladies got nearby and looked at him. He felt awkward and wanted to move. Then one of the ladies said, "You know, I have a special gift, I can read minds."

"Impossible," said the embarrassed man, "You really know what I think?"

"Yes," the lady replied, "I know that you think that the bucket you're holding has a bottom in it."

• • •

A man went to his doctor's and said, "Doc, I've just been raped by an elephant!"

The stunned doctor replied, "What makes you say that?"

"Well," says the man holding his hands about a foot or so apart, "My asshole feels this big!"

"Bend over, and let me have a look." asked the doctor.

The patient bent over and sure enough, his anus was about ten inches in diameter.

"But I thought that elephants only had a long, thin penis?" stated the doctor.

"Yeah, I know," says the agitated man, "but it fingered me first!"

• • •

Americans Jeff & Jim are Siamese twins joined at the hip. They walked into a bar in New York and ordered a couple of beers.

The barman served them and asked "You guys been on vacation yet?"

"We're off to England next week" replied Jeff "We go every year."

The barman said "England's great; the culture, history, the Queen."

Jeff responded "We don't go for that rubbish, it's the only chance Jim gets to drive the fucking car."

• • •

In 1993, the American Government funded a study to see why the head of a penis was bigger than the rest of it. After one year and $180,000.00, they concluded that the reason the head was larger than the shaft was to give the man more pleasure during sex.

After the U.S. published the study, France decided to do their own. After $250,000.00, and 3 years of research, they concluded that the reason was to give the woman more pleasure during sex.

Poland, unsatisfied with these findings, conducted their own study. After two weeks and a cost of around $75.46, they concluded that it was to keep a man's hand from flying off and hitting him in the forehead.

• • •

A lady in her late 401s went to a plastic surgeon for a facelift. The Doctor told her of a new procedure called "The Knob". This small knob is implanted on the back of a woman's head and can be turned to tighten up the skin to produce the effect of a brand new facelift forever.

Of course, the woman wanted "The Knob."

Fifteen years later the woman went back to the surgeon with two problems:

"All of these years everything had been working just fine. I've had to turn the knob on lots of occasions and I'\e loved the results. But now I've developed two rather annoying problems: First of all, I'\e got these terrible bags under my eyes and the knob won't get rid of them."

The doctor looked at her, nodded wisely, and said, "Those aren't bags, those are your breasts."

She replied, "Well, I guess that explains the goatee!"

• • •

A woman was helping her computer-illiterate husband set up his computer. At the appropriate point in the process, she told him that he would now need to choose and enter a password. Something he will use to log on.

The husband was in a rather amorous mood and figured he would try for the shock effect to bring this to his wife's attention. So, when the computer asked him to enter his password, he made it plainly obvious to his wife that he was keying in, "p..e..n..i..s".

His wife nearly fell off her chair laughing when the computer replied:

\*\*\*PASSWORD REJECTED. NOT LONG ENOUGH\*\*\*

• • •

### That Spare Rib

After three weeks in the Garden of Eden, God came to visit Eve. "So, how is everything going?" inquired God. It is all so beautiful, God," she replied, "the sunrises and sunsets are breathtaking, the scents, the sights, everything is wonderful, but I have just this one minor problem. It is these three breasts that you have given me. The middle one pushes the other two out, and I am constantly knocking them with my arms, catching them on branches, snagging them on bushes, they are a real pain," reported Eve. And Eve went on to tell God that since many other parts of her body came in pairs, such as her limbs, eyes, ears, etc., that she felt that having only two breasts might leave her body more "symmetrically balanced," as she put it.

"That is a fair point," replied God, "but it was my first shot at this, you know. I gave the animals four, six, or more breasts, so I figured that you needed only half of those, but I see that you are right. I will fix it right away." And God reached down, removed the middle breast, and tossed it into the bushes.

Three weeks passed, and God once again visited Eve in the garden.

"Well, Eve, how is my favorite creation?"

"Just fantastic," she replied, "but for one oversight on your part. You see, all the animals are paired off. The ewe has a ram and the cow has her bull, all the animals have a mate except me. I feel so alone."

God thought for a moment and said, "You know, Eve, you are right, how could I have overlooked this? Of course, you do need a mate and I will immediately create a man from a part of you. "Now let's see.... where did I put that useless boob?"

• • •

### Ripe Tomatoes

Once there was a beautiful woman who loved to work in her vegetable garden, but no matter what she did, she couldn't get her tomatoes to ripen. Admiring her neighbor's garden, which had beautiful, bright red tomatoes, she went one day and inquired of him his secret.

"It's really quite simple – twice each day, in the morning and in the evening, I expose myself in front of the tomatoes and they turn red with embarrassment."

Desperate for the perfect garden, she tried his advice and proceeded to expose herself to her plants twice daily.

Two weeks passed and her neighbor stopped by to check her progress.

He asked if she had had any luck with her tomatoes.

"No" she replied, "but you should see the size of my cucumbers!!!

• • •

There was this yellow toad wandering around in the forest kind of pissed off because he doesn't want to be yellow. Life would be easier if he were brown like the other toads. He would sure be less visible to predators for one thing.

Anyway, the yellow toad bumped into a fairy godmother. "Fairy godmother, please make me brown like the other toads," he begged her. "I'm hacked off being so visible to predators. The stress is like, killing me, you know?"

"Okay" said the fairy godmother, who whipped out her magic wand and exclaimed: "Abracapokus! You're brown!"

The toad looks down and sees that he is brown — Except— for his weenie, which was still yellow.

"Hang about lady," he says to the fairy godmother, "My pecker's still yellow!"

"Yeah, well I don't do weenies," she said, "You'll have to go see the Wizard of Oz for that."

So the toad thanked her and hopped off on his way.

There is also a purple bear wandering about the very same woods. As luck would have it, he encountered the very same fairy godmother (yes, okay, it's a coincidence, but it's true).

"Fairy Godmother! You're just the person I need!" said the purple bear, "I can't pull any lady bears 'cuz they don't want to be seen with a purple bear on account of the hunters. They can spot me from a mile off."

Being a fairly nice fairy godmother, she took out her magic wand. "Oh for goodness sake, what is the matter with you lot round here" she said, and with that, she yelled: "Pokuscadabra!
You're brown!"

The bear looked down and sees that he is, in fact, brown. Except for his goolies, which remained purple.

"Hold up sweetheart!", he said to the fairy Godmother, "My goolies are still purple!"

"Yeah, well I don't do those goolie things," she replied, "You'll have to go see the Wizard of Oz for that."

"Well that's just dandy, innit?" the bear replied, "How the hell do I find the Wizard of Oz?"

"Easy," says the fairy godmother as she flew off.

"Just follow the yellow-prick toad!"

• • •

Two women were playing golf. One teed off and watched in horror as her ball headed directly toward a foursome of men playing the next hole. The ball hit one of the men. He immediately clasped his hands together at his groin, fell to the ground and proceeded to roll around in agony.

The woman rushed down to the man, and immediately began to apologize.

"Please allow me to help. I'm a physical therapist and I know I could relieve your pain if you woulod allow me", she told him.

"Oh, no, I'll be all right. I'll be fine in a few minutes, the man replied. He was in obvious agony, lying in the fetal position, still clasping his hands there at his groin. At her persistence, however, he finally allowed her to help. She gently took his hands away and laid them to the side, loosened his pants and put her hands inside. She administered tender and artful massage for several long moments and asked,

"How does that feel?"

"Feels great", he replied, "but I think my thumb's still broken!"

• • •

During the service, the pastor asked if anyone in the congregation would like to express thanks for prayers which had been answered. A lady stood up and came forward.

She said, "I have a reason to thank the Lord. Two months ago, my husband, Jim, had a terrible bicycle wreck and his scrotum was completely crushed. The pain was excruciating and the doctors didn't know if they could help him."

You could hear an audible gasp from the men in the congregation as they imagined the pain that poor Jim experienced.

She continued, "Jim was unable to hold me or the children and every move caused him terrible pain. We prayed as the doctors performed a delicate operation. They were able to piece together the crushed remnants of Jim's scrotum and wrap wire around it to hold it in place."

Again, the men in the Congregation squirmed uncomfortably as they imagined the horrible surgery performed on Jim.

She continued, "Now, Jim is out of the hospital and the doctor's say, with time, his scrotum should recover completely."

All the men sighed with relief.

The pastor rose and tentatively asked if any one else had anything to say.

A man rose and walked slowly to the podium. He said, "Hi, I'm Jim and I would like to tell my wife, the word is 'sternum.'"

• • •

A duck hunter was out enjoying a nice morning on the marsh when he decided to take a leak. He walked over to a tree and propped up his gun. Just then a gust of wind blew, the gun fell over, and discharged... shooting him in the genitals.

Several hours later, lying in a hospital bed he was approached by his doctor.

'Well sir, I have some good news and some bad news. The good news is that you are going to be OK. The damage was localized to your groin, there was very little internal damage, and we were able to remove all of the birdshot pellets

"What's the bad news?" asked the hunter.

"The bad news is that there was some pretty extensive birdshot damage done to your penis. I'm going to have to refer you to my brother.

"Oh, well I guess that isn't too bad,' the hunter replied. 'Is your brother a plastic surgeon?"

"Not exactly." answered the doctor. 'He's a flute player in the local symphony and he's going to teach you where to put your fingers so you don't piss in your eye."

• • •

Bruce, an Australian who was working on contract for 3 months in Dublin was drinking in O'Donoghue's pub in Merrion Row when he got a call on his mobile phone. He hung up grinning from ear to ear, ordered a round of drinks for everyone in the bar, because, he announced, his wife back home has just produced a typical baby boy weighing 25 pounds.

Nobody can believe that any baby can weigh in at 25 pounds but Bruce just shrugs, "That's about average in Oz. Like I said my boy is a typical Australian baby boy."

Congratulations showered him from all around and many exclamations were heard. One woman even fainted due to sympathy pains.

Two weeks later Bruce returned to the bar. Greg, the bartender said, "You're the father of that typical Australian baby that weighed 25 pounds at birth. Everybody's been having bets about how big he'd be in 2 weeks we were going to call you. So how much does he weigh now?

The proud father answers "17 pounds."

Greg was puzzled and concerned. "What happened? He weighed 25 pounds the day he was born.

Bruce took a long s-l-o-w swig from his beer, wiped his lips on his shirt sleeve, leaned onto the bar and proudly said .... "Had him circumcised mate"

• • •

Students in an advanced Biology class were taking their mid-term exam. The last question was, 'Name seven advantages of Mother's Milk.' The question was worth 70 points or none at all.

One student, in particular, was hard put to think of seven advantages. However, he wrote:

1) It is perfect formula for the child.
2) It provides immunity against several diseases.
3) It is always the right temperature.
4) It is inexpensive.
5) It bonds the child to mother, and vice versa.
6) It is always available as needed.

And then the student was stuck. Finally, in desperation, just before the bell rang indicating the end of the test, he wrote:

7) It comes in two attractive containers and it is high enough off the ground where the cat can't get it.
    He got an A.

• • •

A cowboy walked into a drug store and asked to talk to a male pharmacist. The elderly woman he was talking to said that she was the pharmacist — and since she and her also widowed elderly sister owned the store – there were no males employed there. She then asked if she could help the gentleman.

The cowboy said that it was something that he would be much more comfortable discussing with a male pharmacist.

The female pharmacist assured him that she was completely professional and whatever it was that he needed to discuss, he could be confident that she would treat him with the highest level of professionalism.

The old bronco-buster agreed and began by saying, "This is tough for me to discuss, but I have a permanent erection. It causes me a lot of problems and severe embarrassment, and I was wondering what you could give me for it."

The pharmacist said, "Just a minute, I'll go talk to my sister."

When she returned, she said, "We discussed it at length – and the absolute best we can do is 1/3 ownership in the store, a company car, and $3,000 a month – plus living expenses."

• • •

A man was sunbathing naked at the beach. For the sake of civility, and to keep it from getting sunburned, he had a hat over his privates.

A woman walked past and said, snickering, "If you were a gentleman you'd lift your hat."

He raised an eyebrow and replied, "If you weren't so ugly it would lift itself."

• • •

## The Human Body

It takes your food seven seconds to get from your mouth to your stomach.

One human hair can support 3 kg (6.6 lb).

The average man's penis is three times the length of his thumb.

Human thighbones are stronger than concrete.

A woman's heart beats faster than a man's.

There are about one trillion bacteria on each of your feet.

Women blink twice as often as men.

The average person's skin weighs twice as much as the brain.

Your body uses 300 muscles to balance itself when you are standing still.

If saliva cannot dissolve something, you cannot taste it.

Women reading this will be finished now.

Men are still busy checking their thumbs.

• • •

A very tall man walked into a bar, and a lady recognized him as a professional rugby player.

They started to talk and eventually go back to his place. They start to kiss, and the man took off his shirt. On his arm, he has a tattoo that says REEBOK.

"What's that for?" the lady questioned.

"Oh, I have this so that when I'm on TV, people will see my tattoo, and Reebok pays me."

Then the man took off his trousers, and on his leg, he has a tattoo that says NIKE.

'What's that?' the lady questioned again.

"Just like the Reebok tattoo, I get paid when this tattoo is seen on TV."

Then the man dropped his underwear and on his penis he has a tattoo that says AIDS.

The lady screamed: "Don't tell me you have AIDS!"

The man replied: "No, no…!!! Calm down…!!!

It will say ADIDAS in a minute."

• • •

## Warning About eBay

If you buy stuff on line, check out the seller carefully. Be careful what you purchase on eBay.

I just spent $100 on a penis enlarger. The bastards sent me a magnifying glass. The instructions said, "Do not use in direct sunlight."

• • •

A man moved into a nudist colony. He received a letter from his grandmother asking him to send her a current photo of himself in his new location. Too embarrassed to let her know that he lived in a nudist colony, he cut a photo in half and mailed it. The next day he discovered that he had accidentally sent the bottom half of the photo. He was really worried but then remembers how bad his grandmother's eyesight is, and hoped she won't notice.

A few weeks later, he received a letter from his Grandmother. It read:

"Thank you for the picture. Change your hairstyle… it makes your nose look too short."

Love, Grandma

• • •

When Jane initially met Tarzan of the jungle, she was attracted to him and during her questions about his life, she asked him how he had sex.

"Tarzan not know sex," he replied.

Jane explained to him what sex was.

Tarzan said, "Oh… Tarzan use hole in trunk of tree."

Horrified, she said, "Tarzan you have it all wrong, but I will show you how to do it properly."

She took off her clothes and lay down on the ground. "Here" she said, "you must put it in here."

Tarzan removed his loin cloth, stepped closer with his huge erection, and then gave her an almighty kick right in the crotch.

Jane rolled around in agony for what seemed like an eternity.

Eventually she managed to gasp for air and screamed, "What did you do that for?"

"Tarzan check for bees."

• • •

### The Pirate in the Bar

A pirate walked into a bar and the bartender said "Hey, I haven't seen you in a while. What happened? You look terrible."

"What do you mean?" said the pirate, "I feel fine."

"What about the wooden leg? You didn't have that before."

"Well," said the pirate, "We were in a battle and I got hit with a cannon ball, but I'm fine now."

The bartender replied, "Well, OK, but what about that hook? What happened to your hand?"

The pirate explained, "We were in another battle. I boarded a ship and got into a sword fight. My hand was cut off. I got fitted with a hook but I'm fine, really."

"What about that eye patch?"

"Oh," said the pirate, "One day we were at sea, and a flock of birds flew over. I looked up, and one of them shat in me eye."

"You're kidding," said the bartender. "You couldn't lose an eye just from bird shit."

"It was my first day with the hook."

• • •

The boss of a Madison Avenue advertising agency called a spontaneous staff meeting in the middle of a particularly stressful week. (This was one pretty sharp boss!). When everyone gathered, the boss, who understood the benefits of having fun, told the burned-out staff the purpose of the meeting was to have a quick contest. The theme: Viagra advertising slogans.

The only rule was they had to use past ad slogans, originally written for other products, that captured the essence of Viagra. Slight variations were acceptable. About 7 minutes later, they turned in their suggestions and created a Top Ten List. With all the laughter and camaraderie, the rest of the week went very well for everyone!

The top 10 were as following:

10. Viagra: Whaazzzz up!
9. Viagra: The quicker pecker picker upper.
8. Viagra: Like a rock!
7. Viagra: When it absolutely, positively has to be there overnight.
6. Viagra: Be all that you can be.
5. Viagra: Reach out and touch someone.
4. Viagra: Strong enough for a man, but made for a woman.

3. Viagra: Home of the whopper!
2. Viagra: We bring good things to Life!

And the unanimous number one slogan:

1. This is your peepee. This is your peepee on drugs.

• • •

Al was getting along in years and finds that he was unable to perform sexually. He finally went to his doctor, who tries a few things but nothing seems to work.

The doctor refers him to an American Indian medicine man. The medicine man declared, "I can cure this." That said, he threw a white powder into a flame, and there was an instant flash with billowing blue smoke. Then he said, "This is powerful medicine. You can only use it once a year. All you have to do is say '123' and it shall rise for as long as you wish!"

Al asked, "What happens when it's over, and I don't want to continue?"

The medicine man replied: "All you or your partner has to say is '1234' and it will go down.

But be warned – it will not work again for another year!"

Al rushed home, eager to try out his new powers and prowess. That night he is ready to surprise Diane. He showered, shaved, and put on his most exotic shaving lotion. He got into bed, and lying next to her says, "123."

He suddenly becomes more aroused than anytime in his life ... just as the medicine man had promised.

Diane, who had been facing away, turned over and asked, "'What did you say 123 for?"

*And that, my friends, is why you shouldn't end a sentence with a preposition.*

• • •

A young woman, heavily burdened with over-stuffed shopping bags of assorted groceries, exited from a produce store and as she stepped over the thresh-hold, the thin paper bags suddenly disintegrated and discharged their contents in a cascade that landed between her legs; the clerk had foolishly placed wet lettuce on the bottom.

Looking down at the resulting disaster comprised of broken eggs, smashed tomatoes, soggy lettuce, and fresh bread that was rapidly absorbing the multihued mess like a white sponge, the woman began to weep as she stared dumbfounded at what now occupied the space lying between her feet.

A moment later, a drunk, reeling up the street stopped for a moment, looked down at what he behold fouling the sidewalk, and shook his head, muttering,

"Now, now, young lady, I shouldn't cry; it wouldn't have lived anyway — its eyes were too close together!"

• • •

A policeman was rushed to the hospital with an inflamed appendix. The doctors operated and advised him that all was well; however, the policeman kept feeling something pulling at his pubic hairs. Worried that it might be a second surgery and the doctors hadn't told him about it, he finally got enough energy to pull his hospital gown up enough so he could look at what was making him so uncomfortable.

Taped firmly across his pubic hair and private parts were three wide strips of adhesive tape, the kind that doesn't come off easily — if at all.

Written on the tape in large black letters was the sentence:

"*Get well soon from the nurse in the Land Rover whom you booked for speeding last week.*"

• • •

Two older women were having lunch together, and discussing the relative merits of cosmetic surgery.

The first woman said, "I need to be honest with you, I'm getting a boob-job."

The second woman responded, "Really? I'm thinking of having my arse-hole bleached!"

"Oh! Dear!" replied the first woman. "I just can't picture your husband as a blonde!"

• • •

A man and a woman were driving down the road, arguing about his deplorable infidelity when suddenly the woman reached over and sliced the man's penis off. Angrily, she tossed it out the car window. Driving behind the couple was a man and his 6-year-old daughter.

The little girl was chatting away at her father when all of a sudden the severed member smacked their car windshield, stuck for a moment, then flew off.

Surprised, the daughter asked her father, 'Daddy, what the heck was that?'

Shocked, but not wanting to expose his little girl to anything sexual at such a young age, the father replied, 'It was only a bug, Honey.'

The daughter sat with a confused look on her face, and after a moment said..

'Sure had a big dick, didn't it.'

• • •

A woman whose hobby was collecting Elvis Presley memorabilia was told by her loving husband that he had purchased a very special birthday gift for her and that she was to collect it for herself at an establishment that was written on a slip of paper that

he handed her.

Diving herself to the address that she was given, she found herself at a tattoo parlor. Thinking that she had been misdirected, she walked into the studio and asked for directions.

"Are you Mrs. Baker?" Asked the tattoo artist.

"Why, yes I am," responded the woman. "Am I in the right place of business?" asked Mrs. Baker.

"Indeed you are; your husband must love you very much because he paid me a large sum to create a special image just for you. Where would you care to have me apply this masterpiece?" The cheerful artist, inquired.

Considering the consequences of her response, the woman smiled demurely and told the tattoo artist to place the portrait of "The King" on the inside of her left thigh.

After several rather painful hours during which the artist applied his talent with multicolored inks, he smiled broadly and gave his patron a hand mirror with which to inspect his handiwork.

Upon first inspection, the woman shrieked, "Oh, how *absolutely AWFUL!*" She was now very distraught as she gazed at her swollen, multi-hued thigh. "How could you have defaced my delicate skin so? My husband and I will sue you for everything you own and he just might come down here and beat you bloody for what you have done to me!"

"Now, now, Madame, you must understand that after so much needling and injection of inks, it is only natural for your skin to a bit swollen. I assure you that after a few days, the swelling will subside and you will be absolutely delighted with my artistry."

The tattooist thought for a moment and said, "Mrs. Baker, I am a fair person; suppose that I create *another* portrait for you at no additional cost; would *that* satisfy you?"

Thinking for a moment, the matron acceded to the offer and told the artist to put yet *another* picture of Elvis on the inner surface of her right thigh, directly opposite the first one.

After enduring another few hours of painful needling, she was again handed the mirror; and again, she was extremely dissatisfied with the result – and again – threatened the tattooist with violence and litigation.

Thinking rapidly, the artist suggested that perhaps a totally disinterested party should be sought to give an impartial opinion of his work. To this suggestion, Mrs. Baker nodded her agreement, whereupon, the tattooist went out to the alley behind his studio and finding a wino, he offered to pay him a five-spot if would go into the shop, look at the tattoos, and give his opinion.

The wino was ushered into the studio and Mrs. Baker was asked to raise her skirt so that the he might get a better view of the pair of Elvises.

"Well, what do you think?" asked the tattoo artist.

"Hey, I don't know who those other fellows are, but the guy in the middle sure looks like Willie Nelson!"

• • •

Sven and Ole were friends since their early childhood in Norway. Sven was bright and had always had his pick of available buxom blond, blue-eyed girls, whereas Ole, was a slower and actually had a few belt loops shy of a full waistband.

One day, Ole asked Sven why it was that he had always been so popular with the girls, whereas, he, Ole, had such trouble meeting eligible lasses. Thinking for a while, Sven rubbed his square chin and opined that it was because most Norwegian girls were as fond of mens' bulges as was any healthy Norwegian man was equally of a girl's smooth curves and bulges.

Shrugging his shoulders, Ole asked Sven what he thought he could do to help attract some girls.

"Try putting a sweet-a-potato in your trousers; ja, girls will certainly notice *THAT*" said Sven.

About a week later, Ole saw Sven on a beach, absolutely surrounded with curvaceous lovely blond lasses.

"Hey Ole, how's it going; did my advice work?" inquired Sven.

"Oh Sven" Ole moaned, "It was awful!"

Always a good friend to Ole, Sven asked what had happened to make him so sad.

"Ja, you betcha, I did what you suggested; I put a nice big sweet-a-potato in my breaches, just like you told me to do. But when I went down to the beach, all of those fine blond girls just laughed and laughed at me; some even kicked sand in my face!"

Sven asked for a demonstration of how Ole had placed the tuberous vegetable in his pants and when he was shown, he exclaimed, "Ach, Ole, you fool; you are supposed to put in the front!"

• • •

After waiting in a line for a few minutes, fellow finally made it into the mens' room during a football game. As he was standing before the urinal trough, he just happened to glance over to his right and spied another fan standing there with an enormous penis in his hand.

"Excuse me sir, I don't usually even glance at another man's "equipment" but, jeez, Luise, that is one righteous tool you have there! Were you born with that thing?!"

"No sir; when I was but a little lad, my pecker was just a little bitty nubbin. Then, I learned that if I soaked it, it would grow bigger and bigger."

"You say that you <u>soak</u> it?!"

"Yeah, that's right."

"What do you soak it in?" asked the first fan.

"Beans"

"Beans? What kind of beans?"

With a glint in his eye, the second fan screamed out "**HUMAN** beans!"

• • •

A fellow was visiting his old high school buddy and founds that he was in deep depression.

"What's the matter, old friend?"

"It's this eye of mine; ever since I lost it in that industrial accident, I can't stand the appearance of my face without that eye" he moaned.

"Well hell, that shouldn't be too difficult to fix; how about having a prosthetic eye fitted? I'll even go with you if you wish."

Agreeing to go, the one-eyed man accompanied his friend. The first eye prostheticist that hey visited showed them some really beautiful examples of his craft; they were truly lifelike and unless one knew that they were replicas of the real thing, they passed perfectly.

"How much?" asked the one-eyed man.

"Sir, these prostheses are made of the finest Venetian glass, hand-blown by old masters; their size, color and tint of the iris is so perfectly matched to your natural one that no one could ever tell that you were not born with it. Because of the artistry and time involved in crafting it, the cost *is* a bit stiff: they are $2,500.00 each."

"Oh, I could never afford to spend so much money on a glass eye. Do you have anything cheaper?"

"Well, yes, I do; we *could* make one for you out of acrylic plastic for a bit less, but it wouldn't look quite as good as the glass one."

"How much?" whined the man."

"$1,500.00" answered the prostheticist. The artistic effort to match your good eye is the same for the Venetian glass one, but the plastic is less expensive." "Couldn't you make one out of even less costly materials?" queried the one-eyed man.

"No, but I do know a colleague who makes fishing lures out of wood that he could paint to at least resemble your good eye."

Going to the address that the prostheticist gave them, the two men approached the fishing lures carver.

"Do you suppose that you could make my friend a false eye?" asked the companion.

Sizing up the problem, the wood carver tells them that yes, he *could* make a false eye but that it wouldn't stand very close scrutiny.

"How much?" asked the man.

"Oh, I could do it for $75.00" answered the carver.

The money was handed over and the one-eyed man was told to come back in two days.

Well, the prosthetic eye looked *ghastly* and, as a result, the poor chap only fell into a deeper depression.

Upon finding his old buddy so deeply down in the dumps, after much persuasion, the friend convinced the one-eyed man to accompany him to a dance. Sitting along one wall like a lump and refusing to approach any woman, the poor chap was encouraged to ask a lone girl who is also sitting on bench across the room.

Immediately upon meeting her, he noticed that she had a poorly repaired hair lip and cleft palate. He asked her whether she would care to dance, to which she replied,

"Oh, *would I, would I*"

Whereupon the one-eyed man screamed "*Hairlip, hairlip!*"

• • •

A fellow was walking along a deserted beach one morning when he stubbed his toe on a half-buried object in the sand. Bending down to inspect what he had stumbled upon, he discovered to his amazement that it was a brass lamp. As he gently brushed away the grains of sand, out popped a genie whose image grew enormously as it issued forth from the lamp's spout.

"What is your wish Oh Master?!" queried the genie.

"How many wishes to I have," replied the greedy man.

"Only one, master, better make it a good one" suggested the genie.

The beachcomber thought for but a moment and responded "I would like to sleep with the three most powerful women in all the world."

The next morning, he woke up in bed with Lorena Bobbitt, Sonya Harding, and Hillary Clinton; and found to his dismay that he had no dick, a very swollen, battered knee, — and no health coverage.

• • •

### Subject: Requesting a raise

I, the Penis, do hearby request a raise for the following reasons:
I do physical labor
I work at great depths
I plunge head first into everything I do
I do not get weekends or holidays off
I work in a damp environment
I do not get paid overtime
I work in a dark workplace that has poor ventilation
I work in high temperatures
My work exposes me to contagious diseases

### In Response:

Dear Penis,
After duly assessing your request, and considering the arguments you have raised, the administration rejects your request on the following reasons: You do not work 8 hours straight.
You fall asleep on the job after brief work periods
You do not always follow the orders of the management team
You do not stay in your allocated position and often visit other areas
You do not take initiative- you need to be pressured and stimulated in order to start working.
You leave the workplace rather messy at the end of your shift
You don't always observe necessary safety regulations, such as wearing the correct protective clothing
You retire well before 65
You're unable to work double shifts
You sometimes leave your allocated position before you have completed a days work and if that were not all, you have been seen constantly entering and leaving the workplace carrying 2 suspicious looking bags.
Sincerely,
The Management

• • •

A little fellow goes into an elevator, looked up and saw a huge muscleman standing next to him.

The big guy sees the little chap staring at him, looks down, and said, "Seven feet, five inches tall, 310 pounds, 16-inch penis, testicles – over a pound each...Turner Brown."

The little guy just faints dead away and falls to the floor. The big dude kneels down and brings him around by slapping his face and shaking him. He asked, "Are you OK?"

In a very weak voice, the little fellow said, "Excuse me, but what did you just say to me?"

The huge guy said, "When I saw the curious look on your face, I just figured that I would give you the answers to the questions everyone always asks me. I am seven feet, five inches tall; I weigh 312 pounds, I have a 16-inch penis, my testicles weigh over a pound each, and my name is Turner Brown."

The little chap said, "Oh, thank God! – I thought that you said "Turn Around!"

• • •

A man and a woman were deeply in love. She, being of a religious nature, had held back the worldly pleasures that he wanted so badly. In fact, he had never even seen her naked.

One day, as they drove down the freeway, she remarked about his slow driving habits.

"I can't stand it anymore," she told him. "Let's play a game. For every 5 miles per hour over the speed limit you drive, I'll remove one article of clothing."

He enthusiastically agreed and sped up the car. The speedometer reached the 55 MPH mark, so she removed her blouse. At 60 MPH, off came her slacks. At 65, it was her brassiere, and at 70, her panties.

Now, seeing her naked for the first time, and traveling faster than he had ever before, he became very excited and lost control of the car. He veered off the road, over an embankment, and wrapped the car around a tree. His girlfriend was thrown clear, but he was trapped within the vehicle. She tried to pull him free but, alas, he was stuck.

"Go up the road and get help!" he shouted.

"But, I haven't anything to cover myself with," she replied.

The man felt around, but could only reach one of his shoes. "You'll have to put this between your legs to cover up," he told her.

She did as she was told and went up the road for help. Along came a truck driver. Seeing a naked, crying woman at the side of the road, he pulled over to hear her story.

"My boyfriend, my poor boyfriend!" she sobbed. "He's stuck and I can't pull him out!"

The truck driver, looking down at the shoe between her legs, replied, "Ma'am, if he's in that far, I'm afraid there's no hope for him!"

• • •

A man and a woman are riding next to each other in first class on a plane. The woman sneezed, then took a tissue and gently wiped it between her legs.

The man isn't sure he saw what she did, and decides he is probably hallucinating.

A few minutes pass. The woman sneezes again. Again, she took a tissue and gently wiped it between her legs.

The man was astonished by what he knows he actually witnessed; however, he could not really believe that he's seeing what he's been seeing.

A few more minutes pass. The woman sneezes yet again. She takes a tissue and gently and with great delicacy, wiped it between her legs.

The man had finally had all he can handle. He turned to the woman and said,

"Three times you've sneezed, and three times you've – well – you have taken a tissue and wiped it between your legs! What kind of signals are you sending me, or are you just trying to drive me crazy?"

The woman replied, "I am so very sorry to have disturbed you, sir. I have a rare condition such that when I sneeze, I have an orgasm."

The man, now feeling badly, says, "Oh, I'm sorry. What are you taking for it?"

The woman looks at him and says, "Ground black pepper."

• • •

Three cowboys -one from Louisiana, one from Arkansas, and the other from Texas are sitting around a campfire, out on the lonesome prairie, each with the bravado for which they are famous. A night of tall tales began.

The guy from Louisiana said, "I must be the meanest, toughest cowboy there is. Why, just the other day a bull got loose in the corral and gored six men before I wrestled it to the ground by the horns, with my bare hands."

The fellow from Arkansas couldn't stand to be bested. "Why, I was walking down the trail yesterday and a 15 foot long rattler slid out from under a rock and made a move for me. I grabbed that snake with my bare hands and bit its head off and sucked the poison down in one gulp. And I'm still here today!"

The Texan remained silent, slowly stirring the coals with his penis.

• • •

There was a young pretty virgin girl who lived with her grandma. She was invited to go on her first date. Before the date her grandma took her aside and said to her, "The boy is going to try to kiss you; and you will like that. But don't let him do it. The boy will try to feel your breast; you will like that too. But don't let him do it. The boy will try to put his hands between your legs; you will like that. But don't let him do that. The boy will try to get on top of you and have his way with you. Most certainly don't let him do that. He will disgrace your dear family if you let him do that."

The girl went on her date and when she came back her grandma asked her how it went.

The young girl said, "It was just like you said Grandma! But to reassure you. When he tried that business with getting on top of me, I rolled him over, got on top of him, and disgraced HIS family!"

• • •

A man with a 25 inch long penis went to his doctor to complain of having a problem with this cumbersome instrument and had had more than one complaint lodged because of its enormous dimensions. "Doctor," he asked, in total frustration, "is there anything you can do for me?"

The doctor replied, "Medically son, there is nothing I can do. But, I do know this witch who may be able to help you."

So the doctor gave him directions to the witch. The man called upon the witch and relayed his story .

"Ms Witch, my penis is 25 inches long and I need help. Can anything be done to help me? You are my only hope."

The witch stared in amazement, scratched her head, and then replied, "I think I may be able to help you with your problem. Do this: Go deep into the forest. You will find a pond. In this pond, you will find a frog sitting on a log. This frog has magic. You say to frog, "Will you marry me?" When the frog says "No," you will find five inches less to your problem."

The man's face lit up and he dashed off into the forest. He called out to the frog, "Will you marry me?"

The frog looked at him dejectedly and replied, "NO."

The man looked down and suddenly his penis was 5 inches shorter.

"WOW," he screamed out loud, "this is great! But it's still too long at 20 inches, so I'll ask the frog to marry me again."

"Frog, will you marry me?" the guy shouted.

The frog rolled its eyes back in its head and screamed back, "NO!'

The man felt another twitch in his penis, looked down, and it was another 5 inches shorter. He man laughed, "This is fantastic." He looked down at his penis again, 15 inches long, and reflected for a moment. Fifteen inches is still a monster, just a little less would be ideal.

Grinning, he looked across the pond and yelled out, "Frog will you marry me?"

The frog looked back across the pond shaking its head, "How many times do I have to tell you? NO, NO, NO!!!"

• • •

The testicles of a Texas dwarf hurt and ached almost all the time. The dwarf went to the doctor and told him about his problem. The doctor told him to drop his pants and he would have a look.

The small chap dropped his pants. The doctor stood him up onto the examining table, and started to examine him. The doctor put one finger under his left testicle and told the midget to turn his head and cough, the usual method to check for an inguinal hernia.

"Hmm..." mumbled the doctor, and as he put his finger under the right testicle, he asked the dwarf to cough again.

"Aha!" said the doctor, and reached for his surgical scissors..

Snip-snip-snip-snip on the right side, then snip-snip-snip-snip on the left side.

The little fellow was so scared he was afraid to look, but noted with amazement that the snipping did not hurt. The doctor then told the midget to walk around the examining room to see if his testicles still hurt.

The dwarf was absolutely delighted as he walked around and discovered his testicles were no longer aching.

The doctor said, "How does that feel now?"

His patient replied, "Perfect Doc, and I didn't even feel it. What did you do?"

The doctor replied, "I cut two inches off the top of your cowboy boots..."

• • •

Renault and Ford have joined forces to create the perfect small car for women. Mixing the Renault "Clio" and the Ford "Taurus" they have designed the "*Clitaurus.*" It comes in pink and the average male car thief won't be able to find it – let alone turn it on – even if someone tells him where it is and how to do it. Rumor has it, though, that it leaks transmission fluid once a month, and can be a real bitch to start in the morning! Some have reported that on cold winter mornings, when you really need it, you can't get it to turn over.

New models are initially fun to own, but very costly to maintain and horribly expensive to get rid of. Used models may initially appear to have great curb appeal but the curb weight typically increases with age.

Used models may initially appear to have curb appeal and a low price, but eventually, they have an increased appetite for fuel. Manufacturers are baffled as to how the size of the trunk increases, but say that the paint may just make it LOOK bigger.

This model is not expected to reach collector status. Most owners find it is best to lease one and replace it each year.

• • •

Rachel, Clare and Samantha haven't seen each other since High School. They rediscover each other via a reunion website and arrange to meet for lunch in a wine bar.

Rachel arrived first, wearing a beige Versace outfit. She ordered a bottle of Pinot Grigio.

Clare arrived shortly afterward, in gray Chanel. After the required ritualized kisses, she joined Rachel in a glass of wine.

Then Samantha walked in, wearing a faded old T-shirt, blue jeans and boots. She, too, shared the wine.

Rachel explained that after leaving high school and graduating from Princeton in Classics, she met and married Timothy, with whom she has a beautiful daughter. Timothy is a partner in one of

New York's leading law firms. They live in a 4000 square feet co-op on Fifth Avenue, where Susanna, the daughter, attends drama school. They have a second home in Phoenix.

Clare related that she graduated from Harvard Medical School and became a surgeon. Her husband, Clive, is a leading Wall Street investment banker. They live in Southampton on Long Island and have a second home in Naples, Florida.

Samantha explained she left school at 17 and ran off with her boyfriend, Ben. They run a tropical bird park in California and grow their own vegetables. Ben can stand five parrots, side by side, on his willy.

Half way down the third bottle of wine and several hours later, Rachel blurted out her husband was actually a cashier at WalMart. They really live in a small apartment in Brooklyn and have a travel trailer parked at a nearby storage facility.

Clare, chastened and encouraged by her old friend's honesty, explained that she and Clive are both nurses' aides in a retirement home. They live in Jersey City and take vacation camping trips to Alabama.

Samantha admitted that the fifth parrot had to stand on one leg

• • •

One evening a man was at home watching TV and eating peanuts. He'd toss them in the air, then catch them in his mouth. In the middle of catching one, his wife asked a question, and as he turned to answer her, a peanut fell in his ear. He tried and tried to dig it out but only succeeded in pushing it in deeper.

He called his wife for assistance, and after hours of trying they became worried and decided to go to local hospital's Emergency Room.

As they were ready to go out the door, their daughter came home with her date. After being informed of the problem, their daughter's date said he could get the peanut out. The young man told the father to sit down, then shoved two fingers up the father's nose and told him to blow hard.

When the father blew, the peanut flew out. The mother and daughter jumped and yelled for joy.

The young man insisted that it was nothing and the daughter brought the young man out to the kitchen for something to eat.

Once he was gone the mother turned to the father and said, "That's so wonderful! Isn't he smart?

What do you think he's going to be when he grows older?"

The father replied "From the smell of his fingers, our son in-law!"

• • •

A flat-chested young lass read an article in a magazine that stated Dr. Bumbutu in Africa could enlarge her breasts without surgery. So, she decided to go to Dr. Bumbutu to see if he could help her.

Dr. Bumbutu advised her, "Every day after your shower, rub your chest and say, "Scooby doobie doobies, I want bigger boobies!"

She did this faithfully for several months and, to her utter amazement, she grew a terrific D-cup rack!

One morning, she was running late, got on the bus, and, in a panic, realized she had forgotten her morning ritual. Frightened that she might lose her lovely boobs if she didn't recite the little rhyme, she stood right there in the middle aisle of the bus closed her eyes and said, "Scooby doobie doobies, I want bigger boobies."

A fellow passenger, sitting nearby looked at her and asked, "Are you a patient of Dr Bumbutu's?"

"Yes I am. How did you know?"

He winked and whispered, "Hickory dickory dock,"

• • •

A group of Year 2, 3 and 4 preschool students, accompanied by two female teachers, went on a field trip to the local racetrack to learn about thoroughbred horses and the supporting industry, mostly to see the "horsies."

When it was time to take the children to the bathroom it was decided that the girls would go with one teacher and the boys would go with the other. The teacher assigned to the boys was waiting outside the men's room when one of the boys came out and told her that none of them could reach the urinal. Having no choice, she went inside, helped the boys with their pants, and began hoisting the little boy's up one by one holding onto their "wee wees" to direct the flow. As she lifted one, she couldn't help but notice that he was unusually well endowed.

Trying not to show that she was staring, the teacher said, "You must be in Year four."

"No, ma'am" he replied. "I'm the jockey riding Silver Arrow in the seventh.

• • •

Michael and Gary got married in California. They couldn't afford a honeymoon so they went back to Michael's Mom and Dad's house in Corner Brook for their first married night together.

In the morning, Johnny, Michael's little brother, got up and had his breakfast. As he is going out of the door to go to school, he asked his mom if Michael and Gary were up yet.

She replied, "No".

Johnny asked, "Do you know what I think?"

His mom replied, "I don't want to hear what you think! Just go to school."

Johnny came home for lunch and asked his mom, "Are Michael and Gary up yet?"

She replied, "No."

Johnny again said, "Do you know what I think?"

His mom replied, "Never mind what you think! Eat your lunch and go back to school "

After school, Johnny came home and inquired again, "Are Michael and Gary up yet?"

His mom said, "No."

He asked, "Do you know what I think?"

His mom responded, "OK, now tell me what you think."

Johnny said: '"Last night Michael came to my room for the Vaseline and I think I gave him my tube of airplane glue."

• • •

A little old lady was walking down the street dragging two large plastic garbage bags behind her. One of the bags was ripped and every once in a while a $20 fell out onto the sidewalk.

Noticing this, a policeman on his beat, stopped her, and said, "Ma'am, there are $20 bills falling out of that bag."

Oh, really? Darn it!" said the little old lady. "I'd better go back and see if I can find them. Thanks for telling me officer."

"Well, now, not so fast," said the cop. Where did you get all that money? You didn't steal it, did you?"

"Oh, no, no," said the old lady. "You see, my back yard is right next to a golf course. A lot of golfers come and pee through a knot hole in my fence, right into my flower garden. It used to really tick me off. Kills the flowers, you know. Then I thought, 'why not make the best of it? So, now, I stand behind the fence by the knot hole, real quiet, with my hedge clippers. Every time some guy sticks his thing through my fence, I surprise him, grab hold of it and say, "O.K., sonny! Give me $20, or off it comes."

"Well, that seems only fair," said the cop, laughing. "OK. Good luck! Oh, by the way, what's in the other bag?"

With a twinkle in her eye, she replied, "Not everybody pays."

• • •

A woman from Los Angeles who was a tree hugger, a liberal Democrat, and an anti-hunter, purchased a piece of timberland near Colville, WA. There was a large tree on one of the highest points in the tract. She wanted a good view of the natural splendor of her land so she started to climb the big tree. As she neared the top she encountered a spotted owl that attacked her. In her haste to escape, the woman slid down the tree to the ground and got many splinters in her crotch. In considerable pain, she hurried to a local ER to see a doctor. She told him she was an environmentalist, a democrat, and an anti-hunter and how she came to get all the splinters.

The doctor listened to her story with great patience and then told her to go wait in the examining room and he would see if he could help her. She sat and waited three hours before the doctor finally reappeared.

The angry woman demanded, "What took you so long?"

He smiled and then told her, "Well, I had to get permits from the Environmental Protection Agency, the Forest Service, and the Bureau of Land Management before I could remove old-growth timber from a "recreational area", so close to a waste treatment facility. I'm sorry, they turned you down."

• • •

### The Indian with One Testicle

There once was an Indian who had only one testicle and whose given name was 'One stone'. He hated that name and asked everyone *not* to call him One Stone.

After years and years of torment, One Stone finally cracked and said, "If anyone calls me One Stone again I will kill them!'

The word got around and nobody called him that any more. Then one day a young woman named Blue Bird forgot and said, 'Good morning, One Stone.'

He jumped up, grabbed her and took her deep into the forest where he made love to her all day and all night. He made love to her all the next day, until Blue Bird died from exhaustion.

The word got around that One Stone meant what he promised he would do. Years went by and no one dared call him by his given name until a woman named Yellow Bird returned to the village after being away. Yellow Bird, who was Blue Bird's cousin, was overjoyed when she saw One Stone. She hugged him and said, "'Good to see you, One Stone."

One Stone grabbed her, took her deep into the forest, then he made love to her all day, made love to her all night, made love to her all the next day, made love to her all the next night, but Yellow Bird wouldn't die!

Why ?....

Everyone knows... You can't kill Two Birds with One Stone!

• • •

While conducting some business at the Court House, I overheard a lady who had been arrested for assaulting a Mammogram Technician say, "Your Honor, I'm guilty but.....there were extenuating circumstances."

The female Judge said, sarcastically, "I'd certainly like to hear those extenuating circumstances."

I did too, so I listened as the lady told her story.

"Your Honor, I had a mammogram appointment, which I actually kept. I was met by this perky little clipboard carrier smiling from ear to ear and she tilted her head to one side and crooned, "Hi! I'm Belinda! All I need you to do is step into this room right here, strip to the waist, then slip on this gown. Everything clear?"

I'm thinking, "Belinda, try decaf. This ain't rocket science."

Belinda then skipped away to prepare the chamber of horrors.

With the right side finished, Belinda flipped me (literally) to the left and said, "Hmmmm. Can you stand on your tippy toes and lean in a tad so we can get everything?"

"Fine", I answered. I was freezing, bruised, and out of air, so why not use the remaining circulation in my legs and neck to finish me off? My body was in a holding pattern that defied gravity (with my other breast wedged between those two 4 inch pieces of square glass) when I heard and felt a zap!

Complete darkness, the power was off!

Belinda said, "Uh-oh, maintenance is working, bet they hit a snag." Then she headed for the door.

"Excuse me! You're not leaving me in this vise alone are you?" I shouted.

Belinda kept going and said, "Oh, you fussy puppy...the door's wide open so you'll have the emergency hall lights. I'll be right back."

Before I could shout "NOOOO!" she disappeared. And that's exactly how Bubba and Earl, "Maintenance Men Extraordinaire" found me...half-naked with part of me dangling from the Jaws of Life and the other part smashed between glass!

After exchanging a polite "Hi, how's it going?" type greeting, Bubba (or possibly Earl) asked, to my utter disbelief, if I knew the power was off.

Trying to disguise my hysteria, I replied with as much calmness as possible, "Uh, yes, I did but thanks anyway."

"OK, you take care now," Bubba replied and waved good-bye as though I'd been standing in the line at the grocery store.

Two hours later, Belinda breezed in wearing a sheepish grin. Making no attempt to suppress her amusement, she said, "Oh I am sooo sorry! The power came back on and I totally forgot about you! And silly me, I went to lunch. Are we upset?"

And that, Your Honor, is exactly how her head ended up between the clamps...."

The judge could hardly contain her laughter as she said "Case Dismissed."

• • •

After a relaxing bath, Monica Lewinsky was looking at herself naked in a mirror, remembering the time with Bill Clinton. Her frustration over her inability to lose weight was depressing her. In an act of desperation, she decided to call on God for help.

"God, if you take away my love handles, I'll devote my life to you," she prayed. And just like that, her ears fell off!

• • •

After having been told my danglies looked like an elderly Rastafarian, I decided to take the plunge and buy some Veet® depilatory gel because previous shaving attempts had only been mildly successful and I nearly put my back out trying to reach the more difficult bits. Being a bit of a romantic I thought I would do the deed on the missus's birthday as a bit of a treat. I ordered the product that was advertised on television well in advance and, working in the North Sea. I considered myself a bit above some of the characters writing the previous reviews and wrote them off as soft office types...oh my fellow sufferers, how wrong I was. I waited until the other half was tucked up in bed and after giving some vague hints about a special surprise I went down to the bathroom. Initially all went well and I applied the gel and stood waiting for something to happen.

I didn't have long to wait. At first there was a gentle warmth which in a matter of seconds was replaced by an intense burning and a feeling I can only describe as like being given a barbed wire *wedgie* by two people intent on hitting the ceiling with my head. Religion hadn't featured much in my life until that night but I suddenly became willing to convert to any religion to stop the violent burning around the turd tunnel and what seemed like the destruction of my twig and berries.

Struggling to not bite through my bottom lip I tried to wash the gel off in the sink and only succeeded in blocking the drain hole with a mat of hair. Through the haze of tears I struggled out of the bathroom across the hall into the kitchen. By this time walking was not really possible and I crawled the final yard to the fridge in the hope of some form of cold relief. I yanked the freezer drawer out and found a tub of ice cream, tore the lid of and positioned it under me. The relief was fantastic but only temporary as it melted fairly quickly and the fiery stabbing soon returned. Due to the shape of the ice cream tub I hadn't managed to give the starfish any treatment and I groped around in the drawer for something else as I was sure my vision was going to fail fairly soon. I grabbed a bag of what I later found out was frozen sprouts and tore it open trying to be quiet as I did so. I took a handful of them and tried in vain to clench some between my ass cheeks. This was not doing the trick as some of the gel had found it's way up the chutney channel and it felt like the space shuttle was running it's engines behind me.

This was probably and hopefully the only time in my life I was going to wish there was a gay snowman in the kitchen which should give you some idea of the depths I was willing to sink to in order to ease the pain. The only solution my pain crazed mind could come up with was to gently ease one of the sprouts where no vegetables had gone before. Unfortunately, alerted by the strange grunts coming from the kitchen the other half chose that moment to come and investigate and was greeted by the sight of me, ass in the air, strawberry ice cream dripping from my bell end pushing a sprout up my ass while muttering..."Ooooh that feels good ".

Understandably this was a shock to her and she let out a scream and as I hadn't heard her come in, it caused an involuntary spasm of shock in myself which resulted in the sprout being ejected at quite some speed in her direction. I can understand that having a sprout farted against your leg at 11 at night in the kitchen probably wasn't the special surprise she was expecting and having to explain to the kids the next day what the strange hollow in the ice cream was didn't improve my status...So to sum it up Veet® gel removes hair, dignity and self respect...)

• • •

A teacher noticed that a little boy at the back of the class was squirming around, scratching his crotch, and not paying attention.

She went back to find out what was going on.

He was quite embarrassed and whispered that he had just recently been circumcised and he was quite itchy. The teacher told him to go down to the principal's office. He was to telephone his mother and ask her what he should do about it. He did and returned to his class.

Suddenly, there was a commotion at the back of the room. She went back to investigate only to find him sitting at his desk with his penis hanging out of his trousers.

"I thought I told you to call your mom!' she said.

"I did," he said, "And she told me that if I could stick it out till noon, she'd come and pick me up from school.

• • •

Professor Higgins at the University of Sydney was giving a lecture on 'Involuntary Muscle Contraction' to the first year medical students. This was not an exciting subject and the professor decided to lighten up the mood.

He pointed to a young woman in the front row and asked, "Do you know what your asshole is doing while you're having an orgasm?'

She replied, "Probably golfing with his buddies."

It took 45 minutes to restore order in the classroom!

• • •

An American tourist went on a trip to China. While there, he was very sexually promiscuous and did not use a condom with each encounter. A week after arriving back home in the United States, he awakened one morning to find his penis covered with bright green and purple bumps. Horrified, he immediately went to see a doctor.

The doctor, never having seen anything like it, ordered some tests and told the man to return in two days.

The patient returned in a couple of days and the doctor said, "I've got bad news for you. You've contracted Mongolian VD. It's very rare and almost unheard of here. We know very little about it".

The man looks perplexed and asked, "Well, give me a shot or something and fix me up, doc."

The doctor answered, "I'm sorry, there's no known cure; We're going to have to amputate your penis."

The man screamed in horror, "Absolutely not! I want a second opinion."

The doctor replied, "Well, it's your choice. Go ahead if you want, but surgery is your only choice."

The next day, the man sought out a Chinese doctor, figuring that he would know more about the disease. The Chinese doctor examined his penis and proclaimed, "Ah yes, Mongolian VD. Vely lare disease."

The guy says to the doctor; "Yeah, yeah, I already know that, but what we can do? My American doctor wants to operate and amputate my penis?"

"What, cut you dick off?!" The Chinese doctor shook his head and laughed. "Stupid Amelican doctas, always want to opelate. Make more money, that way. No need to opelate!"

"Oh, thank God!" the man replied with relief.

"Yes," says the Chinese doctor. "You no worry! Wait two weeks, fall off by itself! You save money."

• • •

An old soldier was celebrating 82 years on this earth. He spoke to his gnarled feet, "Hello toes!" he said, "how are you, toes? You know, you are 82 today; the times we've had! Remember when we walked in the park in summer every Sunday afternoon? Oh, the times we waltzed on the dance floor? Happy birthday, toes!"

"Hello knees", he continued. "How are you, knees? You know you're 82 years-old today. Oh, the grand times we've had! Remember when we marched in the parade? Oh, and the hurdles we've jumped together. Happy Birthday, knees!"

Then, he looked down at his crotch "Hello Willy! If you were alive today, you'd be 82 years old!"

• • •

Snow in the forecast and the female TV weather person said she was expecting 8 inches tonight. I thought to myself, 'fat chance,' with a face like that!

• • •

An old cowboy walked into the barbershop for a shave and a haircut and he told the barber he could not get all his whiskers off because his cheeks are wrinkled from age.

The barber got a little wooden ball from a cup on the shelf and instructed the old cowboy to put it inside his cheek to spread out the skin. When the barber was finished, the old cowboy told the barber that was the cleanest shave he's had in years. But he wanted to know what would have happened if he had swallowed that little ball.

The barber replied, "Just bring it back in a couple of days like everyone else does."

• • •

**Penis Surgery**

A man awakened in the hospital bandaged from head to foot. The doctor came in and said, "Ah, I see you've regained consciousness. Now you probably won't remember, but you were in a huge pile-up on the freeway. You're going to be okay, you'll walk again and everything, however, your penis was severed in the accident and we couldn't find it."

The man groaned, but the doctor goes on, "You have $9000 in insurance compensation coming and we now have the technology to build a new penis. They work great but they don't come cheap. It's roughly $1000 an inch."

The man perked up.

"So," the doctor said "You must decide how many inches you want. But I understand that you have been married for over thirty years and this is something you should discuss with your wife. If you had a five incher before and get a nine incher now she might be a bit put out. If you had a nine incher before and you decide to only invest in a five incher now, she might be disappointed. It's important that she plays a role in helping you make a decision."

The man agreed to talk it over with his wife.

The doctor returned the next day, "So, have you spoken with your wife?"

"Yes I have," replied the man.

"And has she helped you make a decision?"

"Yes" says the man.

"What is your decision?" asks the doctor

"We're getting granite counter tops."

• • •

Being nervous, and embarrassed about my upcoming colonoscopy on a recommendation I decided to have it done while visiting friends in San Francisco, where the beautiful nurses are allegedly more gentle and accommodating.

As I lay naked on my side on the table, the gorgeous nurse began my procedure.

"Don't worry, at this stage of the procedure it's quite normal to get an erection," the nurse told me.

"I haven't got an erection," I replied.

"No, but I have," replied the nurse.

Don't get a colonoscopy in San Francisco

# BODILY FUNCTIONS

Little Johnny blew up a balloon and started flicking it all around the house with his finger.

His mother told him to stop it because he was liable to break something, but the boy continued.

"Johnny!" Mom screamed. "Knock it off." You're going to break something.

He stopped and eventually Mom left for a short trip to the shopping center.

Johnny started up with the balloon again after his mom had left for the store. He gave it one last flick and it lands in the toilet where he left it.

Mom returned and, while putting away the grocery got the urge....a diarrhea run. She could hardly make it to the toilet in time and SPLASH, out it came. When she's finished, she looked down and cold not believe what she saw. She was not sure what this big brown thing was in the toilet!

She called her physician. The doctor was baffled as she described the situation, but he assured her he would be over shortly to examine everything. When he arrived she led him to the bathroom and he got down on his knees to more closely examine the object of his patient's concern. He took a long, hard look at the thing. Finally, he took out his pen and touched it to see what it might be and POP! The balloon exploded and poop was everywhere. on him, the walls, floor, ceiling, shower door, etc.

"Doctor! Doctor! Are you all right?" she asked.

He said, "I've been in this profession for over 30 years, and this is the first time I've ever actually **seen** a fart !"

• • •

An elderly couple were attending church services. About halfway through, she wrote a note and handed it to her husband.

It read: "I just let out a silent fart, what do you think I should do?"

He scribbled back, "Put a new battery in your hearing aid."

• • •

Once upon a time, there lived a woman who had a maddening passion for baked beans. She loved them but unfortunately, they had always induced a very embarrassing and somewhat lively reaction in her. Then one day she met a man and fell in love. When it became apparent that they would marry she thought to herself, "He is such a sweet and gentle man, he would never go for this carrying on."

So she made the supreme sacrifice and gave up beans. Some months later her car broke down on the way home from work. Since she lived in the country she called her husband and told him that she would be late because she had to walk home. On her way, she passed a small diner and the fragrance of the baked beans was more than she could stand. Because she still had miles to walk, she figured that she would walk off any ill effects by the time she reached home. So, she stopped at the diner and before she knew it, she had consumed three large orders baked beans.

All the way home she putt-putted, and upon arriving home she felt reasonably sure she could control it. Her husband seemed excited to see her and exclaimed delightedly, "Darling, I have a surprise for dinner tonight."

He then blindfolded her and led her to her chair at the table. She seated herself and just as he was about to remove the blindfold from his wife, the telephone rang. He made her promise not to touch the blindfold until he returned. He then went to answer the telephone. The baked beans she had consumed were still affecting her and the pressure was becoming almost unbearable, so while her husband was out of the room she seized the opportunity, shifted her weight to one leg and let go a mighty eye-watering sulfurous blast. It was not only loud, but it smelled like a fertilizer truck running over a skunk in front of pulpwood mill. She took her napkin and fanned the air around her vigorously. Then, she shifted to the other cheek and ripped three more, which reminded her of cooked cabbage. Keeping her ears tuned to the conversation in the other room, she went on like this for another ten minutes.

When the telephone farewells signaled the end of her freedom, she fanned the air a few more times with her napkin, placed it on her lap, and folded her hands upon it, smiling contentedly to herself.

She was the picture of innocence when her husband returned, apologizing for taking so long, he asked her if she peeked, and she assured him that she had not. At this point, he removed the blindfold, and she was surprised!

There were twelve dinner guests seated around the table to wish her a "Happy birthday!"

• • •

An old man and his wife have gone to bed. After laying there a few minutes the old man farted and exclaimed, "Seven Points."

His wife rolled over and said, "What in the world was that?"

The old man replied, "It's fart football."

A few minutes later the wife lets one go and announced, "Touchdown, tie score."

After about five minutes the old man farted again and said, "Touchdown, I'm ahead 14 to 7."

Not to be out done the wife rips another one and exclaimed, "Touchdown, tie score."

Five seconds go by and she let out a squeaker and said, "Field goal, I lead 17 to 14."

By now the pressure was on and the old man refused to get beaten by a woman, so he strained very hard but to no avail. Realizing that defeat is totally unacceptable, he gave it everything he had, but instead of farting, he shits in the bed. The wife looked and said, "What the hell was that?"

The old man replied, "Half-time, Switch sides."

• • •

The doctor told him that masturbating before sex often helped men last longer during the act. The man decided, "What the heck, I'll try it." He spent the rest of the day thinking about where to do it. He couldn't do it in his office. He thought about the restroom, but that was too open. He considered an alley, but figured that was too unsafe. Finally, he realized his solution. On his way home, he pulled his truck over on the side of the highway. He got out and crawled underneath to pose as if he was examining the truck. Satisfied with the privacy, he undid his pants and started to masturbate. He closed his eyes and thought of his lover. As he grew closer to orgasm, he felt a quick tug at the bottom of his pants. Not wanting to lose his mental fantasy or the orgasm, he kept his eyes shut and replied, "What?"

He heard, "This is the police. What's going on down there?"

The man replied, "I'm checking out the rear axle, it's busted."

Came the reply, "Well, you might as well check your brakes too while you're down there because your truck rolled down the hill 5 minutes ago!"

• • •

Sometimes when you cry no one sees your tears....
    Sometimes when you are worried no one sees your pain....
    Sometimes when you are happy no one sees your smile....
    But fart just one time....

• • •

Two elderly gentlemen, who had been without sex for several years, decided they needed to visit a cat-house. When they arrived, the madam took one look at them and decided she wasn't going to waste any of her girls on these two old men. So she used "blow-up" dolls instead. She put the dolls in each man's room and left them to their business.

After the two men were finished, they started for home and got to talking.

The first man said, "I think the girl had was dead. She never moved, talked, or even groaned; how was yours?"

The second man replied, "I think mine was a witch."

The first man asked, "How's that?"

"Well," said the second man, "when I nibbled on her breast, she farted, then flew out the window."

• • •

We have all been there but don't like to admit it. We've all kicked back in our cubicles and suddenly felt something brew down below. As much as we try to convince ourselves otherwise, the WORK POOP is inevitable. For those who hate pooping at work, following is the 2001 Survival Guide for taking a dump at work. memorize these definitions and pooping at work will become a pure pleasure.

### ESCAPEE

Definition: a fart that slips out while taking a leak at the urinal or forcing a poop in a stall. This is usually accompanied by a sudden wave of panic embarrassment. This is similar to the hot flash you receive when passing an unseen police car and speeding. If you release an escapee, do not acknowledge it. Pretend it did not happen. If you are standing next to the farter in the urinal, pretend you did not hear it. No one likes an escapee; it is uncomfortable for all involved. Making a joke or laughing makes both parties feel uneasy.

**JAILBREAK** (Used in conjunction with **ESCAPEE**).

Definition: When forcing poop, several farts slip out at a machine gun pace. This is usually a side effect of diarrhea or a hangover. If this should happen, do not panic. Remain in the stall until everyone has left the bathroom so to spare everyone the awkwardness of what just occurred.

**COURTESY FLUSH**

Definition: The act of flushing the toilet the instant the nose cone of the poop log hits the water and the poop is whisked away to an undisclosed location. This reduces the amount of airtime the poop has to stink up the bathroom. This can help you avoid being caught doing the WALK OF SHAME.

**WALK OF SHAME**

Definition: Walking from the stall, to the sink, to the door after you have just stunk up the bathroom. This can be a very uncomfortable moment if someone walks in and busts you. As with all farts, it is best to pretend that the smell does not exist. Can be avoided with the use of the COURTESY FLUSH.

**OUT OF THE CLOSET POOPER**

Definition: A colleague who poops at work and damn proud of it. You will often see an Out Of The Closet Pooper enter the bathroom with a newspaper or magazine under their arm. Always look around the office for the Out Of The Closet Pooper before entering the bathroom.

**THE POOPING FRIENDS NETWORK (PFN)**

Definition: A group of coworkers who band together to ensure emergency pooping goes off without incident. This group can help you to monitor the whereabouts of Out Of The Closet Poopers, and identify SAFE HAVENS.

### SAFE HAVENS

Definition: seldom-used bathrooms somewhere in the building where you can least expect visitors. Try floors that are predominantly of the opposite sex. This will reduce the odds of a pooper of your sex entering the bathroom.

### TURD BURGLAR

Definition: A pooper who does not realize that you are in the stall and tries to force the door open. This is one of the most shocking and vulnerable moments that can occur when taking a dump at work. If this occurs, remain in the stall until the Turd Burglar leaves. This way you will avoid all uncomfortable eye contact

### CAMO-COUGH

Definition: A phony cough that alerts all new entrants into the bathroom that you are in a stall. This can be used to cover-up a WATERMELON, or to alert potential Turd Burglars. Very effective when used in conjunction with an ASTAIRE.

### ASTAIRE

Definition: A subtle toe-tap that is used to alert potential Turd Burglars that you are occupying a stall. This will remove all doubt that the stall is occupied. If you hear an Astaire, leave the bathroom immediately so the pooper can poop in peace.

### WATERMELON

Definition: A turd that creates a loud splash when hitting the toilet water. This is also an embarrassing incident. If you feel a Watermelon coming on, create a diversion. See CAMO-COUGH.

### HAVANA OMELET

Definition: A load of diarrhea that creates a series of loud splashes in the toilet water. Try using a Camo Cough with an Astaire.

## UNCLE TED

Definition: A bathroom user who seems to linger around forever. Could spend extended lengths of time in front of the mirror or sitting on the pot. An Uncle Ted makes it difficult to relax while on the crapper, as you should always wait to drop your load when the bathroom is empty. This benefits you as well as the other bathroom attendees.

## FLY BY

Definition: The act of scouting out a bathroom before pooping. Walk in and check for other poopers. If there are others in the bathroom, leave and come back again. Be careful not to become a FREQUENT FLYER. People may become suspicious if they catch you constantly going into the bathroom.

• • •

Two men were sitting at a bar. After a bunch of drinks over several hours, one guy hiccupped, dropped his head down to his chest, pushed himself away from the bar, and proceeded to hurl all over himself. Wiping his mouth off on his shirt sleeve, he said, "Man, I gotta go home. I'm already 2 hours late, and now I've thrown up all over myself. The ol' lady is gonna kill me.

The second guy turned to the first and said, "Naw she won't. Listen, you got twenty bucks?"

The first said, "Yeah, why?"

The second drunk said, "Take the twenty and put it in your front pocket. When you get home and your wife asks what happened you tell her some guy threw up on your shirt and he gave you twenty bucks for the dry cleaning. I do it all the time."

The first guys said, "Great idea! Let's have another round," and the two continued to drink for the next couple of hours.

Eventually they head home. Sure enough, the first guy's wife was waiting up for him. As he walked through the door, she took a look at him and said, "Look at you! You're pathetic!! You're five hours late, drunk as a skunk, and you've got dried puke all over the front of you! What have you got to say for yourself?"

He said, "Wait honey, listen for a second. This drunk guy threw up on me and gave me twenty bucks to get my shirt dry cleaned, I swear. Check my front pocket."

She reached in and pulls out two twenty dollar bills.

She said, "Wait there's 40 bucks in here!"

He said, "Oh yeah, he crapped in my pants too!!

• • •

A man went to his doctor complaining of bad headaches.

His doctor says, "We just got this new machine. You take a urine sample and feed it into the machine, and it tells you everything that is wrong with you."

Thinking this is pretty amazing, the man gives a sample and the doctor feeds it into the machine. It spits out a piece of paper, which the doctor reads: "According to this, you have tennis elbow."

"But there's nothing wrong with my elbow," the man replies. "It's my head."

The doctor gives him a specimen cup and tells him to bring in a new sample the next day, and they will try again.

When he gets home, the man is angry and thinks to himself, "I'll show that doctor." So he takes the dipstick from his car and puts some oil in the cup. When his wife and daughter get home, he has each of them urinate in the cup, then he finishes by whacking off in it.

The next day he goes back to the doctor and hands him the specimen. The doctor feeds it into the machine, then reads the printout.

"Well, what does it say?" the man asks, laughing.

"According to this," the doctor replies, "your car needs an oil change, your wife has crabs, your daughter is pregnant, and your tennis elbow won't get better if you keep whacking off!".

• • •

My mother was a fanatic about public toilets. As a little girl, she'd bring me in the stall, teach me to wad up toilet paper and wipe the seat. Then, she'd carefully lay strips of toilet paper to cover the seat. Finally, she'd instruct, "Never, never sit on a public toilet seat." And she'd demonstrate "The Stance" which consisted of balancing and hovering over the toilet in a sitting position without actually letting any of your flesh make contact with the toilet seat. But by this time, I'd have peed down my leg. And we'd go home.

That was a long time ago. I've had lots of experience with public toilets since then, but I'm still not particularly fond of public toilets, especially those with powerful, red-eye sensors. Those toilets know when you want them to flush. They are psychic toilets. But I always confuse their psychic ability by following my mother's advice and assuming The Stance.

The Stance is excruciatingly difficult to maintain when one's bladder is especially full. This is most likely to occur after watching a full-length feature film. During the movie pee, it is nearly impossible to hold The Stance. You know what I mean. You drink a two liter cup of Diet Coke, then sit still through a three-hour saga because even if you didn't wipe or wash your hands in the bathroom, you'd still miss the pivotal part of the movie or the second scene, in which they flash the leading man's naked derriere. So, you cross your legs and you hold it. And you hold it until that first credit rolls and you sprint to the bathroom, like superwoman, about ready to explode all over your internal organs.

And at the bathroom, you find a line of women that makes you think there's a half- price sale on Mel Gibson's underwear in there. So, you wait and smile politely at all the other ladies, also crossing their legs and smiling politely. And you finally get closer. You check for feet under the stall doors. Every one is occupied. You hope no one is doing frivolous things behind those stall doors, like blowing her nose or checking the contents of her wallet. Finally, a stall door opens and you dash, nearly knocking down the woman leaving the stall. You get in to find the door won't latch. It doesn't matter. You hang your handbag on the door hook, yank down your pants and assume The Stance.

Relief. More relief. Then your thighs begin to shake. You'd love to sit down but you certainly hadn't taken time to wipe the seat or lay toilet paper on it, so you hold The Stance as your thighs experience a quake that would register an eight on the Richter scale. To take your mind off it, you reach for the toilet paper. Might as well be ready when you are done. The toilet paper dispenser is empty. Your thighs shake more.

You remember the tiny napkin you wiped your fingers on after eating buttered popcorn. It would have to do. You crumble it in the puffiest way possible. It is still smaller than your thumbnail. Someone pushes open your stall door because the latch doesn't work and your pocketbook whams you in the head. "Occupied!" you scream as you reach out for the door, dropping your buttered popcorn napkin in a puddle and falling backward, directly onto the toilet seat. You get up quickly, but it's too late. Your bare bottom has made contact with all the germs and other life forms on the bare seat because YOU never laid down toilet paper, not that there was any, even if you had enough time to. And your mother would be utterly ashamed of you if she knew, because her bare bottom never touched a public toilet seat because, frankly, "You don't know what kind of diseases you could get."

And by this time, the automatic sensor on the back of the toilet is so confused that it flushes, sending up a stream of water akin to a fountain and then it suddenly sucks everything down with such force that you grab onto the toilet paper dispenser for fear of being dragged to China. At that point, you give up. You've finished peeing. You are soaked by the splashing water. You are exhausted. You try to wipe with a Chicklet wrapper you found in your pocket, then slink out inconspicuously to the sinks. You can't figure out how to operate the sinks with the automatic sensors, so you wipe your hands with spit and a dry paper towel and walk past a line of women, still waiting, cross-legged and unable to smile politely at this point.

One kind soul at the very end of the line points out that you are trailing a piece of toilet paper on your shoe as long as the

Mississippi River. You yank the paper from your shoe, plunk it in the woman's hand and say warmly, "Here. You might need this." At this time, you see your spouse, who has entered, used and exited his bathroom and read a copy of War and Peace while waiting for you.

"What took you so long?" he asks, annoyed. This is when you kick him sharply in the shin and go home. This is dedicated to all women everywhere who have ever had to deal with a public toilet.

And it finally explains to all you men what takes us so long.

• • •

### All the Queen's Horses

At Heathrow Airport, a 300-foot long red carpet stretched out to Air Force One and Mr. Bush strode to a warm but dignified hand shake from Queen Elizabeth II. They rode in a silver 1934 Bentley limousine to the edge of central London where they then boarded an open 17th century coach pulled by six magnificent white matching horses. They rode toward Buckingham Palace, each looking sideways and waving to the thousands of cheering Britons. So far everything is going well. Suddenly the right rear horse let fly with the most horrendous, earth-rending, eye-smarting blast of flatulence ever heard in the British Empire and so powerful that it shook the coach. Uncomfortable, but under control, the two Dignitaries of State did their best to ignore the incident. But, embarrassed, the Queen decided that it was impossible to ignore it. "Mr. President, please accept my regrets. I'm sure you understand that there are some things not even a Queen can control."

Ever the Texas gentleman, the President replied, "Your Majesty, please don't give the matter another thought. You know, if you hadn't said something, I would have thought it was one of the horses."

• • •

A very attractive, refined, well-attired lady walks into a Lexus dealership. She browsed around briefly, then spotted the perfect car and walked over to inspect it. As she bent over to feel the fine leather upholstery, a loud fart escaped her. Very embarrassed, she looked around nervously to see if anyone had noticed her little accident, and hoped a sales person wouldn't pop up right now. She turned back, and in her worst nightmare, there standing next to her is an older, refined salesman.

"Good day to you Madame. How may we help you this lovely day?"

Very uncomfortably she asks, "My good man, what is the price of this stunning vehicle?"

He answered, "Madame, if just touching it made you fart, you are going to shit when you hear the price."

• • •

A woman who was rather old-fashioned, delicate, and elegant - especially in her language – was planning a week's vacation in Florida so she wrote to a particular campground and asked for a reservation.

She wanted to make sure the campground was fully equipped, but didn't quite know how to ask about the toilet facilities. She just couldn't bring herself to write the word "TOILET" in her letter. After much deliberation, she finally came up with the old-fashioned term "BATHROOM COMMODE." But when she wrote that down, she still thought she was being too forward. So, she started all over again, rewrote the letter and referred to the bathroom commode merely as the B.C. "Does the campground have it's own B.C.?" is what she actually wrote.

Well, the campground owner wasn't old-fashioned at all and when he got the letter, he just couldn't figure out what the woman was talking about. That B.C. business really stumped him. After worrying about it for a while, he showed the letter to several campers, but they couldn't imagine what the lady meant either. So the campground owner, finally coming to the conclusion that the lady must be asking about the location of the local Baptist Church, sat down and wrote the following reply:

"Dear Madam: Regret very much in the delay in answering you letter. I now take the pleasure in informing you that a B.C. is located nine miles north of the campground and is capable of seating 250 people at one time. I admit it is quite a distance away if you are in the habit of going regularly, but no doubt you will be pleased to know that a great number of people usually take their lunches along and make a day of it. They usually arrive early and stay late."

"The last time my wife and I went was six years ago and it was so crowded that we had to stand up the whole time we were there. It may interest you to know that right now, there is a supper being planned to raise money to buy more seats. They're going to hold it in the basement of the B.C."

"I would like to say it pains me very much not to be able to go more regularly but it is sure no lack of desire on my part. As we grow older, it seems to be more of an effort, particularly in cold weather."

"If you do decide to come down to our campground, perhaps I could go with you the first time you go, sit with you, and introduce you to all the other folks."

"Remember, this is a friendly community."

• • •

For all of you who have or have had small children can relate! And the rest of us can just laugh until we pee!

My three year old son had a lot of problems with potty training; and I was on him constantly. One day we stopped at Taco Bell for a quick lunch in between errands. It was very busy, with a full dining room.

While enjoying my taco, I smelled something funny, so of course, I checked my seven month old daughter, and she was clean. The I realized that Matt had not asked to go potty in a while, so I asked him and he said, "No." I kept thinking, "Oh Lord, that child has had an accident and I didn't have any clean clothes with me."

Then I said, "Matt are you sure you did not have an accident?"

"No," he replied.

I just knew that he must have, because the smell was getting worse! Sooooo.... I asked one more time, "Matt, did you have an accident?"

Matt jumped up, yanked down his pants, bent over and spread his cheeks and yelled,."SEE, MOM, IT'S JUST FARTS!!!" While 100 people nearly choked to death on their tacos, he calmly pulled up his pants and sat down to eat his food as if nothing had happened. I was mortified! Some kind elderly people made me feel a lot better, when they came over and thanked me for the best laugh they had ever had!!!

Another old gentleman stopped us in the parking lot as we were leaving, bent over to my son and said, "Don't worry son, my wife accuses me of the same thing all the time, but I just never had the nerve to make the point like you did."

• • •

An office manager was given the task of hiring an individual to fill a job opening. A fter sorting through a stack of resumes he found four people who were equally qualified. He decided to call the four in and ask them one question and their answer would determine who would get the job.

The day came and as the four sat around the conference room table the interviewer asked "What is the fastest thing you know of?" pointing to the man on his right.

The first man replied, "A thought. It pops into your head. There's no forewarn- ing that it's on the way, it's just there. A thought is the fastest thing I know of."

"That's very good!" replied the interviewer. "And now you sir?" he asked the second man.

"Hmm....let me see, a blink! It comes and goes and you don't know it ever happened. A blink is the fastest thing I know of."

"Excellent!" said the interviewer "The blink of an eye. That's a very popular cliché for speed."

He turned to the third man who was contemplating his reply.

"Well, out at my Dad's ranch, you step out of the house and on the wall there's a light switch; when you flip that switch, way out across the pasture the light at the barn comes on in an instant. Turning on a light is the fastest thing I can think of."

The interviewer was very impressed with the third answer and thought he had found his man. "It's hard to beat the speed of light," he said.

Turning to the fourth man, he posed the question. "After hearing the three previous answers, it's obvious to me that the fastest thing known is diarrhea."

"WHAT?" said the interviewer, stunned by the response.

"Oh I can explain." said the fourth man. "You see, the other day I wasn't feeling so well and ran for the bathroom. But, before I could think, blink or turn on the light, I'd shit my pants!"

He got the job!

• • •

A woman approached a Wal-Mart associate standing there wearing dark shades. She said, "Excuse me, Sir ... can you tell me anything about this rod and reel?"

He replied, "Ma'am, I'm blind, but if you will drop them on the counter I can tell you everything you need to know about it from the sound that it makes."

She didn't believe him but dropped the items on the counter anyway.

He said, "That's a 6' graphite rod with a Zebco 202 reel and 10 lb test line...It's a good all around rod and reel, and it's $20.00."

She exclaimed, "It is amazing that you can tell all that just by the sound of it dropping on the counter. I think it's what I'm looking for, so I'll take it."

He walked behind the counter to the register, she bent down to get her purse and let go an unexpected blast of intestinal gas. At first she was embarrassed but then realized that there was no way that he could tell it was her. Being blind, he wouldn't know that she was the only person around.

He rang up the sale and said, "That will be $25.50."

She replied, "But didn't you say it was $20.00?"

He responded, "Yes ma'am, the rod and reel are $20.00, the duck call is $3.00, and the catfish bait is $2.50. And thank you for shopping Wal-Mart."

• • •

Annie and Sam were on the brink of divorce, so they went to visit a marriage counselor.

The counselor asked Annie about the problem.

She responded, "Sam suffers from premature ejaculation."

The counselor turned to Sam and inquired, "Is that true?"

Sam replied, "Well, not exactly. She's the one that suffers, not me."

• • •

A graduate student in speech therapy had two days to cure her patients of their stuttering and earn her PhD. She came to a therapy session in a revealing outfit and offered a blow job to anyone who could pronounce the name of the city in which they were born without stuttering.

The first man stood up and said, "B-b-b-b-b-b-Boston." Dejected, he shook his head and sat back down.

The next guy stood and said, "Ca-ca-ca-ca-ca-ca-Cleveland." He slapped his thigh in frustration and sat back down.

The third guy stood and without hesitation said, "Miami."

The female instructor fell to her knees and began performing oral sex on the man.

After finishing, she looked up and said, "What do you now have to say?" He replied, "B-b-b-b-b-b-Beach!"

• • •

I was in the pub yesterday when I suddenly realized that I desperately needed to fart. The music was really, really loud, so I timed my farts with the beat.

After a couple of songs, I started to feel better. I finished my pint and noticed that everybody was staring at me.

Then I suddenly remembered that I was listening to my iPod.

• • •

### Baby's first examination with the Doctor

A woman and a baby were in the doctor's examining room, waiting for the doctor to come in for the baby's first exam.

The doctor arrived, and examined the baby, checked his weight, and being a little concerned, asked if the baby was breast-fed or bottle-fed?

"Breast-fed," she replied. "Well, strip down to your waist," the doctor ordered.

She did.

He pinched her nipples, pressed, kneaded, and rubbed both breasts for a while in a very professional and detailed examination. Motioning to her to get dressed, the doctor said, "No wonder this baby is underweight. You don't have any milk."

"I know," she said, "I'm his Grandma, but I'm glad I brought him in.

• • •

This is a story about a couple who had been happily married for years. The only friction in their marriage was the husband's habit of farting loudly every morning when he awoke. The noise would wake his wife and the smell would make her eyes water and make her gasp for air. Every morning she would plead with him to stop ripping them off because it was making her sick.

He told her he couldn't stop it and that it was perfectly natural.

She told him to see a doctor; she was concerned that one day he would blow his guts out.

The years went by and he continued to blast them out! Then one Thanksgiving morning as she was preparing the turkey for dinner and he was upstairs sound asleep, she looked at the bowl where she had put the turkey innards and neck, gizzard, liver and all the pare parts and a malicious thought came to her. She took the bowl and went upstairs where her husband was sound asleep and, gently pulling back the bed covers, she pulled back the elastic waistband of his underpants and emptied the bowl of turkey guts into his shorts.

Some time later she heard her husband waken with his usual trumpeting which was followed by a ghastly, blood curdling scream and the sound of frantic footsteps as he ran into the bathroom.

The wife could hardly control herself as she rolled on the floor laughing, tears in her eyes! After years of suffering the torture of flatulence, she reckoned she had got him back pretty good.

About twenty minutes later, her husband came downstairs in his bloodstained underpants with a look of horror on his face. She bit her lip as she asked him the nature of his problem.

He said, "Honey, you were right! All these years you have warned me and I didn't listen to you."

"What do you mean?" asked his wife.

"Well, you always told me that one day I would end up farting my guts out, and today it finally happened. But by the grace of God, some Vaseline, and two fingers, I think I got most of them back in."

• • •

### An Ode to Flatulence

> A fart it is a pleasant thing,
> It gives the belly ease,
> It warms the bed in winter,
> And suffocates the fleas.

## BODILY FUNCTIONS

A fart can be quiet,
A fart can be loud,
Some leave a powerful,
Poisonous cloud

A fart can be short,
Or a fart can be long,
Some farts have been known
To sound like a song

A fart can create
A most curious medley,
A fart can be harmless,
Or silent, and deadly.

A fart might not smell,
While others are vile,
A fart may pass quickly,
Or linger a while

A fart can occur in a number of places,
And leave everyone there,
With strange looks on their faces.

From wide-open prairie,
To small elevators,
A fart will find all of us
Sooner or later.

But farts are all bad,
Is simply not true-
We must never forget
Sweet old farts like you!

Kinda brings a tear to your eye doesn't it?

### The Agony of Dyslexia

After Daylight Savings Time ended I stopped in to visit my dyslectic friend.

He was busy covering his penis with black shoe polish.

I said to him, "You idiot! You're supposed to turn your clock back!

• • •

1. Schizophrenia — Do You Hear What I Hear?
2. Multiple Personality Disorder — We Three Kings Disoriented Are
3. Dementia — I Think I'll be Home for Christmas
4. Narcissistic — Hark the Herald Angels Sing About Me
5. Manic — Deck the Halls and Walls and House and Lawn and Streets and Stores and Office and Town and Cars and Buses and Trucks and Trees and..
6. Paranoid — Santa Claus is Coming to Town to Get Me
7. Borderline Personality Disorder — Thoughts of Roasting on an Open Fire
8. Personality Disorder — You Better Watch Out, I'm Gonna Cry, I'm Gonna Pout, Maybe I'll Tell You Why
9. Attention Deficit Disorder — Silent night, Holy ooooh look at the Froggy - can I have a chocolate, why is France so far away?
10. Obsessive Compulsive Disorder - – Jingle Bells, Jingle Bells, Jingle Bells, Jingle Bells, Jingle Bells, Jingle Bells, Jingle Bells, Jingle Bells, Jingle Bells, Jingle Bells, Jingle Bells, Jingle Bells, Jingle Bells, Jingle Bells, Jingle Bells, Jingle Bells, Jingle Bells, Jingle Bells, Jingle Bells, Jingle Bells, Jingle Bells, Jingle Bells, Jingle Bells, Jingle Bells, Jingle Bells….

## Ask the Paid-for Diploma Doctor

Q: Doctor, I've heard that cardiovascular exercise can prolong life. Is this true?
A: The heart is only good for so many beats, and that's it... Don't waste time and effort on exercise. Everything wears out eventually. Speeding up your heart not make you live longer; it is like saying you extend life of car by driving faster. Want to live longer? Take a nap.

Q: Should I reduce my alcohol intake?
A: Oh no. Wine is made from fruit. Brandy is distilled wine; that means they take water out of fruity bit so you get even more of goodness that way.
Beer is also made of grain. Bottoms up!

Q: How can I calculate my body/fat ratio?
A: Well, if you have a body and you have fat; your ratio one to one. If you have two bodies, your ratio two to one.

Q: What are some of the advantages of participating in a regular exercise program?
A: Can't think of single one, sorry. My philosophy is No pain...good!

Q: Aren't fried foods bad for you?
A: YOU NOT LISTENING! Food is fried in vegetable oil. How is getting more vegetable a bad thing?

Q: Will sit-ups help prevent me from getting a little soft around the middle?
A: Oh no! When you exercise muscle, it gets bigger. You should only be doing sit-up if you want a bigger stomach.

Q: Is chocolate bad for me?
A: Are you crazy?!? HEL-LO-O!! Cocoa bean! Another vegetable!

It good to eat the best. food around!

Q: Is swimming good for your figure?
A: If swimming good for figure, explain whale to me.

Q: Is getting in shape important for my lifestyle?
A: Hey! 'Round' is shape!

Well... I hope this has cleared up any misconceptions you may have had about food and diets.

And remember: Life should NOT be a journey to the grave with the intention of arriving safely in an attractive and well-preserved body, but rather to skid in sideways – Zinfandel in one hand – chocolate in the other - body thoroughly used up, totally worn out and screaming "WOO-HOO, what a ride!!"

• • •

AND..... For those of you who watch what you eat, here's the final word on nutrition and health. It's a relief to know the truth after all those conflicting nutritional studies.

1. The Japanese eat very little fat and suffer fewer heart attacks than Americans.
2. The Mexicans eat a lot of fat and suffer fewer heart attacks than Americans.
3. The Chinese drink very little red wine and suffer fewer heart attacks than Americans.
4. The Italians drink a lot of red wine and suffer fewer heart attacks than Americans.
5. The Germans drink a lot of beer and eat lots of sausages and fats and suffer fewer heart attacks than Americans.

*CONCLUSION:* Eat and drink what you like. Speaking English is apparently what kills you.

## BODILY FUNCTIONS

• • •

Three men – an Italian, a Frenchman, and an Israeli were reminiscing about their respective sex lives during recent encounters

The Italian said, "Last week my wife and I had great sex when I rubbed her body all over with olive oil and we made passionate love and she screamed for five full minutes at the end."

The Frenchman boasted, "Last week when my wife and had sex, I rubbed her body all over with butter and made passionate love and she screamed for fifteen minutes."

The Israeli said, "Well last week my wife and I also had sex and I rubbed her body all over with Schmaltz (chicken fat) and we made love and she screamed for over six hours.

The other two were stunned and the astonished Frenchman asked, "What could you have possibly done to make your wife scream for six hours?"

The Israeli said, "I wiped my hands on the drapes!"

• • •

# ON BLONDES

### One Blonde Leading Another

A blonde was driving home after a Steelers game, and got caught in a really bad hailstorm. Her car was covered with dents, so the next day she took it to a repair shop. The shop owner saw that she was a blonde, so he decided to have some fun. He told her just to go home and blow into the tail pipe really hard, and all the dents would pop out.

So, the blonde went home, got down on her hands and knees and started blowing into her cars tailpipe. Nothing happened. She blew a little harder, and still nothing happened.

Her roommate, another blonde, came home and said, "What are you doing?"

The first blonde told her how the repairman had instructed her to blow into the tailpipe in order to get all the dents to pop out.

Her roommate rolled her eyes and said, "HELLLLOOOOOOOO. You need to roll up the windows!"

• • •

Two blondes were driving through Louisiana. As they were approaching Natchitoches, they started arguing over how to pronounce the name of the town. They argued back and forth until they stopped for lunch.

"Would you please pronounce where we are very slowly?" asked one of the blondes to the counterman.

Overhearing the question, manager leaned over the counter and said "Burrrrrrr–Gerrrrrrr—Kiiiiing!

• • •

Three blondes died and were at the Pearly Gates. St. Peter told them that they could enter if they could answer a simple question.

St. Peter asked the first blond, "What is Easter?"

The blonde replied. "Oh, that is easy! Easter is the holiday in November when everyone gets together, eats turkey, and are thankful."

"Wrong!" scowled St. Peter who proceeded to ask the second blonde the same question.

"What is Easter?"

The second blonde replied, "Easter is the holiday in December when we put up a nice tree, exchange presents, and celebrate the birth of Jesus."

St. Peter looked at the second blonde, shook his head in disgust, and told her she is wrong.

He then peered over his glasses at the third blonde and asked, "What is Easter?"

The third blonde smiled confidently and looked St. Peter in the eyes, "I know what Easter is.

"Oh?" replied St. Peter, incredulously.

"Oh, yes," said the third blonde, "Easter is the Christian holiday that coincides with the Jewish celebration Passover. Jesus and his disciples were eating at the last supper and Jesus was later deceived and turned over to the Romans by one of his disciples. The Romans took him to be crucified and he was stabbed in the side, made to wear a crown of thorns, and was hung on a cross with nails through his hands. He was buried in a nearby cave which was sealed off by a large boulder."

St. Peter smiled broadly with delight.

The third blonde continued, "Every year the boulder is moved aside so that Jesus can come out ... and, if he sees his shadow, there will be six more weeks of winter."

• • •

Three girls all worked in the same office with the same female Boss.

Each day, they noticed the boss left work early. One day, the girls decided that, when the boss left, they would leave right behind her. After all, she never called or came back to work, so how would she know they went home early?

The brunette was thrilled to be home early. She did a little gardening, spent playtime with her son, and went to bed early.

The redhead was elated to be able to get in a quick workout at the spa before meeting a dinner date.

The blond was happy to get home early and surprise her husband, but when she got to her bedroom, she heard a muffled noise from inside. Slowly and quietly, she cracked open the door and was mortified to see her husband in bed with her boss! Gently she closed the door and crept out of her house.

The next day, at their coffee break, the brunette and redhead planned to leave early again, and they asked the blond if she was going to go with them.

"No way," the blond exclaimed "I almost got caught yesterday."

• • •

Joe got on the bus with both of his front trouser pockets full of golf balls and sat down next to a beautiful blonde.

The puzzled blonde kept looking at him and his bulging pockets. Finally, after many glances from her, he said, "It's golf balls."

The blonde continued to look at him for a very long time, thinking deeply about what he had said. After several minutes, not being able to contain her curiosity any longer, she asked, "Does it hurt as much as tennis elbow?"

• • •

Last year I replaced all the windows in my house with that expensive double-pane energy-efficient kind, and today, I got a call from the contractor who installed them. He was complaining that the work had been completed a whole year ago and I still hadn't paid for them.

Hellloooo, just because I'm blonde doesn't mean that I am automatically stupid. So, I told him just what his fast-talking sales guy had told me last year, that in *one year these windows would pay for themselves! Well –It's been a year*!

I told him. There was only silence at the other end of the line, so I finally just hung up. He never called back. I bet he felt like an idiot.

• • •

A policeman was interrogating 3 blondes who were training to become detectives. To test their skills in recognizing a suspect, he showed the first blonde a picture for 5 seconds and then hid it from view.

"This is your suspect, how would you recognize him?"

The first blonde answered, "That's easy; we'll catch him fast because he only has one eye!"

The policeman says, "Well...uh...that's because the picture shows his profile."

Slightly flustered by this ridiculous response, he flashed the picture for five seconds at the second blonde and asked her, "This is your suspect, how would you recognize him?"

The second blonde giggles, flips her hair and says, "Ha! He'd be too easy to catch because he only has one ear!"

The policeman angrily responded, "What's the matter with you two? Of course only one eye and one ear are showing because it's a picture of his profile! Is that the best answer you can come up with?"

Extremely frustrated at this point, he shows the picture to the third blonde and in a very testy voice asked, "This is your suspect, how would you recognize him?"

He quickly adds, "Think hard before giving me a stupid answer."

The blonde looks at the picture intently for a moment and says, "Hmmmm... the suspect wears contact lenses."

The policeman is surprised and speechless because he really doesn't know himself if the suspect wears contacts or not. "Well, that's an interesting answer...wait here for a few minutes while I check his file and I'll get back to you on that."

He left the room and went to his office, checked the suspect's file in his computer, and came back with a beaming smile on his face. "Wow! I can't believe it... it's true! The suspect does, in fact, wear contact lenses. Good work! How were you able to make such an astute observation?"

"That's easy," the blonde replied. "He can't wear regular glasses because he only has one eye and one ear."

• • •

A blond woman walks into the doctors office and said, "Doctor I hurt allover."

The' doctor says, "That's impossible."

"No really! Just look, when I touch my arm, ouch! It hurts! When I touch my leg, ouch! It hurts. When I touch my head, ouch! It hurts. When I touch my chest, ouch!! it really hurts!" she replied.

The doctor just shakes his head and says, "You're a natural blonde aren't you?"

The woman smiles and says, "Why yes I am. How did you know?"

The physician replied, "Because your finger is broken."

• • •

A depressed young blond woman was so desperate that she decided to end her life by throwing herself into the sea. When she went down the docks, a handsome young sailor noticed her in tears and took pity on her.

"Look, you've got a lot to live for," he said. "I'm off to America in the morning and if you like, I can stow you away on my ship. I'll take good care of you and bring you food every day." Moving closer, he slipped his arm around her shoulder and added, "I'll keep happy, and you'll keep me happy."

The girl nodded. After all, what did she have to lose? That night, the sailor brought her aboard and hid her in a lifeboat. From then on, every night he brought three sandwiches and a piece of fruit and they made passionate love until dawn.

Three weeks later during a routine search, the captain discovered her.

"What are you doing here?" the captain asked.

"I have an arrangement with one of the sailors", she explained. "He's taking me to America, and he's feeding me."

"What are you doing for him?" said the captain.

"He's shagging me" said the girl.

"He certainly is," replied the captain. "This is the Isle of Wight ferry"

• • •

### She Was *Sooooooo* Blond:

She studied for a blood test.

She thought she needed a token to get on "Soul Train"

She sold the car for gas money!

When she missed the 44 bus, she took the 22 bus twice instead

When she went to the airport and saw a sign that said "Airport Left," she turned around and went home.

When she heard that 90% of all crimes occur around the home, she moved

She thinks Taco Bell is the Mexican phone company

If she spoke her mind, she'd be speechless

She thought that she could not use her AM radio in the evening

She had a shirt that said "TGIF," which she thought stood for "This Goes In Front."

She took a ruler to bed to see how long she slept

She sent me a fax with a stamp on it

She thought a quarterback was a refund.

She tried to put M&M's in alphabetical order

She thought Boyz II Men was a day care center.

She thought Eartha Kitt was a set of garden tools

She thought General Motors was in the army

She thought Meow Mix was a CD for cats

She thought TuPac Shakur was a Jewish holiday

Under "education" on her job application, she put "Hooked On Phonics She tripped over a cordless phone

She spent 20 minutes looking at the orange juice can because it said "concentrate"

She told me to meet her at the corner of "WALK" and "DON'T WALK."

At the bottom of the application where it says "sign here," she put "Sagittarius."

She asked for a price check at the Dollar Store.

• • •

A blonde decided to try horseback riding, even though she has had no lessons or prior experience. She mounted the horse unassisted and the horse immediately sprung into motion. It galloped along at a steady and rhythmic pace, but the blonde began to slip from the saddle. In terror, she grabbed for the horse's mane, but could not seem to get a firm grip. She tried to throw her arms around the horse's neck, but she slid down the side of the horse anyway.

The horse galloped along, seemingly ignorant of its slipping rider. Finally, giving up her frail grip, the blonde attempted to leap away from the horse and throw herself to safety. Unfortunately, her foot became entangled in the stirrup, and she was now at the mercy of the horse pounding hooves as her head is struck against the ground over and over. As her head is battered against the ground, she was mere moments away from unconsciousness when to her great fortune, Bobby, the Wal-Mart greeter, saw her and unplugged the horse.

Thank God for heros.

• • •

A blonde dialed 911 to report that her car has been broken into. She was hysterical as she explained her situation to the police dispatcher.

"They've stolen the dashboard, the steering wheel, the brake pedal, and even the accelerator!" she cried.

The 911 dispatcher said, "Stay calm. An officer is on the way. He will be there in two minutes."

Before the police get to the crime scene, however, the 911 dispatcher's telephone rang a second time, and the same blonde is on the line again . "Never mind," giggled the blonde, "I got in the back seat by mistake."

• • •

One night a blonde nun was praying in her room when God appeared before her.

"My daughter, you have pleased me greatly. Your heart is full of love for your fellow creatures and your actions and prayers are always for the benefit of others. I have come to you, not only to thank and commend you, but to grant you anything you wish," said God.

"Dear Heavenly Father, I am perfectly happy. I am a bride of Christ. I am doing what I love. I lack for nothing material since the Church supports me. I am content in all ways," said the nun."

"There must be something you would have of me," said God.

"Well, there is one thing," she said.

"Just name it," said God.

"It's those blonde jokes. They are so demeaning to blondes everywhere, not just to me. I would like for blonde jokes to stop."

"Consider it done," said God. "Blonde jokes shall be stricken from the minds of humans everywhere. But surely there is something that I could do just for you."

"There is one thing. But it's really small, and not worth your time," said the nun.

"Name it. Please," said God.

"It's the M&M's," said the nun. "They're so hard to peel."

• • •

An Irishman, a Mexican and a blonde guy were doing construction work on scaffolding on the 20th floor of a building. They were eating lunch and the Irishman said, "Corned beef and cabbage! If I get corned beef and cabbage one more time for lunch I'm going to jump off this building."

The Mexican opened his lunch box and exclaimed, "Burritos again! If I get burritos one more time I'm going to jump off, too."

The blonde opened his lunch and said, "Bologna again. If I get a bologna sandwich one more time I'm jumping too."

The next day the Irishman opened his lunch box, saw corned beef and cabbage and jumped to his death.

The Mexican opened his lunch, saw a burrito and jumped too. The blonde opened his lunch, saw the bologna and jumped to his death as well.

At the funeral the Irishman's wife was weeping. She said, "If I'd known how really tired he was of corned beef and cabbage I never would have given it to him again!"

The Mexican's wife also wept and said, "I could have given him tacos or enchiladas! I didn't realize he hated burritos so much."

Everyone turned and stared at the blonde's wife.

"Hey, don't look at me," she said, "He made his own lunch."

• • •

A blond, wanting to earn some money, decided to hire herself out as a handyman type. She started canvassing a wealthy neighborhood. She went to the front door of the first house and asked the owner if he had any jobs for her to do.

"Well, you can paint my porch for me", he said. "How much do you charge?"

The blonde said $50. The man agreed, and told her that the paint and any other materials she needed could be found in the garage.

The man's wife, inside the house, heard the conversation and said to her husband, "Does she realize that the porch goes all the way around the house?"

The man replied "She should- she was standing on it."

A short time later the blonde came to the door to collect her money.

"You're finished already?" The man asked.

"Yes", said the blonde, "and I had paint left over so I gave it two coats."

Impressed, the man reached in his pocket for the $50. "And by the way", said the blonde. "It's not a Porch. It's a Ferrari.

• • •

A young ventriloquist was touring the clubs and one night he was performing his act at a small club in a in a town in Arkansas. With his dummy on his knee, he' was going through his usual dumb blonde jokes when a blonde woman in the 4th row stood up on a chair and starts shouting: "I've heard enough of your stupid blonde jokes. What makes you think you can stereotype women that way? What does the color of a person's hair haw to do with her worth as a human being? It's guys like you who keep women like me from being respected at work and in the community and from reaching our full potential as a person... because you and your kind continue to perpetuate discrimination against, not only blondes, but women in general...and all in the name of humor!"

The ventriloquist was embarrassed and began to apologize, when the blonde yelled, "You stay out of this mister! I was talking to that little fucker on your knee!"

• • •

A blonde man is sitting on a train across from a busty woman wearing a tiny mini-skirt. Despite his efforts, he is unable to stop staring at the top of her thighs. To his delight, he realized that she has gone without underwear.

The woman realized he is staring and inquires, "Are you looking at my pussy?"

"Yes, I'm sorry," replies the man and promises to avert his eyes.

"It's quite alright," replied the woman, "It's very talented, watch this, I'll make it blow a kiss to you." Sure enough the pussy blew him a kiss.

The man, who is completely absorbed, inquired what else her wonderful pussy can do.

"I can also make it wink,' said the woman.

The man stares in amazement as the pussy winked at him.

"Come and sit next to me," suggested the woman, patting the seat.

The man moves over and is asked, "Would you like to stick a couple of fingers in?"

Stunned, the blond man replied, "Good grief! Can it whistle too?

• • •

The blonde was crossing the road when she was struck by a speeding Corvette. As she was lying on the ground, the driver stopped with a screech of braked tires and rushed out of his sports car to ascertain whether the blond was injured.

"I am so very sorry luv! I didn't see you. Are you OK?" he blurted out.

"Everything is just a blur; I can't see a thing," she said tearfully.

Concerned, the driver leans over the woman to test her eyesight.

He asked, "How many fingers have I got up?"

"Oh my God!" She screamed, "Don't tell me that I'm paralyzed from the waist down too!"

• • •

A blonde woman named Brandi finds herself in dire trouble. Her business has gone bust and she's in serious financial trouble. She's so desperate that she decided to ask God for help. She began to pray.

"God, please help me. I've lost my business and if I don't get some money, I'm going to lose my house as well. Please let me win the lotto."

Lotto night comes and somebody else wins it. Brandi again prays. "God, please let me win the lotto! I've lost my business, my house and I'm going to lose my car as well."

Lotto night comes and Brandi still has no luck. Once again, she prays fervently, "My God, why have you forsaken me? I've lost my business, my house, and my car. My children are starving. I don't often ask you for help and I have always been a good servant to you. *Please* just let me win the lotto this one time so I can get my life back in order."

Suddenly there is a blinding flash of light as the heavens open and Brandi is confronted by the voice of God Himself:

"Brandi, meet me halfway on this. Buy a ticket!"

• • •

A blonde bought a handgun at a local pawnshop because she thinks that Her husband is cheating on her. When she got home, she found her husband in bed with another woman. The blonde grabbed the gun out of her purse, loaded it and pointed it at her own head.

Her husband seeing this starts screaming at her not to shoot. The blonde replied, "Shut up stupid! You're next!"

• • •

A plane was on its way to Houston when a blonde in Economy Class got up and moved to the First Class section and sat down. The flight attendant watched her do this and asked to see her ticket. She then told the blonde that she paid for Economy and that she must sit in the back. The blonde replied, "I'm blonde, I'm beautiful, I'm going to Houston and I'm staying right here!"

The flight attendant went into the cockpit and told the pilot and copilot that there is some blonde bimbo sitting in First Class that belongs in economy and won't move back to her seat. The copilot went back to the blonde and tried to explain that because she only paid for Economy she will have to leave and return to her seat.

The blonde replied, "I'm blonde, I'm beautiful, I'm going to Houston and I'm staying right here!"

The copilot replied to the pilot that he probably should have the police waiting when they land to arrest this blonde woman that won't listen to reason.

The pilot said, "You say she's blonde? I'll handle this. I'm married to a blonde. I speak blonde!" He walked back to the blonde, whispered in her ear, and she said, "Oh, I'm sorry," and she got up and moved back to her seat in the Economy section.

The flight attendant and copilot were astonished and asked him what he said to make her move without any fuss.

"I told her First Class isn't going to Houston."

• • •

A blonde was terribly overweight, so her doctor put her on a diet. "I want you to eat regularly for 2 days, then skip a day, and repeat this procedure for 2 weeks. The next time I see you, you'll have lost at least 5 pounds."

When the blonde returned, she shocked the doctor by losing nearly 20 pounds.

"Why, that's amazing!" the doctor said, "Did you follow my instructions?"

The blonde nodded. "I'll tell you though, I thought I was going to drop dead that 3rd day."

"From hunger, you mean?"

"No, from skipping.

• • •

A blonde named Pam is appearing on "Who Wants To Be A Millionaire" with Regis Philbin.

Regis: "Pam, you're up to $500,000 with one lifeline left: phone a friend. If you get it right, the next question is worth one million dollars. If you get it wrong, you drop back to $32,000. Are you ready?"

Pam: "Yes."

Regis: "Which of the following birds does not build its own nest? Is it

> A) robin,
> B) sparrow,
> C) cuckoo, or
> D) thrush."

Pam: "I'd like to phone a friend. I'd like to call Carol."
Carol (also a blonde) answerd the phone: "Hello?"

Regis: "Hello Carol, it's Regis Philbin from Who Wants to be a Millionaire. I have your friend Pam here who needs your help to answer the one million dollar question. The next voice you hear will be Pam's."

Pam: "Carol, which of the following birds does not build it's own nest? Is it

A) robin,
B) sparrow,
C) cuckoo, or
D) thrush."

Carol: "Oh jeez, Pam. That's simple. It's a cuckoo."
Pam: "Are you sure?"
Carol: "I'm sure."
Regis: "Pam, you heard Carol. Do you keep the $500,000 or play for the million?"
Pam: "I want to play; I'll go with C) cuckoo."
Regis:" Is that your final answer?"
Pam: "Yes."
Regis: "Are you confident?"
Pam: "Yes; I think Carol's pretty smart."
Regis: "You said C) cuckoo, and you're right! Congratulations, you have just won one million dollars!"

To celebrate, Pam flies Carol to New York. That night they went out on the town. As they're sipping champagne, Pam looks at Carol and asks her, "Tell me, how did you know that it was the cuckoo that does not build its own nest?"

"Pam, it was easy," replies her friend. "Everybody knows that cuckoos live in clocks."

• • •

As a trucker stopped for a red light, a blonde caught up. She jumped out of her car, ran up to his truck, and knocked on the door. The trucker lowered the window and she said, "Hi, my name is Heather and you are losing some of your load."

The trucker ignored her and proceeded down the street. When the truck stopped for another red light, the girl caught up again. She jumped out of her car, ran up to his truck, and knocked on the door. Again, the trucker lowered the window. As if they've never spoken, the blonde said brightly, "Hi, my name is Heather and you are losing some of your load!"

Shaking his head, the trucker ignored her again and continues down the street. At the third red light, the same thing happened again. All out of breath the blonde got out of her car, ran up to his truck, and knocked on the truck door. The trucker lowered the window. Again she says "Hi, my name is Heather and you are losing some of your load!"

When the light turns green, the trucker revved up and raced to the next light. When he stopped this time, he hurriedly got out of the truck and ran back to the blonde. He knocked on her window and as she lowered it, he said..."Hi, my name is Kevin, it's winter in Minnesota and I'm driving the *salt truck!!*"

• • •

A young man wanted to get his beautiful blonde wife something nice for their first wedding anniversary. So he decided to buy her a cell phone. She was all excited, she loved her phone. He showed her and explained to her all the features on the phone.

The next day the blonde went shopping. Her phone rang and it was her husband, "Hi hon," he said. How do you like your new phone?"

She replies, "I just love it, it's so small and your voice is clear as a bell but there's one thing I don't understand though."

"What's that, baby?" asked the husband.

"How did you know I was at WalMart?"

• • •

A Russian, an American, and a Blonde were talking one day. The Russian said, "We were the first in space!"

The American said, "We were the first on the moon!"

The Blonde said, "So what, we're going to be the first on the sun!"

The Russian and the American looked at each other and shook their heads. "You can't land on the sun, you idiot! You'll burn up!" said the Russian.

To which the Blonde replied, "We're not stupid, you know. We're going at night!"

• • •

A blonde was playing Trivial Pursuit one night. It was her turn. She rolled the dice and she landed on "Science Nature." Her first question was, "If you are in a vacuum and someone calls your name, can you hear it?"

She thought for a time and then asked, "Is it on or off?"

• • •

A blonde went to an electronic store and approached the salesman and said, "I'd like to buy this TV" the salesman replied "Sorry, I don't sell to blondes."

The blonde, very angry went home. The next day she dressed up very professionally, pinned her hair up and put on a pair of glasses. She went back to the store and said to the same salesman, "I'd like to buy this TV."

The salesman again responded, "Sorry but I don't sell to blondes."

Again, the blonde was very angry.

The next day she dyed her hair brown and put on the glasses and returned to the appliance store. Again she said to the salesman "I'd like to buy this TV."

And again the salesman replied "Sorry I don't sell to blondes."

The blonde started yelling "I'm not blonde. Look, my hair is brown. Why won't you just sell me the damn TV?"

The salesman replied, "Because it's a microwave".

• • •

A blonde walked into a pharmacy and asked the assistant for some bottom deodorant. The pharmacist, a little bemused, explained to the woman that they don't sell bottom deodorant, and never have.

Unfazed, the blonde assured the pharmacist that she has been buying the stuff from this store on a regular basis, and would like some more.

"I'm sorry," says the pharmacist, "we don't have any."

"But I always get it here," said the blonde

"Do you have the container it comes in?"

"Yes!" said the blonde, "I will go and get it." She returned with the container and handed it to the pharmacist who looked at it, and said to her, "This is just a normal stick of underarm deodorant."

The annoyed blonde snatched the container back and read out loud from the container, "To apply, push up bottom."

● ● ●

A blonde tried to sell her old car. She was having a lot of problems selling it, because the car had 250,000 miles on it. One day, she spoke about her problem with a brunette she worked with at a salon. The brunette told her, "There is a possibility to make the car easier to sell, but it's not legal."

"That doesn't matter," replied the blonde, "as long as I can sell the car."

"Okay," said the brunette. "Here is the address of a friend of mine. He owns a car repair shop. Tell him I sent you and he will turn the counter in your car back to 50,000 miles. Then it shouldn't be problem to sell it anymore."

The following weekend, the blonde made the trip to the mechanic.

About one month after that, the brunette asked the blonde, "Did you sell your car?"

"No," replied the blonde, "why should I? It only has 50,000 miles on it."

● ● ●

A red head, a brunette, and a blonde walked into a bar. The bartender told them that in the bathroom there's a magical mirror that will give you something good if you tell it the truth but you lie you get sucked in.

The girls liked the idea so they all walked into the bathroom. The brunette said, "I think I'm the best looking person in this bar" and out popped out her prize.

Next the red-head and went up and said, "I think I'm the smartest girl in this bar" it was the truth so a prize popped out of the mirror.

Next the blonde went "I think...." She was sucked into the mirror and never seen again.

• • •

A blind man, entered a lesbian bar by mistake. He found his way to a bar stool, and ordered a drink. After sitting there for a while, the blind guy yelled to the bartender, "Hey, you wanna hear a blonde joke?"

The bar immediately becomes absolutely quiet. In a husky, deep voice, the woman next to him said, "Before you tell that joke, you should know something. The bartender is blonde, the bouncer is blonde and I'm a 6' tall, 200 lb. blonde with a black belt in karate. What's more, the woman sitting next to me is blonde and she's a weight lifter. The lady to your right is a blonde, and she's a pro wrestler. Think about it seriously, Mister. You still wanna tell that joke?"

The blind guy said, "Nah, you're right, not if I'm gonna have to explain it five times."

• • •

Three friends, a blonde, a brunette and a redhead were stuck on an island. One day, the three of them are walking along the beach and discover a magic lamp.

They rub and rub, and sure enough, out popped a genie. The genie exclaimed, "Since I can only grant three wishes, you may each have one."

The brunette says, "I've been stuck here for years. I miss my family, my husband, and my life. I just want to go home."

*POOF!* The brunette gets her wish and she is returned to her family. Then, the red head said, "I've been stuck here for years as well. I miss my family, my husband, and my life. I wish I could go home too."

*POOF!* The redhead got her wish and she was returned to her family.

The blonde started crying uncontrollably.

The genie asks, "My dear, what's the matter?"

The blonde whimpers, "I wish my friends were still here."

• • •

### First Degree

A married couple were asleep when the phone rang at 2 in the morning. The wife (undoubtedly blonde), picked up the phone, listened a moment and said, "How should I know, that's 200 miles from here!" and hung up.

The husband said, "Who was that?"

The wife said, "I don't know, some woman wanting to know if the coast is clear."

### Second Degree

Two blondes are walking down the street. One notices a compact on the sidewalk and leaned down to pick it up. She opened it, looks in the mirror and said, "Hmm, this person looks familiar."

The second blonde said, "Here, let me see!"

So the first blonde hands her the compact.

The second one looks in the mirror and says, "You dummy, it's me!"

### Third Degree

A blonde was bragging about her knowledge of state capitols. She proudly said, "Go ahead, ask me, I know all of them."
A friend challenged, "OK, what's the capital of Wisconsin?"
The blonde replies, "Oh, that's easy: W."

### Fourth Degree

What did the blonde ask her doctor when he told her she was pregnant? "Is it mine?"

### Fifth Degree

Bambi, a blonde in her fourth year as a UCLA freshman, sat in her US government class. The professor asked Bambi if she knew what Roe vs. Wade was about. Bambi pondered the question then finally said, "That was the decision George Washington had to make before he crossed the Delaware."

### Sixth Degree

Returning home from work, a blonde was shocked to find her house ransacked and burglarized. She telephoned the police at once and reported the crime.

The police dispatcher broadcast the call on the radio, and a K-9 unit, patrolling nearby was the first to respond. As the K-9 officer approached the house with his dog on a leash, the blonde ran out on the porch, shuddered at the sight of the cop and his dog, then sat down on the steps.
Putting her face in her hands, she moaned, "I come home to find all my possessions stolen. I call the police for help, and what do they do? They send me a *BLIND* policeman."

• • •

A blonde called her boyfriend and said, "Please come over here and help me. I have a killer jigsaw puzzle, and I can't figure out how to get it started.

Her boyfriend asked, "What is it supposed to be when it's finished?"

The blonde replied, "According to the picture on the box, it's a tiger."

Her boyfriend decides to go over and help with the puzzle. She let him in and showed him where she has the puzzle spread all over the table.

He studied the pieces for a moment, then looks at the box, then turns to her and said, "First of all, no matter what we do, we're not going to be able to assemble these pieces into anything resembling a tiger." He held her hand and said, "Second, I'd advise you to relax. Let's have a cup of coffee, then," he sighed, "let's put all these Frosted Flakes back in the box."

• • •

A blonde went out for a walk along a river. She came to a river and saw another blonde on the opposite bank. "Yoo-hoo," she shouted, "How can I get to the other side?"

The second blonde looked up the riverbank then down the riverbank then shouted back, "You're already on the other side."

• • •

## Auto Repair

A blonde pushed her BMW into a gas station. She tells the mechanic it died. After he worked on it for a few minutes, it is idling smoothly. She says, "What's the story?"

He replied, "Just crap in the carburetor."

She asks, "How often do I have to do that?"

• • •

## Speeding Ticket

A police officer stopped a blonde for speeding and asked her very nicely if he could see her license, vehicle registration, and proof of insurance.

She replied in a huff, "I wish you guys would get your act together. Just yesterday you take away my license and then today you expect me to show it to you!"

• • •

## Exposure

A blonde was walking down the street with her blouse open and her right breast hanging out of her silk blouse. A policeman approached her and said, "Ma'am, are you aware that I could cite you for indecent exposure?"

She inquired, "Why, officer?"

"Because your breast is hanging out." He replied.

She looked down and exclaimed, "Oh my god, I left the baby on the bus again!"

• • •

## Knitting

A highway patrolman pulled alongside a speeding car on the freeway. Glancing at the car, he was astounded to see that the blonde behind the wheel was knitting! Realizing that she was oblivious to his flashing lights and siren, the trooper cranked down his window, turned on his bullhorn and yelled, "PULL OVER!"

"NO!" the blonde yelled back, "IT'S A SCARF!"

• • •

## Final Exam

The blonde reported for her university final examination that consisted of yes/no type questions. She took her seat in the examination hall, stared at the questions printed on the paper for five minutes and then, in a fit of inspiration, took out her purse, removed a coin and started tossing the coin, marking the answer sheet: Yes, for Heads, and No, for Tails.

Within half an hour she is all done, whereas the rest of the class was still sweating it out.

During the last few minutes she was seen desperately throwing the coin, muttering and sweating.

The proctor, alarmed, approached her and asked what was going on.

"I finished the exam in half an hour, but now I'm rechecking my answers."

• • •

There was a blonde woman who was having financial troubles so she decided to kidnap a child and demand a ransom. She went to a local park, grabbed a little boy, took him behind a tree and wrote this note: "I have kidnapped your child. Leave $10,000 in a plain brown bag behind the big oak tree in the park tomorrow at 7 A.M. Signed, The Blonde

She pinned the note inside the little boy's jacket and told him to go straight home.

The next morning, she returned to the park to find the $10,000 in a brown bag behind the big oak tree, just as she had instructed. Inside the bag was the following note....'Here is your money. I cannot believe that one blonde would do this to another!'

• • •

A blonde went into a world wide message center to send a message to her mother overseas. "But I don't have any money. But I'd do ANYTHING to get a message to my mother."

The man arched an eyebrow (as we would expect) *"Anything?"* he asked

"Yes, yes, anything" the blonde promised.

'Well then, just follow me" said the man as he walked towards the next room.

The blonde did as she was told and followed the man.

"Come in and close the door" the man said. She did. He then said, Now get on your knees." She did.

"Now take down my zipper." She did.

"Now go ahead ...take it out."

She reached it and grabbed it with both hands ...then paused.

The man closed his eyes and whispered "Well. go ahead."

The blonde slowly brought her mouth closer to it, and while holding it close to her lips, tentatively said, "Hello, mum can you hear me?"

• • •

A Blonde went over to her friends' house wearing a T.G.I.F. tee-shirt.

"Why are you wearing a 'Thank God it's Friday' tee-shirt on Monday?"

Oh shit!" the blonde says, "I thought it meant Tits Go In Front!"

• • •

Blonde and brunette friends were walking down the street and passed a flower shop, where the Brunette happens to see her boyfriend buying flowers. She sighed and said, "Oh, crap, my boyfriend is buying me flowers again for no reason."

The blonde looked quizzically at her and said, "What's the big deal, don't you like getting flowers?"

The brunette answered, "Oh, sure...but he always has expectations after getting me flowers, and I just don't feel like spending the next three days on my back with my legs in the air."

The blonde says, "Don't you have a vase?"

• • •

## On Blondes

A blonde guy got home early from work and heard strange noises coming from the bedroom. He rushed upstairs to find his wife naked on the bed, sweating and panting.

"What's up?" he asked.

"I'm having a heart attack!" cried the woman.

He rushed downstairs to grab the phone, but just as he's dialing 911, his 4-year-old son came up and said, "Daddy! Daddy! Uncle Ted's hiding in your closet and he's got no clothes on!

The guy slammed the phone down and stormed upstairs into the bedroom, past his screaming wife, and ripped open the wardrobe door. Sure enough, there was his brother, totally naked, cowering on the closet floor.

"You rotten bastard!" shouted the husband. "My wife's having a heart attack and you're running around naked scaring the kids!"

• • •

### or – the reverse:

A blonde gets home early from shopping and hears strange noises coming from the bedroom. She rushes upstairs only to find her husband naked lying on the bed, sweating and panting.

"What's up?" she asked.

"I think I'm having a heart attack," cries the husband..

The blonde rushes downstairs to grab the phone, but just as she's dialing, her four-year-old son comes up and says, "Mummy! Mummy! Aunty Shirley is hiding in your wardrobe and she's got no clothes on!"

The blonde slams the phone down and storms back upstairs into the bedroom, right past her husband, rips open the wardrobe door and sure enough, there is her sister, totally naked and cowering on the floor.

"You rotten bitch", she screamed, "My husband's having a heart attack, and
you're running around naked playing hide and seek with the kids!!"

• • •

A blonde wanted to go ice-fishing. She'd seen many books on the subject, and finally, after gathering all the necessary "tools" together, she made for the nearest frozen lake.

After positioning her comfy footstool, she started to make a circular cut in the ice.

Suddenly, from the sky -a voice boomed, "THERE ARE NO FISH THERE."

Startled, the Blonde moved further down the ice, sat upon her stool, poured a thermos of steaming cappuccino, and began to cut yet another hole.

Again, from the heavens, the voice bellowed, "THERE ARE NO FISH THERE!"

She stopped, looked skyward, and asked, "Who are you – God?"

The voice replied, "No, I am the manager of this ice skating rink.

• • •

A couple of blond men in a pickup truck drove into a lumberyard. One of the blond men walked in the office and said, "We need some four-by-twos."

The clerk said, "You mean two-by-fours, don't you?"

The man said, "I'll go check," and went back to the truck.

He returned a minute later and said, "Yeah, I meant two-by-fours."

"O.K.,. How long do you need them?"

The customer paused for a minute and said, "I'd better go check."

After awhile, the customer returned to the office and said, "A long time. We're gonna build a house."

• • •

What should do you do when a blonde throws a pin at you?

Run like hell; she's got a grenade in her other hand.

• • •

What do you call a smart blonde
   A golden retriever.

• • •

A brunette, a blonde, and a redhead are all in third grade. Who has the biggest boobs?
   The blonde, because she's 18.

• • •

Bob, a handsome dude, walked into a sports bar around 9:58 PM. He sat down next to a blonde at the bar and stared up at the TV. The 10:00 PM news was coming on. The news crew was covering a story of a man on a ledge of a large building preparing to jump.
   The blonde looked at Bob and said, "Do you think he'll jump?" Bob says, "You know, I bet he'll jump."
   The blonde replied, "Well, I bet he won't."
   Bob placed a $20 bill on the bar and said, "You're on!"
   Just as the blonde placed her money on the bar, the guy on the ledge did a swan dive off the building, falling to his death.
   The blonde was very upset, but willingly handed her $20 to Bob, saying, "Fair's fair. Here's your money."
   Bob replied, "I can't take your money, I saw this earlier on the 5 PM news and so I knew he would jump."
   The blonde replied, "I did too; but I didn't think he'd do it again."
   Bob took the money.

• • •

A business man got on an elevator. When he entered, there was a blonde already inside who greeted him with a bright, "T-G-I-F."
   He smiled at her and replied, "S-H-I-T."
   She looked puzzled and repeated, "T-G-I-F," more slowly.

He again answered, "S-H-I-T."

The blonde was trying to keep it friendly, so she smiled her biggest smile, and said as sweetly as possibly, "T-G-I-F."

The man smiled back to her and once again, "S-H-I-T."

The exasperated blonde finally decided to explain.

'T-G-I-F' means 'Thank God, It's Friday.' Get it, duuhhh?"

The man answered, "'S-H-I-T' means 'Sorry, Honey, It's Thursday'– duuhhh."

. . .

A Sheriff in a small town in Texas walked out in the street and sees a blond haired cowboy coming toward him with nothing on but his cowboy hat, his gun and his boots. He arrests him for indecent exposure.

As he is locking him up, he asks, "Why in the world are you walking around like this?"

The cowboy says, "Well it's like this Sheriff .... I was in this bar down the road and this pretty little red head asks me to go out to her motor home with her. So I did. We go inside and she pulled off her top and asks me to pull off my shirt... So I did. Then she pulls off her skirt and asks me t o pull off my pants. So I did. Then she pulls off her panties and asks me to pull off my shorts...So I did. Then she gets on the bed and looks at me kind of sexy and says, '"Now go to town cowboy."'

"And here I am."

Son of a Gun. Blonde Men *do* exist.

. . .

A blonde city girl named Amy marries a Colorado rancher.

One morning, on his way out to check on the cows, the rancher said to his wife, Amy, "The insemination man is coming over to impregnate one of our cows today, so I drove a nail into the 2 by 4 just above where the cow's stall is in the barn. Please show him where the cow is when he gets here, OK?"

The rancher leaves for the fields. After a while, the artificial insemination man arrives and knocks on the front door. Amy took him down to the barn. They walk along the row of cows and when Amy sees the nail, she tells him, 'This is the one right here."

The man, assuming he is dealing with an air head blonde, asks, "Tell me lady, 'cause I'm dying to know; how would YOU know that this is the right cow to be bred?"

"That's simple she said, by the nail that's over its stall," she explains very confidently.

Laughing rudely at her, the man says, "And what, pray tell, is the nail for?"

The blonde turns to walk away and says sweetly over her shoulder, "I guess it's to hang your pants on."

(It's nice to see a blonde winning once in awhile.)

• • •

Two Mexicans are on a bicycle about 15 miles outside of Lafayette, Louisiana. One of the bike's tires goes flat and they start hitching a lift back into town. A friendly trucker stops to see if he can help, and the Mexicans ask him for a ride. He tells them he has no room in the trailer as he is carrying 20,000 bowling balls. The Mexicans put it to the driver that if they can manage to fit into the back with their bike, will he take them back into town and he agrees. They manage to squeeze themselves and their bike into the back and the driver shuts the doors and gets on his way. By this time he is really late and so puts the hammer down and sure enough, a blonde cop pulls him over for speeding. The lady officer asked the driver what he is carrying, to which the driver jokingly replied "Mexican eggs."

The blonde Lady Cop obviously doesn't believe this so wants to take a look in the trailer. She opened the back door and quickly shuts it and locks it. She gets on her radio and calls for immediate backup from as many officers as possible, plus the Swat Team. The dispatcher asks what emergency she has that require so many officers.

"I've got a Tractor-Trailer stopped with 20,000 Mexican eggs in it. Two have hatched and they've already managed to steal a bicycle."

• • •

A blonde travels to Canada to seek her fortune as a lumberjack. She met a foreman of a logging organization who offers to give her a job.

"Now, I hope you realize we expect you to cut down at least 100 trees a day," the foreman told her.

The blonde woman didn't see this as a problem, so she went out with the chainsaw and did her best.

She came back drenched in sweat.

"Geez lady, how many trees did you cut down?" asked the foreman. "6" she replied.

"What!? You have to do better than that. Get up earlier tomorrow!"

So she did. Out she went with the chainsaw, and came back that night ... exhausted.

"How many this time?" asked the foreman.

"12" she said.

The foreman said, "That does it. I'm coming out there with you tomorrow morning!"

The next morning, the foreman reached the first tree and said, "This is how to cut down trees really quickly." He pulls the rope on the chainsaw and it gave off a loud BRRRRRRUUUMMM.

He notices the blonde is looking at him frantically, so he asks her ..."What's wrong?"

And she replied, "What the hell is that noise?"

• • •

A blonde entered a very upscale shoe store in New Orleans, Louisiana. She browsed the many pricey shoes and settled on purchasing a pair of Italian Salvatore Farangamo alligator pumps.

When she inquired as to the price of the pair, she Was informed that they were $3,500.

"Why are they so expensive? she inquired.

"Madame, these are made from leather selected from only the very most soft and supple, matched grain and defect-free parts of the alligator's skin. It is so rare that only a single pair of shoes can be mad from one hide. Our stock is very, very exclusive, perhaps you are in the wrong store," he intoned arrogantly.

After becoming very frustrated with the shopkeeper's attitude, the young blonde declared, "Well, then, maybe I'll just go out and catch my own alligator and get a pair of alligator shoes for free!"

The shopkeeper replied with a sly smile, "Well, little lady, why don't you go give it a try?"

The blonde headed off to a near-by swampy bayou, determined to catch an alligator. Later in the day, the shopkeeper was driving home, and spotted the young woman standing waist deep in the murky water, shotgun in hand. He saw a huge 9-foot gator swimming rapidly toward her.

With lightning reflexes, the blond took aim, shot the creature and hauled it up onto the slippery bank. Nearby were 7 more dead gators all lying belly up.

The shopkeeper watched in amazement as the blond struggled with the gator. Then, rolling her eyes, she screamed in frustration. Sonofabitch!! THIS ONE'S BAREFOOT, TOO!

• • •

A blonde drops off a shirt a the Surfside cleaners —

On the way our the door, the lady at the counter said "Come again"

The blonde replied, "No, it's toothpaste this time, you nosey bitch"

• • •

# BARS AND DRUNKS

Two buddies, Jeff and Steve, were getting very drunk at a bar when suddenly Jeff threw up all over himself.

"Oh, no, Jane will kill me!!" Steve said.

"Don't worry, pal. Just tuck a twenty in your breast pocket and tell Jane that someone threw up on you and gave you twenty dollars for the dry cleaning bill."

So they stay for another couple hours and get even drunker. Eventually Jeff rolled into home and his Jane started to give him a bad time.

"You reek of alcohol and you puked all over yourself! My God you are disgusting "

Speaking very carefully so as not to slur, Jeff replied, "Nowainaminit, I can e'splain everything! Itsh not what you thinks, I only had a couple drinks! But this other guy got sick on me... He'd had one too many and couldn't hold his liquor! He said he was sorry an' gave me twenty bucks for the cleaning bill! "

Jane looks in his breast pocket and says "But this is forty dollars!"

"Oh yea..." says Jeff. "I almost forgot! He shit in my pants too!"

• • •

A drunk went into a bar and after looking around, spied a good looking woman at the end of the bar. As he studied her more closely, he noticed that she didn't shave under her arms.

## Bars And Drunks

"Bartender, give that ballerina a drink of her choice."

"How do you know she's a ballerina?" asked the bartender.

"Anyone that can kick that high, has to be a ballerina!" said the drunk.

• • •

A drunk wandered down the street looking for a whorehouse to frequent. But he stumbled into a podiatrist's office by mistake!

When he walked in, the nurse handed him a fenestrated surgical drape told him to go behind a curtain and "put it through the hole."

He did as he was told.

The nurse screamed, "That's not a foot!"

The drunk yelled back, "I didn't know there was a minimum!!!"

• • •

Two men were sitting next to each other at a bar. After awhile, one guy looked at the other and said, "I can't help but think, from listening to you, that you're from Ireland."

The other guy responds proudly, "Yes, that I am, I am!"

The first guy says, "So am I! And where about from Ireland might you be?"

The other guy answers, "I'm from Dublin, I am."

The first guy responds, "Faith 'n Begorrah, so am I!"

"Sure and, and what street did you live on in Dublin?"

The other guy says, "And, a lovely little area it was. I lived on McCleary Street in the old central part of town."

The first guy says, "Ah, and it's a small world. So did I! So did I! And to what school would you have been going?"

The other guy answered, "Well now, I went to St. Mary's, of course."

The first guy gets really excited and exclaimed, "And so did I. Tell me, what year did you graduate?"

The other guy answered, "Well, now, let's see. I graduated in 1964."

The first guy exclaims, "The Good Lord must be smiling down upon us! I can hardly believe our good luck at winding up in the same bar tonight. Can you believe it? I graduated from St. Mary's in 1964 my own self!"

About this time, Vicky walks into the bar, sits down and orders a beer.

Brian, the bartender, walks over to Vicky, shaking his head and mutters, "It's going to be a long night tonight"

Vicky asks, "Why do you say that, Brian?"

The Murphy twins are pissed again."

• • •

When life hands you lemons, ask for a bottle of Tequila and salt.

• • •

I was standing in a bar in town yesterday and this little Chinese guy came in, stands next to me and starts drinking a beer.

I said to him, "Do you know any of those Asian martial arts things, like Kung-Fu, Karate or Ju-Jitsu?"

He said, "No, why the fluck you ask me dat, is it coz I Chinee"?

"No." I say, "It's because you're drinking my beer you little prick!"

• • •

Bob came home drunk one night, slid into bed beside his sleeping wife, and fell into a deep slumber. He awoke before the Pearly Gates, where St. Peter said, "You died in your sleep, Bob"

Bob was stunned. "I'm dead? No, I can't be! I've got too much to live for. Please send me back!"

St. Peter said, "I'm sorry, but there's only one way you can go back, and is was a chicken."

Bob was devastated, but begged St. Peter to send him to a farm near his home. The next thing he knew, he was covered with feathers, clucking and pecking the ground.

A rooster strolled past. "So, you're the new hen, huh? How's your first day here?"

"Not bad" replied Bob the hen, but I have this strange feeling inside like I'm gonna explode!"

"You're ovulating," explained the rooster. Don't tell me you've never laid an egg before?"

"Never," replied Bob.

"Well, just relax and let it happen," said the rooster. "It's no big deal."

He did, and a few uncomfortable seconds later, out popped an egg! He was overcome with emotion as he experienced motherhood. He soon laid another egg – his joy was overwhelming. As he was about to lay his third egg, he felt a smack on the back of his head, and heard....."BOB...BOB, wake up! Your shitting in the bed!"

• • •

From Southern Ireland where driving while under the influence is considered a sport, comes this story.

Recently a routine police patrol was parked outside a bar in Donegal Town. After last call, the officer noticed a man leaving the bar so apparently intoxicated that he could barely walk. The man stumbled around the parking lot for a few minutes, with the officer quietly observing. After what seemed an eternity, in which he tried his keys on five different vehicles, the man managed to find his car and fall into it. He sat there for a few minutes as a number of other patrons left the bar and drove off. Finally, he started the car, switched the wipers on and off; it was a fine, dry summer night, flicked the blinkers on and off a couple of times, honked the horn and then switched on the lights. He moved the vehicle forward a few inches, reversed a little, and then remained still for a few more minutes as some more of the other patrons' vehicles left. At last, when his was the only car left in the parking lot, he pulled out and drove slowly down the road.

The police officer, having waited patiently all this time, now started up his patrol car, put on the flashing lights, and promptly pulled the man over and administered a breathalyzer test. To his amazement, the breathalyzer indicated no evidence that the man had consumed any alcohol at all!

Dumbfounded, the officer said, "I'll have to ask you to accompany me to the police station. This breathalyzer equipment must be broken."

'I doubt it,' said Paddy, truly proud of himself. "'Tonight I'm the designated decoy!"

• • •

A fellow walked into a tavern and placed a beautiful lacquered wooden box onto the bar.

"What's in the box?" inquired the barman with natural curiosity.

"Look for yourself," said the patron. The bartender opened the box and was astonished to see a little man, about a foot tall, wearing an impeccable tuxedo and sitting at a tiny Steinway grand piano, playing melodious classic music.

"That's absolutely fantastic; where in the world did you ever find such a marvel, asked the tavern keeper?"

The patron responded "I was walking along a beach one day and saw this brass bottle sticking part-way out of the sand. Well, when I reached down and, as I brushed off the sand and dust, out popped a genie, offering to grant me any wish."

"Do you suppose that I could have a try at making a wish too?" asked the bartender.

"Be my guest," said the patron, with a smile.

Rubbing the bottle briskly, the bartender waited expectantly. Almost immediately, the genie materialized out of the bottle's neck and folding his burly arms across his chest, instructed the tavern-keeper to make a wish of his own.

"I'd like to have a million bucks!" responded the bartender.

The genie immediately returned to his brass bottle and within mere moments, the tavern door burst open and a vast number of ducks flew into the bar – to the accompaniment of thousands of feathers and scattering gobs of foul brown and green manure.

"Jeez!" screamed the bartender, "What the hell happened?"

"Did you really think that I asked for a twelve-inch pianist?" responded the patron.

• • •

A fellow walked into a bar with a pet alligator by his side. He put the 'gator up on the bar and turned to the astonished patrons.

"I'll make you a small wager. I'll open this alligator's mouth and place my genitals inside. Then, the alligator will close his jaws for one minute. He'll then open his mouth and I'll remove my unit unscathed. In return for witnessing this remarkable spectacle, each of you will buy me a drink."

The crowd murmured their approval, whereupon, the man dropped his trousers, and placed his privates into the alligator's open mouth. The 'gator closed his mouth. After a minute, the grabbed a beer bottle and rapped the alligator hard on the top of its head; animal opened his jaws and the man removed his genitals, undamaged as the crowd of patrons cheered and the first of his free drinks was served.

The fellow stood up again and made another offer. "I'll pay $100.00 to anyone who'll give it a try."

A hush fell over the crowd. After a while, a hand went up in the back of the bar. A woman timidly spoke up, "I'll try, but you have to promise that you won't hit me on the head with the beer bottle."

• • •

We went to a Wine Tasting party, and surprisingly, we both got under the influence. Knowing we were wasted, we did something that we have never done before, we took a bus home! We arrived home safe and sound, which is really surprising, as neither of us had ever driven a city bus before.

• • •

A businessman went up to a bar, located at the top of the Empire State Building in Manhattan. He took a seat at the bar next to another fellow.

"This is a really nice place," the first man said.

The other replied, "It's a very special bar."

"Oh, why is that?"

"Well, you see that painting on the far wall? That's an original Van Gogh. And this stool I'm sitting on was on the Titanic."

"Gee, that's amazing!" said the first fellow.

"Not only that, but you see that window over there, the fourth one from the right? Well, the wind does strange things outside that window. If you jump out, you'll fall only about 50 feet before an updraft catches you and you're pushed back up."

"No way; that's impossible!"

"Not at all; take a look," the other man replied and walked over to the window, opened it, and jumped out. He dropped 10...20...30...40...50...feet, came to a stop, and whoosh! He came right back up and floated in through the window, none the worse for his short trip.

"See, it's fun! You should try it," he said. "Try it? I don't even believe that I saw it!" he exclaimed.

"It's easy. Watch, I'll do it again." And with that, he jumped again. He dropped 0...20...30...40...50 feet. Once again, he came to a stop, and whoosh, he floated safely right back through the window.

"Give it a try, it's a blast!" he said.

"Well, what the heck, it does look like fun. I believe I *will* give it a try," the first man said. He climbed up on the windowsill and proceeded to jump out the window. He fell 10...20...30...40...50...60...70...80...90...100 feet, and splat! He ended up on the sidewalk.

After watching the first man fall to his death, the other guy casually closed the window and headed back to the bar. He sat down and ordered another drink.

As the bartender arrived with the drink and said, "You know, Superman, you're a real asshole when you're drunk!"

• • •

A wealthy socialite had a night out on the town with her friends. When she awakend the next morning, totally naked and with a monster of a hang-over. So she rang for the butler and asked for a cup of strong black coffee.

"Jeeves" she said, "I can't remember a thing about last night. How did I get to bed?"

"Well Madam, I carried you upstairs and put you to bed."

"But my dress?"

"It seemed a pity to crumple it, so I took it off and hung it up."

"But what about my underwear?"

"I thought the elastic might stop the circulation, so I took the liberty of removing them."

"What a night!" she said. "I must have been tight'."

"Only the first time, Madame."

• • •

One day, after striking gold in Alaska, a lonesome miner came down from the mountains and walked into a saloon in the nearest town.

"I'm lookin' for the meanest toughest and roughest hooker in the Yukon," he said to the bartender.

"We got her" replied the bartender. "She's upstairs in the second room the right. The miner handed the bartender a gold nugget to pay for the hooker and two beers. He grabbed the bottles, stomped up the stairs, kicked the door open on the second door on the right and yelled, "I'm looking for the meanest roughest and toughest hooker in the Yukon."

The woman inside the room looked at the miner and said, "You found her!" Then she stripped naked, bent over and grabbed her ankles.

"How do you know I want that position first?" asked the miner.

"I don't," replied the hooker, "but I thought you might want to open those beers first."

• • •

**How to rate your hangovers for the festive season!!**

1 star hangover * No pain. No real feeling of illness. Your sleep last night was a mere disco nap which is giving you a whole lot of is placed energy. Be glad that you are able to function relatively well. However, you are still parched. You can drink 10 bottles of water and still feel this way. Even vegetarians are craving a cheeseburger and a side of fries.

2 star hangover I I I No pain. Something is definitely amiss. You may look okay but you have the attention span and mental capacity of a stapler. The coffee you chug to try and remain focused is only exacerbating your rumbling gut, which is craving a full on English breakfast. Last night has wreaked havoc on your bowels and even though you have a nice demeanor about the office, you are costing your employer valuable money because all you really can handle is aimlessly surfing the net and writing junk e-mails.

3 star hangover I I I* Slight headache. Stomach feels crappy. You are definitely a space cadet and so not productive. Anytime a girl walks by you gag because her perfume reminds you of the random gin shots you did with your alcoholic friends after t he bouncer kicked you out at 1 :45 a.m. Life would be better right now if you were in your bed with a dozen donuts and a liter of coke watching *Good Morning* with Richard and Judy. You've had 4 cups of coffee, a gallon of water, 2 Sausage Rolls and a liter of diet coke; yet you haven't peed once.

4 star hangover | | || | | You have lost the will to live. Your head is throbbing and you can't speak too quickly or else you might honk. Your boss has already lambasted you for being late and has given you a lecture for reeking of booze. You wore nice clothes, but that can't hide the fact that you missed an oh-so crucial spot shaving, (girls, it looks like you put your make-up on while riding the bumper cars), your teeth are wearing sweaters, your eyes look like one big win and your hair style makes you look like a reject from the class picture of Mossy Side secondary school circa 1976. You would give a weeks pay for one the following ( A) Home time (B) A duvet and someone to be alone (C) a time machine so you could go back and NOT have gone out he night before.

5 star hangover, a.k.a. Dante's 4th Circle of Helll | || | |*You have a second heartbeat in your head which is actually annoying the employee who sits next to you. Vodka vapor is seeping out of every pour and making you dizzy. You still have toothpaste crust in the corners of your mouth from brushing your teeth. Your body has lost the ability to generate saliva, so your tongue is suffocating you. You'd cry but that would take the last of the moisture left in your body. Death seems pretty good right now. Your boss doesn't even get mad at you and your co-workers think that your dog just died because you look so pathetic. You should have called in sick because, let's face it, all you can manage to do is breathe... *very gently.*

• • •

**Before you order a drink in public, you should read this!**

Seven New York City bartenders were asked if they could nail a woman's personality based on what she drinks. Though interviewed separately, they concurred on almost all counts. Their results:

*Drink: Beer*
Personality: Causal, low-maintenance, down to earth.
Your Approach: Challenge her to a game of pool.

*Drink: Blender Drinks*
Personality: Flaky, whiny, annoying; a pain in the ass.
Your approach: Avoid her, unless you want to be her cabana boy.
*Drink: Mixed Drinks*
Personality: Older, more refined, high maintenance, has very picky taste; knows
EXACTLY what she wants.
Your Approach: You won't have to approach her. If she's interested, she'll send *YOU* a drink.
*Drink: Wine (does not include White Zinfandel)*
Personality: Conservative and classy, sophisticated, yet giggles.
Your Approach: Tell her you love to travel and spend quiet evenings with friends.

*Drink: White Zinfandel*
Personality: Easy, thinks she is classy and sophisticated, actually she has NO clue.
Your Approach: Make her feel smarter than she is - this should be an easy target.
*Drink: Shots*
Personality: Likes to hang with frat-boy pals and looking to get totally drunk...and naked.
Your Approach: Easiest hit in the joint. You have been blessed. Nothing to do but wait, however, be careful not to make her mad!
*Drink: Tequila*
No explanations required - everyone just KNOWS what happens there.

**Then, there is the MALE addendum —**

The deal with guys is, as always, very simple and clear cut::
*Domestic Beer*: He's poor and wants to get laid.
*Imported Beer*: He likes good beer and wants to get laid.
*Wine*: He's hoping that the wine will give him a sophisticated image to help him get laid.

*Whiskey*: He doesn't give a damn about ANYTHING but getting laid.

*Tequila*: He is thinking he has a chance with the toothless waitress.

*White* Zinfandel: He's gay!

• • •

Into a Belfast pub comes Paddy Murphy, looking like he'd just been run over by a train. His arm was in a sling, his nose was broken, his face was cut and bruised, and he was walking with a limp.

"What happened to you?" asked Sean, the bartender.

"Jamie O'Conner and me had a fight," replied Paddy.

"That little shit, O'Conner?" exclaimed Sean with passion. "He couldn't do that to you; he must have had something in his hand."

"Aye, an' that he did," replied Paddy. "A shovel is what he had, and a terrible lickin' he gave me with it."

"Well," says Sean, "you should have defended yourself. Didn't you have something in *your* hand?"

"Aye, and that I did," said Paddy. "Mrs. O'Conner's breast, and a thing of beauty it was, but useless in a fight."

• • •

An Irishman who had a wee too much to drink was driving home from the city one night and, of course, his car was weaving violently all over the road.

A cop pulled him over.

"So," said the cop to the driver, "Where have ya been?"

"Why, I've been to the pub of course," slurred the drunk.

"Well," says the cop, "it looks like you've had quite a few to drink this evening."

"I did all right," the drunk said with a smile.

"Did you know," asked the cop, standing straight and folding his arms across his chest, "That a few intersections back, your wife fell out of your car?"

"Oh, thank heavens," sighed the drunk. "For a minute there, I thought I'd gone deaf."

• • •

Brenda O'Malley was home making dinner, as usual, when Tim Finnegan arrived at her door.

"Brenda, may I come in?" he implored. "I've somethin' to tell ya."

"Of course you can come in. You're always welcome, Tim. But where's my husband?"

"That's what I'm here to be tellin' ya, Brenda. There was an accident down at the Guinness brewery...."

"Oh, God, no!" cries Brenda. "Please don't tell me!"

"I must, Brenda. Your husband Sean is dead and gone. I'm so very sorry."

Finally, she looked up at Tim. "How did it happen, Tim?"

"It was terrible, Brenda. He fell into a vat of Guinness Stout and drowned."

"Oh my dear Jesus! But you must tell me true, Tim. Did he at least go quickly?"

"Well, no Brenda ... no. Fact is, he got out three times to pee."

• • •

A drunk staggers into a Catholic church, enters a confessional booth, sits down, but says nothing. The priest coughed a few times to get his attention but the drunk just sat there. Finally, the priest pounded three times on the wall.

The drunk mumbled, "Ain't no use knockin'. There's no paper on this side either!"

• • •

A man picked up a young woman in a bar and convinces her to come back to his hotel. When they are relaxing afterwards, he asked, "Am I the first man you ever made love to?"

She looked at him thoughtfully for a second before replying.

"You might be," she said. "Your face looks familiar."

• • •

## Tequila

José was strolling down the street in Mexico City and kicked a bottle lying in the street. Suddenly, out of the bottle came a genie. The Mexican was stunned and the Genie said, "Hello master, I will grant you one wish, anything you want."

José began thinking, "Well, I really like drinking tequila. "I wish to drink tequila whenever I want, so make me piss tequila."

The Genie granted him his wish.

When José returned home he got a glass out of the cupboard and peed into it. He looked at the glass and it's clear contents. Sure looks like tequila. Then he sniffed the liquid. Si, si, it smelled like tequila too. So, he took a wee taste and it is the best tequila he has ever tasted. José yelled to his wife, "Consuela, Consuela, come quickly!"

She came running down the hall and José took another glass out of the cupboard and directed a forceful stream into it. He told his wife her to drink it. Naturally, Consuela was reluctant but went ahead and took a sip. It was the best tequila she has ever tasted also. The two drank and partied all night.

The next night the José came home from work and told Consuela to get two glasses from the cupboard. He proceeded to pee into the two glasses. The result was the same, the tequila is excellent and the couple drink until the sun comes up.

Finally Friday night came and José came home and told his wife, "Consuela grab one glass from the cupboard and we will drink tequila."

His wife got the glass from the cupboard and set it on the table. José began to urinate into the glass and when it was full, his wife asked him, "But José, why do we need only one glass?"

José raised the glass and replied, "Because tonight, my love, you drink from the bottle!!"

• • •

A young woman, heavily burdened with over-stuffed shopping bags of assorted groceries, exited from a produce store and as she stepped over the thresh-hold, the thin paper bags suddenly disintegrated and discharged their contents in a cascade that landed between her legs; the clerk had foolishly placed wet lettuce on the bottom.

Looking down at the resulting disaster comprised of broken eggs, smashed tomatoes, soggy lettuce, and fresh bread that was rapidly absorbing the multihued mess like a white sponge, the woman began to weep as she stared dumbfounded at what now occupied the space lying between her feet.

A moment later, a drunk, reeling up the street stopped for a moment, looked down at what he beheld fouling the sidewalk, and shook his head, muttering, "Now, now, young lady, I shouldn't cry; it wouldn't have lived anyway — its eyes were too close together!"

• • •

A pastor walked into a neighborhood pub. The place was hopping with music and dancing but every once in a while the lights would turn off. Each time after the lights would go out the place would erupt into cheers. However, when the revelers saw the town pastor, the room went dead silent. He walked up to the bartender, and asked, "May I please use the restroom?"

The bartender replied, "I really don't think you should."

Why not?" the pastor asked.

"Well, there is a statue of a naked woman in there, and her most private part is covered only by a fig leaf."

"Nonsense," said the pastor, "I'll just look the other way."

So the bartender showed the clergyman the door at the top of the stairs, and he proceeded to the restroom. After a few minutes, he came back out, and the whole place was hopping with music and dancing again. However, they did stop just long enough to give the pastor a loud round of applause.

He went to the bartender and said, "Sir, I don't understand. Why did they applaud for me just because I went to the restroom?"

"Well, now they know you're one of us." said the bartender. "Would you like a drink?"

"But, I still don't understand," said the puzzled pastor.

"You see," laughed the bartender, "every time the fig leaf is lifted on the statue, the lights go out in the whole place. Now, how about that drink?

• • •

For those who wish to have a glass of wine. And those who don't... this is something to think about.

As Ben Franklin said: In wine there is wisdom, in beer there is freedom, in water there is bacteria. In a number of carefully controlled trials, scientists have demonstrated that if we drink 1 liter of water each day, at the end of the year we would have absorbed more than 1 kilo of *Escherichia coli*, (*E.coli*) bacteria found in feces.

In other words, we would be consuming 1 kilo of poop. However, we do **NOT** run that risk when drinking wine & beer (or tequila, rum, whiskey or other liquor) because alcohol has to go through a purification process of boiling, filtering and/or fermenting.

Remember: Water = Poop, Wine = Health

Therefore, it's better to drink wine and talk stupid, than to drink water and be full of shit.

• • •

Three old ladies were walking home from shopping and the stopped in a pub. When they were drinking their gin and tonics they began discussing what they were planning on giving to their doorman for Christmas.

The first old lady said "Oh I'm going to give the little dear money. He looks like he needs some"

The second old lady said "I've seen him down here before so I'll get him some imported beer."

The first and second old ladies looked at the third and asked her what she'd give him.

The third one replied "I'm going to give him sex."

"Sex?"

"Yes, when I asked my husband what we should give him last night he just said "The doorman? Fuck the doorman!"

. . .

Patrick, Mike, and Sean were sitting in a Dublin pub comparing their favorite toasts for an impromptu contest. After several hours of this excuse for quaffing a few gallons of Guinness, they finally settled upon Sean's which was: "Sure and I would like to spend the rest o' me life between the legs of that fine lass, me wife, Maggie."

The next day, Maggie was walking to the market when she met Mike, who congratulated Sean on his thoughtful toast. When asked by Maggie to recite the winning toast, Mike didn't hesitate for a moment and replied, "Well Maggie, Sean said 'Sure and I would like to spend the rest of me life in church with me sweet wife, Maggie."

To which Maggie responded, "That's strange, he was there only twice, and the first time, he fell asleep; the second time, I had to grab him by ears to make him come."

. . .

Two women go out one weekend without their husbands. As they came back, right before dawn, both of them drunk, they felt the urge to pee. They noticed the only place to stop was a cemetery. Scared and drunk, they stopped and decided to go there anyway. The first one did not have anything to wipe herself with, so she took off her panties and used them to clean herself and then discarded them.

The second woman, not finding anything either, thought, "I'm not getting rid of my panties'...so she used the ribbon of a flower wreath that was leaning against a headstone to dry herself.

The morning after, the two husbands were talking to each other on the phone, and one says to the other:

"We have to be on the lookout, it seems that these two were up to no good last night, my wife came home without her panties...."

The other one responded: "You're lucky, mine came home with a card stuck to her ass that read, "We will never forget you."

• • •

## Alcohol Warning Labels

Due to increasing products liability litigation, American liquor manufacturers have accepted the FDA's suggestion that the following warning labels be placed immediately on all varieties of alcohol containers:

WARNING: The consumption of alcohol may leave you wondering what the hell happened to your bra and panties.

WARNING: The consumption of alcohol may make you think you are whispering when you are not.

WARNING: The consumption of alcohol is a major factor in dancing like a retarded fool.

WARNING: The consumption of alcohol may cause you to tell your friends over and over again that you love them.

WARNING: The consumption of alcohol may cause you to think you can sing.

WARNING: The consumption of alcohol may lead you to believe that ex-lovers are really dying for you to telephone them at four in the morning.

WARNING: The consumption of alcohol may make you think you can logically converse with other members of the opposite sex without spitting.

WARNING: The consumption of alcohol is the leading cause of inexplicable rug burns on the forehead, knees and lower back.

WARNING: The consumption of alcohol may create the illusion that you are tougher, smarter, faster and better looking than most people.

WARNING: The consumption of alcohol may lead you to think people are laughing *with* you.

WARNING: The consumption of alcohol may cause pregnancy.

WARNING: The crumsumpten of alcahol may Mack you tink you can tipe real gode.

• • •

"Sometimes when I reflect back on all the beer I drink I feel shamed. Then I look into the glass and think about the workers in the brewery and all of their hopes and dreams. If I didn't drink this beer, they might be out of work and their dreams would be shattered. Then I say to myself, "It is better that I drink this beer and let their dreams come true than be selfish and worry about my liver." Jack Handy

"I feel sorry for people who don't drink. When they wake up in the morning, that's as good as they're going to feel all day." Frank Sinatra

"When I read about the evils of drinking, I gave up reading." Henny Youngman

"24 hours in a day, 24 beers in a case. Coincidence? I think not." Stephen Wright

"When we drink, we get drunk. When we get drunk, we fall asleep. When we are asleep, we commit no sins. When we commit no sins, we go to heaven. Sooooo, let's all get drunk and go to heaven!" Brian O'Rourke

"Beer is proof that God loves us and wants us to be happy." Benjamin Franklin

"Without question, the greatest invention in the history of mankind is beer. Oh, I grant you that the wheel was also a fine invention, but the wheel does not go nearly as well with pizza." Dave Barry

## BEER: HELPING UGLY PEOPLE HAVE SEX SINCE 3000 B.C.!!! Annon.

Remember "I" before "E", except in Budweiser.
To some it's a six-pack, to me it's a Support Group. Salvation in a can!

And saving the best for last, as explained by Cliff Clavin, of *Cheers*.
One afternoon at Cheers, Cliff was explaining the Buffalo Theory to his buddy Norm.

Here's how it went: "Well ya see, Norm, it's like this... A herd of buffalo can only move as fast as the slowest buffalo. And when the herd is hunted, it is the slowest and weakest ones at the back that are killed first. This natural selection is good for the herd as a whole, because the general speed and health of the whole group keeps improving by the regular killing of the weakest members.
In much the same way, the human brain can only operate as fast as the slowest brain cells. Excessive intake of alcohol, as we know, kills brain cells. But naturally, it attacks the slowest and weakest brain cells first. In this way, regular consumption of beer eliminates the weaker brain cells, making the brain a faster and more efficient machine! That's why you always feel smarter after a few beers."

• • •

The police arrested Patrick Lawrence, 22 year old white male, in a pumpkin patch late Friday night. Saturday morning Lawrence was charged at the Gwinnett County (GA) courthouse with lewd and lascivious behavior, public indecency, and public intoxication.
The suspect explained that as he was passing a pumpkin patch on his way home from a drinking session when he decided to stop,

"You know how a pumpkin is soft and squishy inside and there was no one around for miles or at least I thought there wasn't anyone around', he stated in a telephone interview.

Lawrence went on to say that he pulled over to the side of the road, picked out a pumpkin that he felt was appropriate to his purpose, cut a hole in it, and proceeded to satisfy his alleged need. "Guess I was really into it, you know?" he commented with evident embarrassment. In the process of doing the deed, Lawrence failed to notice an approaching police car and was unaware of his audience until Officer Brenda Taylor approached him. "It was an unusual situation, that's for sure," said Officer Taylor. "I walked up to Lawrence and he's just banging away at this pumpkin."

Officer Taylor went on to described what happened when she approached Lawrence. "I said, 'Excuse me sir, but do you realize that you're having sex with a pumpkin? He froze and was clearly very surprised that I was there and then he looked me straight in the face and said..."A pumpkin? Damn is it midnight already?"

This was in the Washington Post. The title of the article was "Best Come Back Line Ever."

• • •

At 3:00 AM a desk clerk at a hotel got a call from a drunk guy asking what time the bar opened.

"It opens at noon," answered the clerk.

About an hour later he received yet another call from the same guy, sounding even drunker. "What time does the bar open?" he asked.

"Same time as before... Noon," replied the clerk.

Another hour passed and he called again, this time thoroughly plastered. "Wha'yoo shay the bar opins at?"

The clerk then answered, "It opens at noon, but if you can't wait, I can have room service send something up to you."

"No... I don't wanna git in... Ah wanna git *OUT!*"

• • •

A man walked into a restaurant with a full-grown ostrich behind him, and as he sat, the waitress came over and asked for their order. The man said, "I'll have a hamburger, fries and a coke," and turned to the ostrich.

"What's yours?"

"I'll have the same," replied the ostrich.

A short time later the waitress returned with the order. "That will be $6.40 please."

The man reached into his pocket and pulled out exact change for payment.

The next day, the man and the ostrich returned and the man said, "I'll have a hamburger, fries and a coke," and the ostrich says, "I'll have the same."

Once again the man reaches into his pocket and pays with exact change.

This becomes a routine until late one evening, the two enter again.

"The usual?" asks the waitress.

"No, this is Friday night, so I will have a steak, baked potato and salad," says the man.

"Same for me," says the ostrich.

A short time later the waitress comes with the order and says, "That will be $12.62."

Once again the man pulls exact change out of his pocket and places it on the table.

The waitress couldn't hold back her curiosity any longer. "Excuse me, sir. How do you manage to always come up with the exact change out of your pocket every time?"

"Well," replied the man, "several years ago I was cleaning the attic and I found an old lamp. When I rubbed it a genie appeared and offered me two wishes. My first wish was that if I ever had to pay for anything, just put my hand in my pocket, and the right amount of money would always be there."

"That's brilliant!" exclaimed the waitress. "Most people would wish for a million dollars or something, but you'll always be as rich as you want for as long as you live!"

"That's right! Whether it's a gallon of milk or a Rolls Royce, the exact money is always there," said the man.

The waitress asked, "One other thing, sir, what's with the ostrich?"

The man sighs and answers, "My second wish was for a tall chick with long legs who agreed with everything I say!"

• • •

Two blokes were painting a Concorde supersonic jet and it was taking a long time. They had just reached the wings and one exclaimed, "Smell this paint, it smells like Vodka!"

The other bloke says "Yeah, you're right, have a swig."

So he took a swig, and it was just about palatable. Come the end of the shift they have consumed 37 cans of paint between them and they were completely pissed.

They stumbled back to their homes and went straight to bed, nearly dead. The first bloke woke up and he had the worst hangover of his life. He climbed out of bed and fell flat on his face. He looked at his feet and he noticed that some little wheels have grown out of the soles of his feet. "What the hell..." he exclaimed. He skated into the bathroom and he could not believe what he saw in the mirror: he had a 7 inch long pointy nose instead of his own, his shoulders were pushed back and his arms were now decidedly flattish.

"Oh, for Christ's sake!"

Suddenly the phone rang, jarring him and making the headache even worse. He answered the telephone and it was his mate from the day before.

"Thank God you've phoned. I've got wheels on my feet, a long pointy nose, flat arms and I don't know what the hell is going on.

The reply came, "Yeah, I know. Whatever you do don't fart, I'm phoning from Bahrain!"

• • •

An Irishman walked into a bar in Dublin, ordered three pints of Guinness and sat in the back of the room, drinking a sip out of each one in turn. When he finished all three, he came back to the bar and ordered three more. The bartender said to him, "You know, a pint goes flat after I draw it; it would taste better if you bought one at a time."

The Irishman replied, "Well, you see, I have two brothers. One is in America; the other in Australia, and I'm here in Dublin. When we all left home, we promised that we'd drink this way to remember the days we all drank together."

The bartender admitted that this is a nice custom, and left it there.

The Irishman became a regular in the bar and always drank the same way: he ordered three pints and drinks the three pints by taking sips from each of them in turn.

One day, he came in and ordered only two pints. All the other regulars' in the bar notice and fall silent. When he came back to the bar for the second round, the bartender asked, "I don't want to intrude on your grief, but I wanted to offer my condolences on your great loss."

The Irishman looked confused for a moment, then the light dawns in his eye and he laughed. "Oh, no," he says, "Everyone is fine. It's me. I've quit drinking!"

• • •

Two builders (Chris and James) were seated either side of a table in a rough pub when a well-dressed man entered, ordered a beer and sat on a stool at the bar. The two builders started to speculate about the occupation of the suit.

Chris: I reckon he's an accountant.

James: No way, he's a stockbroker.

Chris: He ain't no stockbroker! A stockbroker wouldn't come in here!

The argument repeated itself for some time until the accumulated volume of beer got the better of Chris and he made for the toilet. On entering the toilet he saw that the suit was standing at a urinal. Curiosity and the several beers get the better of the builder...

Chris: 'Scuse me no offence meant, but me and me mate were wondering what you do for a living?

Suit: No offence taken! I'm a Logical Scientist by profession!

Chris: Oh! What's that then?

Suit:-I'll try to explain by example... Do you have a goldfish at home?

Chris: Er...mmm... well yeah, I do as it happens!

Suit: Well, it's logical to follow that you keep it in a bowl or in a pond. Which is it?

Chris: It's in a pond!

Suit: Well then it's reasonable to suppose that you have a large garden then?

Chris: As it happens, yes I have got a big garden!

Suit: Well then it's logical to assume that in this town that if you have a large garden that you have a large house?

Chris: As it happens I've got a five bedroom house... built it myself!

Suit: Well given that you've built a five bedroom house it is logical to assume that you haven't built it just for yourself and that you are quite probably married?

Chris: Yes I am married, I live with my wife and three children!

Suit: Well then it is logical to assume that you are sexually active with your wife on a regular basis?

Chris: Yep! Four nights a week!

Suit: Well then it is logical to suggest that you do not masturbate very often?

Chris: Me? Never!

Suit: Well there you are! That's logical science at work!

Chris: How's that then?

Suit: Well from finding out that you had a goldfish, I've told you about the size of garden you have, the size of house, your family and your sex life!

Chris: I see! That's pretty impressive... thanks mate!

Both leave the toilet and Chris returned to his friend.
James: I see the suit was in there. Did you ask him what he does for a living?
Chris: Yep! He's a logical scientist!
James: -What's that then?
Chris: I'll try and explain. Do you have a goldfish?
James: Nope
Chris: Well then, you're a wanker!

• • •

What's the difference between Beer Nuts and Deer Nuts?
Beer Nuts are $1.50, and Deer Nuts are always under a buck.

• • •

A guy walked into a bar and sat down next to an extremely gorgeous woman. The first thing he noticed about her though, were her pants. They were skin-tight high-waisted and had no obvious mechanism (zipper, buttons or Velcro) for opening them.
After several minutes of puzzling over how she got the pants up over her hips, he finally worked up the nerve to ask her, Excuse me miss, but how do you get into your pants?"
"Well," she replied, "you can start by buying me a drink."

• • •

Bubba went to a psychiatrist. "I've got problems. Every time I go to bed I think there's somebody under it. I'm scared. I think I'm going crazy."
"Just put yourself in my hands for one year," said the shrink. "Come talk to me three times a week, and we should be able to rid you of those fears."
"How much do you charge?"
"Eighty dollars per visit, replied the doctor."

"I'll sleep on it," said Bubba.

Six months later the doctor met Bubba on the street. "Why didn't you ever come to see me about those fears you were having?" asked the psychiatrist.

"Well Eighty bucks a visit three times a week for a year is an awful lot of money! A bartender cured me for $10. I was so happy to have saved all that money that I went and bought me a new pickup!"

"Is that so! And how, may I ask, did a bartender cure you?"

"He told me to cut the legs off the bed! - Ain't nobody under there now!!!"

• • •

A man walks into a bar and asks for six shots of vodka.

The bartender says, "Six shots?! What's wrong?"

"I found out my older brother is gay," replied the man.

The next night, he walked into the bar again and asked for six shots of vodka.

"What now?" asked the barman

"I found out my younger brother is gay," replied the man.

The night after that, the man walked into the bar again and asked for six shots of vodka.

"Jeez, does ANYBODY in your family like women?" asked the bartender.

The man replied, "Yeah, my wife does!"

• • •

A man and his wife were awakened at 3:00 am by a loud pounding on the door. The man gets up and goes to the door where a drunken stranger, standing in the pouring rain, is asking for a push.

"Not a chance," says the husband, "it is 3:00 in the morning!" He slammed the door and returned to bed.

"Who was that?" asked his wife.

"Just some drunken fool asking for a push," he answered.

"Did you help him?" she inquired.

"No, I did not, it is 3:00 in the morning and it is pouring rain out there!"

"Well, you have a short memory,' says his wife. "Can't you remember about three months ago when we broke down, and those two guys helped us? I think you should help him, and you should be ashamed of yourself!"

The man did as he was told, gets dressed, and went out into the pounding rain. He called out into the dark, "Hello, are you still there?"

"Yes," came back the answer.

"Do you still need a push?" called out the husband.

"Yes, please!" was the reply from the dark.

"Where are you?" asked the husband.

"Over here on the swing," replied the drunk.

• • •

# CHILD-RELATED HUMOR

Antonio came home from school one day and walked into the kitchen.

Grandma Maria asked him, "Antonio, what did you learn in school today?"

Antonio replied, "Well, we learned about penises, and vaginas, sexual intercourse, and masturbation."

Grandma hauled off and slapped Antonio, hard. He ran up to his room, crying.

Antonio's mother walked in and cried, "Ma! Why did you go and hit Antonio?"

Grandma replied, "Well, I asked him what he learned in school today. He started talking about sex, and penises, and masturbation!"

Antonio's mother said, "Ma! That's what they learn. It's called sex education!"

Grandma Maria felt terrible about hitting Antonio, so she went upstairs to apologize. When she opened his bedroom door she found him on him on his bed masturbating.

Without a blink, she said, "Antonio, when you're finished with your homework, come downstairs and talk to me."

• • •

Little Johnny was dressed up in his cowboy outfit, and walked into an ice cream shop. Behind the counter was a good-looking, well-endowed, female employee.

Little Johnny walked up to the counter, and said, "Give me an ice cream sundae."

She said, "Okay." Then she asked him if he wanted vanilla ice cream.

He pulled out his six-shooters, and stated loudly, "You're damn right", and then put them back in the holsters.

Then she asked if he wanted chocolate ice cream.

Again he pulled out his guns and stated "You damn right."

After putting all the ingredients on the sundae, she asked him if he wanted his nuts crushed.

Little Johnny pulled his guns out, and said; "Only if you want your boobs blown off!"

• • •

The mother of a 17-year old daughter was concerned that the girl was sexually active. Worried that the girl might become pregnant, which would adversely her future and impact her family status, the mother consulted the family physician for advice.

The doctor told the mother that teenagers today were rather willful and any attempt to stop the girl would probably result in rebellion. He advised the mother to arrange to have the girl placed on birth control medication and to also buy her a package of condoms and explain how there were to be used.

Later that evening, as her daughter was preparing for a date, the mother told her daughter about the situation and handed her the package of foil-wrapped condoms.

The girl burst out laughing and reached over to hug her mom, saying, 'Oh Mom, you don't have anything to worry about that, I am dating Susan!"

• • •

Brenda and Steve took their six-year-old son, Terry, to the family doctor. With hesitation, they explained to the physician that their little angel appeared to be in good health; they were concerned about the lad's rather small penis.

After examining Terry, the doctor confidently declared, "Just feed him pancakes, that should solve the problem."

The next morning, when the boy arrived at the breakfast table, there was a stack of steaming pancakes on the table.

"Gee mom," the boy exclaimed, "For me?"

"Just take two," Brenda replied, The rest are for your father."

• • •

A little boy on his first day of school was asked by his mother what he had learned.

"Bow wow!" replied the lad.

"Now that you are a big boy, you should not use baby language!" responded his mother.

The next day, when the boy returned form school, he was again asked what he had learned.

"Meow, meow!" piped the little boy.

"Remember what I told you yesterday when you came home from school?

Now that you are a BIG boy, you must not use baby talk!" admonished his mother.

On the third day, when asked what he had learned that day, the boy chirped,

"We learned about Winnie the Shit!"

• • •

The college professor had just finished explaining an important research project to his class. He emphasized that this paper was an absolute requirement for passing his course and that there would be only two acceptable excuses for being late: those students with medically certifiable illness or death in the student's immediate family.

A smart-ass student in the back of the classroom waved his hand excitedly and spoke up, "But what about extreme sexual exhaustion, professor?"

As one would expect, the classroom erupted in raucous laughter. When the students had finally settled down, the professor froze the young man with a glaringlook, "Well," he responded, "I guess you'll just have to learn to write with your other hand!"

• • •

Jimmy had been away for the weekend visiting his uncle who ran a farm.

"Did you have a good time?" asked his mother.

"Yes, I really did, Mom," said the lad.

"What animals did you see, Jimmy?" asked Mother.

"Well, I saw Piggy Wigs, and I saw Moo Cows, and I saw the Chooky Hens, and I saw the Baabaa Lambs, and I saw the Fuckers."

"You saw *WHAT?*" cried Mother.

"Well, Uncle called them 'Effers,' but I knew what he meant!"

• • •

Little Johnny was all out of sorts one morning. When his father asked him what the problem was, the kid said, "I am mad at Mommy, because she eats birds."

His father asked him what Little Johnny was talking about.

Little Johnny replied," I was up late last night and heard noises coming from your bedroom. When I listened at your door, I heard Mom say, "Should I swallow it or let it fly?"

• • •

Nancy was in the garden filling in a hole when her neighbor peered over the fence.

"What are up to Nancy?"

"My goldfish died," replied the little girl tearfully, without looking up, "and I've just buried him."

The neighbor commented, "That's an awfully big hole for a goldfish, isn't it?"

Nancy patted down the last heap of soil and then replied, "That's because he's inside your fucking cat!"

• • •

Teacher asked the kids in class: "What do you want to be when you grow up?

"Little Johnny: "I wanna be a billionaire, going to the most expensive clubs, take the best bitch with me, give her a Ferrari worth over a million bucks, an apartment in Copacabana, a mansion in Paris, a jet to travel through Europe, an Infinite Visa Card and to make love to her three times a day."

The teacher, shocked, and not knowing what to do with the bad behavior of the child, decided not to give importance to what he said and then continues the lesson.

And you, Susie; What do you want to be when you grow up?

"I wanna be Johnny's bitch!"

• • •

A boy, about 12 years-old, shows up at a whorehouse dragging a dead frog at the end of a string and is introduced to the madam.

"Well hello, young man, and what can I do for you?"

The kid responds that he wanted to have a woman.

"Come back when you've grown up," answers the madam.

At this point, the boy reaches into his pocket and withdraws a fifty dollar bill.

"Splendid," says the madam, as she tucked the bill into her ample bosom. "Go upstairs; the room you want is on the left, at the end."

"And the woman that I want to visit must have herpes" added the kid, as he pulled out another $50 and handed it to the woman.

"Just to satisfy my curiosity, why for heaven's sake would you want to have sex with an infected person?" inquired the madam.

"Because, when I get home, I'm going screw the baby sitter; then, when my father drives her home, he'll stop on the way and screw her too; then, when he gets home, he'll screw my mom.

Tomorrow morning, after he's gone to work, Mom will screw the milkman — and he's the bastard who ran over and killed my frog!

• • •

A mother and her son were flying Southwest Airlines. The son (who had been looking out the window) turned to his mother and said, 'In big dogs have baby dogs and big cats have baby cats, why don't big planes have baby planes?"

The mother (who couldn't think of an answer) told her son to ask the flight attendant.

So the boy walked down the aisle and asked the flight attendant, "If big dogs have baby dogs and big cats haw baby cats, why don't big planes have baby planes?"

The flight attendant asked the young man, "Did your mother tell you to ask me?"

He said that she had.

The flight attendant knelt down and whispered in the little boy's ear, "Tell your mother that it's because Southwest always pulls out on time."

• • •

A father was explaining the facts of life to his teenage son. After covering the basics of biology, he moved on to the finer points of love-making. Their conversation went as follows:

The Dad: "One thing to keep in mind, son, is that different women say different things during the sex act, even if you are doing the same thing."

The Son: "What do you mean, Dad?"

The Dad: "Well, for example, their words will vary according to their occupation. For example, a prostitute will tend to say, 'Are you done yet?' On the other hand, a nymphomaniac will ask, 'Are you done already?'"

The Son: "What do other women say?"

The Dad: "Well, a school teacher will say, 'We are going to do this over and over again until you get it right!' A nurse will say 'This won't hurt one bit.'"

The Son: "I thought they said, "Pull down your pants and bend over."

The Dad: "That's male nurses. But let's move on, a bank teller will say, 'Substantial penalty for early withdrawal.' A stewardess will say, '"Place this over your mouth and nose and breathe normally.'"

The Son: "And what does mom say?"

The Dad: "She says, 'Beige... beige... I think we should paint the ceiling beige.'"

• • •

## The Perfect Gift

Three sons left home, went out on their own and prospered. Getting back together they discussed the gifts they were able to give their elderly mother.

The first said, "I built a big house for our mother."

The second said," I sent her a Mercedes with a livered driver."

The third son smiled and said, "I've got you, both beat. You know how Mom enjoys the Bible, and you know she can't see very well. I sent her a parrot that can recite the entire Bible. It took 20 monks in a monastery 12 years to teach him. I had to pledge contribute $100,000 a year for 10 years, but it was worth it. Mom just has to name the chapter and verse, and the parrot will recite it."

Soon thereafter, Mom sent out her letters of thanks: "Milton," she wrote the first son, "The house you built is so huge. I live in only one room, but I have to clean the whole house."

# CHILD-RELATED HUMOR

"Marvin," she wrote to another, "I am too old to travel. I stay home all the time, so I never use the Mercedes. And the driver is so rude!"

"Dearest Melvin," she wrote to her third son, "You were the only son to have the good sense to know what your mother likes. That chicken was delicious

• • •

## Should Children Witness Childbirth?
Here's your answer.

Due to a power outage, only one paramedic responded to the call. The house was very dark so the paramedic asked Kathleen, a 3-yr old girl to hold a flashlight high over her mommy so he could see while he helped deliver the baby. Very diligently, Kathleen did as she was asked. Heidi pushed and pushed and after a little while, Connor was born.

The paramedic lifted him by his little feet and spanked him on his bottom. Connor began to cry. The paramedic then thanked Kathleen for her help and asked the wide-eyed 3-yr old what she thought about what she had just witnessed.

Kathleen quickly responded, 'He shouldn't have crawled in there in the first place.

• • •

A pastor was presenting a children's sermon. During the sermon, he asked the children if they knew what the resurrection was.

Now, asking questions during children's sermons is crucial, but at the same time, asking children questions in front of a congregation can also be very dangerous.

Having basked the children if they knew the meaning of the resurrection, a little boy raised his hand.

The pastor called on him and the little boy said, "I know that if you have a resurrection that lasts more than four hours you are supposed to call the doctor."

It took over ten minutes for the congregation to subside sufficiently from their laughter for the worship service to be continued.

• • •

Stories about children and their views of the world are always touching.

A father watched his young daughter playing in the garden. He smiled as he reflected on how sweet and pure his little girl was. Tears formed in his eyes as he thought about her seeing the wonders of nature through such innocent eyes.

Suddenly she just stopped and stared at the ground.

He went over to her to see what work of God had captured her attention. He noticed she was looking at two spiders mating.

"Daddy, what are those two spiders doing?" she asked.

"They're mating," her father replied.

"What do you call the spider on top?" she asked.

"A Daddy Longlegs," her father answered.

"So, the other one is a Mommy Longlegs?" the little girl asked.

As his heart soared with the joy of such a cute and innocent question he replied, "'No sweetheart, *both* of them are Daddy Longlegs."

The little girl, looking a little puzzled, thought for a moment, then lifted her foot and stomped them flat.. "Well, she said, that may be OK in California, but we're not having any of that shit in Texas."

• • •

On the first day of school, the children brought gifts for their teacher.

The supermarket manager's daughter brought the teacher a basket of assorted fruit.

The florist's son brought the teacher a bouquet of flowers.

The candy-store owner's daughter gave the teacher a pretty box of candy.

Then the liquor-store owner's son brought up a big, heavy box. The teacher lifted it up and noticed that it was leaking a little bit. She touched a drop of the liquid with her finger and tasted it.

"Is it wine?" she guessed.

"No," the boy replied.

She tasted another drop and asked, "Champagne?"

"No," said the little boy... "It's a puppy!"

• • •

An atheist was seated next to a little girl on an airplane and he turned to her and said, "Do you want to talk? Flights go quicker if you strike up a conversation with your fellow passenger.

The little girl, who had just started to read her book, replied to the total stranger, " What would you want to talk about?

Oh, I don't know," said the atheist. "How about why there is no God, or no Heaven or Hell, or no life after death?" as he smiled smugly.

"OK," she said. "Those could be interesting topics but let me ask you a question first. A horse, a cow, and a deer all eat the same stuff – grass. Yet a deer excretes little pellets, while a cow turns out a flat patty, but a horse produces clumps. Why do you suppose that is?"

The atheist, visibly surprised by the little girl's intelligence, thinks about it and said, "Hmmm, I have no idea."

To which the little girl replied, "Do you really feel qualified to discuss God, Heaven and Hell, or life after death, when you obviously don't know shit?"

And then she went back to reading her book.

• • •

A teenager came home from school with a writing assignment. He asked his father for help. "Dad, can you tell me the difference between *potential* and *reality*?"

His father looked up thoughtfully and then said, "Son, I'll display it to you. Go ask your mother if she would sleep with Robert Redford for a million dollars. Then ask your sister if she would sleep with Brad Pitt for a million dollars. Then come back and tell me what you've learned."

The kid was puzzled, but he decided to see whether he could figure out what his father meant.

He asked his mother, "Mom, if someone gave you a million dollars, would you sleep with Robert Redford?" His mother looked around slyly, and then with a little smile on her face, said, "Don't tell your father, but, yes, I would."

The boy then went up to his sister's room and asked her, "Sis, if someone gave you a million dollars, would you sleep with Brad Pitt?" His sister looked up and said, "Omigod! Definitely!"

The kid went back to his father and said, "Dad, I think that I've figured it out. *Potentially*, we are sitting on two million bucks, but in *reality*, we are living with a couple of whores!"

• • •

An old man was rocking on his front porch down in Louisiana watching the sunrise when he noticed the neighbor's kid walk by carrying something big under his arm. He yelled out, "Hey boy, whatcha got there?"

The boy yelled back, "Roll of chicken wire."

The old man asked, "Whatcha goin' to do with it, boy?"

The lad replied, "Gonna catch me some chickens."

"You damned fool, you cain't catch no chickens with chicken wire!"

The boy just laughed and kept on walking. That evening about sundown, the Old chap was astonished to see the boy walk past his porch, dragging the chicken wire with about 30 chickens caught in it.

The next day, the elderly fellow spied the same lad walking past his porch carrying something round and shiny in his hand.

"Whatcha got there boy?"

The boy replied, "Roll of duct tape."

## Child-Related Humor

The old man inquired, "Whatcha goin' to do with that?"

The kid answered, "Going to catch me some ducks."

Hearing that, the old man leaned back in his rocker and roared, "You damned fool, you cain't catch no ducks with duct tape!"

The boy just laughed and kept on walking. Late that afternoon, the lad passed by the porch and to the old man's amazement, the boy unrolled the tape and revealed that he had captured about fat 25 mallards and 10 sleek teal.

Sure enough, the third morning in a row, the same boy ambles past the old fellow's porch dragging a long reed-like stick with a tuft of fuzzy stuff at the tip.

"Whatcha got there, lad?" inquired the old man.

"It's a pussy willow," answered the boy.

The old fellow bellowed out, "Hey boy, I'll get my hat!"

• • •

# ENGLISH FOR FOREIGNERS

The following signs have been found in various locations, using the English language somewhat creatively:

In a Cocktail lounge, Norway:
**LADIES ARE REQUESTED NOT TO HAVE CHILDREN IN THE BAR.**

At a Budapest zoo:
**PLEASE DO NOT FEED THE ANIMALS. IF YOU HAVE ANY SUITABLE FOOD, GIVE IT TO THE GUARD ON DUTY.**

At a Doctor's office in Rome:
**SPECIALIST IN WOMEN AND OTHER DISEASES.**

At a Hotel in Acapulco:
**THE MANAGER HAS PERSONALLY PASSED ALL THE WATER SERVED HERE.**

In a booklet about using a hotel air conditioner in Japan:
**COOLES AND HEATES: IF YOU WANT CONDITION OF WARM AIR IN YOUR ROOM, PLEASE CONTROL YOURSELF.**

In a car rental brochure in Tokyo:
**WHEN PASSENGER OF FOOT HEAVE IN SIGHT, TOOTLE THE HORN.**

**TRUMPET HIM MELODIOUSLY AT FIRST, BUT IF HE STILL OBSTACLES YOUR PASSAGE THEN TOOTLE HIM WITH VIGOUR.**

In men's rest room in Japan:
**TO STOP LEAK TURN COCK TO THE RIGHT**

In a Nairobi restaurant:
**CUSTOMERS WHO FIND OUR WAITRESSES RUDE OUGHT TO SEE THE MANAGER.**

On the grounds of a private school:
**NO TRESPASSING WITHOUT PERMISSION.**

On an Athi River highway:
**TAKE NOTICE: WHEN THIS SIGN IS UNDER WATER, THIS ROAD IS IMPASSABLE.**

On a poster at Kencom:
**ARE YOU AN ADULT THAT CANNOT READ? IF SO, WE CAN HELP.**

In a City restaurant:
**OPEN SEVEN DAYS A WEEK, AND WEEKENDS TOO.**

On one of the Mathare, Kenya buildings:
**MENTAL HEALTH PREVENTION CENTRE.**

A sign seen on an automatic restroom hand dryer:
**DO NOT ACTIVATE WITH WET HANDS.**

In a Pumwani maternity ward:
**NO CHILDREN ALLOWED.**

In a cemetery:
**PERSONS ARE PROHIBITED FROM PICKING FLOWERS FROM ANY BUT THEIR OWN GRAVES.**

In Japanese public bath:
**FOREIGN GUESTS ARE REQUESTED NOT TO PULL COCK IN TUB.**

In a Perugia, Italy fast food ristaurante:
**"FISH & CHEAP"**

On a sign of a Tokyo hotel's rules and regulations:
**GUESTS ARE REQUESTED NOT TO SMOKE OR DO OTHER DISGUSTING BEHAVIOURS IN BED.**

On the menu of a Swiss restaurant:
**OUR WINES LEAVE YOU NOTHING TO HOPE FOR.**

In a Tokyo bar:
**SPECIAL COCKTAILS FOR THE LADIES WITH NUTS.**

In a Bangkok temple:
**IT IS FORBIDDEN TO ENTER A WOMAN EVEN A FOREIGNER, IF DRESSED AS A MAN.**

On a Hotel room notice, Chiang-Mai, Thailand:
**PLEASE DO NOT BRING SOLICITORS INTO YOUR ROOM.**

In a Hotel brochure, Italy:
**THIS HOTEL IS RENOWNED FOR ITS PEACE AND SOLITUDE. IN FACT, CROWDS FROM ALL OVER THE WORLD FLOCK HERE TO ENJOY ITS SOLITUDE.**

In a Hotel lobby, Bucharest:
**THE LIFT IS BEING FIXED FOR THE NEXT DAY. DURING THAT TIME WE REGRET THAT YOU WILL BE UNBEARABLE.**

In a Hotel elevator, Paris:
**PLEASE LEAVE YOUR VALUES AT THE FRONT DESK.**

In a Hotel, Yugoslavia:
**THE FLATTENING OF UNDERWEAR WITH PLEASURE IS THE JOB OF THE CHAMBERMAID.**

In lobby of a Hotel, Japan:
**YOU ARE INVITED TO TAKE ADVANTAGE OF THE CHAMBERMAID.**

In the lobby of a Moscow hotel across from a Russian Orthodox monastery:
**YOU ARE WELCOME TO VISIT THE CEMETERY WHERE FAMOUS RUSSIAN AND SOVIET COMPOSERS, ARTISTS, AND WRITERS ARE BURIED DAILY EXCEPT THURSDAY.**

In a Hotel catering to skiers, Austria:
**NOT TO PERAMBULATE THE CORRIDORS IN THE HOURS OF REPOSE IN THE BOOTS OF ASCENSION.**

Taken from a menu, Poland:
**SALAD AFIRM'S OWN MAKE; LIMPID RED BEET SOUP WITH CHEESY DUMPLINGS IN THE FORM OF A FINGER; ROASTED DUCK LET LOOSE; BEEF RASHERS BEATEN IN THE COUNTRY PEOPLE'S FASHION.**

In a Supermarket, Hong Kong:
**FOR YOUR CONVENIENCE, WE RECOMMEND COURTEOUS, EFFICIENT SELF-SERVICE.**

From the "Soviet Weekly":
**THERE WILL BE A MOSCOW EXHIBITION OF ARTS BY 15,000 SOVIET REPUBLIC PAINTERS AND SCULPTORS. THESE WERE EXECUTED OVER THE PAST TWO YEARS.**

In an East African newspaper:
**A NEW SWIMMING POOL IS RAPIDLY TAKING SHAPE SINCE THE CONTRACTORS HAVE THROWN IN THE BULK OF THEIR WORKERS.**

A sign posted in Germany's Black Forest:
**IT IS STRICTLY FORBIDDEN ON OUR BLACK FOREST CAMPING SITE THAT PEOPLE OF DIFFERENT SEX, FOR INSTANCE, MEN AND WOMEN, LIVE TOGETHER IN ONE TENT UNLESS THEY ARE MARRIED WITH EACH OTHER FOR THIS PURPOSE.**

In a Hotel room in Vienna:
**IN CASE OF FIRE, DO YOUR UTMOST TO ALARM THE HOTEL PORTER.**

In a Hotel in Zurich:
**BECAUSE OF THE IMPROPRIETY OF ENTERTAINING GUESTS OF THE OPPOSITE SEX IN THE BEDROOM, IT IS SUGGESTED THAT THE LOBBY BE USED FOR THIS PURPOSE.**

An advertisement by a Hong Kong dentist:
**TEETH EXTRACTED BY THE LATEST METHODISTS.**

In a laundry in Rome:
**LADIES, LEAVE YOUR CLOTHES HERE AND SPEND THE AFTERNOON HAVING A GOOD TIME.**

Tourist agency, Czechoslovakia:
**TAKE ONE OF OUR HORSE-DRIVEN CITY TOURS. WE GUARANTEE NO MISCARRIAGES.**

An advertisement for donkey rides, Thailand:
**WOULD YOU LIKE TO RIDE ON YOUR OWN ASS?**

The box of a clockwork toy made in Hong Kong:
**GUARANTEED TO WORK THROUGHOUT ITS USEFUL LIFE.**

In a Swiss mountain inn:
**SPECIAL TODAY - NO ICE-CREAM.**

## English For Foreigners

Airline ticket office, Copenhagen:
**WE TAKE YOUR BAGS AND SEND THEM IN ALL DIRECTIONS.**

On the door of a Moscow hotel room:
**IF THIS IS YOUR FIRST VISIT TO THE USSR, YOU ARE WELCOME TO IT.**

Dry cleaners, Bangkok:
**DROP YOUR TROUSERS HERE FOR THE BEST RESULTS.**

In a City restaurant:
**OPEN SEVEN DAYS A WEEK AND WEEKENDS**.

And, then, there are signs in English but written by those whose English leaves a wee bit to desire. Here are a few:

Spotted in a toilet of a London office: **TOILET OUT OF ORDER. PLEASE USE FLOOR BELOW.**

In a Laundromat in Surrey: **AUTOMATIC WASHING MACHINES: PLEASE REMOVE ALL YOUR CLOTHES WHEN THE LIGHT GOES OUT.**

In a London department store: **BARGAIN BASEMENT UPSTAIRS**

In a Bristol office: **THE PERSON WHO TOOK THE STEP LADDER YESTERDAY PLEASE BRING IT BACK OR FURTHER STEPS WILL BE TAKEN**

In an office in London: **AFTER TEA BREAK STAFF SHOULD EMPTY THE TEAPOT AND STAND UPSIDE DOWN ON THE DRAINING BOARD.**

Outside a secondhand shop in Liverpool: **WE EXCHANGE ANYTHING - BICYCLES, WASHING MACHINES, ETC. WHY**

**NOT BRING YOUR WIFE ALONG AND GET A WONDERFUL BARGAIN?**

Notice in health food shop window in London: **CLOSED DUE TO ILLNESS.**

Spotted in a safari park: **ELEPHANTS PLEASE STAY IN YOUR CAR.**

Seen during a conference: **FOR ANYONE WHO HAS CHILDREN AND DOESN'T KNOW IT, THERE IS A DAY CARE ON THE FIRST FLOOR.**

Notice in a field: **THE FARMER ALLOWS WALKERS TO CROSS THE FIELD FOR FREE, BUT THE BULL CHARGES**

Message on a leaflet: **IF YOU CANNOT READ, THIS LEAFLET WILL TELL YOU HOW TO GET LESSONS**

On a repair shop door: **WE CAN REPAIR ANYTHING. (PLEASE KNOCK HARD ON THE DOOR - THE BELL DOESN'T WORK)**

• • •

A little lady from North Carolina had worked in and around family dairy farms since she was old enough to walk...with hours of hard work and little compensation .and when canned Carnation Milk became available in grocery stores (1940's or 50's???) she read an advertisement offering $5,000 for the best slogan...rhyme beginning with "Carnation Milk is best of all...." and she said, I know all about milk and dairy farms...I can do this!!!!

She sent in her entry and about a week later, a black limo drove up in front of her house...a man got out and said, Carnation LOVED your entry so much, we are here to award you $1000, even though we will not be able to use it....Here is her entry:

Carnation milk is best of all,
no tits to pull, no shit to haul
no buckets to wash, no hay to pitch,
just poke a hole in the son-of-a-bitch!

• • •

Coors put its slogan, "Turn It Loose," into Spanish, where it was read as "Suffer From Diarrhea."

Scandinavian vacuum manufacturer Electrolux used the following in an American campaign: "Nothing sucks like an Electrolux."

When Gerber started selling baby food in Africa, they used the same packaging as in the US, with the smiling baby on the label. Later they learned that in Africa, companies routinely put pictures on the labels of what's inside, since many people can't read.

Colgate introduced a toothpaste in France called Cue, the name of a notorious porno magazine.

Pepsi's "Come Alive With the Pepsi Generation" translated into "Pepsi Brings Your Ancestors Back From the Grave" in Chinese.

When American Airlines wanted to advertise its new leather first class seats in the Mexican market, it translates its "Fly In Leather" campaign literally, which meant "Fly Naked" (vuela en cue) in Spanish!

• • •

### Some Tee Shirt Emblazonings of Note

"MY WILD OATS HAVE TURNED TO SHREDDED WHEAT"
"Filthy, Stinking Rich –Well, Two Out of Three Ain't Bad "
"Real Men Don't Waste Their Hormones Growing Hair"
"Upon the Advice of My Attorney, My Shirt Bears No Message at This Time"
"That's It! I'm Calling Grandma!" (seen on an 8 year old)
"Wrinkled Was Not One of the Things I Wanted to Be When I Grew Up"

"Procrastinate Now"

"Rehab Is for Quitters"

"My Dog Can Lick Anyone"

"I Have a Degree in Liberal Arts –Do You Want Fries With That?"

"Party –My Crib –Two A.M." (On a baby-size shirt)

"If a woman's place is in the home WHY AM I ALWAYS IN THIS CAR!"

"A hangover is the wrath of grapes"

"STUPIDITY IS NOT A HANDICAP. Park elsewhere!"

"They call it "PMS" because "Mad Cow Disease" was already taken"

"He who dies with the most toys is nonetheless dead"

"POLICE STATION TOILET STOLEN Cops have nothing to go on."

"HECK IS WHERE PEOPLE GO WHO DON'T BELIEVE IN GOSH"

"A PICTURE IS WORTH A THOUSAND WORDS– But it uses up a thousand times the memory "

"Time flies like an arrow. Fruit flies like a banana."

"HAM AND EGGS A day's work for a chicken; A lifetime commitment for a pig."

"HARD WORK WILL PAYOFF LATER. LAZINESS PAYS OFF NOW!"

The trouble with life is there's no background music.

"The original point and click interface was a Smith & Wesson."

"Two rights do not make a wrong. They make an airplane."

"Computer programmers don't byte, they nybble a bit."

"Quoting one is plagiarism. Quoting many is research."

"Bombing for Peace — Is like Fucking for Chastity"

On a forest green tee shirt showing a tall tree: "Who Cut One?"

• • •

# THE RESULTS OF OUR CURRENT EDUCATIONAL SYSTEM

The following questions and answers were collated from SAT tests given in Springdale, Arkansas in 2000 to 16 year old students! (Don't laugh too hard–one of these may be the president someday. Also, more recent scores have not improved materially.)

Q: Name the four seasons.
A: Salt, pepper, mustard and vinegar.

Q: Explain one of the processes by which water can be made safe to drink.
A: Flirtation makes water safe to drink because it removes large pollutants like grit, sand, dead sheep and canoeists.

Q: How is dew formed?
A: The sun shines down on the leaves and makes them perspire.

Q: What is a planet?
A: A body of earth surrounded by sky.

Q: What causes the tides in the oceans?
A: The tides are a fight between the Earth and the Moon. All water tends to flow towards the moon, because there is no water

## The Results Of Our Current Educational System

on the moon, and nature abhors a vacuum. I forget where the sun joins in this fight.

Q: In a democratic society, how important are elections?
A: Very important. Sex can only happen when a male gets an election.

Q: What are steroids?
A: Things for keeping carpets still on the stairs.

Q: What happens to your body as you age?
A: When you get old, so do your bowels and you get intercontinental.

Q: What happens to a boy when he reaches puberty?
A: He says good-bye to his boyhood and looks forward to his adultery.

Q: Name a major disease associated with cigarettes.
A: Premature death.

Q: How can you delay milk turning sour?
A: Keep it in the cow.

Q: How are the main parts of the body categorized? (e.g., abdomen.)
A: The body is consisted into three parts – the brainium, the borax and abdominal cavity. The brainium contains the brain, the borax contains the heart and lungs, and the abdominal cavity contains the five bowels,
A,E,I,O and U.

Q: What is the Fibula?
A: A small lie.

Q: What does "varicose" mean?
A: Nearby.

Q: What is the most common form of birth control?
A: Most people prevent contraception by wearing a condominium.

Q: Give the meaning of the term "Caesarean Section."
A: The caesarean section is a district in Rome.

Q: What is a seizure?
A: A Roman emperor.

Q: What is a terminal illness?
A: When you are sick at the airport.

Q: Give an example of a fungus. What is a characteristic feature?
A: Mushrooms. They always grow in damp places and so they look like umbrellas.

Q: What does the word "benign" mean?
A: Benign is what you will be after you be eight.

Q: What is a turbine?
A: Something an Arab wears on his head.

Q: What is a Hindu?
A: It lays eggs.

• • •

## Math Through the Ages

### Teaching Math in 1950:

A logger sells a truckload of lumber for $100. His cost of production is 4/5 of the price. What is his profit?

# The Results Of Our Current Educational System

**Teaching Math in 1960:**
A logger sells a truckload of lumber for $100. His cost of production is 4/5 of the price, or $80. What is his profit?

**Teaching Math in 1970:**
A logger exchanges a set "L" of lumber for a set "M" of money. The cardinality of set "M" is 100. Each element is worth one dollar. Make 100 dots representing the elements of the set "M." The set "C." the cost of production contains 20 fewer points than set "M." Represent the set "C" as a subset of set "M" and answer the following question: What is the cardinality of the set "P" of profits?

**Teaching Math in 1980:**
A logger sells a truckload of lumber for $100. His cost of production is $80 and his profit is $20. Your assignment: Underline the number 20.

**Teaching Math in 1990:**
By cutting down beautiful forest trees, the logger makes $20. What do you think of this way of making a living? Topic for class participation after answering the question: How did the forest birds and squirrels feel as the logger cut down the trees? There are no wrong answers.

**Teaching Match in 2010:**
A logger sells a truckload of lumber for $100. His cost of production is $120. How does Arthur Andersen determine that his profit margin is $60?

• • •

or:

**Teaching Math in 1950:**
A logger sells a truckload of lumber for $100. His cost of production is 4/5 of The price. What is his profit?

**Teaching Math in 1960:**
A logger sells a truckload of lumber for $100. His cost of production is 4/5 of the price, or $80. What is his profit?

**Teaching Math in 2010:**
El hachero vende un camion carga por $100. El costo de produccion es....

### More Math through the Ages

Q: How does a home schooler change a light bulb?

A: First, mom checks three books on electricity out of the library, then the kids make models of light bulbs, read a biography of Thomas Edison and do a skit based on his life. Next, everyone studies the history of lighting methods, wrapping up with dipping their own candles.

Next, everyone takes a trip to the store where they compare types of light bulbs as well as prices and figure out how much change they'll get if they buy two bulbs for $1.99 and pay with a five dollar bill. On the way home, a discussion develops over the history of money and also Abraham Lincoln, as his picture is on the five dollar bill. Finally, after building a homemade ladder out of branches dragged from the woods, the light bulb is installed. And there is light.

### English Class 101

Remember the book "Men are from Mars, Women are from Venus"? Well, here's a prime example offered by an English professor at a U.S. University.

"Today we will experiment with a new form called the tandem story. The process is simple. Each person will pair off with the person sitting to his or her immediate right. One of you will then write the first paragraph of a short story. The partner will read the first paragraph and then add another paragraph to the story. The first person will then add a third paragraph, and so on back and forth. Remember to reread what has been written each time in order to keep the story coherent. There is to be absolutely NO talking and anything you wish to say must be written on the paper. The story is over when both agree a conclusion has been reached."

# The Results Of Our Current Educational System

The following was actually turned in by two of my English students: Rebecca and Gary.

## STORY
(First paragraph by Rebecca)

At first, Laurie couldn't decide which kind of tea she wanted. The chamomile, which used to be her favorite for lazy evenings at home, now reminded her too much of Carl, who once said, in happier times, that he liked chamomile. But she felt she must now, at all costs, keep her mind off Carl. His possessiveness was suffocating, and if she thought about him too much her asthma started acting up again. So chamomile was out of the question.

(Second paragraph by Gary)

Meanwhile, Advance Sergeant Carl Harris, leader of the attack squadron now in orbit over Skylon 4, had more important things to think about than the neuroses of an air-headed asthmatic bimbo named Laurie with whom he had spent one sweaty night over a year ago. "A.S. Harris to Geostation 17," he said into his transgalactic communicator. "Polar orbit established. No sign of resistance so far..." But before he could sign off a bluish particle beam flashed out of nowhere and blasted a hole through his ship's cargo bay. The jolt from the direct hit sent him flying out of his seat and across the cockpit.

(Third paragraph by Rebecca)

He bumped his head and died almost immediately but not before he felt one last pang of regret for psychically brutalizing the one woman who had ever had feelings for him. Soon afterwards, Earth stopped its pointless hostilities towards the peaceful farmers of Skylon 4. "Congress Passes Law Permanently Abolishing War and Space Travel," Laurie read in her newspaper one morning.

The news simultaneously excited her and bored her. She stared out the window, dreaming of her youth, when the days had passed unhurriedly and carefree, with no newspapers to read, no television todistract her from her sense of innocent wonder at all the beautiful things round her. "Why must one lose one's innocence to become a woman?" she pondered wistfully.

(Fourth paragraph by Gary)

Little did she know, but she had less than 10 seconds to live. Thousands of miles above the city, the Anu'udrian mothership launched the first of its lithium fusion missiles. The dimwitted wimpy peaceniks who pushed the Unilateral Aerospace Disarmament Treaty through the congress had left Earth a defenseless target for the hostile alien empires who were determined to destroy the human race. Within two hours after the passage of the treaty the Anu'udrian ships were on course for Earth, carrying enough firepower to pulverize the entire planet. With no one to stop them, they swiftly initiated their diabolical plan. The lithium fusion missile entered the atmosphere unimpeded. The President, in his top-secret Mobile submarine headquarters on the ocean floor off the coast of Guam, felt the inconceivably massive explosion, which vaporized poor, stupid, Laurie and 85 million other Americans. The President slammed his fist on the conference table. "We can't allow this! I'm going to veto that treaty! Let's blow 'em out of the sky!"

(Fifth paragraph by Rebecca)

This is absurd. I refuse to continue this mockery of literature. My writing partner is a violent, chauvinistic semiliterate adolescent.

(Sixth paragraph by Gary)

Yeah? Well, you're a self-centered tedious neurotic whose attempts at writing are the literary equivalent of Valium. "Shall I

## The Results Of Our Current Educational System

have chamomile tea? Or shall I have some other sort of FRIGGING TEA??? Oh no, I'm such an air-headed bimbo who reads too many Danielle Steele novels."

(Seventh paragraph by Rebecca)

Asshole.

(Eight paragraph by Gary)

Bitch.

(Ninth paragraph by Rebecca)

Wanker.

(Tenth paragraph by Gary)

Slut.

(teacher: A⁺ - I *really* liked this one)

• • •

The teacher of the earth science class was lecturing on map reading. After explaining about latitude, longitude, degrees and minutes the teacher asked, "Suppose I asked you to meet me for lunch at 23 degrees, 4 minutes north latitude and 45 degrees, 15 minutes east longitude?"

After a confused silence, a voice volunteered, "I guess you'd be eating alone."

• • •

## The following is a list of similes used by high school students in actual essays:

Her face was a perfect oval, like a circle that had its two other sides gently compressed by a Thigh Master. –Sue Lin Chong, Washington

His thoughts tumbled in his head, making and breaking alliances like underpants in a dryer without Cling Free. –Chuck Smith, Woodbridge

The little boat gently drifted across the pond exactly the way a bowling ball wouldn't. –Russell Beland, Springfield

McBride fell 12 stories, hitting the pavement like a Hefty bag filled with Vegetable soup. –Paul Sabourin, Silver Spring

From the attic came an unearthly howl. The whole scene had an eerie, surreal quality, like when you're on vacation in another city and "Jeopardy" comes on at 7:00 p. m. instead of 7:30. –Ashley, Washington

Her hair glistened in the rain like nose hair after a sneeze. –Chuck Smith, Woodbridge

Her eyes were like two brown circles with big black dots in the center. –Russell Beland, Springfield

Bob was as perplexed as a hacker who means to access T:flw.quid55328.com\ aaakk/ch@ung but gets T:\flw.quidaaakk/ch@ung by mistake. –Ken Krattenmaker, Landover Hills

Her vocabulary was as bad as, like, whatever. –Unknown

He was as tall as a six-foot-three-inch tree. –Jack Bross, Chevy Chase

# The Results Of Our Current Educational System

The hailstones leaped from the pavement, just like maggots when you fry them in hot grease. –Gary F. Hevel, Silver Spring

Long separated by cruel fate, the star-crossed lovers raced across the grassy field toward each other like two freight trains, one having left Cleveland at 6:36 p.m. traveling at 55 mph, the other from Topeka at 4:19 p.m. at a speed of 35 mph. –Jennifer Hart, Arlington

The politician was gone but unnoticed, like the period after the Dr. on a Dr Pepper can. –Wayne Goode, Madison, AL

John and Mary had never met. They were like two hummingbirds who had also never met. –Russell Beland, Springfield

The thunder was ominous sounding, much like the sound of a thin sheet of metal being shaken backstage during the storm scene in a play. –Barbara Fetherolf, Alexandria

He fell for her like his heart was a mob informant and she was the East River. –Brian Broadus, Charlottesville

Even in his last years, Grandpappy had a mind like a steel trap, only one that had been left out so long, it had rusted shut. – Sandra Hull, Arlington

Shots rang out, as shots are wont to do. –Jerry Pannullo, Kensington

The plan was simple, like my brother-in-law Phil. But unlike Phil, this plan just might work. –Unknown

The young fighter had a hungry look, the kind you get from not eating for a while. –Malcolm Fleschner, Arlington

He was as lame as a duck. Not the metaphorical lame duck, either, but a real duck that was actually lame. Maybe from stepping on a land mine or something. –John Kammer, Herndon

Her artistic sense was exquisitely refined, like someone who can tell butter from I Can't Believe It's Not Butter. –Barbara Collier, Garrett Park

She had a deep, throaty, genuine laugh, like that sound a dog makes just before it throws up. –Susan Reese, Arlington

It came down the stairs looking very much like something no one had ever seen before. –Marian Carlsson, Lexington

The ballerina rose gracefully *en pointe* and extended one slender leg behind her, like a dog at a fire hydrant. –Jennifer Hart, Arlington

The revelation that his marriage of 30 years had disintegrated because of his wife's infidelity came as a rude shock, like a surcharge at a formerly surcharge-free ATM. –Paul J. Kocak, Syracuse

The dandelion swayed in the gentle breeze like an oscillating electric fan set on medium. –Unknown

It was an American tradition, like fathers chasing kids around with power tools. –Brian Broadus, Charlottesville

He was deeply in love. When she spoke, he thought he heard bells, as if she were a garbage truck backing up. –Susan Reese, Arlington

She was as easy as the "TV Guide" crossword. –Tom Witte, Gaithersburg

Her eyes were like limpid pools, only they had forgotten to put in any pH cleanser. –Chuck Smith, Woodbridge

## The Results Of Our Current Educational System

She grew on him like she was a colony of *E. coli* and he was room-temperature Canadian beef. –Brian Broadus, Charlottesville

She walked into my office like a centipede with 98 missing legs. –Jonathan Paul, Garrett Park

It hurt the way your tongue hurts after you accidentally staple it to the wall. –Brian Broadus, Charlottesville

• • •

On the first day of University, the Dean addressed the students, pointing out some of the rules:
"The female Halls will be out-of-bounds for all male students, and the male halls to the female students. Anybody caught breaking this rule will be fined twenty dollars the first time." He continued, "Anybody caught breaking this rule the second time will be fined sixty dollars. Being caught a third time will cost you a fine of one hundred and eighty dollars. Are there any questions?"
A male student in the crowd inquired: "How much for a season pass?"

• • •

### The Applicant

After being interviewed by the school administration, the eager teaching prospect said, "Let me see if I've got this right; you want me to go into that room with all those kids, and fill their every waking moment with a love for learning. And I'm supposed to instill a sense of pride in their ethnicity, modify their disruptive behavior, observe them for signs of abuse and even censor their T-shirt messages and dress habits. You want me to wage a war on drugs and sexually transmitted diseases, check their backpacks for weapons of mass destruction, and raise their self esteem. You want me to teach them patriotism, good citizenship, sportsmanship, fair play, how to register to vote, how to balance a checkbook, and how to apply for a job. I am to check their heads for lice, maintain a safe environment, recognize signs of antisocial behavior, offer advice, write letters of recommendation for student employment and scholarships, encourage respect for the cultural diversity of others, and oh, make sure that I give the girls in my class fifty percent of my attention."

"My contract requires me to work on my own time after school, evenings and weekends grading papers. Also, I must spend my summer vacation at my own expense working toward advance certification and a Masters degree. And on my own time you want me to attend committee and faculty meetings, PTA meetings, and participate in staff development training. I am to be a paragon of virtue, larger than life, such that my very presence will awe my students into being obedient and respectful of authority. And I am to pledge allegiance to family values and this current administration."

"You want me to incorporate technology into the learning experience, monitor web sites, and relate personally with each student. That includes deciding who might be potentially dangerous and/or liable to commit a crime in school. I am to make sure all students pass the mandatory state exams, even those who don't come to school regularly or complete any of their assignments. Plus, I am to make sure that all of the students with handicaps get an equal education regardless of the extent of their mental or physical handicap. And I am to communicate regularly with the parents by letter, telephone, newsletter and report card. All of this I am to do with just a piece of chalk, a computer, a few books, a bulletin board, a big smile AND on a starting salary that qualifies my family for food stamps!"

"You want me to do all of this and yet you expect me NOT TO PRAY?"

• • •

# The Results Of Our Current Educational System

Recently, when I went to McDonald's I saw on the menu that you could have an order of 6, 9 or 12 Chicken McNuggets. I asked for a half dozen nuggets.

"We don't have half dozen nuggets," said the teenager at the counter.

"You don't?" I replied.

"We only have six, nine, or twelve," was the reply.

"So I can't order a half dozen nuggets, but I can order six?"

"That's right." So I shook my head and ordered six McNuggets.

The paragraph above doesn't amaze me because of what happened a couple of months ago. I was checking out at the local Foodland with just a few items and the lady behind me put her things on the belt close to mine. I picked up one of those "dividers" that they keep by the cash register and placed it between our things so they wouldn't get mixed. After the girl had scanned all of my items, she picked up the "divider" looking it all over for the bar code so she could scan it. Not finding the bar code she said to me, "Do you know how much this is?"

I said to her "I've changed my mind, I don't think I'll buy that today."

She said "OK" and I paid her for the things and left. She had no clue to what had just happened.

• • •

A lady at work was seen putting a credit card into her floppy drive and pulling it out very quickly.

When inquired as to what she was doing, she said she was shopping on the Internet and they kept asking for a credit card number, so she was using the ATM "thingy."

• • •

I recently saw a distraught young lady weeping beside her car.

"Do you need some help?" I asked.

She replied, "I knew I should have replaced the battery to this remote door unlocker. Now I can't get into my car. Do you think they (pointing to a distant convenient store) would have a battery to fit this?"

"Hmmm, I dunno. Do you have an alarm too?" I asked.

"No, just this remote thingy," she answered, handing it and the car keys to me.

As I took the key and manually unlocked the door, I replied, "Why don't you drive over there and check about the batteries. It's a long walk."

• • •

Several years ago, we had an Intern who was none too swift. One day she was typing and turned to a secretary and said, "I'm almost out of typing paper. What do I do?"

"Just use copier machine paper," the secretary told her.

With that, the intern took her last remaining blank piece of paper, put it on the photocopier and proceeded to make five "blank" copies.

• • •

I was in a car dealership a while ago, when a large motor home was towed into the garage. The front of the vehicle was in dire need of repair and the whole thing generally looked like an extra in "Twister."

I asked the manager what had happened. He told me that the driver had set the "cruise control" and then went in the back to make a sandwich.

• • •

My neighbor works in the operations department in the central office of a large bank. Employees in the field call him when they have problems with their computers. One night he got a call from a woman in one of the branch banks who had this question: "I've got smoke coming from the back of my terminal. Do you guys have a fire downtown?"

• • •

Police in Radnor, Pennsylvania, interrogated a suspect by placing a metal colander on his head and connecting it with wires to a photocopy machine. The message "He's lying" was placed in the copier, and police pressed the copy button each time they thought the suspect wasn't telling the truth.

Believing the "lie detector" was working, the suspect confessed.

• • •

**Temperature of Hell**

The following is an actual question given on a University of Washington chemistry mid-term exam.

The answer by one student was so "profound" that the professor shared it with colleagues, via the Internet, which is of course why we now have the pleasure of enjoying it as well.

Bonus Question: Is Hell exothermic (emits heat) or endothermic (absorbs heat)?

Most of the students wrote proofs of their beliefs using Boyle's Law (gas cools off when it expands and heats up when it is compressed) or some variant. One student, however, wrote the following:

First, we need to know how the mass of Hell is changing in time. So we need to know the rate that souls are moving into Hell and the rate they are leaving. I think that we can safely assume that once a soul gets to Hell, it will not leave.

Therefore, no souls are leaving.

As for how many souls are entering Hell, let's look at the different religions that exist in the world today. Some of these religions state that if you are not a member of their religion, you will go straight to Hell. Since there are more than one of these religions and since people do not belong to more than one religion, we can project that all souls go to Hell.

With birth and death rates as they are, we can expect the number of souls in Hell to increase exponentially. Now, we look at the rate of change of the volume in Hell, because Boyle's Law states that in order for the temperature and pressure in Hell to stay the same, the volume of Hell has to expand proportionately as souls are added. This gives two possibilities:

(1) If Hell is expanding at a slower rate than the rate at which souls enter Hell, then the temperature and pressure in Hell will increase until all Hell breaks loose.

(2) If Hell is expanding at a rate faster than the increase of souls in Hell, then the temperature and pressure will drop until Hell freezes over.

So which is it?

If we accept the postulate given to me by a certain girl I dated back when I was a freshman, that it will be a cold day in Hell before I sleep with you", and take into account the fact that I still have not succeeded in having sexual relations with her, then No. 2 cannot be true, and thus I am sure that Hell is exothermic and will not freeze.

The student received the only "A"

• • •

### You So Smart?

In an article called "The Intelligence on Stupidity" by The New York Times' Emily Eakin, we learn that in 1976, British journalist Stephen Pile created the "Not Terribly Good Club" where members were accepted on the basis of their incompetence. But at the club's opening event "at a hand-picked, third-rate restaurant" the founder blundered by catching a tureen of soup in mid-air and "for this blatant display of adroitness, was instantly demoted."

Undaunted, he penned "The Incomplete Book of Failures" which catalogs notable imbecility such as the worst tourist – a man who stayed two days in New York believing he was in Rome, and the slowest solution of a crossword puzzle – 34 years.

The book also included a membership application for the Club which immediate-ly received 20,000 applications and "Thus was in violation of its commitment to failure" and had to be disbanded. Now we have "The Encyclopedia of Stupidity" by Matthijs van Boxsel, a lapsed middle-aged Dutch academic who cited research on "the effect of side winds on arithmetic sums," "the specific gravity of a kiss" and "the surface of God," and reveals recent "technological advances" like "filters for water purification that are breeding grounds for bacteria; suntan lotions that cause skin cancer and cushioned running shoes designed to protect the knees but at the expense of increasing stress on the hips."

He also guides readers to Darwin awards.com to read about those who improve our gene pool by removing themselves from it – such as "the leader of a Christian sect who died after slipping on a bar of soap while trying to walk on the water in his bathtub." "On the one hand, stupidity poses a daily threat to civilization," states van Boxel, "on the other it constitutes the mystical foundation of our existence. Stupidity is the engine that drives our society." Full speed ahead!

• • •

### No Parent Left Behind

These are *real* notes written by *parents* in a Tennessee school district. Spellings have been left intact. Most of them are funny, but some are just sad.

1– MY SON IS UNDER A DOCTOR'S CARE AND SHOULD NOT TAKE PE TODAY. PLEASE EXECUTE HIM.
2– PLEASE EXKUCE LISA FOR BEING ABSENT SHE WAS SICK AND I HAD HER SHOT

3– DEAR SCHOOL : PLEASE ECSC's JOHN BEING ABSENT ON JAN. 28, 29, 30, 31, 32 AND ALSO 33.
4– PLEASE EXCUSE GLORIA FROM JIM TODAY. SHE IS ADMINISTRATING.
5– PLEASE EXCUSE ROLAND FROM P.E. FOR A FEW DAYS. YESTERDAY HE FELL OUT OF A TREE AND MISPLACED HIS HIP.
6– JOHN HAS BEEN ABSENT BECAUSE HE HAD TWO TEETH TAKEN OUT OF HIS FACE.
7– CARLOS WAS ABSENT YESTERDAY BECAUSE HE WAS PLAYING FOOTBALL. HE WAS HURT IN THE GROWING PART.
8– MEGAN COULD NOT COME TO SCHOOL TODAY BECAUSE SHE HAS BEEN BOTHERED BY VERY CLOSE VEINS.
9– CHRIS WILL NOT BE IN SCHOOL CUS HE HAS AN ACRE IN HIS SIDE.
10– PLEASE EXCUSE RAY FRIDAY FROM SCHOOL. HE HAS VERY LOOSE VOWELS.
11– PLEASE EXCUSE PEDRO FROM BEING ABSENT YESTERDAY. HE HAD (DIAHRE, DYREA, DIREATHE), THE SHI I IS. NOTE: [WORDS IN ( )'s WERE CROSSED OUT.
12– PLEASE EXCUSE TOMMY FOR BEING ABSENT YESTERDAY. HE HAD DIARRHEA, AND HIS BOOTS LEAK.
13– IRVING WAS ABSENT YESTERDAY BECAUSE HE MISSED HIS BUST.
14– PLEASE EXCUSE JIMMY FOR BEING. IT WAS HIS FATHER'S FAULT.
15– I KEPT BILLIE HOME BECAUSE SHE HAD TO GO CHRISTMAS SHOPPING BECAUSE I DON'T KNOW WHAT SIZE SHE WEAR.
16– PLEASE EXCUSE JENNIFER FOR MISSING SCHOOL YESTERDAY. WE FORGOT TOGET THE SUNDAY PAPER OFF THE PORCH, AND WHEN WE FOUND IT MONDAY. WE THOUGHT IT WAS SUNDAY.
17– MY DAUGHTER WAS ABSENT YESTERDAY BECAUSE SHE WAS TIRED. SHE SPENT A WEEKEND WITH THE MARINES.
18– PLEASE EXCUSE JASON FOR BEING ABSENT YESTERDAY. HE HAD A COLD AND COULD NOT BREED WELL.

# The Results Of Our Current Educational System

19– PLEASE EXCUSE MARY FOR BEING ABSENT YESTERDAY. SHE WAS IN BED WITH GRAMPS.
20– GLORIA WAS ABSENT YESTERDAY AS SHE WAS HAVING A GANGOVER.
21– PLEASE EXCUSE BRENDA. SHE HAS BEEN SICK AND UNDER THE DOCTOR.
22– MARYANN WAS ABSENT DECEMBER 11-16, BECAUSE SHE HAD A FEVER, SORE THROAT, HEADACHE AND UPSET STOMACH. HER SISTER WAS ALSO SICK, FEVER AN SORE THROAT, HER BROTHER HAD A LOW GRADE FEVER AND ACHED ALL OVER. I WASN'T THE BEST EITHER SORE THROAT AND FEVER. THERE MUST BE SOMETHING GOING AROUND, HER FATHER EVEN GOT HOT LAST NIGHT.

Now we know why parents are screaming for better education for our kids

• • •

A Roadway driver was driving east on Route 66 when he saw a truck driving west when the CB radio crackled to life...Hey Roadway driver, who are the two biggest a-holes in America?" came from the CB.

Roadway driver replied, "I don't know."

The other trucker says, "You and your brother."

The Roadway driver got annoyed but the other driver told him, "It's just a joke – tell it to the next truck you see."

So the Roadway driver drives for about an hour and finally sees another truck. He gets on the CB and transmits, "Hey other truck, do you know who the two biggest a-holes in the world are?"

The other trucker said, "I don't know, who?"

The Roadway driver replied, "Me and my brother!"

• • •

On September 17, 1994, Alabama's Heather Whitestone was selected as Miss America 1995.

Question: If you could live forever, would you and why?

Answer: "I would not live forever, because we should not live forever, because if we were supposed to live forever, then we would live forever, but we cannot live forever, which is why I would not live forever."

• • •

"Whenever I watch TV and see those poor starving kids all over the world, I can't help but cry. I mean I'd love to be skinny like that, but not with all those flies and death and stuff." Mariah Carey

• • •

"Smoking kills. If you're killed, you've lost a very important part of your life." Brooke Shields, during an interview to become spokesperson for federal anti-smoking campaign.

• • •

"I've never had major knee surgery on any other part of my body," Winston Bennett, University of Kentucky basketball forward.

• • •

"Outside of the killings, Washington has one of the lowest crime rates in the country," Mayor Marion Barry, Washington, DC.

• • •

I'm not going to have some reporters pawing through our papers. We are the president." Hillary Clinton commenting on the release of subpoenaed documents.

• • •

## The Results Of Our Current Educational System

"That lowdown scoundrel deserves to be kicked to death by a jackass, and I'm just the one to do it." A congressional candidate in Texas .

• • •

"Half this game is ninety percent mental." Philadelphia Phillies manager, Danny Ozark

• • •

"It isn't pollution that's harming the environment. It's the impurities in our air and water that are doing it." Al Gore, Vice President

• • •

"We are ready for an unforeseen event that may or may not occur." Al Gore, VP

• • •

"I love California. I practically grew up in Phoenix." Dan Quayle, V.P.

• • •

"We've got to pause and ask ourselves: How much clean air do we need ?" Lee Iacocca

• • •

"The word "genius" isn't applicable in football. A genius is a guy like Norman Einstein." Joe Theisman, NFL football quarterback and sports analyst.

• • •

"We don't necessarily discriminate. We simply exclude certain types of people." Colonel Gerald Wellman, ROTC Instructor.

• • •

If we don't succeed, we run the risk of failure." Bill Clinton, President

• • •

"Traditionally, most of Australia's imports come from overseas." Keppel Enderbery

• • •

"Your food stamps will be stopped effective March 1992 because we received notice that you passed away. May God bless you. You may reapply if there is a change in your circumstances." Department of Social Services, Greenville, South Carolina

• • •

"If somebody has a bad heart, they can plug this jack in at night as they go to bed and it will monitor their heart throughout the night. And the next morning, when they wake up dead, there'll be a record." Mark S. Fowler, FCC Chairman

• • •

**History Test**

Insight into the minds of 6th graders: The following were answers provided by 6th graders during a history test. Watch the spelling! Some of the best humor is in the misspelling.

# The Results Of Our Current Educational System

The Greeks were a highly sculptured people, and without them we wouldn't have history. The Greeks also had myths. A myth is a female moth.

Socrates was a famous Greek teacher who went around giving people advice. They killed him. Socrates died from an overdose of wedlock. After his death, his career suffered a dramatic decline.

In the Olympic games, Greeks ran races, jumped, hurled biscuits, and threw Java.

Julius Caesar extinguished himself on the battlefields of Gaul. The Ides of March murdered him because they thought he was going to be made king. Dying, he gasped out: "Tee hee, Brutus."

Joan of Arc was burnt to a steak and was canonized by Bernard Shaw.

Queen Elizabeth was the "Virgin Queen." As a queen she was a success. When she exposed herself before her troops they all shouted "hurrah."

It was an age of great inventions and discoveries. Gutenberg invented removable type and the Bible. Another important invention was the circulation of blood. Sir Walter Raleigh is a historical figure because he invented cigarettes and started smoking.

Sir Francis Drake circumcised the world with a 100-foot clipper.

The greatest writer of the Renaissance was William Shakespeare. He was born in the year 1564, supposedly on his birthday. He never made much money and is famous only because of his plays. He wrote tragedies, comedies, and hysterectomies, all in Islamic pentameter. Romeo and Juliet are an example of a heroic couple. Romeo's last wish was to be laid by Juliet.

Writing at the same time as Shakespeare was Miguel Cervantes. He wrote Donkey Hote. The next great author was John Milton. Milton wrote Paradise Lost. Then his wife died and he wrote Paradise Regained.

Delegates from the original 13 states formed the Contented Congress. Thomas Jefferson, a Virgin, and Benjamin Franklin were two singers of the Declaration of Independence. Franklin discovered electricity by rubbing two cats backward and declared, "A horse divided against itself cannot stand." Franklin died in 1790 and is still dead.

Abraham Lincoln became America's greatest Precedent. Lincoln's mother died in infancy, and he was born in a log cabin, which he built with his own hands. Abraham Lincoln freed the slaves by signing the Emasculation Proclamation. On the night of April 14, 1865, Lincoln went to the theater and got shot in his seat by one of the actors in a moving picture show. They believe the assinator was John Wilkes Booth, a supposingly insane actor. This ruined Booth's career.

Johann Bach wrote a great many musical compositions and had a large number of children. In between he practiced on an old spinster which he kept up in his attic. Bach died from 1750 to the present. Bach was the most famous composer in the world and so was Handel. Handel was half German, half Italian, and half English. He was very large.

Beethoven wrote music even though he was deaf. He was so deaf he wrote loud music. He took long walks in the forest even when everyone was calling for him. Beethoven expired in 1827 and later died for this.

The nineteenth century was a time of a great many thoughts and inventions. People stopped reproducing by hand and started reproducing by machine. The invention of the steamboat caused a network of rivers to spring up. Cyrus McCormick invented the McCormick raper, which did the work of a hundred men. Louis Pasteur discovered a cure for rabbits. Charles Darwin was a naturalist who wrote the Organ of the Species. Madman Curie discovered the radio. Karl Marx became one of the Marx Brothers.

# BUMPER STICKERS

These are actual bumper stickers hat have been seen on cars

JESUS IS COMING; EVERYONE LOOK BUSY

A BARTENDER IS JUST A PHARMACIST
WITH A LIMITED INVENTORY

HORN BROKEN – WATCH FOR FINGER

THE MORE YOU COMPLAIN, THE
LONGER GOD LETS YOU LIVE

MY KID HAD SEX WITH YOUR HONOR STUDENT

IF AT FIRST YOU DO SUCCEED, TRY
NOT TO APPEAR ASTONISHED

HELP WANTED TELEPATH: YOU KNOW WHERE TO APPLY

JESUS LOVES YOU ... EVERYONE ELSE
THINKS YOU'RE AN ASSHOLE!

I.R.S.: WE'VE GOT IT TAKES TO TAKE WHAT YOU'VE GOT

## Bumper Stickers

I'M JUST DRIVING THIS WAY TO PISS YOU OFF

JESUS PAID FOR OUR SINS...NOW LET'S GET OUR MONEY'S WORTH

REALITY IS A CRUTCH FOR PEOPLE WHO CANNOT HANDLE DRUGS

I LOVE CATS ... THEY TASTE JUST LIKE CHICKEN

OUT OF MY MIND. BACK IN FIVE MINUTES

KEEP HONKING; I'M RELOADING

HANG UP AND DRIVE

LAUGH ALONE AND THE WORLD THINKS YOU'RE AN IDIOT

I DON'T HAVE TO BE DEAD TO DONATE MY ORGAN

LORD SAVE ME FROM YOUR FOLLOWERS

GUNS DON'T KILL PEOPLE ... POSTAL WORKERS DO

CATS ... THE OTHER WHITE MEAT

CHANGE IS INEVITABLE ... EXCEPT IN VENDING MACHINES

IT *IS* AS *BAD* AS YOU THINK; THEY *ARE* OUT TO GET YOU!

WHEN YOU DO A GOOD DEED, GET A RECEIPT, IN CASE HEAVEN IS THE I.R.S.

FRIENDS DON'T LET FRIENDS DRIVE NAKED

**FRIENDS HELP YOU MOVE. REAL FRIENDS
HELP YOU MOVE BODIES**

**SEX ON TELEVISION CAN'T HURT
YOU UNLESS YOU FALL OFF**

**DAS AUTO IST NICHTGEFERLECH**
(this car is not too bad) – on a Smart Car

# DARWIN AWARD NOMINEES

For those of you not familiar with the Darwin awards, they are awarded annually for the most extreme act of (occasionally terminal) stupidity - they are now in for several years enjoy. Some of these individuals obviously hail from the shallow end of our gene pool.

NOMINEE No.1 [San Jose Mercury News]: An unidentified man, using a shotgun like a club to break a former girlfriend's windshield, accidentally shot himself to death when the gun discharged, blowing a hole in his gut.

• • •

NOMINEE No.2 [Kalamazoo Gazette]: James Burns, 34, a mechanic of Alamo, Michigan, was killed as he was trying to repair what police described as a "farm-type truck." Bums got a friend to drive the truck on a highway while Burns hung underneath so that he could ascertain the source of the troubling noise. Bums' clothes caught on something, however, and the other man found Burns wrapped in the drive shaft."

• • •

NOMINEE No.3: [Hickory Daily Record]: Ken Charles Barger, 47 accidentally shot himself to death in Newton, N.C. Awakening to the sound of a ringing telephone beside his bed, he reached for the phone, but grabbed instead a Smith & Wesson .38 Special, which discharged when he drew it to his ear.

• • •

NOMINEE No.4: [UPI, Toronto]: Police said a lawyer, demonstrating the safety of windows in a downtown Toronto skyscraper, crashed through a pane with his shoulder and plunged 24 floors to his death. A police spokesman said Carl Y. Hoy, 39, fell into the courtyard of the Toronto Dominion Bank Tower early Friday evening as he was explaining the strength of the building's windows to visiting law students. Hoy previously has conducted demonstrations of window strength, according to police reports. Peter Lawyers, managing partner of the firm, Holden Day Wilson, told the Toronto Sun that Hoy was "one of the best and brightest" members of the 200-man association.

• • •

NOMINEE No.5: Michael Anderson Godwin made news posthumously. He spent several years awaiting South Carolina's electric chair for a murder conviction before successfully having his sentence reduced to life imprisonment. While sitting on a metal toilet in his cell and attempting to fix his small TV set, he bit a wire and was electrocuted.

• • •

NOMINEE No.6: [The Indianapolis Star]: A cigarette lighter may have triggered a fatal explosion. A Jay County man, using a lighter to check the barrel of muzzleloader, was killed when the weapon discharged in his face. Sheriff's investigators said Gregol Y. David Pryor died in his parents' rural Dunkirk home while cleaning a 54-caliber muzzleloader that had not been firing properly. He was using the lighter to look into the barrel when the gunpowder ignited.

• • •

NOMINEE No.7: [AP, St. Louis]: Robert Pueblo, 32, was apparently behaving in a disorderly fashion in a St. Louis market, when the clerk threatened to call the police. Pueblo grabbed a hot dog, shoved it in his mouth, and walked out without paying for it. Police found him unconscious in front of the store. Paramedics removed the six-inch wiener from his throat after he had choked to death.

• • •

NOMINEE No.8: [Unknown]: Poacher Marino Malerba shot a stag standing above him on an overhanging cliff and was killed instantly when the dead stag fell on him.

• • •

NOMINEE No.9: [Associated Press, Kincaid, W. VA]: Blasting Cap Explodes in Man's Mouth at Party. A man at a party popped a blasting cap into his mouth and bit down, triggering an explosion that blew off his lips, teeth and tongue, State Police said. Jerry Stromyer, 24, of Kincaid, bit the blasting cap as a prank during a party.

• • •

NOMINEE No.10: [UPI, Portland, Oregon]: Doctors at Portland's University Hospital said an Oregon man, shot through the skull by a hunting arrow, is lucky to be alive and will be released soon. Tony Roberts, 25, lost his right eye during an initiation into Mountain Men Anonymous, a men's rafting club in Grants Pass, Oregon. A member tried to shoot a beer can off his head, but the arrow entered Robert's right eye instead. Doctors said that if the arrow had gone one millimeter to the left, a major blood vessel would have been severed and Roberts would have died instantly. Neurosurgeon Dr. John Delashaw said the arrow went through 8 to 10 inches brain, with the tip protruding at the rear of Roberts' skull, yet somehow, it managed to miss all major blood vessels. Delashaw also said that if Roberts had tried to pull the arrow out, he surely would have killed himself. Roberts admitted that he and his friends had been drinking that afternoon. Roberts said, "I feel so dumb about this."

• • •

NOMINEE No.11 : [The Calgary Sun (CP)] : A man arguing over a love triangle accidentally shot himself in the groin, taking off his testicles and part of his penis. Police said the man was waving a .357 Magnum revolver around during a shouting match, but when he stuffed it back into his pants, the gun went off.

• • •

NOMINEE No.12: [Arkansas Democrat Gazette]: Two local men were seriously injured when their pick-up truck left the road and struck a tree near Cotton Patch on State Highway 38. Thurston Poole, 33, of Des Arc and Billy Ray Wallis, 38, of Little Rock are listed in serious condition at Baptist Medical Center. The accident occurred as the two men were returning to Des Arc after a frog-gigging trip. On an overcast Sunday night, Poole's pick-up truck headlights malfunctioned. The two men concluded that the headlight fuse on the older model truck had burned out. A replacement fuse was not available, and Wallis noticed that a .22 caliber bullet from his pistol fit perfectly into the fuse box next to the steering wheel column. Upon inserting the bullet, the headlights began to operate and the two men proceeded eastbound toward White River bridge. After traveling approximately 20 miles and just before crossing the river, the bullet apparently overheated, discharged and struck Poole in the right testicle. The vehicle swerved sharply to the right and struck a tree. Poole suffered only minor cuts and abrasions from the accident, but will require surgery to repair the other wound. Wallis sustained a broken clavicle and was treated and released.

"Thank God we weren't on the bridge when Thurston shot his balls off or we might both be dead," stated Wallis. "I've been a trooper for 10 years in this part of the world, but this is a first for me," said the reporting officer, Dovey Snyder. "I can't believe those two would admit how this accident happened."

Upon being notified of the wreck, Poole's wife Lavinia asked how many frogs the boys had caught and did anyone get them from the truck.

• • •

NOMINEE No.13: When his 38 caliber revolver failed to fire at his intended victim during a holdup in Long Beach, California, would be robber James Elliot did something that can only inspire wonder: He peered down the barrel and tried the trigger again. This time it worked.

• • •

NOMINEE No.14: The chef at a hotel in Switzerland lost a finger in a meat-cutting machine and, after a little hopping around, submitted a claim to his insurance company. The company, suspecting negligence, sent out one of its men to have a look for himself. He tried the machine out and lost a finger. The chef's claim was approved.

• • •

NOMINEE No.15: A man who shoveled snow for an hour to clear a space for his car during a blizzard in Chicago returned with his vehicle to find a woman had taken the space. Understandably, he shot her.

• • •

NOMINEE No.16: After stopping for drinks at an illegal bar, a Zimbabwean bus driver found that the 20 mental patients he was supposed to be transporting from Harare to Beltway had escaped. Not wanting to admit his incompetence, the driver went to a nearby bus stop and offered everyone waiting there a free ride. He then delivered the passengers to the mental hospital, telling the staff that the patients were very excitable and prone to bizarre fantasies. The deception wasn't discovered for 3 days.

• • •

NOMINEE No.17: An American teenager was in the hospital yesterday recovering from serious head wounds received from an oncoming train. When asked how he received the injuries, the lad told police that he was simply trying to see how close he could get his head to a moving train before he was hit.

• • •

NOMINEE No.18: A man walked into a Louisiana Circle-K, put a $20 bill on the counter, and asked for change. When the clerk opened the cash drawer, the man pulled a gun and asked for all the cash in the register, which the clerk promptly provided. The man took the cash from the clerk and fled, leaving the $20 bill on the counter. The total amount of cash he got from the drawer? $15. (If someone points a gun at you and gives you money, was a crime committed?)

• • •

NOMINEE No.19: A thief burst into a Florida bank one day wearing a ski mask and carrying a gun. Aiming his gun at the guard, the thief yelled, "FREEZE, MOTHERSTICKERS, THIS IS A FUCK-UP!" For a moment, everyone was silent. Then the snickers started. The guard completely lost it and doubled over laughing. It probably saved his life, because he'd been about to draw his gun. He couldn't have drawn and fired before the thief got him. The thief ran away and is still at large. In memory of the event, the banker later put a plaque on the wall engraved with the words, "Freeze, mother-stickers, this is a fuck-up!"

• • •

NOMINEE No.20: Seems this Arkansas guy wanted some beer pretty badly. He decided that he'd just throw a cinderblock through a liquor store window, grab some booze, and run. So he lifted the cinderblock and heaved it over his head at the window. The cinderblock bounced back and hit the would-be thief on the head, knocking him unconscious. Seems the liquor store window was made of Plexiglas. The whole event was caught on videotape.

• • •

NOMINEE No.21: As a female shopper exited a New York convenience store, a man grabbed her purse and ran. The clerk called 911 immediately, and the woman was able to give them a detailed description of the snatcher. Within minutes, the police apprehended the snatcher. They put him in the car and drove back to the store. The thief was then taken out of the car and told to stand there for a positive I D. To which he replied, "Yes, officer, that's her. That's the lady I stole the purse from."

• • •

NOMINEE No.22: The Ann Arbor News crime column reported that a man walked into a Burger King in Ypsilanti, Michigan, at 5 a.m., flashed a gun, and demanded cash. The clerk turned him down because he said he couldn't open the cash register without a food order. When the man ordered onion rings, the clerk said they weren't available for breakfast. The man, frustrated, walked away.

• • •

NOMINEE No.23: Paduca, Kentucky: Two men tried to pull the front off a cash machine by running a chain from the machine to the bumper of their pickup truck. Instead of pulling the front panel off the machine, though, they pulled the bumper off their truck. Scared, they left the scene and drove home. With the chain still attached to the machine. With their bumper still attached to the chain. With their vehicle's license plate still attached to the bumper. They were quickly arrested.

• • •

NOMINEE No.24: A 5-STAR STUPIDITY AWARD WINNER! When a man attempted to siphon gasoline from a motor home parked on a Seattle street, he got much more than he bargained for. Police arrived at the scene to find a very sick man curled up next to a motor home near spilled sewage. A police spokesman said that the man admitted to trying to steal gasoline and plugged his siphon hose into the motor home's sewage tank by mistake. The owner of the vehicle declined to press charges, saying that it was the best laugh he'd ever had.

• • •

NOMINEE No.25: A San Anselmo, California man died when he hit a lift tower at the Mammoth Mountain ski area while riding down the slope on a foam pad. The 22-year old David Hubal was pronounced dead at Central Mammoth Hospital. The accident occurred about 3 a.m., the Mono County Sheriff's department said. Hubal and his friends apparently had hiked up a ski run called Stump Alley and undid some yellow foam protectors from lift towers, said Lt. Mike Donnelly of the Mammoth Lakes Police Department. The pads are used to protect skiers who might hit towers. The group apparently used the pads to slide down the ski slope and Hubal crashed into a tower. It has since been investigated and determined the tower he hit was the one with its pad removed.

• • •

NOMINEE No.26: "Man loses face at party" is what the headline read: A man at a West Virginia party (probably related to the winner last year, a man in Arkansas who used the .22 bullet to replace the fuse in his pickup truck) popped a blasting cap into his mouth and bit down, triggering an explosion that blew off his lips, teeth, and tongue. Jerry Stromyer, 24, of Kincaid, bit the blasting cap as a prank during the party late Tuesday night, said Cpl. M.D. Payne. "Another man had it in an aquarium hooked to battery and was trying to explode it. It wouldn't go off and Stromyer said: 'I'll show you how to set it off.' He put it into his mouth, bit down and it blew all his teeth out and his lips and tongue off", Payne added. Stromyer was listed in guarded condition Wednesday with extensive facial injuries, according to a spokesperson at Charleston Area Medical Division. "I just can't imagine anyone doing something like that," Payne said.

• • •

NOMINEE No.27: The late John Pernicky and his friend, the late Sal Hawkins, of the great state of Washington, decided to attend a local Metallica concert at the George Washington amphitheater. Having no tickets (but having had 18 beers between them), they thought it would be easy to "hop" over the nine foot fence and sneak into the show. They pulled their pickup truck over to the fence and the plan was for Mr. Pernicky, who was 100-pounds heavier than Mr. Hawkins to hop the fence and then assist his friend over. Unfortunately for Mr. Pernicky, there was a 30-foot drop on the other side of the fence. Having heaved himself over, he found himself crashing through a tree. His fall was abruptly halted (and broken, along with his arm) by a large branch that snagged him by his shorts. Dangling from the tree with a broken arm, he looked down and saw some bushes below him. Possibly figuring the bushes would break his fall, he removed his pocket knife and proceeded to cut away his shorts to free himself from the tree. Finally free, Mr. Pernicky crashed into holly bushes. The sharp leaves scratched his entire body and worse, without the protection of his shorts, a holly branch penetrated his rectum. To make matters worse still, on landing, his pocket knife penetrated his thigh. Mr. Hawkins, seeing his friend in considerable pain and agony, threw him a rope and tried to pull him to safety by tying the rope to the pickup truck and slowly driving away. However, in his drunken state, he put the truck into reverse and crashed through the fence, landing 30' below atop his friend, killing him. Police arrived to find the crashed pickup with its driver thrown 100' from the truck and dead from massive internal injuries. Upon moving the truck, they found John under it half-naked, scratches on his body, a holly stick in his rectum, a knife in his thigh, and his shorts dangling from a tree branch 25-feet in the air.

• • •

## The *Stella* Awards

Most of the country has heard of the Darwin Awards given annually to the individuals who do the most for mankind by removing themselves from the gene pool. Now, we have the Stella Awards given to the individuals who win the most frivolous lawsuits ever. The Stella Awards are named in honor of 81 year-old Stella Liebeck, the woman who won $2.9 million for spilling a cup of MacDonald's coffee on herself.

The following are candidates for the award:

Kathleen Robertson of Austin, Texas, was awarded $780,000 by a jury of her peers after breaking her ankle, tripping over a toddler who was running amuck inside a furniture store. The owners of the store were understandably surprised at the verdict, considering that the misbehaving little fellow was Robertson's son.

19-year-old Carl Truman of Los Angeles won $74,000 and medical expenses when his neighbor ran over his hand with a Honda Accord. Mr. Truman apparently didn't notice there was someone at the wheel of the car when he was trying to steal his neighbor's hub caps.

Terrence Dickson of Bristol, Pa., was leaving a house he had just finished robbing by way of the garage. He was not able to get the garage door to go up, because the automatic door opener was malfunctioning. He couldn't re-enter the house because the door connecting the house and garage locked when he pulled it shut. The family was on vacation. Mr. Dickson found himself locked in the garage for eight days. He subsisted on a case of Pepsi he found in the garage and a large bag of dry dog food. Mr. Dickson sued the homeowner's insurance claiming the situation caused him undue mental anguish. The jury agreed to the tune of one half million dollars.

Jerry Williams of Little Rock Arkansas was awarded $14,500 and medical expenses after being bitten on the buttocks by his next door neighbor's beagle. The dog was on a chain in its owner's fenced-in yard at the time. Mr. Williams was also in the fenced-in yard. The award was less than sought because the jury felt the dog may have been provoked by Mr. Williams who, at the time, was repeatedly shooting it with a pellet gun.

A Philadelphia restaurant was ordered to pay Amber Carson of Lancaster, Pa., $113,500 after she slipped on a soft drink and broke her coccyx. The beverage was on the floor because Ms. Carson threw it at her boyfriend 30 seconds earlier during an argument.

Kara Walton of Delaware, successfully sued the owner of a night club when she fell from the bathroom window to the floor and knocked out her two front teeth. This occurred while Ms. Walton was trying to sneak through the window in the ladies room to avoid paying the $3.50 cover charge. She was awarded $12,000 and dental expenses.

• • •

# WHY CHICKENS CROSS ROADS

### A Chicken Crossing the Road is Poultry in Motion

**MOSES:**
And God came down from the heavens, and He said unto the chicken, "Fowl, thou shalt cross the road!" And the chicken crossed the road, and there was rejoicing.

**AL GORE**
I fight for the chickens and I am fighting for the chickens right now. I will not give up on the chickens crossing the road! I will fight for the chickens and I will not disappoint them.

**GEORGE W. BUSH**
I don't believe we need to let the chickens cross the road. I say give the road to the chickens and let them decide. The government needs to let go of strangling the chickens so they can get across the road.

**JOE LIEBERMAN**
I believe that every chicken has the right to worship their God in their own way. Crossing the road is a spiritual journey and no chicken should be denied the right to cross the road in their own way.

**JERRY FALWELL**

Because the chicken was gay! Isn't it obvious? Can't you people see the plain truth in front of your face? The chicken was going to the "other side." That's what "they" call it -the "other side." Yes, my friends, that chicken is gay. And, if you eat that chicken, you will become gay too. I say we boycott all chickens until we sort out this abomination that the liberal media whitewashes with seemingly harmless phrases like "the other side." That chicken should not be free to cross the road. It's as plain and simple as that.

**DR. SEUSS**

Did the chicken cross the road? Did he cross it with a toad? Yes! The chicken crossed the road, but why it crossed, I'm not been told!

**ERNEST HEMINGWAY** To die. In the rain.

**MARTIN LUTHER KING, JR.**

I envision a world where all chickens will be free to cross without having their motives called into question.

**GRANDPA**

In my day, we didn't ask why the chicken crossed the road. Someone told us that the chicken crossed the road, and that was good enough fur us.

**DICK CHENEY**

Chickens are big time because they have wings. They could fly if they wanted to. Chickens don't want to cross the road. They don't need help crossing the road. In fact, I'm not interested in crossing the road myself.

**RALPH NADER** Chickens are misled into believing there is a road by the evil tire makers. Chickens aren't ignorant, but our society pays tire makers to create the need for these roads and then lures chickens into believing that there is an advantage to crossing them. Down with the roads, up with chickens!

**FOX MULDER**: "You saw it cross the road with your own eyes. How many more chickens have to cross the road before you believe it?"

**RICHARD NIXON**: "The chicken did not cross the road. Repeat, the chicken did NOT cross the road."

**JERRY SEINFELD**: "Why does anyone cross the road? I mean, why doesn't anyone ever think to ask, "What the hell was the chicken doing walking around all over the place anyway?"

**SIGMUND FREUD**: "The fact that you are all concerned that the chicken crossed the road reveals your underlying insecurity."

**BILL GATES**: "I have just released the new Chicken Office 2000, which will not only cross roads, but will lay eggs, file your important documents, and balance your checkbook."

**OLIVER STONE**: "The question is not, 'Why did the chicken cross the road?' Rather, it is 'Who was crossing the road at the same time and whom did we overlook in our haste to observe the chicken crossing?"

**CHARLES DARWIN**: Chickens, over great periods of time, have been naturally selected in such a way that they are now genetically disposed to cross roads."

**LOUIS FARRAKHAN**: The road, you will see, represents the Black Man; the chicken 'crossed' the black man in order to trample him and keep him down."

**MACHIAVELLI**: So that its subjects will view it with admiration, as a chicken which has the daring and courage to boldly cross the road, but also with fear, for whom among them has the strength to contend with such a paragon of avian virtue? In such a manner is the princely chicken's dominion maintained.

**ALBERT EINSTEIN**: "Whether the chicken crossed the road, or the road moved beneath the chicken depends upon your frame of reference."

**BUDDAH**: "Asking this question denies your own chicken nature."

**RALPH WALDO EMERSON**: "The chicken did not cross the road; it transcended it."

**COLONEL SANDERS**: "I missed one?!"

**BILL CLINTON**: "I categorically deny any involvement with the chicken! I did not cross the road with *THAT* chicken. What do you mean by 'chicken?' Could you define 'chicken' please."

**HILLARY CLINTON**: "Because I told it to!"

**PLATO:** For the greater good.

**KARL MARX**: It was a historical inevitability.

**HAMLET**: Because 'tis better to suffer in the mind the slings and arrows of outrageous road maintenance than to take arms against a sea of oncoming vehicles.

**DOUG HOFSTADTER**: To seek explication of the correspondence between appearance and essence through the mapping of the external road-object onto the internal road-concept.

**HIPPOCROTES**: Because of an excess of light pink gooey stuff in its pancreas.

**H.P. LOVECRAFT**: To futilely attempt escape from the dark powers which even then
Pursued it, hungering after the stuff of its soul!

**ROBERT ANTON WILSON**: Because agents of the Ancient Illuminated Roosters of Cooperia were controlling it with their Orbital Mind-Control Lasers as part of their master plan to take over the world's egg production.

**ALEISTER LEISTER CROWLEY**: Because it was its True Will to do so.

**SAPPHO**: For the touch of your skin, the sweetness of your lips...

**J.R.R. TOLKIEN**: The chicken, sunlight coruscating off its radiant yellow-white coat of feathers, approached the dark, sullen asphalt road and scrutinized it intently with its obsidian-black eyes. Every detail of the thoroughfare leapt into blinding focus: the rough texture of the surface, over which countless tires had worked their relentless tread through the ages; the innumerable fragments of stone embedded within the lugubrious mass, perhaps quarried from the great pits where the Sons of Man labored not far from here; the dull black asphalt itself, exuding those waves of heat which distort the sight and bring weakness to the body; the other attributes of the great highway too numerous to give name.

**MALCOM X**: Because it would get across that road by any means necessary.

**GARY GYGAX**: Because I rolled a 64 on the "Chicken Random Behaviors" chart on page 497 of the Dungeon Master's Guide.

**DOROTHY PARKER**: Travel, trouble, music, art / A kiss, a frock, a rhyme / The chicken never said they fed its heart / But still they pass its time.

**T.S. ELLIOT**: It's not that they cross, but that they cross like chickens.

**JEAN-LUC PICARD**: To see what's out there.

**DARTH VADER**: Because it could not resist the power of the Dark Side.

**RICHARD NIXON**: That part of our conversation was accidentally erased.

**JOHN LE CARRE** : Because it knew, at the core of its being where none could ever reach, that its only course of action now that its cover was blown wide open was to try and slip away into the grey, foggy, bleak evening before Smiley came, accompanied by his silent shadow Peter Guillam, asking questions for which there could never be answers.

**JACQUES DERRIDA**: Any number of contending discourses may be discovered within the act of the chicken crossing the road, and each interpretation is equally valid as the authorial intent can never be discerned, because structuralism is DEAD, DAMMIT, DEAD!

**THOMAS de TORQUEMADA**: Give me ten minutes with the chicken and I'll find out.

**TIMOTHY LEARY**: Because that's the only kind of trip the Establishment would let it take.

**E.E. (DOC) SMITH**: Your humble narrator can barely do justice to this climactic event that rent asunder the fundamental ether of space itself, as the chicken, embodying all that is good and hard and straight and keen in the Avian world, fearlessly approached, bridged, and conquered the road for Civilization.

**NIETZE**: Because if you gaze too long across the Road, the Road gazes also across to you.

**JANE AUSTEN**: Because it is a truth universally acknowledged that a single chicken, being possessed of a good fortune and presented with a good road, must be desirous of crossing.

**B.F. SKINNER**: Because the external influences which had pervaded its sensorium from birth had caused it to develop in such a fashion that it would tend to cross roads, even while believing these actions to be of its own free will.

**CARL JUNG**: The confluence of events in the cultural gestalt necessitated that Individual chickens cross roads at this historical juncture, and therefore synchronistically brought such occurrences into being.

**CARL SAGAN**: To see the billions and billions of stars.

**JEAN-PAUL SARTRE**: In order to act in good faith and be true to itself, the chicken found it necessary to cross the road.

**LUGWIG WITTENGENSTEIN**: The possibility of "crossing" was encoded into the objects "chicken" and "road," and circumstances came into being which caused the actualization of this potential occurrence.

**ROBERT HEINLEIN**: Because with the freedom the chicken was given, it was the chicken's responsibility to do so.

**ARISTOTLE**: To actualize its potential.

**GENERAL JACK D. RIPPER**: To maintain the purity of its precious bodily fluids.

**JULIUS CAESAR**: It came, it saw, it crossed.

**JOHN CONSTANTINE**: Because it'd made a bollocks of things over on this side of the road and figured it'd better get out right quick.

**GANDALF**: O chicken, do not meddle in the affairs of roads, for you are tasty and good with barbecue sauce.

**BALDRICK**: It had a cunning plan.

**ROSEANNE BARR**: Urrrrrp. What chicken?

**CANDIDE**: To cultivate its garden.

**BUDDAH**: If you ask this question, you deny your own chicken-nature.

**JOSEPH CONRAD**: Mistah Chicken, he dead.

**FRANK BUNKER GILBERETH**: To minimize its *therbligs*

**BILL GATES**: For the money

**HOWARD COSELL**: It may very well have been one of the most astonishing events to grace the annals of history. An historic, unprecendented avian biped with the temerity to attempt such an herculean achievement formerly relegated to *homo sapien* pedestrians is truly a remarkable occurence.

**SALVADOR DALI**: The Fish.

**DARWIN**: It was the logical next step after coming down from the trees.

**FOGHORN LEGHORN**: To get to that damn Dawg, Boah!

**EMILY DICKINSON**: Because it could not stop for death.

**GEORGE LUCAS**: Because the Force was with it.

**GERALD R. FORD**: It probably fell from an airplane and couldn't stop its forward momentum.

**SIGMUND FREUD**: The chicken obviously was female and obviously interpreted the pole on which the crosswalk sign was mounted as a phallic symbol of which she was envious, selbstverstaendlich.

**BASIL FAWLTY**: Oh, don't mind that chicken. It's from Barcelona.

**LEE IACOCCA**: It found a better car, which was on the other side of the road.

**JOHN PAUL JONES**: It has not yet begun to cross!

**MARTIN LUTHER KING**: It had a dream.

**JAMES TIBERIUS KIRK**: To boldly go where no chicken has gone before.

**STAN LAUREL**: I'm sorry, Ollie. It escaped when I opened the run.

**EPICURUS**: For fun.

**RALPH WALDO EMERSON**: It didn't cross the road; it transcended it.

**COLONEL KILGORE**: "I love the smell of chickens in the morning"

**JOHANN FRIEDRICH von GOETHE**: The eternal hen-principle made it do it.

**WERNER HEISENBERG**: We are not sure which side of the road the chicken was on, but it was moving very fast.

**DAVID HUME**: Out of custom and habit.

**SADDAM HUSSEIN**: This was an unprovoked act of rebellion and we were quite justified in dropping 50 tons of nerve gas on it.

**JACK NICHOLSON**: 'Cause it (censored) wanted to. That's the (censored) reason.

**GEORGE ORWELL**: Because Big Brother was watching to make sure that it did cross the road, although in its heart, the chicken never did.

**PYYRHO THE SKEPTIC**: What Road?

**DOCTOR STRANGELOVE**: Because it could not afford to be caught on the wrong side of the road-side gap.

**ROBERT BURNS**: Fair Fa Your Honest Sonsie Face Great Chieftain O' The Chicken Race The blackened road 'ahind ye said Ye best run quick ere ye be deid!

**JOHN SUNUNU**: The Air Force was only too happy to provide the transportation, so quite understandably the chicken availed himself of the opportunity.

**THE SPHINX**: You tell me.

**TOM CLANCY**: The Mark 84 gargleblaster that the chicken carried, at the heart of which was an inferior ex-Soviet excimer laser system, had insufficient range to allow the chicken to carry out its mission from this side of the road.

**HENRY DAVID THOREAU**: To live deliberately ... and suck all the marrow out of life.

**LEDA**: Are you sure it wasn't Zeus dressed up as a chicken? He's into that kind of thing, you know.

**GOTTFRIED von LEIBNIZ**: In this best possible world, the road was made for it to cross.

**GROUCHO MARX**: Chicken? What's all this talk about chicken? Why, I had an uncle who thought he was a chicken. My aunt almost divorced him, but we needed the eggs.

**KARL MARX**: (Again) To escape the bourgeois middle-class struggle.

**GREGOR MENDEL**: To get various strains of roads.

**JOHN MILTON**: To justify the ways of God to men.

**SIR ISAAC NEWTON**: Chickens at rest tend to stay at rest. Chickens in motion tend to cross the road.

**THOMAS PAINE**: Out of common sense.

**MICHAEL PALIN**: Nobody expects the banished inky chicken!

**WOLFGANG PAULI**: There already was a chicken on the other side of the road.

**GEORG FRIEDRICH RIEMANN**: The answer appears in Dirichlet's lectures.

**SISYPHUS**: Was it pushing a rock, too?

**SOCRATES**: To pick up some hemlock at the corner druggist.

**MARGARET THATCHER**: There was no alternative.

**DYLAN THOMAS**: Dylan Thomas: To not go (sic) gentle into that good night.

**MAE WEST**: 'Cause I invited it to come up and see me sometime.

**WALT WHITMAN**: To cluck the song of itself.
**WILLIAM WORDSWORTH**: To have something to recollect in tranquility.

**MOLLY YARD**: It was a hen!

**HENNY YOUNGMAN**: Take this chicken ... please.

**ZENO OF ELEA**: To prove it could never reach the other side.

**MR SCOTT**: 'Cos ma wee transporter beam was na functioning properly. Ah cannawork miracles, Captain, wi' no dilithium crystals left to speak of!

**JIM GILLIS**: The chicken crossed the road to show the gophers it could be done.

**JERRY WHITE**: Why does a chicken cross the road only half-way? So she can lay it on the line.

**MARK TWAIN**: The news of its crossing has been greatly exaggerated.

**TOM WAITS**: ...and the chicken, decked out in Foster Grant wraparounds and Purina checkerboard slacks, cruised across La Cieniga Boulevard in a 1959 monkey-shit- brown Buick Super, while the yellow biscuit of a buttery cue-ball moon came rolling maverick across an obsidian sky, and why? you say? Cause that's life, and that's what all the chickens say. You're one side in April, and you're seriously run down in May.

**MONTY PYTHON**: For Something Completely Different

**GROUCHO MARX** (again): This morning I shot an elephant in my pyjamas – and lemme tell ya, that chicken ran out in a second!

**GEORGE W. BUSH**: We don't really care why the chicken crossed the road. We just want to know if the chicken is on our side of the road or not. The chicken is either with us or it is against us. There is no middle ground here.

**JACQUES CHIRAC:** The chicken has rights, mais oui? We care not whether the chicken crosses the road since we will claim her eggs regardless of on which side of the road she lays them, n'est pas? Should les Americains succeed in seizing them, we shall insist on coq au vin!

**TONY BLAIR:** It is clear to Her Majesty's government that the chicken has disguised and hidden her eggs, which, under extraordinary circumstances, particularly on All Hallow's E'en, can certainly be used as weapons of mass destruction.

**AL GORE:** I invented the chicken. I invented the road. Therefore, the chicken crossing the road represented the application of these two different functions of government in a new, reinvented way designed to bring greater services to the American people.

**COLIN POWELL:** Now at the left of the screen, you clearly see the satellite image of the chicken crossing the road.

**HANZ BLIX:** (U.N. weapons of mass destruction inspector) We have reason to believe there is a chicken, but we have not yet been allowed access to the other side of the road.

**MOHAMMED ALDOURI** (Iraq ambassador): The chicken did not cross the road. This is a complete fabrication. We don't even have a chicken.

**SADDAM HUSSEIN:** (Again) This was an unprovoked act of rebellion and we were quite justified in dropping 50 tons of nerve gas on it.

**RALPH NADER:** The chicken's habitat on the original side of the road had been polluted by unchecked industrialist greed. The chicken did not reach the unspoiled habitat on the other side of the road because it was crushed by the wheels of a gas-guzzling SUV.

**PAT BUCHANAN:** To steal a job from a decent, hardworking American.

**RUSH LIMBAUGH:** I don't know why the chicken crossed the road, but I'll bet it was getting a government grant to cross the road, and I'll bet someone out there is already forming a support group to help chickens with crossing-the-road syndrome. Can you believe this? How much more of this can real Americans take? Chickens crossing the road paid for by their tax dollars, and when I say tax dollars, I'm talking about your money, money the government took from you to build roads for chickens to cross.

**MARTHA STEWART:** No one called to warn me which way that chicken was going. I had a standing order at the farmer's market to sell my eggs when the price dropped to a certain level. No little bird gave me any insider information.

**BARBARA WALTERS:** Isn't that interesting? In a few moments we will be listening to the chicken tell, for the first time, the heart-warming story of how it experienced a serious case of molting and went on to accomplish its life-long dream of crossing the road.

**JOHN LENNON:** Imagine all the chickens crossing roads in peace.

• • •

# HAIKU AND ZEN FOR THE MASSES

In Japan, Toshiba has replaced the impersonal and unhelpful MS Windows messages on its notebook computers with its own Japanese haiku poetry of 17 syllables: five in the first line; seven in the second; five in the third. Perhaps a lesson for Bill Gates?

A file that big?
It might be very useful
But now it is gone

• • •

Chaos reigns within
Reflect, repent. and reboot
Order shall return

• • •

Aborted effort
Close all that you have worked on
You ask far too much

• • •

## Haiku And Zen For The Masses

The Zen that is seen
Is not the true Zen
Until You bring fresh toner.

• • •

Stay the patient course Of little worth
is your ire The network is down.

• • •

A crash reduces Your expensive computer
To a simple stone

• • •

You step in the stream
But the water has moved on
This page is not here.

• • •

Out of memory.
We wish to hold the whole sky
But we never will

• • •

Having been erased
The document you're seeking
Must now be retyped

• • •

Serious error
All shortcuts have disappeared
Screen; mind; both are blank

• • •

Your file was so big.
It might be very useful.
But now it is gone.

• • •

The Web site you seek
Cannot be located,
But Countless more exist.

• • •

Chaos reigns within.
Reflect, repent, and reboot.
Order shall return.

• • •

Program aborting:
Close all that you have worked on.
You ask far too much.

• • •

Windows NT crashed.
I am the Blue Screen of Death.
No one hears your screams.

• • •

Yesterday it worked.
Today it is not working.
Windows is like that.

• • •

First snow, then silence.
This thousand-dollar screen dies
So beautifully.

• • •

With searching comes loss
And the presence of absence:
"My Novel" not found.

• • •

I am in style with
my ergonomic keyboard.
If I could just type.

• • •

The Tao that is seen
Is not the true Tao-
until You bring fresh toner.

• • •

Stay the patient course.
Of little worth is your ire.
The network is down.

• • •

A crash reduces
Your expensive computer
To a simple stone.

• • •

Three things are certain:
Death, taxes and lost data.
Guess which has occurred.

• • •

You step in the stream,
But the water has moved on.
This page is not here.
Having been erased,
The document you're seeking
Must now be retyped.

• • •

Serious error.
All shortcuts have disappeared.
Screen. Mind. Both are blank.

• • •

Need report today?
sorry, system is down,
call back tomorrow!

• • •

Data entered but
lights dim, quick save!
Aaagh! Too late, so now all is lost.

• • •

Thursday tomorrow
But yesterday on Friday
Then it's the Weekend

• • •

Toppled Mountain Dew
A waste of precious caffeine.
Oh, yes, and the mouse.

• • •

Cryptic initials
That nobody understands
Telling me nothing

• • •

Useless messages
About strange device drivers
Telling me nothing

• • •

Everyone says
Reboot, reformat, reload
Telling me nothing

• • •

Post More Tomorrow
For Now A Big Good-bye
Friday Here Soon!

• • •

"Send error report?"
Sartre would say,
Life is defined by choices.

• • •

"Send error report?"
Why, who will answer?
My emails are like arrows.

• • •

"Send error report?"
To that great repository
Of errors between earth and sky?

• • •

## The Zen of Sarcasm

Do not walk behind me, for I may not lead. Do not walk ahead of me, for I may not follow. Do not walk beside me either. Just pretty much leave me the hell alone.

• • •

The journey of a thousand miles begins with a broken fan belt and leaky tire.

• • •

Its always darkest before dawn. So if you're going to steal your neighbor's newspaper, that's the time to do it.

• • •

Don't be irreplaceable. If you can't be replaced, you can't be promoted.

• • •

Always remember that you're unique. Just like everyone else.

• • •

Never test the depth of the water with both feet.

• • •

If you think nobody cares if you're alive, try missing a couple of car payments.

• • •

Before you criticize someone, you should walk a mile in their shoes. That way, when you criticize them, you're a mile away and you have their shoes.

• • •

If at first you don't succeed, skydiving is probably not for you.

• • •

Give a man a fish and he will eat for a day. Teach him how to fish, and he will sit in a boat and drink beer all day.

• • •

If you lend someone $20 and never see that person again, it was probably a wise investment.

• • •

If you tell the truth, you don't have to remember anything.

• • •

Everyone seems normal until you get to know them.

• • •

A closed mouth gathers no foot.

• • •

Never miss a good chance to shut up.

# GROWING OLD GRACEFULLY

A group of Britons were traveling by tour bus through The Netherlands. As they stopped at a cheese farm, a young guide led them through the process of cheese making, explaining that goat's milk was used with this particular cheese variety. She showed them a group of lovely goats that were grazing peacefully on a gentle slope.

She then asked, What do you do in England with your old goats?"

A spry elderly gentleman answered, "They send us on bus tours."

• • •

The elderly Mr. Shapiro and the widow Joyce Levy were sitting in the lobby of the retirement home.

Mr. Shapiro, a widower himself, said to Joyce, "For five dollars, I'll have sex with you on that rocking chair over there. For ten dollars, I'll have sex with you on that couch. But for twenty dollars, I'll take you to my room, light a few candles and give you a romantic evening of passion you'll never forget."

Joyce considers this for a moment and then, after digging through her purse, produces a twenty dollar bill.

Mr. Shapiro says, "So, you want the romantic night in my room, eh?"

Joyce says, "No, I want four times in the rocker!"

• • •

A 90-year old man went to his doctor for his annual check-up. The doctor asked him how he was feeling.

The 90-year old said, "I've never felt better. I have an 18 year old bride who is pregnant with my child. What do you think about that?"

The doctor considered his question for a minute and then began, "I have a friend who is an avid hunter and never missed a season. One day when he was going out in a bit of a hurry, he accidentally picked up his umbrella instead of his gun. When he got to the creek he saw a prime beaver sitting beside the stream of water. He raised his umbrella and went 'Bang, bang' and the beaver fell over dead. "What do you think about that?"

The 90-year-old said, "I'd say somebody else shot that beaver."

The doctor replied…"Exactly."

• • •

A woman consulted her physician, complaining of lower back pain. She was told that in order to strengthen her back and abdominal muscles, she should do some exercises by raising her feet over her head, while lying on her back upon a firm bed. The next morning, while her husband was in the bathroom shaving, the woman removed her nightgown and began raising her feet over her head and touching the wall; soon she got her feet stuck in the headboard grillwork.

Re-entering the bedroom, her husband saw his wife in an inverted, ass-up position, pinioned by her captured ankles, and said, "Ethel, comb your hair and put your teeth in; you are getting to look more like your mother every day!"

• • •

When I was ready to pay for my purchases of gun powder and bullets the cashier said, "Strip down, facing me."

Making a mental note to complain about the gun registry people running amok, I did just as she had instructed.

When the hysterical shrieking and alarms finally subsided, I found out that she was referring to my credit card.

I have been asked to shop elsewhere in the future. They REALLY need to make their instructions to us seniors a little clearer!

• • •

A couple in their nineties are both having problems remembering things. During a checkup, the doctor tells them that they're physically okay, but they might want to start writing things down to help them remember. Later that night, while watching TV, the old man got up from his chair.

"Want anything while I'm in the kitchen?" he asked.

"Will you get me a bowl of ice cream?"

"Sure."

"Don't you think you should write it down so you can remember it?" she asked.

"No, I can remember it."

"Well, I'd like some strawberries on top, too. Maybe you should write it down, so as not to forget it?"

He says, 'I can remember that. You want a bowl of ice cream with strawberries."

"I'd also like whipped cream. I'm certain you'll forget that, write it down?" she suggests.

Irritated, he replied, "I don't need to write it down, I can remember it! Ice cream with strawberries ....and whipped – I got it, for goodness sake!"

Then he toddles into the kitchen. After about 20 minutes, the old man returned and handed his wife a plate of bacon and eggs. She stares at the plate for a moment and says "Where's my toast?"

• • •

An elderly couple had dinner at another couple's house, and after eating, the wives left the table and went into the kitchen.

The two gentlemen were talking, and one said, "Last night we went out to a new restaurant and it was really great. I would recommend it very highly."

The other man said, "What is the name of the restaurant?"

The first man thought and thought and finally said, "What is the name of that flower you give to someone you love? You know.... The one that's red and has thorns."

"Do you mean a rose?"

"Yes, that's the one," replied the man.

He then turned towards the kitchen and yelled, "Rose, what's the name of that restaurant we went to last night?"

• • •

Hospital regulations require a wheel chair for patients being discharged.

However, while working as a student nurse, I found one elderly gentleman already dressed and sitting on the bed with a suitcase at his feet, who insisted he didn't need my help to leave the hospital. After a chat about rules being rules, he reluctantly let me wheel him to the elevator. On the way down I asked him if his wife was meeting him.

"I don't know," he said. "She's still upstairs in the bathroom changing out of her hospital gown."

• • •

A senior citizen said to his eighty-year old buddy:
"So I hear you're getting married?"
"Yep!"
"Do I know her?"
"Nope!"
"This woman, is she good looking?"
"Not really."

"Is she a good cook?"
"Naw, she can't cook too well."
"Does she have lots of money?"
"Nope! Poor as a church mouse."
"Well, then, is she good in bed?"
"I don't know."
"Why in the world do you want to marry her then?"
"Because she can still drive!"

• • •

Three old guys are out walking.
First one says, "Windy, isn't it?"
Second one says, "No, it's Thursday!"
Third one says, "So am I. Let's go get a beer."

• • •

A man was telling his neighbor, "I just bought a new hearing aid. It cost me four thousand dollars, but it's state of the art.. It's perfect."
"Really," answered the neighbor . "What kind is it?"
"Twelve thirty."

• • •

A little old man shuffled slowly into an ice cream parlor and pulled himself slowly, painfully, up onto a stool... After catching his breath, he ordered a banana split. The waitress asked kindly, "Crushed nuts?"
"No," he replied, "Arthritis."

• • •

Jacob, age 92, and Rebecca, age 89, living in Florida, are all excited about their decision to get married. They go for a stroll to discuss the wedding, and on the way they pass a CVS Pharmacy. Jacob suggests they go in.

Jacob addresses the man behind the counter: "Are you the Pharmacist?"

The pharmacist answers, "Yes."

Jacob: "We're about to get married. Do you sell heart medication?"

Pharmacist: "Of course we do."

Jacob: "How about medicine for circulation?"

Pharmacist: "All kinds."

Jacob: "Medicine for rheumatism and scoliosis?"

Pharmacist: "Definitely."

Jacob: "How about Viagra?"

Pharmacist: "Of course."

Jacob: "Medicine for memory problems, arthritis, jaundice?"

Pharmacist: "Yes, a large variety. The works."

Jacob: "What about vitamins, sleeping pills, Geritol, antidotes for Parkinson's disease?"

Pharmacist: "Absolutely."

Jacob: "You sell wheelchairs and walkers?"

Pharmacist: "All speeds and sizes."

Jacob: "We'd like to use this store as our Bridal Registry."

• • •

Russ and Sam, two friends, met in the park every day to feed the pigeons, watch the squirrels and discuss world problems.

One day Russ didn't show up. Sam didn't think much about it and figured maybe he had a cold or something. But after Russ hadn't shown up for a week or two, Sam really got worried. However, since the only time they ever got together was at the park, Sam didn't know where Russ lived, so he was unable to find out what had happened to him.

A month had passed, and Sam figured he had seen the last of Russ, but one day, Sam approached the park and – lo and behold!

—there sat Russ! Sam was very excited and happy to see him and told him so. Then he said, "For crying out loud Russ, what in the world happened to you?"

Russ replied, "I have been in jail."

"Jail?" cried Sam. "What in the world for?"

"Well," Russ said, "You know Sue, that cute little blonde waitress at the coffee shop where I sometimes go?"

"Yeah," said Sam, "I remember her. What about her?"

"'Well, one day she filed rape charges against me; and, at 89 years old, I was so proud that when I got into court, I pleaded "guilty; the damn judge gave me 30 days for perjury."

• • •

Two businessmen in Florida were sitting down for a break in their soon-to-be new store. As yet, the store wasn't ready, with only a few shelves set up. One said to the other, "I bet any minute now some senior is going to walk by, put his face to the window, and ask what we're selling."

No sooner were the words out of his mouth when, sure enough, a curious senior walked to the window, had a peek, and in a soft voice asked, "What are you sellin' here?"

One of the men replied sarcastically, "We're selling ass-holes."

Without skipping a beat, the old timer said, "You're doing well, only two left."

• • •

You can say what you want about Florida, but you never hear of anyone retiring and moving north. Advertisements seen in "The Villages" a Florida newspaper. (Who says seniors don't have a sense of humor?)

**Foxy Lady**

Sexy, fashion-conscious blue-haired beauty, 80's, slim, 5'4' (used to be 5'6'), Matching white shoes and belt a plus. LONG-TERM

COMMITMENT: Recent widow who has just buried fourth husband, looking for someone to round out a six-unit plot. Dizziness, fainting, shortness of breath not a problem.

• • •

### Serenity Now

I am into solitude, long walks, sunrises, the ocean, yoga and meditation. If are the silent type, let's get together, take our hearing aids out and enjoy quiet times.

• • •

### Winning Smile

Active grandmother with original teeth seeking a dedicated. flosser to share rare steaks, corn on the cob and caramel candy.

### Beatles or Stones

I still like to rock, still like to cruise in my Camaro on Saturday nights and still like to play the guitar. If you were a groovy chick, or are now a groovy hen, let's get together and listen to my eight-track tapes.

• • •

### Memories

I can usually remember Monday through Thursday. If you can remember Friday, Saturday and Sunday, let's put our two heads together.

• • •

## Mint Condition

Male, 1932 model, high mileage, good condition, some hair, many new parts including hip, knee, cornea, valves. Not in running condition, but walks well.

• • •

A couple had been married for 50 years. They were sitting at the breakfast table in the morning when the wife said, "Just think, fifty years ago we were sitting here at this breakfast table together."

"I know," her husband said. "We were probably sitting here naked as the day we were born. "

"Well," his wife snickered. "Let's relive some old times."

Where upon, the two stripped to the buff and sat down at the table.

"You know, honey," the wife breathlessly replied, "My nipples are as hot for you today as they were fifty years ago."

I wouldn't be surprised," replied her husband. "One's in your coffee and the other is on your toast..

• • •

An elderly man goes into a pharmacy to buy some Viagra.

"Can I have 6 tablets, cut in quarters?"

"I can cut them for you," said the pharmacist, "But a quarter tablet will not give you a full erection."

"I am 96, said the gentleman . "I don't want an erection; I just want it sticking out far enough so I don't piss on my slippers."

• • •

A 60 year-old man complained to his buddies that he had a problem passing his urine early in the morning. His 70 year-old friend complained that *his* problem was being able to produce an adequate bowel movement in the morning. Their 80 year-old friend then piped up and said, "I can't believe you old farts! Every morning at 8:00 o'clock sharp, I take a good piss; then at about 8:45, I have a healthy b.m. MY only problem is that I don't wake up until noon!"

• • •

The eighty-three year old lady finished her annual physical examination, the doctor said, "You are in fine shape for your age, Mrs. Green, but tell me, do you still have intercourse?"

"Just a minute, I'll have to ask my husband, "she said. She stepped out into the crowded reception room and yelled out loud: "Bob, do we still have intercourse?"

There was a complete hush - you could have heard a pin drop.

Bob answered impatiently, "If I told you once, Irma, I've told you a hundred times...what we have is Blue Cross!"

• • •

An old soldier was celebrating 82 years on this earth. He spoke "Hello toes!" He said, "how are you, toes? You know, you are 82 today; the times we've had! Remember when we walked in the park in summer every Sunday afternoon? The times we waltzed on the dance floor? Happy Birthday, toes! "Hello knees", he continued. "How are you, knees? You know you're 82 years-old today. Oh, the times we've had! Remember when we marched in the parade? Oh, the hurdles we've jumped together. Happy Birthday, knees!" Then, he looked down at his crotch "Hello Willy! If you were alive today, you'd be 82 years old!"

### Advice on Heart Attacks

The Japanese eat very little fat and suffer fewer heart attacks than the British or Americans. On the other hand, the French eat a lot of fat and also suffer fewer heart attacks than the British or Americans. The Chinese drink very little red wine and suffer fewer heart attacks than the British or Americans. The Italians drink excessive amounts of red wine and also eat a lot of fat, but suffer fewer heart attacks than the British or Americans.

Conclusion: Eat & drink what you like. It's speaking English that kills you.

• • •

### O.M.G., I'm rich!

> Silver in the Hair
> Gold in the Teeth
> Crystals in the Kidneys
> Sugar in the Blood
> Lead in the Ass
> Iron in the Arteries
> And an inexhaustible supply of Natural Gas.

• • •

One day, while going on a trip to the store, I passed by a nursing home. There on the front lawn were six elderly ladies lying naked as the day they were born on the grass.

I thought this was a bit more than unusual, but continued on my way to the store. On my return trip, I passed by the nursing home again and there they were, the same six old women lying stark naked on the lawn.

This time my curiosity got the best of me, so I went inside to talk to the Nursing Home Administrator.

"Do you know there are six ladies lying naked on your front lawn?"

"Yes, she said, "They're retired prostitutes and they're having a yard sale."

• • •

An old man was in a hospital bed. He leaned to the right; a nurse immediately entered the room and propped him up with a plump pillow. He then leaned to the left; again, the nurse propped him up with another pillow. The fellow then leaned forward and again, the nurse came up to him and slipped another pillow behind him.

"Do you like it here? Are they treating you well?" Asked a friend.

"Oh, it's O.K.," said the patient "but it's sure hard to fart!"

• • •

An elderly man on a moped, looking about 100 years old, pulled up next to a doctor at a street light. The old man looked over at the sleek shiny car and asks, "What kind of car ya got there, sonny?"

The doctor replies, "A Ferrari GTO. It cost half a million dollars!"

"That's a lot of money," says the old man. "Why does it cost so much?"

"Because this car can do up to 320 miles an hour!" states the doctor proudly.

The moped driver asked, "Mind if I take a look inside?"

"No problem,' replied the doctor"

The old man poked his head in the window and looked around. Then, sitting back on his moped, the old man said, "That's a pretty nice car, all right.. But I'll stick with my moped!"

Just then the light changes, so the doctor decided to show the old man just what his car could do. He floored it, and within 30 seconds the speedometer reads 160 mph. Suddenly, he noticed a dot In his rear view mirror. It seems to be getting closer!

He slowed down to see what it could be. And suddenly, WHOOOSSSHHH! Something whips by him going much faster!

"What on earth could be going faster than my Ferrari?" The doctor asks himself.

He pressed harder on the accelerator and took the Ferrari up to 250 mph.

Then, up ahead of him, he sees that it's the old man on the moped! Amazed that the moped could pass his Ferrari, he gave it more gas and passed the moped at 275 mph. He's feeling pretty good until he looks in his mirror and sees the old man gaining on him AGAIN! Astonished by the speed of this old guy, he floors the gas pedal and takes the Ferrari all the way up to 320 mph.

Not ten seconds later, he sees the moped bearing down on him again! Ferrari is flat out, and there's nothing he can do!

Suddenly, the moped plows Into the back of his Ferrari, demolishing the rear end.

The doctor stopped and jumped out and unbelievably the old man was still alive. He ran up to the banged-up old guy and says, 'I'm a doctor.... Is there anything I can do for you?'

The old man whispers, "Perhaps you can unhook my suspenders from your side view mirror."

• • •

An elderly woman on her deathbed was ready to meet her maker when all of a sudden, God said to her, "Mildred, you have always led an exemplary life and because of that, I am granting you an extra twenty five years of life!"

Delighted with that wonderful news, she immediately jumped from her bed, got dressed, scheduled an appointment to get her hair and nails done and called a highly recommended plastic surgeon to perform a face-lift, boob job, and liposuction. After that was accomplished, she stepped from her doctor's office and was immediately struck by a truck and died on the spot.

Arriving in heaven, she asked God why, after he had promised her an extra twenty five years of life.

God responded, "I am SO sorry; I didn't recognize you!"

• • •

Q. What is 30 feet long and smells like urine?
A. A line dance at a nursing home.

• • •

An elderly man consulted his physician and after a lengthy examination is told that the news was "Bad and Worse." Asking the doctor what the diagnosis was, the man was told that he both lung cancer *and* Alzheimer's disease.

"Well, at least I don't have lung cancer" said the man cheerfully.

• • •

An elderly fellow became quite friendly with an equally elderly woman and after a few weeks struck up a relationship where they talked and fondled each other; she hold his penis in her hand until he dozed off; he would massage her sagging breasts and rub her thighs and pubis while telling her about his life until she nodded off. After several months of this routine, his visits stopped abruptly. Thinking that he had suffered another stroke or had died, she was surprised to see him one morning at breakfast. After he told her that he had found another love interest, the first woman asked what the new one had that she did not; his answer:

"Parkinson's disease."

• • •

A woman went to her physician for a routine medical examination and was told at the end of her physical examination and many laboratory tests that she was suffering from an incurable disease; she had but about two months to live. Upon reaching her home, she told her husband the awful news. Her loving mate asked her if she would like him to book a cruise to spend her remaining time having as much fun as possible.

"No, honey, I would only keep thinking of the little time remaining." Her husband then asked what special things she would like to do. "Well, I've always had this fantasy about you giving me oral sex." So, morning, noon, afternoon, and evenings, she was treated to every form of cunnilingus known to the *Kama Sutra*. She was elated!

Upon returning to her physician for a follow up examination, she astonished her doctor by her return to vigorous health.

"Why, what kind of medications or vitamins have you been taking?"

"Absolutely nothing, doctor," she answered.

Then, forgetting her initial embarrassment, she finally told him that for the past several weeks, she had been receiving grand oral sex from her loving husband.

"Ah gee!" the physician moaned, "I could have saved Mom!"

• • •

An 86-year-old man walked into a crowded physician's office. As he approached the reception desk, the receptionist said, "Yes sir, may we help you?"

"There's something wrong with my penis" he replied.

The receptionist became aggravated and said, "You shouldn't come into a crowded office and say things like that!"

"Why not? You asked me what was wrong and I told you," he said.

The receptionist replied angrily, "You obviously caused some embarrassment in this room full of patients. You should have said that there is something wrong with you ear or something else and then discussed the problem further with the doctor in private."

The man walked out, waited several minutes, and then re-entered the office.

The receptionist smiled smugly and asked, "Yes?"

"There's something wrong with my ear," he stated firmly.

The receptionist nodded approvingly and smiled, knowing he had taken her advice.

"And what is wrong with you ear sir?"

"I can't pee out of it!" he replied.

• • •

An elderly lady in a nursing home was wheeling up and down the halls in her wheelchair making sounds like she was driving a car. As she was going down the hall, and old man jumped out of his room and declared "Excuse me lady, but you were speeding. May I please see your driver's License?"

She dug around in her purse a little, pulled out a candy wrapper and handed it to him.

He looked it over, gave her a warning, and sent her on her way.

Up and down the halls she went again. Again, the same old man jumped out of his room and said, "Excuse me, ma'am but I saw you cross over the center fine back there. May I see our registration please?"

Again, she rummaged around in her purse and finally pulled out a store receipt and handed it to him. He examined it carefully, issued another warning to drive more carefully, and sent her on her way.

She zoomed off again – up and down the halls, weaving all over. As she came to the old man's room, he jumped out once more. This time, he was stark naked and had an erection!

The old lady in the wheelchair stopped, looked up and exclaimed, "Oh no, not the Breathalyzer again!"

• • •

An elderly couple married for more than fifty years, hadn't had sex for a very long time and the wife was becoming very frustrated.

One night when the old fellow was sitting on the couch watching a football game, she went into the bedroom and took off all of her clothes, except for a red towel that she put around her neck like a cape.

She then leapt into the living room exclaiming, "IT'S SUPERPUSSY!"

The old fellow replied, "Ill take the soup."

• • •

Willow and Jason, both 91, lived in a senior citizen's residence. They met in the social center and discovered over time that they enjoyed each other's company. After several weeks of meeting for coffee, Jason asked Willow out for dinner and she accepted. They had a lovely evening. Afterward, Jason asked Willow to join him at his place for an after-dinner drink. Things continued along a natural course and, age being no inhibitor, Willow soon joined Jason for a most enjoyable roll in the hay.

As they were basking in the glow of the magic moments that they had just shared, each was lost for a time in their own thoughts.

Jason was thinking: "If I had known that she was a virgin, I would have been more gentle."

Willow was thinking: "If I had know that he could still get it up, I would have taken off my pantyhose."

• • •

Three sisters ages 92, 94 and 96 live in a house together. One night the 96 year old drew a bath. She put her foot in and paused. She yelled down the stairs, "Was I getting in or out of the bath?"

The 94 year old yelled back, "I don't know, I'll come up and see."

She started up the stairs and paused. "Was I going up the stairs or down?"

The 92 year old was sitting at the kitchen table having tea listening to her sisters. She shook her head and said, "I sure hope that I never get that forgetful."

She knocked on wood for good measure.

She then yelled, "I'll come up and help both of you as soon as I see who's at the door."

• • •

An elderly couple were celebrating their 50th wedding anniversary, so they decided to return to the little town where they first met. They sat in a small coffee shop in the town and were telling the waitress about their love for each other and how they met at this same spot. Sitting next to them was the local cop and he smiled as the old couple spoke.

After the waitress left the table, the old man said to his wife, "Remember the first time we made love, it was up in that field across the road, when I put you against the fence. Why don't we do it again for old times sake?"

His wife giggled like crazy and said, "Sure, why not."

So off they went out the door and across to the field. The cop smiled to himself, thinking how sweetly romantic this was and decided he better keep an eye on the couple so they didn't run into any harm.

The old couple walked to the field and as they approached the fence they began to undress.

The old man picked up his wife when they were naked and leaned her against the fence. The cop was watching from the bushes and was surprised at what he saw. With the vitality of youth, the wife bounced up and down excitedly, while the husband thrashed around like a wild man, then they both fell to the ground in exhaustion. Eventually they stood up, shook themselves, and got dressed.

As they walked back towards the road, the cop stepped from his hiding spot and said, "That is the most wonderful love making I have ever seen. You must have been a wild couple when you were young."

"Not really," said the old man, "when we were young, that fence wasn't electrified."

• • •

In a small town, an elderly couple had been dating each other for a long time. At the urging of their friends, they decided it was finally time for marriage. Before the wedding, they went out to dinner and had a long conversation regarding how their marriage might work. They discussed finances, living arrangements and so on.

Finally, the old gentleman decided it was time to approach the subject of their physical relationship. "How do you feel about sex?" he asked, rather hesitantly.

"Well," she said, responding very carefully, "I'd have to say... I would like it infrequently."

The old gentleman sat quietly for a moment, then over his glasses, he looked her in the eye and casually asked "Is that one word or two words?"

• • •

A man was sitting on a lawn sunning and reading, when he was startled by a fairly late model car crashing through a hedge and coming to rest on his lawn. He helped the elderly driver out and sat her on a lawn chair.

"My goodness" he exclaimed, "you are quite old to be driving!"

"Yes," she replied," I am old enough that I don't need a license anymore. The last time I went to my doctor he examined me, and asked if I had a driver's license. I told him yes and handed it to him. He took scissors out of a drawer, cut the license into pieces and threw them in the wastebasket."

"You won't be needing this anymore," he said.

"So I thanked him and left."

• • •

## Some Germane Observations

It is well documented that for every mile that you jog, you add one minute to your life. This enables you at 85 years old to spend an additional 5 months in a nursing home at $7,000 per month.

My grandmother started walking five miles a day when she was 60. She's 97 now and we don't know where the hell she is.

The only reason I would take up jogging is so that I could hear heavy breathing again.

I joined a health club last year, spent about 400 bucks. Haven't lost a pound. Apparently you have to show up.

I have to exercise early in the morning before my brain figures out what I'm doing.

I don't exercise at all. If God meant us to touch our toes, he wouldn't have put them further up on our body.

I like long walks, especially when they are taken by people who annoy me.

I have flabby thighs, but fortunately my stomach covers them.

The advantage of exercising every day is that you die healthier.

If you are going to try cross-country skiing, start with a small country .

I don't jog, it makes the ice jump right out of my glass.

• • •

A woman decided to have a facelift for her birthday. She spent $5,000.00 and felt pretty good about the results. On her way home she stopped at a news stand to buy a paper. Before leaving, she asked the sales clerk, "I hope you don't mind my asking, but how old do you think I am?"

"About 32", the clerk replied.

"I'm actually 47," the woman says happily.

A little while later she went into McDonalds and upon getting her order, asked the counter girl the same question. She replied, "I'd guess about 29."

The woman replied, "Nope, I am 47." Now she was feeling really good about herself.

While waiting for the bus home, she asked an old man the same question.

He replied, "I'm 78 and my eyesight is starting to go. Although, when was young, there was a sure way to tell how old a woman was, but it requires you to let me put my hands up your shirt and feel your breasts. Then I can tell exactly how old you are."

They waited in silence on the empty street until curiosity got the best of the woman and she finally said,

"What the hell, go ahead."

The old man slips both hands up her shirt, under her bra, and began to feel around. After a couple of moments she exclaimed, "Okay, Okay. How old am I?"

He removes his hands and says, "You are 47."

Stunned the woman exclaimed, "That is amazing. How did you know?"

The old man replied, "I was behind you in line at McDonalds."

• • •

"OLD" is when your sweetie says, "let's go upstairs and make love," and you answer, "Honey, I can't do both!"

"OLD" is when your friends compliment you on your new alligator shoes and you're barefoot.

"OLD" is when a sexy babe catches your fancy and your pacemaker opens the garage door.

"OLD" is when going bra-less pulls all the wrinkles out of your face.

"OLD" is when you don't care where your spouse goes, just as long as you don't have to go along.

"OLD" is when you are cautioned to slow down by the doctor instead of by the police.

"OLD" is when. "Getting a little action" means I don't need to take any fiber today.

"OLD" is when "Getting lucky" means you find your car in the parking lot.

"OLD" is when an *"all nighter"* means not getting up to pee.

• • •

There was a merry family gathering with all generations around the table. The little children (naughty little rascals) smuggled a Viagra tablet into Grandpa's drink. After a short time, Grandpa excused himself because he had to go the bathroom. When he returned to the room, however, his trousers were wet all over.

Grandma just looked and shook her head in disbelief but those kids quickly asked, "What happened Grandpa?"

"Well," he said, I had to go to the bathroom to urinate. So I took it out, but then I saw that it wasn't mine, so I put it back!"

• • •

Sadie lost her husband almost four years ago and has not gotten out of her depression...mourning as if it were only yesterday. Her daughter is constantly calling her and urging her to get back into the world.

Finally, Sadie said she'd go out, but didn't know anyone. Her daughter immediately replied, "Mama, I have someone for you to meet."

Well, it was an immediate hit. They took to one another and after dating for six weeks, he asked her to join him for a weekend in the Catskills. And we know what that meant.

Their first night there she undressed, as does he. She stood there nude except for a pair of black lacy panties. He is in his birthday suit.

Looking at her he asked, "Why the black panties?"

She replied, "My breasts you can fondle, my body is yours to explore, but down there I am still in mourning."

He knows he's not getting lucky that night.

The following night the same scenario. She was standing there with the black panties on and he is in his birthday suit; except that he has an erection, on which he has a black condom.

She looked at him and asks, "What's with this...a black condom?"

He replies, "I'd like to offer my condolences."

• • •

### Why I Want an Older Woman
Andy Rooney

"As I grow in age, I value older women most of all. Here are just a few reasons why:

An older woman will never wake you in the middle of the night to ask, "What are you thinking?"

She doesn't care what you think.

An older woman knows herself well enough to be assured in who she is, what she is, what she wants and from whom. Few women past the age of 50 give a damn what you might think about her.

An older single woman usually has had her fill of "meaningful relationships" and "commitment." The last thing she needs in her life is another dopey, clingy, whiny, dependent lover!

Older women are dignified. They seldom have a screaming match with you at the opera or in the middle of an expensive restaurant. Of course, if you deserve it, they won't hesitate to shoot you if they think they can get away with it.

Most older women cook well. They care about cleanliness and are generous with praise, often undeserved.

An older woman has the self-assurance to introduce you to her women friends. A younger woman with a man will often ignore even her best friend because she doesn't trust the guy with other women. Older women couldn't care less.

Women get psychic as they age. You never have to confess your sins to an older woman. They *always* know.

An older woman looks good wearing bright red lipstick. This is not true of younger women or drag queens.

Older women are forthright and honest. They'll tell you right off you are a jerk if you are acting like one.

Yes, we praise older women for a multitude of reasons. Unfortunately, it's not reciprocal. For every stunning, smart, well-coifed babe of 70 there is a bald, paunchy relic in yellow pants making a fool of himself with some 22 year old waitress.

Ladies, I apologize for all of us. That men are genetically inferior is no secret. Count your blessings that we die off at a far younger age, leaving you the best part of your lives to appreciate the exquisite woman you've become, without the distraction of some demanding old man clinging and whining his way into your serenity.

• • •

A 82-year old man went to his doctor's office to get a sperm count. The doctor gave the man a specimen jar and said, "Take this jar home and bring me back a sample tomorrow."

The next day, the 82-year old man reappeared at the doctor's office and gave him the jar, which was as clean and empty as on the previous day.

The doctor asked, What happened, why is the specimen jar empty?

The old fellow replied, "Well, doc, it's like this. First I tried with my right hand, but nothing. Then I tried with my left hand, but nothing. Then I asked my wife for help. She tried with her right hand, but nothing. Then her left, but nothing. She even tried with her mouth, first with the teeth in, then with the teeth out, and still nothing. Hell, we even called up the lady next door, and she tried with both hands and her mouth too, but nothing."

The doctor was shocked, "You asked your neighbor?"

The old man replied, "Yep, but no matter what we tried, we couldn't get the damn jar open!"

• • •

Lulu was a prostitute, but she didn't want her grandma to know. One day the police raided a whole group of prostitutes at a sex party in a hotel, and Lulu was among them. The police took them outside and had all the prostitutes lined up along the driveway when suddenly, Lulu's grandma came around the corner. Grandma asked, "Why are you standing in line here, dear?"

Not willing to let her grandmother know the truth, Lulu told her grandmother that the policemen were there passing out free oranges and she was lining up for some.

"Wow, that's awfully nice of them. I think I'll get some for myself", and she proceeded to the back of the line. A policeman was going down the line asking for information from all of the prostitutes. When he got to Grandma, he was bewildered and exclaimed, "Wow, still going at it at your age? How do you do it?"

Grandma replied, "Oh, it's easy, dear. I just take my dentures out, rip the skin back and suck them dry."

• • •

An 85-year-old couple, after being married for almost 60 years, died in a car crash. They had been in good health the last ten years, mainly due to her interest in health food and exercising. When they reached the Pearly Gates, St. Peter took them to their mansion, which was decked out with a beautiful kitchen, master bath suite and a Jacuzzi.

As they looked around, the old man asked St. Peter how much all this was going to cost.

"It's free," St. Peter replied, "this is Heaven."

Next, they went out in the backyard to survey the championship-style golf course that the home was located. They would have golfing privileges every day and each week, the course changed to a new one representing the great golf courses on earth. The old man asked, "What are the green fees?"

St. Peter replied, "This is heaven, you play for free."

Next, they went to the club house and saw the lavish buffet lunch with the cuisine of the World laid out.

"How much to eat?" asked the old man.

"Don't you understand yet? This is heaven, it is free!" St. Peter replied, with some exasperation.

"Well, where are the low fat and low cholesterol tables?" the old man asked timidly.

St. Peter lectured, "That's the best part - you can eat as much as you like of whatever you like and you never get fat and you never get sick. This is Heaven."

With that, the old man went into a fit of anger, throwing down his hat and stomping on it, and screaming wildly.

St. Peter and his wife both tried to calm him down, asking him what was wrong.

The old man looked at his wife and said, "This is all your fault! If it weren't for your fucking bran muffins, I could have been here ten years ago!"

• • •

Do you realize that the only time in our lives when we like to get old is when we're kids? If you're less than 10 years old, you're so excited about aging that you think in fractions. "How old are you?" "I'm four and a half!" You're never thirty-six and a half. You're four and a half, going on five!

That's the key. You get into your teens, now they can't hold you back. You jump to the next number, or even a few ahead. "How old are you?" "I'm gonna be 16!" You could be 13, but hey, you're gonna be 16!

And then the greatest day of your life . . . you become 21. Even the words sound like a ceremony . . . You *become* 21. . . YESSSS!!!

But then you turn 30. Oooohh, what happened there? Makes you sound like bad milk. He *turned*, we had to throw him out. There's no fun now, you're just a sour-dumpling. What's wrong? What's changed?

You *become* 21, you *turn* 30, then you're *pushing* 40.

Whoa! Put on the brakes, it's all slipping away. Before you know it, you *reach* 50 . . . and your dreams are gone.

But wait!!! You *make it* to 60. You didn't think you would!

So you *become* 21, *turn* 30, *push* 40, *reach* 50 and *make it* to 60. You've built up so much speed that you *hit* 70! After that it's a day-by-day thing; you *hit* Wednesday!

You get into your 80s and every day is a complete cycle; you *hit* lunch; you *turn* 4:30; you *reach* bed time.

And it doesn't end there. Into the 90s, you start going backwards; "I was *just* 92."

Then a strange thing happens. If you make it over 100, you become a little kid again. "I'm 100 and a half!"

May you all make it to a healthy 100 and a half!!

• • •

## How to Stay Young

1. Throw out nonessential numbers. This includes age, weight and height. Let the doctor worry about them. That is why you pay him/her.
2. Keep only cheerful friends. The grouches pull you down.
3. Keep learning. Learn more about the computer, crafts, gardening, whatever. Never let the brain idle. "An idle mind is the devil's workshop." And the devil's name is Alzheimer's.
4. Enjoy the simple things.
5. Laugh often, long and loud. Laugh until you gasp for breath.
6. The tears happen. Endure, grieve, and move on. The only person who is with us our entire life, is ourselves. Be *ALIVE* while you are alive.
7. Surround yourself with what you love, whether it's family, pets, keepsakes, music, plants, hobbies, whatever. Your home is your refuge.
8. Cherish your health: If it is good, preserve it. If it is unstable, improve it. If it is beyond what you can improve, get help.
9. Don't take guilt trips. Take a trip to the mall, to the next county, to a foreign country, but *NOT* to where the guilt is.
10. Tell the people you love that you love them, at every opportunity.

*And always remember —*

Life is not measured by the number of breaths we take, but by the moments that take our breath away.

• • •

## **Deficit Disorder.**

This is how it is manifested:

I decided to wash my car. As I start toward the garage, I notice that there is mail on the hall table. I decide to go through the mail before I wash the car. I lay my car keys down on the table, put the junk mail in the trashcan under the table, and notice that the trashcan is full.

So, I decide to put the bills back on the table and take out the trash first. But then I think, since I'm going to be near the mailbox when I take out the trash anyway, I may as well pay the bills first. I take my checkbook off the table, and see that there is only one check left. My extra checks are in my desk in the study, so I go to my desk where I find the bottle of coke that I had been drinking.

I'm going to look for my checks, but first I need to push the coke aside so that I don't accidentally knock it over. I see that the coke is getting warm, and I decide I should put it in the refrigerator to keep it cold.

As I head toward the kitchen with the coke a vase of flowers on the counter catches my eye—they need to be watered. I set the coke down on the counter, and I discover my reading glasses that I've been searching for all morning. I decide I better put them back on my desk, but first I'm going to water the flowers.

I set the glasses back down on the counter, fill a container with water and suddenly I spot the TV remote. Someone left it on the kitchen table. I realize that tonight when we go to watch TV, we will be looking for the remote, but nobody will remember that it's on the kitchen table, so I decide to put it back in the den where it belongs, but first I'll water the flowers. I splash some water on the flowers, but most of it spills on the floor. So, I set the remote back down on the table, get some towels and wipe up the spill. Then I head down the hall trying to remember what I was planning to do.

At the end of the day: the car isn't washed, the bills aren't paid, there is warm bottle of coke sitting on the counter, the flowers aren't watered, there is still only one check in my checkbook, I can't find the remote, I can't find my glasses, and I don't remember what I did with the car keys.

Then when I try to figure out why nothing got done today, I'm really baffled because I know I was busy all day long, and I'm really tired. I realize this is a serious problem, and I'll try to get some help for it, but first I'll check my e-mail.

• • •

An old farmer had owned a large farm for several years. He had a large pond in the back, fixed up nicely with picnic tables, horseshoe courts, basketball court, etc. The pond was properly shaped and fixed up for swimming when it was built.

One evening the old farmer decided to go down to the pond, as he hadn't been there for a while, and look it over. As he neared the pond, he heard voices shouting and laughing with glee. As he came closer he saw it was a bunch of young women skinny dipping in his pond. He made the women aware of his presence and they all went to the deep end of the pond.

One of the women shouted to him, 'We're not coming out until you leave!'

The old man replied, "I didn't come down here to watch you ladies swim or make you get out of the pond naked."

"Then what do you want?" said the girls.

'I only came to feed the alligator'.

Moral: Old age and cunning will triumph over youth and aggression every time.

• • •

An elderly couple who were childhood sweethearts had married and settled down in their old neighborhood and were celebrating their fiftieth wedding anniversary. They walked down the street to their old school. There, they hold hands as they find the old desk they 'd shared and where he had carved "I love you, Sally."

On their way back home, a bag of money fell out of an armored car practically at their feet. She quickly picked it up, but they don't know what to do with it so they take it home. There, she counted the money, and it amounted to fifty thousand dollars.

The husband said, "We've got to give it back."

She says, "Finders keepers." And she put the money back in the bag and hid it up in their attic.

The next day, two FBI men were going door-to-door in the neighborhood looking for the money and show up at their home. They say, "Pardon me, but did either of you find any money that fell out of an armored car yesterday?"

She says, "No."

The husband says, "She's lying. She hid it up in the attic."

She says, "Don't believe him, he's getting senile."

But the agents sit the man down and begin to question him. One said, "Tell us the story from the beginning.."

"The old man replied, "Well, when Sally and I were walking home from school yesterday..."

The FBI guy looked at his partner and said, "Let's get out of here."

• • •

An old man uses his life's savings to buy his dream car, a Rolls Royce. The salesman gives him a walk through of the vehicle, pointing out all the different knobs, handles and switches, and explaining how they all work.

The salesman explains how the old man is to start the car's engine, had to warm it up, how to fill the car's petrol tank, had to occasionally replenish the water the car's radiator, and how to handle the car while driving. The old man was overwhelmed with all the gadgetry and technology.

The elderly fellow drove off shakily, and about 2 miles down the road, the car stalled. The old man was devastated and was sitting there when a truck pulled up and a young man jumped out and offered to help out. He checked under the hood and in no time he reappeared.

"I found it", says the young man, "just crap in the carburetor".

The old man groaned, "I have to do that too?"

• • •

As a senior citizen was driving down the freeway, his car phone rang. Answering, he heard his wife's voice urgently warning him, "Herman, I just heard on the news that there's a car going the wrong way on Interstate 280. Please be careful!"

"It's not just one car," said Herman. "It's hundreds of them!"

• • •

Seems an elderly gentleman had serious hearing problems for a number of years. He went to the doctor and the doctor was able to have him fitted for a set of hearing aids that allowed the gentleman to hear 100%.

The elderly gentleman went back in a month to the doctor and the doctor said, "Your hearing is perfect. Your family must be really pleased that you can hear again."

To which the gentleman said, "Oh, I haven't told my family yet. I just sit around and listen to the conversations. I've changed my will three times!"

• • •

An elderly couple were enjoying the evening by swinging on the front porch and looking at the beautiful sunset. After a few minutes the old woman reached over and knocks the hell out of her husband who went flying off the porch and into the bushes.

The poor chap man slowly got up and made his way back to his seat next to his wife on the swing. He sat there for a few minutes and then asked, "What was that for Ma?"

She replied: "That's for having a small one!"

A few more minutes go by and the old fellow reached over and knocked the hell out of his wife, who also went flying off the porch and into the bushes.

She slowly got up and made her way back to her seat next to Pa. She sat there a few minutes and then asked, "What was that for Pa?"

He replies: "That's for knowing there was more than one size."

• • •

There was a man who really took care of his body. He lifted weights and jogged six miles every day. One morning he looked into the mirror, admiring his toned body, and noticed that he was suntanned all over with the exception of his penis. So he decided to do something about that. He went to the beach, undressed completely, and buried himself in the sand, except for his penis, which he left sticking out of the sand.

A bit later, two little old ladies came strolling along the beach, one using a cane to help her get along. Upon seeing the thing sticking out of the sand, the lady with the cane began to move the penis around with her cane.

Remarking to the other little old lady, she said, "There really is no justice in the world."

The other little old lady asked, "What do you mean by that?"

The first little old lady replied, "Look at that. When I was 20, I was curious about it. When I was 30, I enjoyed it. When I was 40, I asked for it. When I was 50, I paid for it. When I was 60, I prayed for it. When I was 70, I forgot about it. Now that I'm 80, the damned things are growing wild, and I'm too old to squat."

• • •

**(To the Music: "When I'm Sixty-four")**

Senior citizens are constantly being criticized for every conceivable deficiency of the modern world, real or imaginary. We know we take responsibility for all we have done and do not blame others. BUT, upon reflection, we would like to point out that it was NOT the senior citizens who took:

>The melody out of music
>The pride out of appearance
>The romance out of love
>The commitment out of marriage
>The responsibility out of parenthood
>The togetherness out of the family
>The learning out of education
>The service out of patriotism
>The religion out of school
>The Golden Rule from rulers
>The nativity scene out of cities
>The civility out of behavior
>The refinement out of language
>The dedication out of employment
>The prudence out of spending

or

>The ambition out of achievement

And we certainly are *not* the ones who eliminated patience and tolerance from personal relationships and interactions with others!!

• • •

Does anyone under the age of 50 know the lyrics to the Star Spangled Banner? Just look at the Seniors with tears in their eyes and pride in their hearts as they stand at attention with their hand over their hearts!

Remember..

Inside every older person is a younger person wondering what the heck happened!

YES, I'M A SENIOR CITIZEN! The life of the party. even if it lasts until 8 p.m. I'm very good at opening childproof caps with a hammer. I'm usually interested in going home before I get to where I am going. I'm awake many hours before my body allows me to get up. I'm smiling all the time because I can't hear a thing you're saying. I'm very good at telling stories, over and over and over and over... I'm aware that other people's grandchildren are not as cute as mine. I'm so cared for – long term care, eye care, private care, dental care.

I'm not grouchy—-I just don't like traffic, waiting, crowds, lawyers, loud music, unruly kids, Toyota commercials, Tom Brokaw, Dan Rather, Peter Jennings, Ashleigh Banfield, barking dogs, politicians and a few other things I can't remember.

I'm sure everything I can't find is in a secure place. I'm wrinkled, saggy, lumpy, and that's just my left leg. I'm having trouble remembering simple words like..I'm realizing that aging is not for wimps. I'm sure they are making adults much younger these days, and when did they let kids become policemen? I'm wondering, if you're only as old as you feel, how could I be alive at 150? I'm a walking storeroom of facts .....I've just lost the key to the storeroom door.

• • •

At the Senior Citizen's luncheon, an elderly gentleman and an elderly lady struck up a conversation and discovered that they both loved to fish. Since both of them were widowed, they decided to go fishing together the next day. The gentleman picked the lady up, and they headed to the river to his fishing boat and started out on their adventure.

They were riding down the river when there was a fork in the river, and the gentleman asked the lady, "Do you want to go up or down?"

All of a sudden the lady stripped off her shirt and pants and made mad passionate love to the man right there in the boat!

When he finished, the man couldn't believe what had just happened, but he had just experienced the best sex that he'd had in years.

They fished for a while and continued on down the river, when soon they came upon another fork in the river. He asked the lady, "Up or Down?"

There she went again, stripped off her clothes, and made wild passionate love to him again.

This really impressed the elderly gentleman, so he asked her to go fishing again the next day. She said yes.

There they were the next day, riding in the boat when they came upon the fork in the river, and the elderly gentleman asked, "Up or Down?"

The woman replied, "Down."

A little puzzled, the gentleman drove the boat down the river when he came upon another fork in the river and he asked the lady, "Up or Down?"

She replied "Up."

This really confused the gentleman, so he asked, "What's the deal?

Yesterday, every time I asked you if you wanted to go up or down, you made mad passionate love to me. Now today, nothing!"

She replied, "Well yesterday I wasn't wearing my hearing aid and I thought the choices were" *fuck or drown.*"

• • •

A man goes to visit his 85-year-old grandpa in the hospital.

"How are you grandpa? he asked.

"Feeling fine," says the old man.

"What's the food like?"

"Terrific, wonderful menus."

"And the nursing?"

"Just couldn't be better. These young nurses really take care of you."

"What about sleeping? Do you sleep OK?"

"No problem at all nine hours solid every night. At 10 o'clock they bring me a cup of hot chocolate and a Viagra tablet ... and that's it. I go out like a light."

The grandson is puzzled and a little alarmed by this, so rushes off to question the nurse in charge.

"What are you people doing," he demanded, "I'm told you're giving an 85-year- old Viagra on a daily basis. Surely that can't be true?"

"Oh, yes," replies the nurse. "Every night at 10 o'clock we give him a cup of chocolate and a Viagra tablet. It works wonderfully well. The chocolate makes him sleep, and the Viagra stops him from rolling out of bed."

• • •

As a new bride, Aunt Edna moved into the small home on her husband's ranch near Snowflake. She put a shoe box on a shelf in her closet and asked her husband never to touch it.

For fifty years Uncle Jack left the box alone, until Aunt Edna was old and dying. One day when he was putting their affairs in order, he found the box again and thought it might hold something important. Opening it, he found two doilies and $82,500 in cash. He took the box to her and asked about the contents.

"My mother gave me that box the day we married," she explained. "She told me to make a doily to help ease my frustrations every time I got mad at you."

Uncle Jack was very touched that in 50 years she'd only been mad at him twice.

"What's the $82,500 for?" he asked.

"Oh, that's the money I made selling the doilies."

• • •

Two elderly women were eating breakfast in a restaurant one morning. Ethel noticed something funny about Mabel's ear and she said, "Mabel, did you know you've got a suppository in your left ear?"

Mabel answered, "What did you say, I can't hear you very well"

Ethel repeated what she had said a bit louder.

Mabel replied, "I have? A suppository? Oh my goodness." She pulled it out and stared at it. Then she said, "Ethel, I'm glad you saw this thing. Now I think I know where my hearing aid is."

• • •

An elderly couple was on a cruise and it was really stormy. They were standing on the back of the ship watching the moon, when a wave came up and washed the old woman overboard. They searched for days and couldn't find her, so the captain sent the old man back to shore with the promise that he would notify him as soon as they found something. Three weeks went by and finally the old man got a fax from the boat. It read: "Sir, sorry to inform you, we found your wife dead at the bottom of the ocean. We hauled her up to the deck and attached to her buttocks was an oyster and in it was a pearl worth $50,000 . .please advise"

The old man faxed back: "Send me the pearl and re-bait the trap"

• • •

A funeral service was being held for a woman who has just passed away. At the end of the service, the pall bearers were carrying the casket out when they accidentally bumped into a wall, jarring the casket.

They heard a faint moan! When they opened the casket they found that the woman was actually alive! She lived for ten more years, and then died. Once again, a ceremony was held, and at the end of it, the pallbearers were again carrying out the casket. As they carry the casket towards the door, the recently widowed husband cried out: "Watch that wall!"

• • •

When I went to lunch today, I noticed an elderly lady sitting on a park bench sobbing her eyes out. I stopped and asked her what was wrong.

She said, "I have a 22 year old husband at home. He makes love to me every morning and then gets up and makes me pancakes, sausage, fresh fruit and freshly ground coffee."

I said, "Well, then why are you crying?"

She said, "He makes me homemade soup for lunch and my favorite brownies and then makes love to me for half the afternoon."

I said, "Well, why are you crying?"

She said, "For dinner he makes me a gourmet meal with wine and my favorite dessert and then makes love to me until 2:00 a.m.

I said, "Well, why in the world would you be crying?"

She said, "I can't remember where I live!"

• • •

Two elderly ladies had been friends for many decades. Over the years they had shared all kinds of activities and adventures. Lately, their activities had been limited to meeting a few times a week to play cards.

One day they were playing cards when one looked at the other and said, "Now don't get mad at me.....I know we've been friends for a long time.....but I just can't think of your name! I've thought and thought, but I can't remember it. Please tell me what your name is.

Her friend glared at her. For at least three minutes she just stared and glared at her.

Finally she said, "How soon do you need to know?

• • •

## The Senility Prayer

Grant me the senility to forget the people I never liked anyway, the good fortune to run into the ones I do, and the eyesight to tell the difference.

• • •

My husband is 83 years old and loves to fish. He was sitting in his boat the other day when he heard a tiny voice say, "Pick me up!"

He looked around and could not see anyone. At first, he thought that he was dreaming, but he then heard the voice again, "Pick me up!" This time when he looked, he saw a floating lily pad on which was perched a green frog. My husband said, "Are you speaking to me?"

The small frog replied, "Yes, I am talking to you. Pick me up and kiss me and, in return, I'll be Transformed into the most beautiful woman that you have ever seen. Furthermore, I shall give you the Very most wonderful sexual experience that you have ever dreamed of ."

My husband looked at the frog for a brief time and then reached over the side of the boat and picked up the frog, placing in his front breast pocket of the fishing vest he was wearing. The frog said in a now muffled voice, "What, are you nuts, didn't you hear what I just said? I Told you to kiss me and that I will give you the most wonderful sexual experience of your entire Life."

Well, he then opened his pocket, looked at the frog, and said, "At my age, I'd rather have a talking frog!"

• • •

A couple, both age 78, went to a sex therapist's office.
The doctor asked, "What can I do for you?"
The man said, "Will you watch us have sexual intercourse?"

The doctor looked puzzled, but agreed. When the couple finished, the doctor said, "There's nothing wrong with the way you have intercourse," and charged them $50.00

This happened several weeks in a row. The couple would make an specific appointment, have intercourse with no problems, pay the doctor, then leave. Finally the doctor asked, "Just exactly what are you trying to find out?"

The old man said, "We're not trying to find out anything. She's married and we can't go to her house. I'm married and we can't go to my house. The Holiday Inn charges $90. The Hilton charges $108. We do it here for $50, and I get $43 back from Medicare!"

• • •

One night, an 87-year-old woman came home from Bingo to find her husband in bed with another woman. Angry, she became violent and ended up pushing him off the balcony of their 20th-floor apartment, killing him instantly.

When brought before the court on the charge of murder, she was asked if she had anything to say in defense of herself.

"Well, Your Honor," she began coolly. "I figured that at 92, if he could fuck, he could fly!"

• • •

A young man walked up to the bench and sat down. He had spiked hair in all different colors: green, red, orange, blue and yellow.

The old man just stared.

The young man said sarcastically, "What's the matter old timer, never done anything wild in your life?"

Without batting an eye, the old man replied, "Got drunk once and had sex with a parrot. I was just wondering if you were my son."

• • •

### Tips For Older Love Makers...

* 1. Put bifocals on. Double check that you're with the right partner.
* 2. Set alarm on your clock for 2 minutes ... in case you doze off in the middle.
* 3. Set the mood with lighting. Turn 'em *ALL OFF!*
* 4. Make sure you put 911 on your speed dial before you begin ... just in case!
* 5. Write partner's name on your hand in case you can't remember what to scream out at the end.

• • •

Sam and Becky were celebrating their 50th wedding anniversary. Sam said to Becky, "Becky, I was wondering ... have you ever cheated on me?"

Becky replies, "Oh Sam, why would you ask such a question now? You don't want to ask that question."

"Yes, Becky, I really want to know. Please."

"Well, all right. Yes, 3 times."

"Three? Well, when were they?" he asked.

"Well, Sam, remember when you were 35 years old and you really wanted to start the business on your own and no bank would give you a loan? Remember, then one day the bank president himself came over the house and signed the loan papers, no questions asked?"

"Oh, Becky, you did that for me! I respect you even more than ever, to do such a thing for me. So, when was number 2?"

"Well, Sam, remember when you had that last heart attack and you were needing that very tricky operation, and no surgeon would touch you? Then remember how Dr. DeBakey came all the way up here, to do the surgery himself, and then you were in good shape again?"

"I can't believe it! Becky, you should do such a thing for me, to save my life. I couldn't have a more wonderful wife. To do such a thing, you must really love me darling. I couldn't be more moved. So, all right then, when was number 3?"

"Well, Sam, remember a few years ago, when you really wanted to be president of the golf club and you were 17 votes short?"

• • •

When I was younger I hated going to weddings. It seemed that all of my aunts and the grandmotherly types used to come up to me, poking me in the ribs and cackling, telling me, 'You're next.'

They stopped that stuff after I started doing the same thing to them at funerals.

• • •

An old man got on a crowded bus and no one gave him a seat. As the bus shook and rattled, the old man's cane slipped on the floor and he fell. As he got up, a thirteen-year-old kid, sitting nearby, turned to him and said, "If you put a little rubber thingy on the end of your stick, it wouldn't slip."

The old man snapped back, "Well, if your daddy did the same thing thirteen years ago, I would have a seat today."

• • •

An elderly couple was vacationing in the West. Sam always wanted a pair of authentic cowboy boots. Seeing some on sale one day, he bought them and wore them back to the hotel, walking proudly.

He walked into their hotel room and said to his wife, "Notice anything different, Bessie?"

Bessie looked him over, "Nope."

Sam says excitedly, "Come on, Bessie, take a GOOD look. Notice anything different about me?"

Bessie looked again. "Nope."

Frustrated, Sam stormed off into the bathroom, undressed, and walked back into the room completely naked except for his boots. Again he asked, a little louder this time, "Notice anything DIFFERENT?"

Bessie looked up and replied, "Sam, what's different? It's hanging down today, it was hanging down yesterday, and it'll be hanging down again tomorrow."

Furious, Sam yells, "AND DO YOU KNOW WHY IT'S HANGING DOWN, BESSIE? IT'S HANGING DOWN BECAUSE IT'S LOOKING AT MY NEW BOOTS!"

To which Bessie responded, "Shoulda bought a hat, Sam. Shoulda bought a hat."

• • •

An old man was on the beach and walked up to a beautiful girl in a bikini.

"I want to feel your breasts" he exclaimed.

"Get away from me, you crazy old man" she replied.

"I want to feel your breasts, I will give you twenty dollars," he says.

"Twenty dollars, are you nuts!? Get away from me!"

"I want to feel your breasts, I will give you ONE HUNDRED DOLLARS" he stated.

"NO! Get away from me!"

"TWO HUNDRED DOLLARS" he offered.

She paused to think about it, but then comes to her senses and said, "I said NO!"

"FIVE HUNDRED DOLLARS if you let me feel your breasts," he countered.

She thought, well he is old, and he seems harmless enough... and $500 *is* a lot of money. "Well, OK...but only for a minute." She loosened her bikini top and while both are standing there on the beach, he slid his hands underneath and began to feel... then he started saying, "OH MY GOD...OH MY GOD...OH MY GOD... " while he was caressing them.

Out of curiosity, she asked him, "Why do you keep saying, 'Oh my god, oh my god'?"

While continuing to feel her breasts he answered, "OH MY GOD...OH MY GOD... OH MY GOD... OH MY GOD, where am I ever going to get five hundred dollars?

• • •

### Subject: Senile Virus Warning

Date: Tue, Jan 7, 2013, 1:29 PM

Just got this in from a reliable source It seems that there is a virus out there called the Senile Virus that even the most advanced programs from Norton and McAfee cannot take care of, so be warned, it appears to affect anyone born before 1960. Symptoms of Senile Virus:

1. Causes you to send same e-mail twice.
2. Causes you to send blank e-mail.
3. Causes you to send to wrong person.
4. Causes you to send back to person who sent it to you.
5. Causes you to forget to attach the attachment.
6. Causes you to hit "SEND" before you've finished the message.

• • •

The American Medical Association researchers have made a remarkable discovery. Good news for all of you that need blood transfusions. Thought this may be of some interest to some of you.

It seems that some patients needing blood transfusions may benefit from receiving chicken blood rather than human blood.

It tends to make the men cocky and the women lay better.

• • •

1. Age is a very high price to pay for maturity.
2. Going to church doesn't make you a Christian, any more than standing in a garage makes you a car.
3. Artificial intelligence is no match for natural stupidity.
4. If you must choose between two evils, pick the one you've never tried before.
5. It is easier to get forgiveness than permission.
6. For every action, there is an equal and opposite government program.
7. If you look like your passport picture, you probably need the trip.
8. A conscience is what hurts when all of your other parts feel so good.
9. Eat well, stay fit, die anyway.
10. No man has ever been shot while doing the dishes.
11. Middle age is when broadness of the mind and narrowness of the waist change places.
12. Opportunities always look bigger going than coming.
13. Junk is something you've kept for years and throw away three weeks before you need it.
14. Experience is a wonderful thing. It enables you to recognize a mistake when you make it again.
15. By the time you can make ends meet, they move the ends.
16. Someone who thinks logically provides a nice contrast to the real world.
17. It ain't the jeans that make your butt look fat.

• • •

An elderly Italian man lay dying in his bed. While suffering the agonies of impending death, he suddenly smelled the aroma of his favorite Italian anisette *biscotti* cookies wafting up the stairs. He gathered his remaining strength, and lifted himself from the bed. Leaning against the wall, he slowly made his way out of the bedroom, and with even greater effort, gripping the railing with both hands, he crawled downstairs. With labored breath, he leaned against the door frame, gazing into the kitchen. Were it not for death's agony, he would have thought himself already in heaven, for there, spread out upon waxed paper on the kitchen table were literally hundreds of his favorite anisette sprinkle cookies.

Was it heaven? Or was it one final act of heroic love from his devoted Italian wife of sixty years, seeing to it that he left this world a happy man?

Mustering one great final effort, he threw himself towards the table, landing on his knees in a rumpled posture. His parched lips parted, the wondrous taste of the cookie was already in his mouth, seemingly bringing him back to life. The aged and withered hand trembled on its way to a cookie at the edge of the table, when it was suddenly smacked with a spatula by his wife.

"Hey-a back-a off!" she said harshly, "They–a for da funeral."

• • •

An elderly man and his wife showed up at a doctors office for an appointment for the old man. Once in the office, the doctor tells the old man he needs a urine sample, as stool sample, and a sperm sample.

Now the old man, being hard of hearing asks his wife, "What, what did he say?"

At which time his wife yelled in his ear, "He wants to see your underwear."

• • •

An old man was living the last of his life in a nursing home. One day he appeared to be very sad and depressed.

The nurse asked if there was anything wrong.

"Yes, nurse," said the old man, "my penis died today, and I am very sad."

Knowing her patients were forgetful and sometimes a little crazy, she replied, "Oh, I'm so sorry. Please accept my condolences."

The following day, the old man was walking down the hall with his penis hanging out of his pajamas, when he met the nurse.

"You shouldn't be walking down the hall like this," she admonished him.

"Please put your penis back inside your pajamas."

"But, nurse," replied the old man, "I told you yesterday that my penis died."

"Yes, you did tell me that, but why is it hanging out of your pajamas?" She asked.

"Well," he replied, "today's the viewing."

• • •

### "The Sound of Music," Done for the AARP

Maalox and nose drops and needles for knitting,
Walkers and handrails and new dental fittings,
Bundles of magazines tied up in string,
These are a few of my favorite things.
Cadillacs and cataracts and hearing aids and glasses,
Polident and Fixodent and false teeth in glasses,
Pacemakers, golf carts and porches with swings,
These are a few of my favorite things.

When the pipes leak,
When the bones creak,
When the knees go bad,
I simply remember my favorite things,
And then I don't feel so bad.

Hot tea and crumpets, and corn pads for bunions,
No spicy hot food or food cooked with onions,
Bathrobes and heat pads and hot meals they bring,
These are a few of my favorite things.

Back pains, confused brains, and no fear of sinning,
Thin bones and fractures and hair that is thinning.

And we won't mention our short shrunken frames,
When we remember our favorite things.

When the joints ache, when the hips break,
When the eyes grow dim,
Then I remember the great life I've had,
And then I don't feel so bad.

• • •

A young man came walking up to the house when he noticed his grandfather sitting on the porch, in his rocking chair, with nothing on from the waist down.

"Grandpa, what are you doing?" he exclaimed.

The old man looked off in the distance without answering.

"Grandpa, what are you doing sitting out here with nothing on below the waist?" he asked again.

The old man slowly looked at him and said, "Well, last week I sat out here with no shirt on, and I got a stiff neck. "This is your grandma's idea."

• • •

A young fellow was about to be married and asked his grandfather about sex. He asked how often you should have it.

His grandfather told him, "When you first get married, you want it all the time and maybe do it several times a day. Later on, sex tapers off and you have it once a week or so. Then as you get older, you have sex maybe once a month. When you get really old, you are lucky to have it once a year maybe on your anniversary.

The young fellow then asked his grandfather, "Well how about you and Grandma now?"

His grandfather replied, "Oh, we just have oral sex now."

"What's oral sex?" The young fellow asked.

"Well," Grandpa said, "She goes to bed in her bedroom, and I go to in my bedroom and she yells, 'Fuck You!' and I holler back, 'Fuck You too!"

• • •

A preacher went to a nursing home to meet an elderly parishioner. As he was sitting there he noticed this bowl of peanuts beside her bed and takes one. As they talk, he can't help himself and eats one after another. By the time they are through talking, the bowl is empty. He said, "I'm so sorry, but I seem to have eaten all of your peanuts,"

"That's okay," she replied. "They would have just sat there. Without my teeth, all I can do is suck the chocolate off and put 'em back in the bowl."

• • •

Upon hearing that her elderly grandfather had just passed away, Katie went straight to her grandparent's house to visit her 95 year old grandmother and comfort her. When she asked how her grandfather had died, her grandmother replied, "He had a heart attack while we were making love on Sunday morning.

Horrified, Katie told her grandmother that 2 people nearly 100 years old having sex would surely be asking for trouble.

"Oh no, my dear," replied granny. "Many years ago, realizing our advanced age, we figured out the best time to do it was when the church bells would start to ring. It was just the right rhythm. Nice and slow and even. Nothing too strenuous, simply in on the Ding and out on the Dong."

She paused to wipe away a tear, "He'd still be alive today if that damned ice cream truck hadn't come along."

• • •

For those who are feeling a little older and missing those great old tunes, there is good news! Some of our favorite artists have re-released their great hits with new lyrics to accommodate their aging audience. These were re-written for those of us who admit to being over 39 years old – like me.....enjoy:

    Herman's Hermits - "Mrs. Brown, You've Got A Lovely Walker"
    The Bee Gees - "How Can You Mend A Broken Hip"
    The Temptations - "Papa's Got A Kidney Stone"
    Nancy Sinatra - "These Boots Aren't Made For Bunions"
    The Beatles - "I Get By With A Little Help From Depends"
    Marvin Gaye - "I Heard It Through The Grape Nuts"
    Purple Harem - "A Whiter Shade Of Hair"
    Johnny Nash - "I Can't See Clearly Now"
    Leo Sayer - "You Make Me Feel Like Napping"
    ABBA - "Denture Queen"
    Paul Simon - "Fifty Ways To Lose Your Liver"
    Roberta Flack - "The First Time I Ever Forgot Your Face"
    Commodores - "Once, Twice, Three Times To The Bathroom"
    Rolling Stones - "You Can't Always Pee When You Want"
    Bobby Darin - "Splish, Splash, I Was Havin' A Flash"

• • •

## My Pills

A row of bottles on my shelf
Caused me to analyze myself
One yellow pill I hope to pop
Goes to my heart so it won't stop,
A little white one that I take,
Goes to my hands so they won't shake.
The blue ones that I use a lot,
Tell me I'm happy when I'm not.
The purple goes to my brain,
And tells me that I have no pain.

> The capsules tell me not to sneeze,
> Or cough, or choke or even wheeze.
> The red ones, smallest of them all,
> Go to my blood so I won't fall.
> The orange ones so big and bright,
> Stop my leg cramps in the night.
> Such an array of brilliant pills,
> Helping to cure all kinds of ills.
> But what I'd really like to know,
> Is what tells each one where to go?

• • •

Q: I've heard that cardiovascular exercise can prolong life. Is this true?

A: Your heart is only good for so many beats, and that's it Don't waste them on exercise. Everything wears out eventually. Speeding up your heart will not make you live longer; that's like saying you can extend the life of your car by driving it faster. Want to live longer? Take a nap.

Q: Should I cut down on meat and eat more fruits and vegetables?

A: You must grasp logistical efficiencies. What does a cow eat? Hay and corn. And what are these? Vegetables. So a steak is nothing more than an efficient mechanism of delivering vegetables to your system. Need grain? Eat chicken. Beef is also a good source of field grass (green leafy vegetable). And a pork chop can give you 100% of your recommended daily allowance of vegetable slop and swill.

Q: Is beer or wine bad for me?

A: Look, it goes to the earlier point about fruits and vegetables. As we all know, scientists divide everything in the world into three categories: animal, mineral, and vegetable. We all know that beer and wine are not animal, and they are not on the periodic table of elements, so that only leaves one thing, right? My advice: Have a burger and a beer and enjoy your liquid vegetables.

Q: How can I calculate my body/fat ratio?

A: Well, if you have a body, and you have body fat, your ratio is one to one. If you have two bodies, your ratio is two to one, etc.

Q: What are some of the advantages of participating in a regular exercise program?

A: Can't think of a single one, sorry. My philosophy is: No Pain... Good.

Q: Aren't fried foods bad for you?

A: You're not listening. Foods are fried these days in vegetable oil. In fact, they're permeated in it. How could getting more vegetables be bad for you?

Q: What's the secret to healthy eating?

A: Thicker gravy.

Q: Will sit-ups help prevent me from getting a little soft around the middle?

A: Definitely not! When you exercise a muscle, it gets bigger. You should only be doing sit-ups if you want a bigger stomach.

Q: Is chocolate bad for me?

A: Are you crazy? HELLO. Cocoa beans. Another vegetable!!! It's the best feel good food around!

Well, I hope this has cleared up any misconceptions you may have had about food and diets. Have a cookie...flour is a veggie! One more thing: When life hands you lemons, ask for a bottle of Tequila and salt.

• • •

Now that I'm 'older' (but refuse to grow up), here's what I've discovered:

1. I started out with nothing, and I still have most of it.
2. My wild oats have turned into prunes and All Bran.
3. I finally got my head together; now my body is falling apart.
4. Funny, I don't remember being absent minded...
5. Funny, I don't remember being absent minded...
6. All reports are in; life is now officially unfair.

7. If all is not lost, where is it?
8. It is easier to get older than it is to get wiser.
9. Some days you're the dog; some days you're the hydrant.
10. I wish the buck stopped here; I sure could use a few...
11. Kids in the back seat cause accidents.
12. Accidents in the back seat cause kids.
13. It's hard to make a comeback when you haven't been anywhere.
14. The only time the world beats a path to your door is when you're in the bathroom.
15. If God wanted me to touch my toes, he would have put them on my knees.
16. When I'm finally holding all the cards, why does everyone decide to play chess?
17. It's not hard to meet expenses... they're everywhere.
18. The only difference between a rut and a grave is the depth.
19. These days, I spend a lot of time thinking about the hereafter; I go somewhere to get something and then wonder what I'm here after.

Tom T. Hall

• • •

An older lady was somewhat lonely, and decided that she needed a pet to keep her company. So off to the pet shop she went. Forlornly, she searched and searched and searched. Nothing seemed to catch her interest, except this one ugly frog. As she walked by the barrel he was in, he looked up and winked at her!

He whispered, I'm lonely too, buy me and you won't be sorry."

The old lady figured what the heck as she hadn't found anything else. So she bought the frog, went to her car and drove off down the road.

Driving along down the road, the frog suddenly whispered, to her, "Kiss me, you won't be sorry."

So, the old lady figured what the heck and kissed the frog.
Immediately, the frog turned into an absolutely gorgeous, sexy handsome,
young prince. Then, the prince kissed her back.
Guess what the old lady turned into?
That's right, the first motel she could find ! (She's old, not dead.)

• • •

**A very senior moment**

Two elderly women were out driving in a large car; both could barely see over the dashboard. As they were cruising along they came to an intersection. The stoplight was red but they just went on through. The woman in the passenger seat thought to herself, "I must be losing it, I could have sworn we just went through a red light".

After a few more minutes they came to another intersection and the light was red again and again they went right though. This time the woman in the passenger seat was almost sure that the light had been red but was really concerned that she was losing it. She was getting nervous and decided to pay very close attention to the road and the next intersection to see what was going on.

At the next intersection, sure enough, the light was definitely red and they went right through and she turned to the other woman and said, "Mildred! Did you know we just ran through three red lights in a row! You could have killed us!

Mildred turned to her and said "Oh SHIT, am I driving?"

• • •

Two old ladies were outside their nursing home, having a smoke when it started to rain. One of the ladies pulled out a condom, cut off the end, and put it over her cigarette, and continued smoking.

Lady 1: What's that?
Lady 2: "A condom, Keeps what I'm smoking dry."
Lady 1: Good idea ...where'd you get it?
Lady 2: You can get them at any drugstore.

The next day, Lady 1 hobbles herself into the local drugstore and announced to the pharmacist that she wanted a package of condoms. The guy looks at her kind of strangely (she is after all, in her 80's) but politely asked her what brand she prefers.

"Doesn't matter" she replies "As long as it fits a camel."

• • •

A married couple of 15 years had an anniversary coming soon. Of course after 15 years the sex was getting a wee bit stale, so the wife decided to go buy some crotchless panties to spice it up a little.

The night of their anniversary, the wife then put them on and greeted her husband in their bedroom by saying, "Honey, you know you want some of this."

The husband looked at her and the crotchless panties and replied, "Hell no, I don't. Look what it did to your panties!"

• • •

A general store owner hires a young female clerk with a penchant for very short skirts. One day a young man entered the store, glanced at the clerk, and glanced at the loaves of bread behind the counter.

"Id like some raisin bread, please," the man says politely.

The clerk nodded and climbed up a ladder to reach the raisin bread, located on the very top shelf. The man, standing almost directly beneath her, is provided with an excellent view. As the clerk retrieved the bread, a small group of male customers gathered around the young man, looking in the same direction.

Pretty soon each person is asking for raisin bread, just to see the clerk climb up and down.

After a few trips the clerk is tired and irritated. She stopped and fumed at the top of the ladder, glaring at the men standing below. She noticed an elderly man standing amongst the throng.

"Is yours raisin too?" the clerk yells testily.

"No," croaks the feeble old man "But it's startin' to twitch."

• • •

A little old lady went to the grocery store and put the most expensive cat food in her basket. She then went to the check out counter where she told the check out girl, "Nothing but the best for my little kitten."

The girl at the cash register said, "I'm sorry, but we cannot sell you cat food without proof that you have a cat. A lot of old people buy cat food to eat, and the management wants proof that you are buying the cat food for your cat."

The little old lady went home, picked up her cat and brought it back to the store. They sold her the cat food.

The next day, the old lady went to the store and bought 12 of the most expensive dog cookies-one for each day of Christmas. The cashier this time demanded proof that she now had a dog, claiming that old people sometimes eat dog food.

Frustrated she went home, came back and brought in her dog. She was then given the dog cookies.

The next day she brought in a box with a hole in the lid.

The little old lady asked the cashier to stick her right index finger into the hole.

The cashier said, "No, you might have a snake in there."

The little old lady assured her that there was nothing in the box that would bite her.

So the cashier inserted her right index finger into the box and pulled it out and exclaimed to the little old lady, "That smells like crap!"

The little old lady grinned from ear to ear, "Now, my dear, can I please buy three rolls of toilet paper?"

• • •

There were three old ladies sitting on a park bench talking amongst themselves when a flasher strolled by. The flasher stood right in front of them and opened his trench coat

Well, the first old lady had a stroke, and then the second old lady had a stroke, and the third old lady, well, she couldn't reach that far.

• • •

An 85 year old man married a lovely 25 year old woman. Because her new husband was so old the woman decides that on their wedding night they should have separate suites. She was concerned that the old fellow could overexert himself.

After the festivities she prepared herself for bed and for the knock on the door she was expecting. Sure enough the knock came and there was her groom ready for action. They unite in conjugal union and all goes well whereupon he took his leave of her and she prepared to go to sleep for the night.

After a few minutes there was a knock on the door and there the old guy was again ready for more action. Somewhat surprised she consented to further coupling which was again successful, after which the octogenarian wished her a fond good night and left.

She was certainly ready for slumber at this point and was close to sleep for the second time when, again, there was another knock at the door and there he was again fresh as a 25 year old and ready for more. Once more they do the horizontal boogie.

As they're lying in afterglow the young bride said to him, "I am really impressed that a guy your age has enough juice to go for it three times. I've been with guys less half your age who were only good for one."

The old fellow looked puzzled and turned to her and asked, "Was I already here?"

• • •

A little old lady wanted to join a biker club. She knocked on the door of a local biker club and a big, hairy, bearded biker with tattoos allover his arms answered the door.

She proclaimed "I want to join your biker club."

The guy was amused and told her that she needed to meet certain biker requirements before she was allowed to join. So the biker asked her "You have a bike?"

The little old lady says "Yea, that's my Harley over there" and pointed to a Harley parked in the driveway.

The biker asks her "Do you smoke?"

The little old lady replied "Yea, I smoke. I smoke four packs of cigarettes a day and a couple of cigars while I'm shooting pool."

The biker was impressed and asked "Well, have you ever been picked up by the fuzz?"

The little old lady answered "No, I've never been picked up by the fuzz, but I've been swung around by my nipples a few times."

• • •

Miss Bea was in her eighties, and much admired for her sweetness and kindness to all. The pastor came to call on her one afternoon early in the spring, and she welcomed him into her Victorian parlor. She invited him to have a seat while she prepared some tea. As he sat facing her old organ, the young minister noticed a glass bowl sitting on top of it, filled with water. In the water floated a condom. Imagine his shock and surprise! Imagine his curiosity! Surely Miss Bea had flipped or something! But, he certainly couldn't mention the strange sight in her parlor.

When she returned with tea and cookies, they began to chat. The pastor tried to stifle his curiosity about the bowl of water and its strange floating contents, but soon it got the better of him, and he could resist no longer.

"Miss Bea," he said, pointing to the bowl, "I wonder if you could tell me about that?"

"Oh, yes," she replied, "isn't it wonderful? I was walking downtown last fall and I found this little package. It said to put it on the organ, keep it wet, and it would prevent disease. And you know I haven't had a cold all winter."

• • •

A banker saw his old friend Tom, an eighty-year old rancher, in town. Tom had lost his wife a year or so before and rumor had it that he was marrying a 'mail order' bride. Being a good friend, the banker asked Tom if the rumor was true.

Tom assured him that it was. The banker then asked Tom the age of his new bride to be.

Tom proudly said, "She'll be twenty-one in November."

Now the banker, being the wise man that he was, could see that the sexual appetite of a young woman could not be satisfied by an eighty-year-old man. Wanting his old friend's remaining years to be happy the banker tactfully suggested that Tom should consider getting a hired hand to help him out on the ranch, knowing nature would take its own course. Tom thought this was a good idea and said he would look for one that afternoon.

About four months later, the banker ran into Tom in town again. "How's the new wife? inquired the banker.

Tom proudly said, "Good - she's pregnant."

The banker, happy that his sage advice had worked out, continued, "And how's the hired hand?"

Without hesitating, Tom said, "Oh, she's pregnant too."

Don't ever underestimate old Guys.

• • •

An 80 year old man went for his annual check-up and the Doctor said, "Friend, for your age, you're in the best shape I've seen."

The old fella replied, "Yep. It comes from clean living. Why, I know I live a good, clean, spiritual life."

The Doctor asked, "What makes you say that?"

The old man replied, "If I didn't live a good, clean life, the Lord wouldn't turn the bathroom lights on for me every time I get up in the middle of the night."

The Doc was concerned, "You mean, when you get up in the night to go to the bathroom, the Lord himself turns the light on for you?"

"Yep," the old man said, "whenever I get up to go to the bathroom, the Lord turns the light on for me."

Well, the Doctor didn't say anything else, but when the old man's wife came in for her check-up, he felt he had to let her know what her husband said, "Your husband's in fine physical shape, but I'm worried about his mental condition. He told me that every night when he gets up to go to the bathroom, the Lord turns the light on for him."

"He What?" She cried.

"He said that every night when he gets up to go to the bathroom, the Lord turns the light on for him."

"AHA!!" She exclaimed. "So he's the one who's been peeing in the fridge!"

• • •

### Great Truths About Growing Old

Growing old is mandatory; growing up is optional.

Forget the health food. I need all the preservatives I can get.

When you fall down, you wonder what else you can do while you're down there.

You're getting old when you get the same sensation from a rocking chair that you once got from a roller coaster.

It's frustrating when you know all the answers, but nobody bothers to ask you the questions.

Time may be a great healer, but it's a lousy beautician.

Wisdom comes with age, but sometimes age comes alone.

• • •

Twin sisters in St. Luke's Nursing Home were turning one hundred years old. The editor of the local newspaper told a photographer to get over there and take pictures of the two 100 year old twins. One of the twins was hard of hearing and the other could hear quite well.

Once the photographer arrived, he asked the sisters to sit on the sofa. The nearly-deaf sister said to her twin, "WHAT DID HE SAY?"

"WE GOTTA SIT OVER THERE ON THE SOFA!", said the other.

"Now get a little closer together," said the cameraman.

Again, "WHAT DID HE SAY?"

"HE SAYS SQUEEZE TOGETHER A LITTLE."

So they wiggled up close to each other.

"Just hold on for a bit longer, I've got to focus a little," said the photographer.

Yet again, "WHAT DID HE SAY?"

"HE SAYS HE'S GONNA FOCUS!"

With a big grin, the nearly-deaf twin shouted out, "OH MY GOD - BOTH OF US!

· · ·

An elderly gentleman had experienced serious hearing problems for a number of years. He went to the doctor and the doctor was able to have him fitted for a set of hearing aids that allowed the gentleman to hear 100%.

The elderly gentleman went back to the doctor for a test a month later.

The doctor said, "Your hearing is perfect. Your family must be really pleased can you hear again."

To which the gentleman replied, "Oh, I haven't told my family yet. I just sit around and listen to the conversations. I've changed my will three times!"

· · ·

A little Jewish grandmother gets on the crowded bus and discovered that she didn't have correct change for the fare. The driver tried to be firm with her, but she placed her hand delicately over her chest and murmured, "Oy, [deep sigh] if you only knew vat I had, you'd be nicer to me."

He caved in and let her ride for free.

She tried to push her way down the crowded aisle, but people wouldn't move over for her. She finally places her hand delicately over her chest and murmured,

"Oy, [deep sigh] if you only knew vat I had, you'd be nicer to me."

The crowd parted like the Red Sea and let her down the aisle. She got to the back of the bus where there were no seats, and looked significantly at several people, none of whom take the hint and get up to offer her their seat. Once again she placed her hand delicately over her chest and murmured, "OY, [even deeper sigh] if you only knew vat I had, you'd be nicer to me."

Several people jumped up and insist that she sit down and ride in comfort. A woman who had been watching all this leaned over and said to her, "I know this is none of my business, but just what is it that you've got, anyway?"

The little grandmother smiles and replied, "Chutzpah!"

• • •

Yesterday my daughter asked why I didn't do something useful with my time. She suggested that I go don to the senior center and hang out with the guys.

I did this and when I got home last night I told my wife that I had joined a parachute club.

She said "Are you nuts? You're almost 67 years old and you're going to start jumping out of airplanes?"

I proudly showed her that I even got a membership card.

She said to me, "You idiot, where are your glasses! This is a membership to a Prostitute Club, not a Parachute Club!"

I'm in trouble again and don't know what to do! I signed up for five jumps a week!

• • •

I went to the store the other day, and I was in there for only about 5 minutes. When I came out there was a damn cop writing out a parking ticket. So I went up to him and said, "Come on, buddy, how about giving a guy a break?"

He ignored me and continued writing the ticket. So I called him a Nazi. He glared at me and started writing another ticket for having worn tires! So I called him a piece of horse shit.

He finished the second ticket and put it on the windshield with the first. Then he started writing a third ticket! This went on for about 20 minutes... the more I abused him, the more tickets he wrote.

I didn't give a shit. My car was parked around the corner. I try to have a little fun each day. It's important at my age.

• • •

A furious pounding in a hotel room in the middle of the night awakened a number of guests. The hotel manager went to the room, and when his knocks went unanswered, he let himself in. He found an elderly man cursing and banging on the wall with both fists.

"Stop that immediately, sir!" the manager ordered. "You're disturbing everyone in the hotel."

"Damn the hotel and everyone in it!" the elderly man hollered. "I just got an erection!"

"Okay," said the hotel manager, "but why must you bang your fists against the wall?"

"Because it's the first erection I've had in years and both of my hands are asleep!"

• • •

## **A Senior Moment**

A very self-important college student attending a recent rugby game, took it upon himself to explain to a senior citizen sitting next to him why it was impossible for the older generation to understand his generation. "You grew up in a different world, actually an almost primitive one," the student said, loud enough for many of those nearby to hear. "The young people of today grew up with television, jet planes, space travel, man walking on the moon, our spaceships have visited Mars. We have nuclear energy, electric and hydrogen cars, computers with light-speed processing and...," pausing to take another drink of beer.

The Senior took advantage of the break in the student's litany and said, "You're right, son. We didn't have those things when we were young . . so we invented them. Now, you arrogant little twit, what are you doing for the next generation?"

The applause was resounding...

• • •

I want to live my next life backwards
(Attributed to Woody Allen).

You start out dead and get that out of the way.

Then you wake up in an old age home feeling better every day.

You get kicked out for being too healthy; go collect your pension.

When you start work, you get a gold watch on your first day.

You work 40 years until you're young enough to enjoy your retirement.

You drink alcohol, you party, you're generally promiscuous and you get ready for high school.

You go to primary school, you become a kid, you play, you have no responsi- bilities, you become a baby, and then...

You spend your last 9 months floating peacefully in luxury, in spa-like conditions; central heating, room service on tap, larger quarters every day, and then, you finish off as an orgasm I rest my case.

• • •

Three old guys were sitting around complaining...

The first guy moaned, "My hands shake so bad that when I shaved this morning I almost cut my ear off."

The second guy said, "My hands shake so bad that when I ate breakfast today, I spilled half my coffee on my toast."

The third guy says, "My hands shake so bad that the last time I went to pee, I ejaculated instead!"

• • •

The first old woman told the second old woman that sometimes she gets her husband excited at night by getting totally naked, lying in bed and putting both legs behind her head, yoga style.

The second old woman thought that this was a great idea, so that night when her husband went in the bathroom to get ready for bed, she got totally naked and began the process of putting her legs behind her head. The first leg was kind of tough to put in place as she was a bit arthritic. However, she finally got it in place. She had an even tougher time with the second leg, so she rocked herself backwards until she finally got it behind her head. However, she had rocked just a little too hard so that she flipped slightly backwards and got stuck with her butt sticking straight up in the air. It was just then that her husband came out of the bathroom.

"'Gladys!' he exclaimed.' For heavens sake, comb your hair and put your teeth in ....you look like an asshole.'"

• • •

## AARP Quiz

Q. Where can men over the age of 50 find younger, sexy women who are interested in them?

A: Try a bookstore——under fiction.

Q: What can a man do while his wife is going through menopause?

A: Keep busy; .if you're handy with tools, you can finish the basement. When you are done you will have a place to live.

Q: Someone has told me that menopause is mentioned in the Bible? Is that true? Where can it be found?

A: Yes. Matthew 14:92: 'And Mary rode Joseph's ass all the way to Egypt.'

Q: How can you increase the heart rate of your 50+ year old husband?

A: Tell him you're pregnant.

Q: What can I do for these crow's feet and all those wrinkles on my face?

A: Go braless. It will usually pull them out.

Q: Why should 50+ year old people use valet parking?

A: Valets don't forget where they park your car.

Q: Is it common for 50+ year olds to have problems with short term memory storage?

A: Storing memory is not a problem, retrieving it is a problem.

Q: As people age, do they sleep more soundly?

A: Yes, but usually in the afternoon.

Q: Where should 50+ year olds look for eye glasses?

A: On their foreheads.

Q: What is the most common remark made by 50+ year olds when they enter antique stores?

A: "Gee, I remember these."

• • •

Two elderly men decide that they are close to their last days and decide to have a last night on the town. After a few drinks, they end up at a local brothel. The madam takes one look at the two old geezers and whispers to her manager, "Go up to the first two bedrooms and put an inflated doll in each bed. These two are so old and drunk, I'm not wasting two of my girls on them; they won't know the difference."

The manager does as she is told and the two old men go upstairs and take care of their business.

As they are walking home, the first man says, "You know, I think that my girl was dead!"

"Dead?" replied his friend, "Why do you say that?"

"Well, she never moved or made a sound all the time I was loving her."

His friend, said, "Could be worse; I think that mine was a witch!"

"A witch?? Why the hell would you say that?"

"Well, I was making love to her, kissing her on the neck, and giving her a little bite, she farted and flew out the window…took my teeth with her!"

• • •

After his exam, the doctor said to the elderly man: "You appear to be in good health. Do you have any medical concerns you would like to ask me about?"

"In fact, I do." said the old man. "After I have sex, I am usually cold and chilly; and then, after I have sex with her the second time, I am usually hot and sweaty."

After examining his elderly wife, the doctor said: "Everything appears to be fine. Do you have any medical concerns that you would like to discuss with me?"

The lady replied that she had no questions or concerns.

The doctor then said to her: "Your husband had an unusual concern. He claims that he is usually cold and chilly after having sex with you the first time; and then hot and sweaty after the second time. Do you know why?"

"Oh, that crazy old fart!' she replied. "That's because the first time is usually in January, and the second time is in August."

• • •

While on a road trip, an elderly couple stopped at a roadside restaurant for lunch. After finishing their meal, they left the restaurant, and resumed their trip. When leaving, the elderly woman unknowingly left her glasses on the table, and she didn't miss them until they had been driving for about forty minutes. By then, to add to the aggravation, they had to travel quite a distance before they could find a place to turn around, in order to return to the restaurant to retrieve her glasses.

All the way back, the elderly husband became the classic grouchy old man. He fussed and complained, and scolded his wife relentlessly during the entire return drive. The more he chided her, the more agitated he became. He just wouldn't let up for a single minute. To her relief, they finally arrived at the restaurant. As the woman got out of the car, and hurried inside to retrieve her glasses, the old geezer yelled to her, "While you're in there, you might as well get my hat and the credit card."

• • •

### When I Say I'M Broke - I'm Broke

A little old lady answered a knock on the door one day, to be confronted by a well-dressed young man carrying a vacuum cleaner. "Good morning Madam," said the young man. 'If I could take a couple minutes of your time, I would like to demon- strate the very latest in high-powered vacuum cleaners.

"'Go away!" said the old lady. "I'm broke and haven't got any money!" and she proceeded to close the door.

Quick as a flash, the young man wedged his foot in the door and pushed it wide open. "Don't be too hasty!" he said. "Not until you have at least seen my demonstration." And with that, he emptied a bucket of horse manure onto her hallway carpet.

"Now, if this vacuum cleaner does not remove all traces of this horse manure from your carpet, Madam, I will personally eat the remainder."

The old lady stepped back and said, "Well sonny, let me get you a fork, 'cause they cut off my electricity this morning."

· · ·

Two ninety year old men, Moe and Sam, have been friends all their lives. It seems that Sam was dying, and Moe comes to visit him every day.

"Sam," says Moe, "You know how we have both loved baseball all our lives, and how we played minor league ball together for so many years. Sam, you have to do me one favor. When you get to Heaven, and I know you will go to Heaven, somehow you've got to let me know if there's baseball in Heaven."

Sam looks up at Moe from his death bed, and says, "Moe, you've been my best friend many years. This favor, if it is at all possible, I'll do for you."

And shortly after that, Sam passed on. It is midnight a couple of nights later. Moe is sound asleep when he is awakened by a blinding flash of white light and a voice calls out to him, "Moe.... Moe...."

"Who is it?" says Moe sitting up suddenly. "Who is it?"

"Moe, it's me, Sam."

"Come on. You're not Sam. Sam just died."

"I'm telling you," insists the voice. "It's me, Sam!"

"Sam? Is that you? Where are you?"

"I'm in heaven," says Sam, "and I've got to tell you, I've got really good news and a little bad news."

"So, tell me the good news first," says Moe.

"The good news," says Sam "is that there is baseball in heaven. Better yet, all our old buddies who've gone before us are there. Better yet, we're all young men again. Better yet, it's always spring time and it never rains or snows. And best of all, we can play baseball all we want, and we never get tired!"

"Really?" says Moe, "That is fantastic, wonderful beyond my wildest dreams! But, what's the bad news?"

"You're pitching next Tuesday."

• • •

An 80 year old woman was arrested for shop lifting. When she went before the judge in Cincinnati he asked her, "What did you steal?"

She replied, "A can of peaches."

The judge then asked her why she had stolen the can of peaches and she replied that she was hungry.

The judge then asked her how many peaches were in the can. She replied 6.

The judge then said, "Then I will give you 6 days in jail."

Before the judge could actually finalize the sentence, the woman's husband spoke up and asked the judge if he could say something.

The judge said, "What is it?"

The husband said, "She also stole a can of peas."

• • •

Two elderly gentlemen from a retirement centre were sitting on a bench under a tree when one turned to the other and said: "Slim, I'm 83 years old now and I'm just full of aches and pains. I know you're about my age. How do you feel?"

Slim said, "I feel just like a newborn baby."

"Really!? Like a newborn baby?"

"Yep. No hair, no teeth, and I think I just wet my pants."

• • •

A man was telling his neighbor, "I just bought a new hearing aid. It cost me four thousand dollars, but it's state of the art. It's perfect."

"Really," answered the neighbor. "What kind is it?"

"12:30," he replied.

Maurice, an 82 year-old man, went to the doctor to get a physical. A few days later the doctor saw Maurice walking down the street with a gorgeous young woman on his arm. A couple of days after that the doctor phoned Maurice and said, "You're really doing great, aren't you?"
Maurice replies, "Just doing what you said Doc: 'Get a hot mamma and be cheerful.'"

The doctor replies, "I didn't say that; .I said, 'You've got a heart murmur, be careful.'"

• • •

Bob, a 70-year-old, extremely wealthy widower, shows up at the Country Club with a breathtakingly beautiful and very sexy 25 year-old blonde who knocks everyone's socks off with her youthful sex appeal and charm. She hung onto Bob's arm and listened intently to his every word. His buddies at the club were all aghast.

At the very first chance, they cornered him and asked, "Bob, how did you get the trophy girlfriend?"

Bob replied, "Girlfriend? She's my wife!"

They're amazed, but continued to ask. "So, how did you persuade her to marry you?"

"I lied about my age", Bob replied.

"What, did you tell her you were only 50?"

Bob smiles and says, "No, I told her I was 90."

• • •

The other day I went up to a local Christian bookstore and saw a "Honk if you love Jesus" bumper sticker. I was feeling particularly sassy that day, because I had just come from a thrilling choir practice followed by a powerful prayer meeting, so I bought the sticker

## Growing Old Gracefully

and put it on my bumper. I was stopped at a red light at a busy intersection, just lost in thought about the Lord and how good He is, and I didn't notice that the light had changed. It is a good thing someone else loves Jesus, because if he hadn't honked, I'd never have noticed. I found that *lots* of people love Jesus. Why, while I was sitting there, the nice man behind me started honking like crazy, and he leaned out of his window and screamed, "For the love of God, GO! GO!" What an exuberant cheerleader he was for the Lord.

Everyone started honking! I just leaned out of my window and started waving and smiling at all these loving people. I even honked my horn a few times to share in the love. There must have been a man from Florida back there, because I heard him yelling something about a sunny beach.

I saw another man waving in a funny way with only his middle finger stuck up in the air. When I asked my teenage grandson in the back seat what that meant, he said that it was a Hawaiian good luck sign or something. Well, I've never met anyone from Hawaii, so I leaned out the window and gave him the good luck sign back. My grandson burst out laughing; why, even he was enjoying this religious experience!

A couple of the people were so caught up in the joy of the moment that they got out of their cars and started walking towards me. I bet they wanted to pray or ask what church I attended, but this is when I noticed the light had changed. So I waved to all my sisters and brothers, smiled at them all, and drove on through the intersection.

I noticed I was the only car that got through the intersection before the light changed again, and I felt kind of sad that I had to leave them after all the love we had shared, so I slowed the car down, leaned out of the window, and gave them all the Hawaiian good luck sign one last time as I drove away.

Praise the Lord for such wonderful folks!

A lawyer and a senior citizen were sitting next to each other on a long flight. The lawyer was thinking that seniors are so dumb that he could get one over on them easily. So, the lawyer asked if the senior would like to play a fun game. The senior was tired and just wanted to take a nap, so he politely declined and tries to catch a few winks.

The lawyer persisted, saying that the game is a lot of fun...."I ask you a question, and if you don't know the answer, you pay me only $5.00. Then you ask me one, and if I don't know the answer, I will pay you $500.00," he said.

This caught the senior's attention and, to keep the lawyer quiet, he agreed to play the game.

The lawyer asked the first question. "What's the distance from the Earth to the Moon?" The senior didn't say a word, but reached into his pocket, pulled out a five- dollar bill, and handed it to the lawyer.

Now, it was the senior's turn. He asked the lawyer, "What goes up a hill with three legs, and comes down with four?"

The lawyer used his laptop to search all references he can find on the Net. He sent E-mails to all the smart friends he knew; all to no avail. After an hour of searching, he finally gave up. He awakens the senior and handed him $500.00. The senior pockets the $500.00 and went right back to sleep.

The lawyer was going nuts not knowing the answer. He awakens the senior again and asked, "Well, so what goes up a hill with three legs and comes down with four?"

The senior reaches into his pocket, hands the lawyer $5.00, and went back to sleep.

• • •

An elderly lady was invited to an old friend's home for dinner one evening. She was impressed by the way her lady friend preceded every request to her husband with endearing terms such as: Honey, My Love, Darling, Sweetheart, etc. The couple had been married almost 70 years and, clearly, they were still very much in love.

While the husband was in the living room, her lady friend leaned over to her hostess to say, "I think it's wonderful that, after all these years, you still call your husband all those loving names."

The elderly lady hung her head, "I have to tell you the truth,' she said, "his name slipped my mind about 10 years ago, and I'm scared to death to ask the cranky old asshole what his name is."

• • •

An old prospector shuffled into town leading an old tired mule. The old man headed straight for the only saloon to clear his parched throat. He walked up and tied his old mule to the hitching rail. As he stood there, brushing some of the dust from his face and clothes, a young gunslinger stepped out of the saloon with a gun in one hand and a bottle of whiskey in the other. The young gunslinger looked at the old man and laughed, saying, "Hey old man, have you ever danced?"

The old man looked up at the gunslinger and said, "No, I never did dance... never really wanted to."

A crowd had gathered as the gunslinger grinned and said, "Well, you old fool, you're gonna dance now," and started shooting at the old man's feet.

The old prospector – not wanting to get a toe blown off – started hopping around like a flea on a hot skillet. Everybody was laughing, fit to be tied.

When his last bullet had been fired, the young gunslinger, still laughing, holstered his gun and turned around to go back into the saloon.

The old man turned to his pack mule, pulled out a double-barreled shotgun, and cocked both hammers. The loud clicks carried clearly through the desert air.

The crowd stopped laughing immediately.

The young gunslinger heard the sounds too, and he turned around very slowly.

The silence was almost deafening. The crowd watched as the young gunman stared at the old timer and the large gaping holes of those twin barrels. Those barrels of the shotgun never wavered in the old man's hands, as he quietly said, "Son, have you ever licked a mule's ass?"

The gunslinger swallowed hard and said, "No sir..... but... I've always wanted to."

There are a few lessons for us all here:

Never be arrogant.

Don't waste ammunition.

Whiskey makes you think you're smarter than you are.

Always, always make sure you know who has the power.

Don't mess with old men, they didn't get old by being stupid.

. . .

An elderly man went into a brothel and told the madam he would like a young girl for the night.

Surprised, she looks at the ancient man and asks how old he is.

"I'm 90 years old," he replied.

"Wow, 90!" replied the woman. "Don't you realize you've had it?"

"Oh, sorry,' says the old man.'How much do I owe you?"'

. . .

An elderly man went to his doctor and said, "Doc, I think I'm getting senile.

Several times lately, I have forgotten to zip up."

"That's not senility,' replied the doctor. '"Senility is when you forget to zip down."

• • •

Two medical students were walking along the street when they saw an old man walking with his legs spread apart. He was stiff-legged and walking slowly.

One student said to his friend: "I'm sure that poor old man has Peltry Syndrome. Those people walk just like that."

The other student says: "No, I don't think so. The old man surely has Zovitzki Syndrome. He walks slowly and his legs are apart, just as we learned in class."

Since they couldn't agree they decided to ask the old man. They approached him and one of the students said to him, "We're medical students and couldn't help but notice the way you walk, but we couldn't agree on the syndrome you might have. Could you tell us what it is?"

The old man said, "I'll tell you, but first you tell me what you two fine medical students think."

The first student said, "I think it's Peltry Syndrome."

The old man said, "You thought - but you are wrong."

The other student said, "I think you have Zovitzki Syndrome."

The old man said, "You thought - but you are wrong."

So they asked him, "Well, old timer, what do you have?"

The old man said, "I thought it was gas - but I was wrong, too!"

• • •

An 80-year-old Italian went to the doctor for a check-up. The physician wais amazed at what good shape the elderly gent was in and asked, "How do you stay in such great physical condition?"

I'm Italian and I am a golfer,"' says the old guy, "and that's why I'm in such good shape. I'm up well before daylight and out golfing up and down the fairways. I have a glass of vino, and all is well."

"Well.", says the doctor, "I'm sure that helps, but there's got to be more to it. How old was your Father when he died?'"

"Who said my Father's dead?"

The doctor is amazed. "You mean you're 80 years old and your Father's still alive. How old is he?"

"He's 100 years old," says the Old Italian golfer. "In fact he golfed with me this morning, and then we went to the topless beach for a walk and had a little vino and that's why he's still alive. He's Italian and he's a golfer, too."

"Well," the doctor says, "that's great, but I'm sure there's more to it than that. How about your Father's Father? How old was he when he died?"

"Who said my Nono's dead?"

Stunned, the doctor asks, "'you mean you're 80 years old and your grand- father's still living! Incredible, how old is he?'"

"He's 118 years old," says the Old Italian golfer.

The doctor is getting frustrated at this point, "So, I guess he went golfing with you this morning too?"

"No, Nono couldn't go this morning because he's getting married today."

At this point the doctor was close to losing it. "Getting married!! Why would a 118 year- old guy want to get married?"

"Who said he wanted to?"

• • •

### Observations on Growing Older

Your kids have become you...and you don't like them...but your grandchildren are perfect!

Going out is good.. Coming home is better!

When people say you look "Great"... they add "for your age!"

When you needed the discount, you paid full price. Now you get discounts on everything...movies, hotels, flights, but you're too tired to use them.

You forget names .... but it's OK because other people forgot they even knew you!

The 5 pounds you wanted to lose is now 15 and you have a better chance of losing your keys than the 15 pounds.

You realize you're never going to be really good at anything .... anymore.

Your spouse/companion is counting on you to remember things you don't remember.

The things you used to care to do, you no longer care to do, but you really do care that you don't care to do them anymore.

You sleep better in a chaise-lounge chair with the TV blaring than you do in bed. It's called your "pre-sleep."

Remember when your mother said, "Wear clean underwear in case you *get* in an accident"? Now you bring clean underwear in case you *have* an accident!

You used to say, "I hope my kids *get* married...Now, "I hope they stay married!"

You miss the days when everything worked with just an "ON" and "OFF" switch.

When GOOGLE, iPod, email, modem ....were unheard of, and a mouse was something that made you climb onto a table.

You tend to use more 4 letter words ..."what?"..."when?"... ???

Now that you can afford expensive jewelry, it's not safe to wear it anywhere.

You might have a night out with the ladies, but you're home by 9:00 P.M. Next week it will be 8:30 P.M.

You read 100 pages into a book before you realize you've read it.

Notice everything they sell in stores is "sleeveless"?!

What used to be freckles are now liver spots.

Everybody whispers.

Now that your spouse/companion has retired ...you'd give anything if they'd find a job!

You have 3 sizes of clothes in your closet ...2 of which you will never wear.

• • •

You are in the middle of some kind of project around the house, putting in a new fence, painting the living room, or whatever. You are hot and sweaty, covered in dirt or paint. You have your old work clothes on. You know the outfit - shorts with the hole in the crotch, old T-shirt with a stain from who knows what, and an old pair of tennis shoes.

Right in the middle of this great home improvement project you realize you need to run to Home Depot to get something to help complete the job.

Depending on your age you might do the following:

**In your 20's:**
Stop what you are doing. Shave, take a shower, blow dry your hair, brush your teeth, floss, and put on clean clothes. Check yourself in the mirror and flex. Add a dab of your favorite cologne because you never know, you just might meet some hot chick while standing in the checkout lane. And you went to school with the pretty girl running the register.

**In your 30's:**
Stop what you are doing, put on clean shorts and shirt. Change shoes. You married the hot chick so no need for much else. Wash your hands and comb your hair. Check yourself in the mirror. Still got it. Add a shot of your favorite cologne to cover the smell. The cute girl running the register is the kid sister to someone you went to school with.

**In your 40's:**
Stop what you are doing. Put on a sweatshirt that is long enough to cover the hole in the crotch of your shorts. Put on different shoes and a hat. Wash your hands. Your bottle of Brute Cologne is almost empty so you don't want to waste any of it on a trip to Home Depot... Check yourself in the mirror and do more sucking in than flexing. The spicy young thing running the register is your daughter's age and you feel weird thinking she is spicy.

**In your 50's:**
Stop what you are doing. Put a hat on, wipe the dirt off your hands onto your shirt. Change shoes because you don't want to get dog doo-doo in your new sports car. Check yourself in the mirror and you swear not to wear that shirt anymore because it makes you look fat. The cutie running the register smiles when she sees you coming and you think you still have it. Then you remember the hat you have on is from Buddy's Bait & Beer Bar and it says, 'I Got Worms.'

**In your 60's:**
Stop what you are doing. No need for a hat anymore. Hose the dog doo-doo off your shoes. The mirror was shattered when you were in your 50's. You hope you have underwear on so that your scrotum hangs out the hole in your pants. The girl running the register may be cute, but you don't have your glasses on so you are not sure.

**In your 70's:**
Stop what you are doing. Wait to go to Home Depot until the drug store has your prescriptions ready, too. Don't even notice the dog doo-doo on your shoes. The young thing at the register smiles at you because you remind her of her grandfather.

**In your 80's:**
Stop what you are doing. Start again. Then stop again. Now you remember you needed to go to Home Depot. Go to Wal-Mart instead and wander around trying to think what it is you are looking for. Fart out loud and you think someone called out your name. You went to school with the old lady who greeted you at the front door.

**In your 90's and beyond:**
What's a home-deep-hoe? Something for my garden? Where am I? Who am I? Why am I reading this? Did I send it? Did you? Who farted?

• • •

A group of chaps, all aged 40, members of London's The Tommy Club, discussed where they should meet for their reunion lunch.

Finally it was agreed that they would meet at Wetherspoons in Brignorth because the waitresses had big chests and wore mini skirts.

Ten years later, at age 50, the friends once again discussed where they should meet for lunch. Finally it was agreed that they would meet at Wetherspoons in Bridgnorth because the food and service was good and the beer was excellent.

Ten years later, at age 60, the friends again discussed where they should meet for lunch. Finally it was agreed that they would meet at Wetherspoons in Bridgnorth because they could dine in peace and quiet and it was good value for money.

Ten years later, at age 70, the friends discussed where they should meet for lunch.Finally it was agreed that they would meet at Wetherspoons in Bridgnorth because the restaurant was wheelchair accessible and had a lift for the disabled.

Ten years later, at age 80, the friends discussed where they should meet for lunch. Finally it was agreed that they would meet at Wetherspoons in Bridgnorth because they had never been there before.

• • •

Walking can add minutes to your life

This enables you at 85 years old to spend an additional 5 months in a nursing home at
$4,000 per month.

Grandpa started walking five miles a day when he was 60. Now he's 97 years old and we have no only reason I would take up walking is so that I could hear heavy breathing again.

I have to walk early in the morning, before my brain figures out what I'm doing.

Every time I hear the dirty word 'exercise.' I wash my mouth out with chocolate.

I do have flabby thighs, but fortunately my stomach covers them.

The advantage of exercising every day is so when you die, they'll look at you there in the coffin and say, 'Well, he looks good doesn't he.'

If you are going to try cross-country skiing, start with a small country.

I know I got a lot of exercise the last few years, .just getting over the hill.

We all get heavier as we get older, because there's a lot more information in our heads. That's my story and I'm sticking to it.

Every time I start thinking too much about how I look, I just find a pub with a Happy Hour and by the time I leave, I look just fine.

You could run this over to your friends but just e-mail it to them! It will save you the walk!

• • •

## Our generation didn't have the green thing in its day

Checking out at the grocery store, the young cashier suggested to the older woman, that she should bring her own grocery bags because plastic bags weren't good for the environment.

The woman apologized and explained, *"We didn't have this green thing back In my earlier days."*

The young clerk responded, "That's our problem today. Your generation did not care enough to save our environment for future generations."

She was right – *our generation didn't have the green thing in its day.* Back then, we returned milk bottles, soda bottles and beer bottles to the store. The store sent them back to the plant to be washed and sterilized and refilled, so it could use the same bottles over and over. So they really were truly recycled. *But we didn't have the green thing back in our day.*

Grocery stores bagged our groceries in brown paper bags, that we reused for numerous things, most memorable besides household garbage bags, was the use of brown paper bags as book covers for our schoolbooks. This was to ensure that public property, (the books provided for our use by the school) was not defaced by our scribbling. Then we were able to personalize our books on the brown paper bags. *But too bad we didn't do the green thing back then.*

We walked up stairs, because we didn't have an escalator in every store and office building. We walked to the grocery store and didn't climb into a 300-horsepower machine every time we had to go two blocks. But she was right. *We didn't have the green thing in our day.*

Back then, we washed the baby's diapers because we didn't have the throw-away kind. We dried clothes on a line, not in an energy-gobbling machine burning up 220 volts wind and solar power really did dry our clothes back in our early days. Kids got hand-me-down clothes from their brothers or sisters, not always brand-new clothing. But that young lady is right; *we didn't have the green thing back in our day.*

Back then, we had one TV, or radio, in the house – not a TV in every room. And the TV had a small screen the size of a handkerchief (remember them?), not a screen the size of the state of Montana. In the kitchen, we blended and stirred by hand because we didn't have electric machines to do everything for us. When we packaged a fragile item to send in the mail, we used wadded up old newspapers to cushion it, not Styrofoam or plastic bubble wrap. Back then, we didn't fire up an engine and burn gasoline just to cut the lawn. We used a push mower that ran on human power. We exercised by working so we didn't need to go to a health club to run on treadmills that operate on electricity. *But she's right; we didn't have the green thing back then.*

We drank from a fountain when we were thirsty instead of using a cup or a plastic bottle every time we had a drink of water. We refilled writing pens with ink instead of buying a new pen, and we replaced the razor blades in a razor instead of throwing away the whole razor just because the blade got dull. *But we didn't have the green thing back then.*

Back then, people took the streetcar or a bus and kids rode their bikes to school or walked instead of turning their moms into a 24-hour taxi service. We had one electrical outlet in a room, not an entire bank of sockets to power a dozen appliances. And we didn't need a computerized gadget to receive a signal beamed from satellites 23,000 miles out in space in order to find the nearest burger joint.

But isn't it sad the current generation laments how wasteful we old folks were just because *we didn't have the green thing back then?*

You just might wish to send this on to another selfish old person who needs a lesson in conservation from a smart ass young person.

• • •

Liam Murphy was at the Senior Centre in Dublin the other day and failed a Health & Safety course quiz that was put on for the elderly.

One of the questions was "In the event of fire, what steps would you take?"

"Fooking big ones" was apparently not the correct answer.

• • •

If you are a senior you will understand this one; if you deal with seniors; this should help you understand them a little better, and if you are not a senior yet…God willing, someday you will be. The $2.99 Special

We went to breakfast at a restaurant where the 'seniors' special' was two eggs, bacon, hash browns and toast for $2.99.

'Sounds good,' my wife said. 'But I don't want the eggs.'

"Then, I'll have to charge you $3.49 because you're ordering a la carte," the waitress warned her.

"You mean I'd have to pay for not taking the eggs?" my wife asked incredulously.

"YES!" 'Stated the waitress.
"'I'll take the special then," my wife said..
"How do you want your eggs?" the waitress asked.
"Raw and in the shell," my wife replied.
She took the two eggs home and baked a cake.

• • •

### Six Basic Rules For Good Health

1. Fl l l*ing once a week is good for your health, every day is even better.
2. Fl l l*ing gives proper relaxation for your mind & body.
3. Fl l l*ing refreshes you.
4. After Fl l l*ing don't eat too much ... Go for more liquids.
5. Fl l l*ing can even reduce your cholesterol level !

### So Remember ...

6. FISHING is good for your health and soul
   *And may the Good Lord cleanse your Filthy Mind*

• • •

Two old fellows, one 80 and one 87, were sitting on their usual park bench one morning..

The 87 year old had just finished his morning jog and wasn't even short of breath.

The 80 year old was amazed at his friend's stamina and asked him what he did to have so much energy.

The 87 year old said, "Well, I eat rye bread every day. It keeps your energy level high and you'll have great stamina with the ladies."

So, on the way home, 80 year old stopped at the bakery. As he was looking around, the lady asked if he needed any help.

He said "Do you have any Rye bread?"

She said, "Yes, there's a whole shelf of it. Would you care for some?"

He said, "I want 5 loaves."

She said, "My goodness, 5 loaves ... By the time you get to the 3rd loaf, it'll be hard."

He replied, "I can't believe it, everybody knows about this shit but me"

• • •

**Seven Thoughts to Ponder:**

Number 7. Good health is merely the slowest possible rate at which one can die.

Number 6. Men have two emotions : Hungry and Horny. They can't tell them apart. If you see a gleam in his eyes, make him a sandwich.

Number 5. Give a person a fish and you feed them for a day. Teach a person to use the Internet and they won't bother you for weeks, months, maybe years.

Number 4. Health nuts are going to feel stupid someday, lying in hospitals, dying of nothing.

Number 3. All of us could take a lesson from the weather. It pays no attention to criticism.

Number 2. In the 60's, people took acid to make the world weird. Now the world is weird and people take Prozac to make it normal.

And Number 1. Don't worry about old age–it doesn't last that long.

• • •

### Scotch with two drops of water.

A lady goes to the bar on a cruise ship and orders a Scotch with two drops of water. As the bartender gives her the drink she says, 'I'm on this cruise to celebrate my 80th birthday and it's today.'

The bartender says, 'Well, since it's your birthday, I'll buy you a drink. This one is on me.'

As the woman finished her drink, the woman to her right said, 'I would like to buy you a drink, too.'

The old woman replied, 'Thank you. Bartender, I want another Scotch with two drops of water.'

'Coming up,' says the bartender.

As she finished that drink, the man to her left offered, 'I would like to buy you one, too.'

The old woman thanked him. "I'll have another Scotch with two drops of water."

'Coming right up,' the bartender confirmed.

As he gave her the drink, he said, "'Ma'am, I'm dying of curiosity. Why the Scotch with only two drops of water?"

The old woman replied, "Sonny, when you're my age, you've learned how to hold your liquor. Holding your water, however, is a wholly different issue.'

• • •

### 'Old' is When —

Your sweetie says, 'Let's go upstairs and make love,' and you answer, 'Pick one; I can't do both!"

A sexy babe catches your fancy and your pacemaker opens the garage door.

Going bra-less pulls all the wrinkles out of your face.

You don't care where your spouse goes, just as long as you don't have to go along.

## Growing Old Gracefully

You are cautioned to slow down by the doctor instead of by the police

Getting a little action" means you don't need to take any fiber today.

Getting lucky" means you find your car in the parking lot.

An 'all nighter' means not getting up to use the bathroom.

You are not sure these are jokes?

• • •

# GLOSSARY AN OTHER USEFUL EXPLANATIONS

**Word "Equations,**
(With thanks to the Washington Post):

Ennui = Boredom + thesaurus
Subpoena = Invitation - RSVP
Surrealism + bowling = Anchor - chicken
Entitlement - experience = Teenager
Fun at 30-year reunion: (Football captain's baldness + cheerleader's obesity) / Yours
Constructive criticism = You suck + here's why
B + $8K = DD
Bird watcher = Voyeur - sex
Big Mac = Special sauce + lettuce + cheese + pickles + onion + cardboard
Helpmate = Husband - recliner
Sharing + caring + loving support + tears of joy = Girl porn
Uncle Sam x 24/7 = Big Brother
Tofu = Protein - fun
Crocs = sandals - dignity
Religion = Cult + 150 years
French = Latin + useless silent letters
Diet program = Anvil - Feather + Anvil

## Glossary An Other Useful Explanations

Movie at theater = movie at home + big screen + 120 db + $10/person + sitter + people texting in front of you + not clicking on 'Pause' when you go to the bathroom
Window of opportunity < door of failure
2009 = 2004 - money + hope
Iranian = Straight - M. Ahmadinejad, Tehran Reality TV = Reality - real life
Chances a Victoria's Secret model will sleep with a guy > 0 > Chances a Victoria's
Secret model will sleep with you.
Chipmunk = Squirrel - rat
National debt problem = Whole lot of zeros + their bosses
401(k) + (2009 - 2008) = 201(k)
Unfashionable = Trendy + 3 months
15 +/- 14 = Express lane
Prostatitis = The urge ÷ the stream
Eccentric = Insane/kind of amusing
Eureka = Wrong + wrong + wrong + wrong + not wrong
? + ? + ? + salt = hot dog
Greenspan + 90dB – 40W = Cramer
Tween applying makeup = Clown face – clown
Husband = Boyfriend + buying feminine items at the supermarket
Snail mail = E-mail + punctuation - instantly regrettable impulse
United Nations = (Lofty ideas - ability to act) + funny blue helmets
Success = Failure + press secretary
Household budget = Income - expenses - Oh, they're having a sale on big-screen TVs!

• • •

The following list of phrases and their definitions might help you understand
The mysterious language of science and medicine. These special phrases are also applicable to anyone working on a Ph.D. dissertation or academic paper anywhere:

**"It has long been known"**........I didn't look up the original reference.

**"A definite trend is evident"**.....These data are practically meaningless.

**"While it has not been possible to provide answers to the questions"**.....An unsuccessful experiment, but I still hope to get it published.

**"Three of the samples were chosen for detailed study"**.....The other results didn't make sense.

**"Typical results are shown"**.....This is the prettiest graph.

**"These results will be published in a subsequent report"**.....I might get around to this sometime, if pushed / funded.

**"In my experience"**.......Once.

**"In case after case"**......Twice.

**"In a series of cases"**...Thrice.

**"It is believed that"** ......I think.

**"It is generally believed that"**......A couple of others think so, too.

**"Correct within an order of magnitude"**.....Wrong

**"According to statistical analysis"**......Rumor has it.

**"A statistically oriented projection of the significance of these findings**...A wild guess.

**"A careful analysis of obtainable data"**.....Three pages of notes were obliterated when I knocked over a glass of pop.

**"It is clear that much additional work will be required before a complete**

**"Understanding of this phenomenon occurs"**......I don't understand it.

**"After additional study by my colleagues"**.....They don't understand it either.

**"Thanks are due to Hugo Shamowitz for assistance with the experiment and to Ms. Rackenzall for their valuable discussions"**....Mr. Shamowitz and Ms. Rackenzall explained to me what it meant.

# Glossary An Other Useful Explanations

**"A highly significant area for exploratory study"**...A totally useless topic selected by my graduate committee.

**"It is hoped that this study will stimulate further investigation in this field"** I quit.

• • •

The Washington Post publishes a yearly contest in which readers are asked to supply alternate meanings for various words. The following were some of this year's winning entries:

1. **Coffee** (n.), a person who is coughed upon.
2. **Flabbergasted** (adj.), appalled over how much weight you have gained.
3. **Abdicate** (v.), to give up all hope of ever having a flat stomach.
4. **Esplanade** (v.), to attempt an explanation while drunk.
5. **Willy-nilly** (adj.), impotent
6. **Negligent** (adj.), describes a condition in which you absent-mindedly answer the door in your nightie.
7. **Lymph** (v.), to walk with a lisp.
8. **Gargoyle** (n.), an olive-flavored mouthwash.
9. **Flatulence** (n.) the emergency vehicle that picks you up after you are run over by a steamroller.
10. **Balderdash** (n.), a rapidly receding hairline.
11. **Testicle** (n.), a humorous question on an exam.
12. **Rectitude** (n.), the formal, dignified demeanor assumed by a proctologist immediately before he examines you.
13. **Oyster** (n.), a person who sprinkles his conversation with Yiddish expressions.
14. **Circumvent** (n.), the opening in the front of boxer shorts.
15. **Frisbeetarianism** (n.), The belief that, when you die, your soul goes upon the roof and gets stuck there.
16. **Pokemon** (n), A Jamaican proctologist
17. **Intaxication:** Euphoria at getting a tax refund, which lasts until you realize it was your money to start with.

18. **Reintarnation:** Coming back to life as a hillbilly.
19. **Foreploy**: Misrepresentation about yourself for the purpose of getting laid.
20. **Giraffiti:** Vandalism painted very, very high.
21. **Sarchasm:** The gulf between the author of sarcastic wit and the person who doesn't get it.
22. **Inoculatte:** To take coffee intravenously when you are running late.
23. **Osteopornosis:** A degenerate disease. (This one got extra credit).
24. **Karmageddon:** It's like, when everybody is sending off all these really bad vibes, right? And then, like, the Earth explodes and it's like, a serious bummer.
25. **Glibido:** All talk and no action.
26. **Dopeler Effect:** The tendency of stupid ideas to seem smarter when they come at you rapidly.

. . .

## Clear Definitions

**Adult**: A person who has stopped growing at both ends and is now growing in the middle.
**Beauty Parlor**: A place where women curl up and dye.
**Cannibal**: Someone who is fed up with people.
**Chickens**: The only creatures you eat before they are born and after they are dead.
**Committee**: A body that keeps minutes and wastes hours.
**Dust**: Mud with the juice squeezed out.
**Egotist**: Someone who is usually me-deep in conversation.
**Gossip**: A person who will never tell a lie if the truth will do more damage.
**Handkerchief**: Cold Storage.
**Inflation**: Cutting money in half without damaging the paper.
**Mosquito**: An insect that makes you like flies better.
**Raisin**: Grape with a sunburn.
**Secret**: Something you tell to one person at a time.

# Glossary An Other Useful Explanations

**Toothache**: The pain that drives you to extraction.
**Tomorrow**: One of the greatest labor saving devices of today.
**Yawn**: An honest opinion openly expressed.
**Wrinkles**: Something other people have. You have character lines.

• • •

**Bozone:** (n.) The substance surrounding stupid people, which stops bright ideas from penetrating. The bozone layer, unfortunately, shows little sign of breaking down in the near future.
**Cashtration:** (n.): The act of buying a house, which renders the subject financially impotent for an indefinite period.
**Hipatitis**: Terminal coolness.
**Decafalon** (n.): The grueling event of getting through the day consuming only things that are good for you.
**Arachnoleptic fit** (n.): The frantic dance performed just after you've accident-ally walked through a spider web.
**Beezlebug:** (n.) Satan in the form of a mosquito that gets into your bedroom at three in the morning and cannot be cast out.
**Caterpallor:** (n.) The color you turn after finding half a grub in the fruit you're eating.
And the pick of the literature:
**Ignoranus:** (N) A person who's both stupid and an asshole.

• • •

The following is a list of commonly employed tools used by some men and even fewer women:
**DRILL PRESS:** A tall upright machine useful for suddenly snatching flat metal bar stock out of your hands so that it smacks you in the chest and flings your beer across the room, denting the freshly-painted project which you had carefully set in the corner where nothing could get to it.

**WIRE WHEEL:** Cleans paint off bolts and then throws them somewhere under the workbench with the speed of light. Also removes fingerprints and hard-earned calluses from fingers in about the time it takes you to say, "Oh shit!"

**SKIL SAW:** A portable cutting tool used to make studs too short.

**PLIERS:** Used to round off bolt heads. Sometimes used in the creation of blood-blisters.

**BELT SANDER:** An electric sanding tool commonly used to convert minor touch-up jobs into major refinishing jobs.

**HACKSAW:** One of a family of cutting tools built on the Ouija board principle... It transforms human energy into a crooked, unpredictable motion, and the more you attempt to influence its course, the more dismal your future becomes.

**VISE-GRIPS:** Generally used after pliers to completely round off bolt heads. If nothing else is available, they can also be used to transfer intense welding heat to the palm of your hand.

**OXYACETYLENE TORCH:** Used almost entirely for lighting various flammable objects in your shop on fire. Also handy for igniting the grease inside the wheel hub out of which you want to remove a bearing race.

**TABLE SAW:** A large stationary power tool commonly used to launch wood projectiles for testing wall integrity.

**HYDRAULIC FLOOR JACK:** Used for lowering an automobile to the ground after you have installed your new brake shoes, trapping the jack handle firmly under the bumper.

**BAND SAW:** A large stationary power saw primarily used by most shops to cut good aluminum sheet into smaller pieces that more easily fit into the trash can after you cut on the inside of the line instead of the outside edge.

**TWO-TON ENGINE HOIST:** A tool for testing the maximum tensile strength of everything you forgot to disconnect.

**PHILLIPS SCREWDRIVER:** Normally used to stab the vacuum seals under lids or for opening old-style paper-and-tin oil cans and splashing oil on your shirt; but can also be used, as the name implies, to strip out Phillips screw heads.

**STRAIGHT (SLOT) SCREWDRIVER:** A tool for opening paint cans. Sometimes used to convert common slotted screws into non-removable screws and butchering your palms.

**PRY BAR:** A tool used to crumple the metal surrounding that clip or bracket you needed to remove in order to replace a 50 cent part.

**HOSE CUTTER:** A tool used to make hoses too short.

**HAMMER:** Originally employed as a weapon of war, the hammer nowadays is used as a kind of divining rod to locate the most expensive parts adjacent the object we are trying to hit. It is especially valuable at being able to find the EXACT location of the thumb or index finger of the other hand.

**UTILITY KNIFE:** Used to open and slice through the contents of cardboard cartons delivered to your front door; works particularly well on contents such as seats, vinyl records, liquids in plastic bottles, collector magazines, refund checks, and rubber or plastic parts. Especially useful for slicing work clothes, but only while in use.

**SON-OF-A-BITCH TOOL:** (A personal favorite!) Any handy tool that you grab and throw across the garage while yelling 'Son of a BITCH!' at the top of your lungs. It is also, most often, the next tool that you will need.

• • •

## Texting Abbreviations for Senior Citizens

ATD: At The Doctor's
BFF: Best Friend Fainted
BTW: Bring The Wheelchair
BYOT: Bring Your Own Teeth
CBM: Covered By Medicare
CGU: Can't get up
CUATSC: See You At The Senior Center
DWI: Driving While Incontinent

FWB: Friend With Beta Blockers
FWIW: Forgot Where I Was
FYI: Found Your Insulin
GGPBL: Gotta Go, Pacemaker Battery Low!
GHA: Got Heartburn Again
HGBM: Had Good Bowel Movement
IMHO: Is My Hearing-Aid On?
LMDO: Laughing My Dentures Out
LOL: Living On Lipitor
LWO: Lawrence Welk's OnOMMR: On My Massage Recliner
OMSG: Oh My! Sorry, Gas.
ROFL... CGU: Rolling On The Floor Laughing... And Can't Get Up
TTYL: Talk To You Louder
WAITT: Who Am I Talking To?
WTFA: Wet The Furniture Again
WTP: Where's The Prunes?
WWNO: Walker Wheels Need Oil
GGLKI: (Gotta Go, Laxative Kicking In)

• • •

# ABOUT THE AUTHOR

**Fredric L. Frye, BSc, DVM, MSc, CBiol, FSB (FIBiol), FRSM**

After his honorable discharge from the U.S. Navy, where he served as a combat air crew member in a blimp squadron engaged in antisubmarine patrols, Fredric Frye earned his degrees at the University of California, Davis and served two residencies: <u>General Surgery</u> at the U.S. Public Service Hospital, San Francisco and <u>Pathology</u> at the University of California, Davis. He is an elected member of two scholastic honor societies: *Alpha Gamma Sigma* and *Phi Zeta*. He was an epidemiologist with the California Cancer Research Program; and then engaged in private clinical practice in Berkeley and Davis, California. Dr. Frye joined the faculties of the University of California, School of Medicine, San Francisco, teaching experimental surgery; University of California, Berkeley's Lawrence Berkeley Laboratory, working on nuclear medicine, immunosuppression, and space-suit design for the NASA Apollo Project; and the University of California Davis, School of Veterinary Medicine, as a Clinical Professor of Medicine serving *pro bono* for 26 years. In 1977 he returned to the University of California, Davis and earned a Master's degree in Comparative Pathology. For 23 years, he was the principal pathologist for a biopharmaceutical research firm until they relocated to the United Kingdom in 2005.

He is now a Visiting Professor of Comparative Medicine and Pathobiology at numerous Universities and Colleges in North

## About The Author

America, UK, Italy, and Japan. He is the author of 23 text-books, 363 papers, 38 CD Rom programs; co-author of 28 textbooks, and numerous chapters in multi-authored textbooks. He was the 1969 recipient of the American Veterinary Medical Association's *Practitioner Research Award*; he was the *Second Edward Elkan Memorial Lecturer* at the University of Kent; the *Richard N. Smith Memorial Lecturer* at the University of Bristol; and the *Peter Wilson Bequest Memorial Lecturer* at the University of Edinburgh. He is an elected *Life Member* of *the American Association for the Advancement of Science, an Elected Fellow of the Royal Society of Medicine,* and the *Institute of Biology,* London. He was named as a *patron of the Charles Louis Davis Foundation for International Advancement of Veterinary and Comparative Pathology* and was elected to the Board of Directors of the German Society for the Study of Comparative Pathology and Oncology in Berlin. In 2001 he was elected as an *Honorary Life Member of the British Veterinary Zoological Society.*

After developing – and maintaining – an intense interest in animals in general, and particularly reptiles, amphibians, and invertebrates, he applied his clinical veterinary skills to these previously overlooked animals and has been credited by his colleagues as the "Father of Herpetological Medicine and Surgery." In January, 2002, he was the honored as the recipient of the first *Association of Reptilian and Amphibian Veterinarians (ARAV) Lifetime Achievement Award,* which now is named the *Fredric L. Frye Lifetime Achievement Award.* In 2010, he was named as the first *Distinguished Honorary member of the Associazione Linnaeus* in Italy. The multi-authored text, INVERTEBRATE MEDICINE in which his chapter on scorpions, received the 2012 *TEXTY Award.* Fred was elected to Life Membership in the Association of Reptile and Amphibian Veterinarians in September, 2013,.

Fred served *pro bono* on the Governor of California's Bioterrorism and Natural Disaster Advanced Preparedness Action Group for two Northern California counties. He consults on difficult clinical cases with colleagues; mentors students; and devotes much of his time to the family certified organic farm, *La Primavera*, where he is engaged in pomological culture and improvement of apple, pear, peach, plum, nectarine, and citrus fruit trees. In the 1980s he was successful in producing viable garlic seeds from a plant that usually reproduces only asexually. Among his avocations are designing and building fine furniture, and sculpting art objects from sustainable tropical forest products, metal, and stone; he has had two one-man shows of his artwork.

Fredric L. Frye, D.V.M.

Made in the USA
Columbia, SC
11 January 2022